CW00953828

PSYCHOSEXUAL TRAINING
AND THE
DOCTOR/PATIENT RELATIONSHIP

INSTITUTE OF PSYCHOSEXUAL MEDICINE DIGESTS

PSYCHOSEXUAL TRAINING

AND THE

DOCTOR/PATIENT RELATIONSHIP

TRANSCRIPTS OF LEADERS WORKSHOPS

EDITED BY

R.L. SKRINE, M.B., Ch.B., M.R.C.G.P.

FOREWORD BY

MARSHALL MARINKER, M.D., F.R.C.G.P.

MONTANA PRESS

©

MONTANA PRESS (1987)

ISBN 1 870786 00 9

PRINTED BY
BROWN, SON & FERGUSON, LTD.
GLASGOW G41 2SG

CONTENTS

SECTION III. THE LEADER AND GROUP IN PSYCHOSEXUAL TRAINING

ACKNOWLEDGEMENTS

Those taking part in these workshops were:

Dr. Tom Main, President and Consultant in Training, Institute of Psychosexual Medicine

Dr. Prudence Tunnadine, Scientific Director, Institute of Psychosexual Medicine

Leader doctors Bramley, Dewsbury, Devereux, Gill, Gilley, Gregson, Hutchinson, Jones, Kilvington, Lincoln, Moore, Morgan, Rogers, Skrine, Snead, Tattersall, Thexton, Tisdall, Wakley

Leader nurse Mrs. Selby

My thanks to all of these for allowing me to use their work, and to Mrs. Judith Grott for making the original transcripts. Special thanks to Dr. Gregson for some suggestions concerning the final text.

R.L.S.

Because these discussions were never intended for publication, considerable steps have been necessary to preserve professional and patient confidentiality. Identities, genders and locations have been disguised. The leader doctor initial does not correspond to the doctor's name.

FOREWORD

This book attempts to communicate the atmosphere and intellectual discipline of a Leaders Workshop concerned with training in psychosexual medicine. A small group of doctors meet regularly over a period of years in order to discuss other small groups of doctors who meet regularly to discuss the medical management of patients with psychosexual problems. What they discuss seems to have little to do with the diagnosis of sexual dysfunction and its treatment. The reader will fail to find reference to the work of Masters and Johnson, Kinsey and Hite in these pages.

Is this then a book about counselling rather than clinical medicine? Mysteriously almost nothing is said about the techniques of counselling. Indeed when the word 'counselling' is used, it clearly has a special meaning for these doctors: the word seems to carry its own quotation marks, and there are overtones of amused disdain.

General practitioners, not least those who are responsible for the development of vocational training, and the thousands of younger doctors who have gone through this training, will instantly recognise the definition of medicine implied in this work. The approach to the patient simultaneously acknowledges the physical, the psychological and the social. In this sense, psychosexual medicine which is the ostensible subject of this book is simply an example, and a particularly apt one, of the whole of medicine. What goes on in these case discussion groups? Are they case conferences? Are they clinical tutorials? If the doctors are learning, who teaches them?

If there is an element of 'case conference' in the work of these seminars, it is hard to discern from this book. The cases discussed are not presented as detailed or coherent clinical histories, but rather as vignettes, glimpses of clinical work which happen at many removes from the discussions which are recreated here. The group discusses the cases which were discussed in other groups.

There is talk about talk about talk: sometimes there is silence about silence about silence.

In the distance we may catch a glimpse of a man and a woman locked into some personal unhappiness. Nearer, but still unclear, we hear the doctor talking about his or her relationship with the patient, or as often avoiding talking about the doctor/patient relationship. Perhaps the impotent lover makes the doctor feel useless: the premature ejaculator makes the doctor respond too impulsively, before the patient can make use of his response. And all of this seems to take place behind the screen of this book, where the figures are shadows and the words are fragmentary whispers.

Nearer and less muffled we hear the voices of the doctors talking in their training seminars. Suddenly it is the doctors who are in focus, and the clearer their voices and images, the clearer we begin to make out the qualities of the doctor/patient relationship. Meanwhile the persons with whom it all began, the patient and his partner, come in and out of focus. The atmosphere of the consulting room, of the seminar, and later the atmosphere of the Leaders Workshop, act as lenses in a spyglass through which we can view the patient's life.

Closest to hand is the Workshop where the leaders meet to discuss their leadership of the doctors seminars, and whose discussions are reproduced here in edited and abridged form. Their voices are always clear. Even though only two of them are named (Dr. Tom Main, leader of the workshop, and Dr. Prudence Tunnadine, the Institute's Scientific Director), each of these doctors becomes a distinct personality, with particular strategies, flairs and fears. The Leaders Workshop becomes the stage for everything that we are to learn from this book. The device is Shakespearean: the play within a play. Bergman in his brilliant *Fanny and Alexander* presents us with a film about a theatrical company, and opens with a child on a stage moving the cardboard characters of his toy theatre. Each play resonates with the other, both resonate with the audience, and with the story that they have to tell.

The book reflects just such a many-layered structure. In clinical work this multi-layered tradition of learning and teaching has its roots in psychoanalysis, and in that particular school of psychoanalytical training which links the training analyst, the trainee analysand and the patient. It is also the basis of the so-called Balint or Tavistock seminars for general practitioners.

In the discussions here presented, we may meet a patient who is sweetly reasonable with her husband, but cannot allow him to penetrate beneath the surface of their lives: the marriage is unconsummated. The doctor tries to understand her patient's feelings, but the sweet reasonableness is too cloying, and in the end the doctor too loses her appetite for the task. Faced with this story about the unconsummated marriage and the unconsummated consultation, the doctors in the seminar try to help. But the reporting doctor begins sweetly, so sweetly to defend her patient, to explain how vulnerable she is, how brutal it would be to attack her with an insight, let alone an interpretation. The group is fed up. Nothing happens.

There is a unity about this work, from the experience in the marital bed, through the encounter in the consulting room, the discussion in the doctors seminar and the *dénouement* of the Leaders Workshop. It may come as no surprise that the feelings and the strategies which the patient expresses in his or her own very personal life, surface again in the consulting room. The trained doctor who is able at once to feel empathically and to think critically, can make important clinical use of this phenomenon. But the feelings are even more contagious than this. Not only does the atmosphere of the patient's sexual relationship transmit itself into the doctor/patient relationship, but the atmosphere in the consulting room transmits itself instantly into the atmosphere of the doctors seminar. Here the doctor not only presents the story of the patient, but somehow comes to represent the patient himself or herself in the group. And a similar contagion affects the Leaders Workshop. The leader may relate a problem encountered with one of the doctors in the seminar. Almost before we are aware of it, the reporting leader seems to act out, almost to become, the doctor whose behaviour is being discussed.

All of this will be instantly recognised by readers who are members of the Institute of Psychosexual Medicine, by doctors who have taken part in Family Planning Association seminars and by general practitioners who have had first-hand experience of Balint and other groups concerned with the doctor/patient relationship. A similar philosophy, and tiered arrangement of the work, is familiar in counselling training under the aegis of the National Marriage Guidance Council.

The book however is concerned with much more than training in psychosexual medicine. It is concerned with case discussion in small groups, and deals at once with learning about the doctor/patient relationship; with learning how to explore the subject in the setting of a small group, and with learning about the function and the competences of such small group leadership. As such it has the greatest relevance to a variety of doctors and others who learn and teach about the care of patients. For small group teachers in general practice, for those concerned with the running of vocational training schemes and young principals groups, the account of these Leaders Workshops will be invaluable. Be warned however that this is no cook book. Those who seek didactic instruction, a list of approved behaviours in small groups, still less a theory of whole person medicine or small group dynamics, will be disappointed. It is certainly true that Dr. Tom Main makes crystal clear his own views on how a group or seminar should be led. In doing so he appears to breach almost every one of the guidelines which he expounds, and we should be very grateful to him for this. This is not a book about theory or about rules, it is about creativity, about risk-taking and about intellectual rigour.

Our most influential theories and models about small group work stem from the developments of group psychotherapy. Bion's theory of group dynamics is based on his experience with psychiatric patients, although one finds reference to this theory throughout the literature on small group teaching in a variety of academic settings. Bion suggests that the small group operates in one of two distinct modes. First it may function as a *work group*. In this mode, members of the group seriously address the task. In this case, the seminar members would constantly return to a consideration of the doctor/patient relationship, and how this illuminates the psychosexual problem of the patient. Bion suggests that at other times, members of the group attend to their own unconscious needs. Group members treat the group as an appropriate setting in which to act out a number of well described strategies, in order to avoid the pain of getting on with the task.

Games are unwittingly played by the members: they pair with one another, they fight, they run from the task and they engage the group leader in their exaggerated fears, and in their unrealistic wishes for fulfilment. This mode of activity Bion describes as the *basic assumption group.*

Bion's model, and other models of small group work which stem from the experience of university teaching, are helpful and influential, but fail to take account of the atmosphere of professional seminars such as those described in this book. Here there is a peculiar relationship between patient and doctor, the seminar and its leader. The members of such groups are practising professionals. The relationship with the patient whose case is being reported, has technical, emotional, ethical and legal aspects. The work in the seminar may directly influence the work which the doctor and patient do together, and so the quality of the care. This imparts a particular quality to the group, to the rôle of the leader, and to the leader/group relationship. For example, here the group leader is not an alien expert, a psychiatrist among patients or a lecturer among students, but rather he is *primus inter pares.*

I found myself reflecting on so many of the difficult issues about small group teaching, which I myself have been engaged in for most of my professional life. New light is thrown on how to begin with a group, the pros and cons of using forenames or surnames, on how to cope with the difficult group member, and how to help a group which gets stuck. In their fascinating interplay, Dr. Tom Main and Dr. Prudence Tunnadine explore and make a very good case for the possibilities of co-leadership.

Even the idea of 'teaching' is uncomfortable in the setting of these seminars, yet the word 'training', preferred by pioneers like Balint and Main seems even more unsatisfactory. This may be because we have assumed that training simply equips people to perform known tasks in an approved fashion. Dr. Jack Norell, a general practitioner doyen of the Balint school, commented that dogs can be trained to jump through hoops. Here, however, the doctors are being trained to listen carefully, to use the imagination, to evaluate self-critically, and to test the validity of professional intuition. Because most scientific endeavour is highly technical, it is easy to forget that at its heart, science is

concerned with ways of thinking and discovering. Bronowski
described three essential characteristics of science as he saw it:
creativity, the habit of truth and the sense of human dignity.
These Leaders Workshops are master classes both in the
leadership of case discussion groups, and in the science of
medicine.

Marshall Marinker
August 1987

INTRODUCTION

A number of doctors experienced in psychosexual medicine, who also act as leaders in psychosexual training seminars, have in their possession large piles of duplicated sheets. These are transcripts recording every word spoken in a series of ongoing discussion groups, specifically a series of Leaders Workshops held in London, in which the doctors took part during the early 1980s. The piles of sheets have increased year by year and I know I was not alone in thinking that this rich collection of verbatim material contained original ideas concerning psychosexual medicine and, in particular, how to train doctors in its practice. Having had some previous editorial experience I have been tempted to try to extract some of the ideas and to organise them into a readable book.

I must admit that it took longer than I expected, not because of any paucity of material but because of its abundance and variety; and for a further reason: the discussions were actually very complex in their nature. As Dr. Marinker has pointed out in his illuminating Foreword, the provenance of this work is a multi-layered tradition of learning and teaching. I soon discovered that any attempt to reproduce the discussions in simple chronological sequence, following the order in which they occurred, would quickly bemuse both editor and reader. Instead I chose to adopt a thematic framework which reflects the three situations inherent in this training system, namely, the doctor with his patient in the consulting room, the doctor with his colleagues in the group and the leaders in the workshop. Not only does this arrangement seem to arise naturally from the material, but it also helps to highlight the levels on which the training of leaders must concentrate: in almost every discussion the leaders can be seen transferring their attention from one level to another. I hope the division into sections will help to clarify the complexity of the ideas.

The general nature of seminar training will, I imagine, be familiar to many readers of this book. However, its use by the

Institute of Psychosexual Medicine needs a word of explanation. The Institute is an independent postgraduate medical training organisation which focusses its attention on the psychosexual area of medicine and the particular problems raised therein. The training which it employs is fundamentally based on the Balint seminar method, where a group of GPs meet with a psychoanalyst to discuss their ongoing work and especially the doctor/patient relations. This training enables doctors to increase their skills and to help patients with a wide range of problems.

One psychoanalyst, Dr. Tom Main, subsequently pioneered a method of training seminar leaders who are not analysts although they are experienced doctors in the psychosexual field. His method, developed in the 1970s at the Cassel Hospital, is to conduct Leaders Workshops, which are similar to the training seminars in that leaders are trained by the discussion of their work, but differ inasmuch as the work under discussion is the *leading of the group*. Further workshops of this kind have been held both in Newcastle upon Tyne and in London. As a result, 'non-analytic' doctors have been acquiring skills in leading both training seminars and leaders workshops for a number of years.

The particular sort of training which has evolved from these origins has some characteristic features. The work is firmly focussed on observing and considering how the doctor and the patient treat each other, on the interactions between them and the light which this throws on the patient's problem. Neither at seminar nor at workshop level is there a syllabus or any body of theory that is taught. In the seminar the study of ongoing work with specific patients presents each meeting with fresh clinical material. There is no discussion of theories about the aetiology of sexual dysfunction, nor are particular Methods of Treatment recommended. In the leaders workshop there is no teaching or discussion of group dynamics although the behaviour of each group, as it considers the work of the member doctor, is studied in detail. The training method is therefore also in a significant sense a research process.

In editing the Digests for publication, deciding which passages to use and which (more painfully) to leave out, I have taken as sole criteria the quality and relevance of the reported discussion. The substance of the case material has played no part in the choice; although when organising the material, I was interested to discover that most common psychosexual problems and anxieties were in fact represented: I have attempted an informal classification of these in the Appendix.

Each leaders workshop lasted two hours and covered the discussion of two or three groups. The whole proceedings — case material, seminar discussion as reported by the leader and subsequent workshop discussion — were tape-recorded at the time and later transcribed by a secretary. In editing, I have included a very bare summary of the case material; no more than was necessary to make sense of the ensuing discussion. The group discussion I have usually left as reported in the words of the leader, so as to give some feeling of the group atmosphere and leadership style; but here too drastic shortening has been needed, so that the bulk of the Digests could be concerned with the main feature: the discussions of the leaders in the workshop. Apart from cutting out irrelevances and making sense of muddled comments, I have left those discussions as far as possible in their original form. I am grateful to the leader doctors for allowing these very private examinations of their work to be recorded in print.

The most difficult part of the editing, not surprisingly, concerned the most important, indeed unique function of the leaders workshop: namely, training leaders to detect elements of the unconscious material in the doctor/patient relationship and to recognise the effect of the material on the group and on the leader. As Dr. Main has remarked, "Life is not easy for the leader. He must be concerned not only with his own understanding of the doctor/patient relationship but the group's understanding of this". In addition, the leader has to consider the relationship between the presenting doctor and the group, as well as between the group and the leader. In the final chapter entitled "Unconscious material 'going down the line'", I have attempted to record the search by the leaders for this material and to show the way it is transferred from level to level.

Finally, on a personal note, I have felt it a privilege to edit this book because it has given the opportunity to put on record the contribution of two remarkable individuals who are named in the text. It is no accident that so many of the digests highlight their interventions. Dr. Main has written elsewhere about the danger of the "hierarchical promotion of ideas", whereby original work is made respectable, revered and turned into rules, thus inhibiting further thought and the development of new ideas. If this book encourages such a trend it will be guilty of biting the hand that fed it. I hope instead that it will stimulate thought and will be read for what it is: a true record of a group of doctors working in a unique training system, with two charismatic leaders, at a particular time in the development of the new discipline of psychosexual medicine.

Ruth Skrine

SECTION ONE

THE INDIVIDUAL DOCTOR

AND

PSYCHOSEXUAL TRAINING

A. TRAINING THE PROFESSIONAL EGO

The primary task of the seminar is the training of doctors. The aim is to help them to become of more use to their patients by providing a training process which enables them to increase their skills in psychosexual medicine.

Doctors as well as patients have psychosexual lives which are personal and private. There is a danger that sometimes personal preferences or problems may be revealed in a training group and this can interfere with the training process. At the leaders workshops the problem of focussing on the professional training is frequently discussed.

1. THE TROUBLE WITH CHRISTIAN NAMES.
The use of christian names during training is considered in some training systems to be helpful and egalitarian. In this work we have found that the conscious and deliberate use of surnames can be a symbolic reminder that it is the professional rôle that is being studied.

2. DOCTOR REVEALING PERSONAL ANXIETIES.
3. MORE PERSONAL REVELATIONS.
Doctors may reveal personal problems directly by referring to their own experience, causing embarrassment for the leader and sometimes for the group as well.

4. 'VELVET' DOCTORING.
Fear of aggressiveness can seriously affect a doctor's technique.

5. IS THE DOCTOR IDENTIFYING WITH THE PATIENT?
6. MORE IDENTIFICATION OF DOCTOR WITH PATIENT.
The leader is sometimes worried that the doctor is in danger of exposing him/herself by identification with the case material.

1. The trouble with christian names

Leader Doctor P.

Doctor P.   One of the doctors in my group complained about the fact that I called everyone 'doctor' — "Why don't we use christian names? We do in my psychiatric training. Why should this work be different?" It seemed that he somehow wanted it to be personal therapy.

Dr. Main   Why didn't you bring that out into the open? This man has been trained in another institution and idealises this and is always comparing the practices there with this training. In some groups it is felt to be the business to examine each others' guts and discuss each others' problems. Some people hold the theory that you can't be any good at this unless you have examined your own whatnots. You've got to learn about your own blind spots, your own neuroses, sexual hang-ups. Plainly he's been in one of those things. Why didn't you bring it out into the open? That's him; that's how he's been trained; and that's how he is thinking; and he's not hearing what is going on in the present group. But, Mary, don't you think that Diana's account makes it awfully cosy?

Dr. G.   I do, Tom.

Dr. Main   Don't you think so, Jeremy? I think so too. — How is your husband, incidentally? . . . We're getting right off the professional relationship.

Doctor P.   They've had this with me before and we are just about on christian name terms, but it's all been terribly awkward because we don't all know each other's christian names.

Dr. Main   You should not use christian names unless it is very clear the difference between Dr. P and Diana P.

Dr. Tunnadine   I think that's right, but there is a further reason to be called "doctor". The wish for christian names is a wish for equality and the other way up it's a patronising business. It gives a model of the sort of doctor who calls the patient by the christian name but does not expect to be called by the christian name back; which puts you into a patronising situation which is quite irrelevant to the doctor/patient relationship. The idea of christian names for patients is a bad idea in therapy just as it is a bad idea for seminars.

Dr. Main   'You call me Doctor Main and I'll call you Janet'.

Dr. Tunnadine   That's what I'm getting at.

Dr. Main   There's another thing. Sometimes doctors would ring me up at hospital and say, "Oh Tom, I wonder if you would see this case". They were saying, 'Look, I've made a mess of this case, but *please* remember our old friendship and don't be so unpleasant as to judge me professionally. I am relying on an old friendship for you to suspend your ordinary professional opinion and I want a favour from you. I know that you, as Dr. Main, wouldn't help Dr. Smith, but as Tom and Dick we have an old obligation and surely you'll make an exception for me'. Things are really messed up from the start. Often you will find a patient and a doctor in a similar situation: they've got mixed up in this and things are a mishmash for the doctor. There's something very damaging about christian name terms. If we're Diana and Tom we can excuse each other and we needn't be honest about it. It'll be friendly and nice. But if we are to have professional criticism we have to be professional.

Mrs. R.   It would make it easier to sort this out at the beginning, to lay down the ground rules that this is how we are going to work. I am obviously up a gum tree because all mine are on christian name terms.

Dr. Main   We are not here to do each other favours or be nice to each other. Outside this room I don't mind what terms we use. I don't call you Dr. S outside this room, but inside the room I always do — well, nearly always! You can have this business as long as it's clear that 'Now we're doing professional work'.

Dr. Tunnadine   And presumably would be free to say at four o'clock: 'Now it's drinking time'.

Dr. Main   Yes, it's absolutely all right as long as it's clear that your name is Diana or Mrs. P, but not Dr. P at that time; and then there's Tom, Dick and Harry and you don't discuss work. But in the group you're not there to know about each other. Your private life is your affair; it's not their affair. Their private life is not your affair. Their *professional* life is your affair, and your *professional* life is their affair. We meet to train the professional ego. We're not there to treat the total ego at all: we're there to train the professional ego and this requires real recognition.

Dr. Tunnadine   I wonder if this difficulty in the group has contributed to some of the discomfort we have been hearing about between one of your doctors and a sexy patient. He seems uneasy about the chumminess, and 'are we meant to be in personal sexy relationships?', and so on.

Doctor P.   Several of the doctors found it very difficult to produce cases at the beginning.

Dr. Main   That's it. If he calls you Diana and you call him John and you get chummy and matey, then you needn't exhibit your professionalism. If I don't want my work to be examined I'll say, "How's the family? Read any good books lately?" — Anything except work. Having one's professional work examined is very painful.

Dr. Tunnadine   Particularly if you're supposed to be a psychiatrist.

Dr. Main   It's not a bad convention. I am addressing your professional ego, Dr. P. I am not doing it to be nice or nasty; just a training job. It respects the part of the ego that we are concerned with. Similarly, private feelings exhibited in the group are not the business of the group. You can detect them in any group — in this group sometimes — personal sensitivities or family difficulties or whatever; but it is not the affair of the work.

The subject of christian names is discussed again in III C 5.

2. Doctor revealing personal anxieties

Leader Doctor N.

During a discussion of the work of an early group the leader raised his anxieties about a doctor who revealed something of his own sexual difficulties.

Doctor N.   Can I divulge — not divulge, *divert* — from the case, to raise a leadership problem? After two meetings of this group I already feel I know quite a lot about the personal sexual situation of one of the doctors. In the discussion of an early case, someone asked, "How often are they having sex?" The presenting doctor replied, "Only occasionally: she doesn't enjoy it — just sits back". The doctor I am anxious about said, "Well, that's quite common for women, don't you think?" The rest of them said, "Certainly not!" Now he keeps coming in with interventions which seem to mean, 'I sympathise with that'. When we were discussing why a particular patient couldn't make the first move towards her husband, he said, "Well, my wife cannot do that". And again, when we discussed oral sex, he said, "That is not something we do". I felt I had to break in here because I thought this man would see this group as a therapeutic thing. The way I dealt with it was —

Dr. Main   Badly!

Doctor N.   Absolutely, of course! You know me — I'm tactful and don't come to the point! I said, "What are the patient's feelings about it? We're here to study the patient's feelings rather than the doctor's own activities. It's the patient; we've all got our own private lives, but let's have a look and see what this meant to the patient".

Dr. Main   Let's discuss technique on that point. The group member revealed an embarrassing amount of his own private life.

Doctor N.   Yes.

Dr. Main   Dr. N. handled it that way. It wasn't well thought out. He didn't have time as we have to sit down and think things out; but we are in a better position, so we can do better.

Dr. I.   One wonders if the others felt embarrassed about it, but then that is only asking another silly question!

Dr. Main   If Dr. N. was the only one embarrassed by it, I was born yesterday!

Dr. I.   But they didn't react either. I don't feel one can just ignore it.

Doctor N.   I could have ignored it, couldn't I? — I nearly did.

Dr. Main   What would have happened?

Dr. I.   There would have been another incident.

Dr. Main   Yes, and other doctors might have joined in.

Dr. S.   I thought the leader let him off the hook rather kindly:

'O.K., we might be interested in what you do, but we aren't interested in it at the moment' — in a rather kind way, not attacking him for it.

Mrs. R. He must project part of his personality, surely, as a doctor working with a patient. It isn't only the patient. Am I right?

Dr. Main Can you take that thought back a bit further?

Mrs. R. If he's going to work with his patients . . .

Dr. Main What is his technique with patients?

Mrs. R. Very directive.

Dr. Main 'I wouldn't do it that way, if I were you: we do it *this* way'. — There's a chance there for a different kind of intervention: to say, "I notice that this doctor is revealing quite a lot of his own personal experiences. We will have to find out how relevant that is to our work. But I presume you are like this with your patients?" Or you could say to the group, "Does it give this group any idea of how this doctor works with patients?" Then let the group discuss the relevance of this or usefulness to the group. That's my first clever thought for an alternative way.

Dr. S. I think that might make the doctor much more vulnerable in his early group than the way Dr. N. did it.

Dr. Main I thought he was very gentle: he just said, "For God's sake, shut up about your private life!" Kindly! — I think he was very direct.

Doctor N. In every case this particular doctor has brought up something about himself.

Dr. Main The question is, what do you do about it? What alternative ways are there? Everyone finds this sooner or later. Dr. Tunnadine's idea is to lay down the ground rules early in the group: 'Private stuff — no; because private stuff is irrelevant. It's a nuisance to your patient — out!' Another way is: 'If that is your usual technique, let's have a case to show how it helps'. Or you might say even more: 'How does the group feel about the doctor discussing his own experiences?' I think the group would say, "It's bloody embarrassing!" — You felt it.

Dr. G. I would have felt that in a new group that would have been very threatening for the doctor.

Dr. Main The question is, does the group depend on Dr. N. for its thinking, or do you require them to think for themselves and face all the pain?

Dr. Tunnadine   Dr. N. did relate his shut-up to the fact that it was irrelevant to the work; and so he didn't just say, "Stop it", but did say, "What effect does it have on the doctor/patient relation?"; which I thought was a good bit of leadership.

3. More personal revelations

Leader Doctor F.

The patient was a 15 year old girl who was brought by her mother to a family planning clinic for a 'physical check'. A few weeks before the girl had been staying with her grandfather on a farm in Devon and had been raped. The mother wanted the girl checked to see if she had V.D. The doctor felt it was not the appropriate place for that sort of check-up and suggested the girl should go to the S.T.D. Clinic. However, the girl then said she wanted the pill, which very much surprised the doctor. She did manage to discover that the girl had acquired a boy friend in the four weeks since the rape, but somehow the doctor put off examining her or giving her the pill at that visit, but asked her to come back.

Doctor F.   The group really saw that this was all terrible and they more or less put the boot in. They said, "Was this rape?" They jumped up and down and said, "Look here, what's all this about? Was it incest with the grandfather in the wilds of Devon?" Someone said, "What about the mother in all this?" — "Oh yes, I didn't tell you: the mother had just found a new partner and wanted to spend some time with him". "Oh! What about the jealousy of this daughter? . . ." They were all tearing around. What they were saying was: 'You failed to do anything for this young woman. She may have come because it was incest; she may have come because she wanted contraception; she may have come because she was raped. But you don't know. You've not done anything with it!' The doctor said: "I can see that I really have managed it all terribly badly and I feel awful"; and at this point one doctor said: "Speaking from my own experience of having been assaulted, yes, you did do it all terribly. The girl, if she was raped, needed to talk about feelings like the pain, dirt and humiliation, all those things: and you gave her no opportunity. In fact, you closed the door on speaking and you reinforced the fact that one should not speak about these painful things. . ." The rest of the group listened to all this, with respect and concern, but they didn't refer to it afterwards. They went on, in a sense, to try and look back to the girl who had been presented and what had gone on between her and the doctor.

Dr. Q.   Were you about to say something to stop her going on about her personal life and then didn't, because the group just went on as though she had said nothing and went back to the case?

Doctor F.   She has revealed personal things about herself before which have been worse. This time it was in the context of the case and she didn't dwell on her own personal details.

Dr. P.   It seems there are two problems. Is this setting an example of self-revelation that may be repeated or copied by others in the group? And is she in need of personal help for herself? If so, maybe . . .

Dr. Main   It's nothing to do with the leader, personal help.

Dr. P.   It is if it's going to upset the work in the group; not to offer her personal help yourself, but someone else . . .

Dr. Main   How about the leader sticking to the job?

Dr. P.   I think she *is* trying to stick to the job.

Dr. Main   Which is what?

Dr. P.   She's afraid that personal revelations are going to upset the work of the group and that this person's going to do it again.

Dr. Main   How about saying, "But what light does this throw on this case?", and getting it back to the work?

Doctor F.   That's in effect what they did do.

Dr. Main   But ask her, "What light does this throw on the case?" — the answer to which is "None".

Doctor F.   It did in a way, you see.

Dr. Main It didn't. It offered her viewpoint of what happened to her. She is not there to have her personal problems attended to.

Dr. Tunnadine What impressed me was that it wasn't apparently necessary; that the group just took it as another . . .

Dr. Q. Or did they do that because they were so embarrassed by it, it was much easier to go back to the case?

Dr. Main It's not bad, if they are embarrassed, saying "Repress that — we don't think like that, it's embarrassing, it's irrelevant — push off!" To ignore, after all, is to aid repression. I would have made it more pointed, by more or less saying, 'We are here to do some work, not to listen to that personal stuff. Does it throw light on the case?'

Doctor F. I think that would have seemed incredibly callous.

Dr. Main No no, not callous: 'Does this help us to examine this case? We are here to work'.

Dr. Tunnadine Not to her, but to the group.

Dr. Main Mmm.

Doctor F. The group certainly went back to the case that had been presented and carried on working on it.

Dr. Q. If they hadn't, would you have come in?

Doctor F. I think I would have had to have done something.

Dr. Main You can say, "Reminiscences are not allowed"; because they aren't: they are useless.

Dr. Tunnadine Dr. F. had handled this doctor that way earlier, when she kept on intervening with anecdotes, and said: "We want your case properly".

Dr. Main Yes: 'Anecdotes are irrelevant here. Let's study this case'. Or put it to the group: "Do these anecdotes help in any way in the study of the case under discussion?" Obviously they don't. My guess is that this doctor is not full of pain and personal trouble, but she has difficulty in working, studying the case under her nose.

Dr. Tunnadine If we think about this doctor and her training needs, it's a terrible burden, isn't it, to believe that the only help you have for your patients comes from your own personal experience? If this doctor is one who thinks that, what a relief it will be to her when she can get to Dr. Main's state of saying, "The great thing about this work is that the doctor knows nothing".

Doctor F.   What she said was in the context of reinforcing how badly that first case had been dealt with.

Dr. Tunnadine   She was saying, "I wouldn't go to a doctor like you". But that doctor didn't get much help, did she, with all this boot coming in?

Dr. D.   I am very disturbed about this idea of letting someone go on producing their personal experience. Surely if one lets this creep in, it is going to happen with everything — 'Like the time I was frigid with my husband', or 'I have just had a stillbirth'. I think I would have found it very difficult not to intervene rather more heavily than just allowing the group to ignore it.

Doctor F.   No-one else has actually been encouraged to do the same thing.

Dr. Main   No. It's as though she has no capability to think for herself. She doesn't realize it's all right to be ignorant as long as you start thinking and putting things together. Her idea is, 'The only knowledge I have is my personal knowledge from my own sexual life — does it fit that?' It doesn't matter as long as you get it back to the group.

Dr. Tunnadine   I share Dr. D's anxieties a bit. How many personal stories do you have to hear before you put a stop to it?

Dr. Main   You have to say, "That's all right. Keep it out of this seminar. It's irrelevant". No matter what personal anguish an individual has, it is irrelevant to the work of the seminar. They can seek help somewhere else but not during the seminar.

Dr. Tunnadine   On that occasion the group and the leader decided to deal with it by ignoring it and getting on with the work. Wouldn't it be marvellous, if she keeps on doing it, and one of the group can eventually say, "We don't want to hear this".

Dr. Main   Or the leader can say, "Are you saying this girl should have been better investigated?" Gear it back. It's a good example for the group of how to deal with an irrelevancy. The other thing I am beginning to feel about the doctor who reported the case and getting hammered, is — I wonder why she did so badly? What are this doctor's anxieties? — because all the others could see it very clearly. This doctor gave them all the ammunition; she said, 'Right, here is the ammunition — now shoot me'; and they all said, 'Right!' She asked for trouble, that doctor; showed quite deliberately how lousy she was.

Doctor F.   She wasn't aware at the beginning how lousy she was, she really wasn't. It sounds so the way I presented it.

Dr. Main   Well, why did she bring the case at all, then?

Doctor F.   She really presented it, I think, because she thought it was interesting material.

Dr. Main   All right, well, let's have a look. No one spotted what the blind spot was about: she was just hammered for it. What *was* it about? Why was she so stupid? A young girl of fifteen, obviously sexy and interested — what was this doctor's trouble with sexuality with a girl of fifteen?

Doctor F.   In part, that the mother was there; that the two were totally inseparable; that one didn't think of the girl in that way with the mother present.

Dr. Main   But the doctor needs to think about sexuality as a positive thing. Is she a young doctor?

Doctor F.   Mmm.

Dr. Tunnadine   I had the feeling that that doctor, like the other one, has to learn that you don't have to do it all out of your own head. You can actually learn to listen.

Dr. Main   When this girl said, "I would like the pill", the woman had no feeling for that at all, and I wonder what that is about.

Doctor F.   The whole situation is loaded with anxieties because this doctor goes into schools and the teachers take her the contraceptive problems. The group recognised that and said, 'What you tried to do was make this into a proper consultation to do with contraception, by saying, "If at some time you find you do need the pill, come back".' Someone else said, "Was it that, or was it that the girl sensed she wasn't going to be allowed to talk about the rape, or what she had really come for, and she wasn't going to be examined; and so she thought, 'You come here for contraception, so I'd better talk about contraception'.

Dr. Tunnadine   It's exciting stuff, isn't it? The one word that has been missing. . .

4. 'Velvet doctoring'

The Institute of Psychosexual Medicine holds an annual Weekend Meeting for seminar leaders and potential leaders. The following digest is one of several appearing in the book taken from Dr. Main's introductory remarks at one such meeting. Further extracts appear elsewhere in the text.

Dr. Main   The leader may sometimes be tempted to conclude that a doctor's handling of a case was affected by his personal neurosis. It is important that the leader makes comments *not* about the doctor's problem but *only* insofar as it affects his professional work.

Let us say — a very common example — that the doctor is concerned to be seen as kind, sweet, loving, sympathetic, sensitive, tactful, wise and unabrasive; the kind of doctor to which we all aspire to be — and which none of us is! The worst instances concern those doctors who are so afraid of being aggressive that they have velvet thoughts, velvet voices, velvet techniques and often velvet interpretations. Their clinical techniques are seriously limited by their fear of being aggressive.

In group discussion of such a doctor's work, it is vital for the leader to distinguish between remarks (from himself or from other group members) which suggest that the doctor has a personal problem in this respect which needs help, and remarks which point out that his treatment of his case is being held up by this tendency towards "velvet doctoring".

In responding to a doctor's application for clinical training we have no sanction to intrude or to make observations upon his/her private and personal views or neuroses. We are not there to diagnose or treat doctors' neuroses, nor to expose them within the group. Personal transferences within the group may be obvious, but these are private matters: reference to them should

B

never be made or allowed.

We are concerned with the doctor's professional ego, and with that alone. Thus we should be quite bold in laying bare neurotic feelings in the *professional* ego: blind spots, evasions and inconsistencies; failures of assertiveness, etc. Our comments must be about the doctor's work problem; never about the doctor's personal problem.

One hopes to illustrate how these matters affect his understanding of the patient, or his understanding of how such feelings have been evoked by the patient. We have every right — indeed, it is our professional duty as a trainer — to talk about such defects in the doctor's professional ego which thus limit his range of understanding and skill in dealing with the patient.

It is difficult — sometimes embarrassingly difficult — when personal neuroses of a particular doctor become obvious to all the group; for the leader must get interest back on to the professional task and away from preoccupation with the personal feelings of the doctor. We need not care whether the doctor is paranoid, sexually inhibited, schizophrenic, homosexual: all we want to study is his doctoring. If his doctoring is all right, his personal diagnosis is irrelevant. If his professional work is blind, or bad, or prejudiced by his internal attitudes, these personal attributes are still irrelevant: it is the flaw in his *work* which should command the group's attention.

5. Is the doctor identifying with the patient?

Leader Doctor L.

A patient came to the doctor saying he was impotent, but it turned out that he had premature ejaculation. He had been quite happy until his girlfriend threw him over because he was "no good at it" and was always too quick.

Doctor L.   The group were unusually silent about this, and then someone jumped in and said it reminded her of a case, and told us

about that. I was embarrassed because I felt the presenting
doctor had some personal problems, and perhaps the group were
somehow sensing some kind of identification with the case which
was making them silent. When the second doctor had finished
her case I took it back to the first case and said, "I wonder what
went on between Dr. X. and that man which made Dr. W. act in
an unusual manner by interrupting and presenting a case of her
own". We did then hear some more about the patient's previous
girlfriends and relationships.

Dr. S.   I like the way you let Dr. W. go on and didn't stop her
but commented afterwards. I think I would have been inclined to
say, "Hey, what are you interrupting for?"

Dr. Q.   But they shied away from talking about this
embarrassment by going back into the details of the case history.

Dr. N.   Was the group embarrassed, or was it just the group
leader who was embarrassed?

Doctor L.   It could well have been just me and I presumed that
Dr. W. had picked it up too.

Dr. Q.   You mean, the rest of the group just didn't know why
she had interrupted?

Mrs. R.   They didn't interpret that.

Dr. N.   No-one interpreted anything here.

Dr. Q.   No. Well, was that embarrassment, or. . . ?

Dr. N.   What stage is this group at?

Doctor L.   It's in its third term.

Dr. N.   Then it is unlikely that the group would see this as
talking about himself.

Doctor L.   I'm sorry — some of them are in their third term;
some have been in longer.

Dr. S.   Dr. X. is in his third term.

Doctor L.   Yes.

Dr. Main   It doesn't matter. It's a very interesting point, this.
Here's a doctor who shows his own difficulties very clearly to the
leader. What relevance has that with the qualities of doctoring?
We're not here to take the slightest notice of people's personal
neuroses; our job is the *work*. The thing that is really important
is, what is this doctor's work like; not what is his private life like?

It is really irrelevant. It is not our job to take the slightest notice of the personal neuroses, but to go on with the work: that is, the professional area of the individual, not the private area.

Dr. Y.   I wasn't sure what we were hearing. . . which bit he was telling us about.

Dr. Main   He was talking about the work, but Dr. L. was concerned about personal neuroses.

Dr. Y.   I wondered if he was talking about his work, and saying, "I have tried and. . ."

Dr. Main   I don't care if this man is a transvestite whose sexual partners are sheep — *what is his work as a doctor like?* What did he do in the group? How did he get on with his patients? The group in fact did discuss this. After Dr. W's interruption, he went back to the case. He didn't do marvellous work, but he did do more than take a routine history. It was all right. There was a chance for the leader to show that she is not interested in personal neuroses. You were too hit between the eyes. You could have emphasised that the personal pains and troubles of the doctor are none of your business.

Doctor L.   I was floored.

Dr. Y.   I think he was like the patient in that he brought you a bit of work and was terrified that you clever doctors were going to turn round and tell him. . .

Dr. Main   *That's irrelevant!* What's his work like? What his anxieties are about *this* patient is relevant. It's a very important technical point, this: his relationship with the group, his seduction of the group. . . — But I doubt whether this man had premature ejaculation: it's taken a long time before he reported this.

Doctor L.   Three terms.

Dr. Main   I wouldn't call that premature. I thought Dr. W's ejaculation was pretty premature. She got too excited and burst out. It's a very interesting event.

Dr. Q.   As a leader, should one stop that and go back to the bursting-in of the other doctor?

Dr. S.   I would have.

Dr. Main   — "Just a minute, we have Dr. So-and-so's work to discuss. . ."

Dr. Q.   Yes, so you go right back to his work, what he is presenting.

Dr. Main   I might even have said to Dr. W.: "This is a case of premature ejaculation, but there is no need for it to be infectious — keep quiet!"

Doctor L.   You mean, at the outcome?

Dr. Main   Yes.

Dr. Q.   Then that would cover the embarrassment, to get back to working.

Dr. Main   Mmm, get back to the work — "We are not concerned with this doctor's personal life". It re-affirms the work task and makes it clear what you are there for.

Mrs. R.   That's very brave, isn't it?

Dr. S.   Stopping someone talking.

Mrs. R.   But by saying, "We are not concerned with your personal life".

Dr. Main   Oh, I wouldn't say *that*! *(Laughter).* No!

Mrs. R.   Sorry, I mis-interpreted you.

Dr. Main   The *attitude* is: we are not concerned with his personal life; the emphasis is on the work. It's important, because we are all aware of this in groups. I will give you an example of a doctor in a group I had. In every case that this doctor reported, she taught the patient how to masturbate. Masturbation was the greatest thing, and this was quite plainly a personal quirk which was revealed. But there was no sense in discussing it. All one could do was say, "How does it help this patient?". . . "This patient has become a very good masturbator" — all one could do was talk about the patient. Everyone realised that this was a thing with this doctor, but it was none of our business. It's what the *work* is like with the patient. Everyone has a group with someone in it like this.

Later in the seminar, another case of premature ejaculation was discussed. This was a young man who was very worried that he could only last thirty seconds, but when he got together with his mates, they boasted they could keep it up all night. The doctor had heard about how he had failed in civilian jobs and hoped to join the army. He also talked about how his father had left home, but come

*back after six months. The doctor tried to get him to talk about
girls, relationships and his feelings; but there didn't seem to be any
relationship that had lasted longer than the second date.*

Doctor L.   The group didn't seem to make much of this. They
asked how the patient felt about his parents, but we weren't
getting anything of what was going on between this doctor and
this boy, who seemed a very shadowy figure. The group went
round and round the houses about 'Yes, he adored his father'.

Dr. Main   And his uncle and cousin.

Doctor L.   That's right.

Dr. Main   You made some remark just now that you didn't talk
much about what happened between the doctor and the patient.
Did you make that remark to them?

Doctor L.   Yes. I said, "Can we try and see what is happening
between the doctor and this boy?"

Dr. Main   And how did you get on?

Doctor L.   Not well. The doctor kept saying, "I felt very sorry
for him. He looked a real wing three-quarter and he ought to
have been able not to have premature ejaculations. He should
have been able to keep it up all night like the other chaps". I think
there was great sympathy going on there.

Dr. N.   But it is all talk about ejaculations, and how many times
you could do it, and how long you could keep it up for; and
nothing about his feelings, and why he was wanting to go out
with these women, and why he was so lonely and didn't have
friends of his own; why he was leaving to go into the army.

Doctor L.   He was leaving because of the set-up at home and the
tension between mum and dad. It was a very unhappy situation.

Dr. Main   Well, we are all unhappy, but there are different kinds
of unhappiness. I have got no picture, even this business of the
family. In a way, interest in *that* is a defence against interest in the
doctor/patient relation; but even so, even in the family, I haven't
got any picture of what goes on there.

Doctor L.   She is a nurse and he is a civil servant — is this the
sort of thing? I think this husband running away in a small village
is pretty traumatic to this family. It isn't as though it happened in
a big city.

Dr. Main What's worse is that father came home — presumably to dominate the family *(ironically)*. The female domination here is clear. This boy's terror is clearly derived from somewhere. The other thing which Dr. N. mentioned is this about the army. He goes out with the boys, and they pick up girls, these boys do — a little homosexual group — and then they tell each other: "How did you get on last night?" There is a great deal of homosexuality here; there's a funny kind of retreat from femininity into the rugger-bugger world. How about saying something like this? I know it's dangerous, but I think it's about time you drew attention to these things. I don't mean preach at them, but this man wants to go away and join a man's organisation because it will make a man of him! *(Laughter).* He's wanting male discipline, has a weak father who can't stand the mother and runs away and comes back. He's in a trap, this young chap, and this doctor is nowhere near seeing it. I would like to hear about what the chap is like with this doctor. How did he tell his story and what did the doctor think of him? The doctor feels sorry for him; no admiration.

Doctor L. No, I didn't get any admiration at all.

Dr. Main So he's not an admirable character. I wonder if he was sorry, or if it was contempt as well. The leader must help this group to start describing events in the consulting room in terms of the relationship. The danger is you will take too much interest in the doctor's attitude rather than the patient's.

6. More identification of doctor with patient

Leader Doctor P.

The leader reported a case that worried her because there seemed to be a lot of identification by the presenting doctor with the patient, who had just been deserted by her boyfriend. The leader knew that the doctor was separated from her husband and was afraid that the group discussion might lead into the doctor's private life. The patient's original complaint was of painful intercourse, but much of the group discussion was about the pain and anguish of this patient, and the awfulness of the boyfriend. At one point there seemed to be a split between the men and the women in the group, with the men finding some good things about the boyfriend from the story, which had been long and complicated and full of the patient's pain. Someone suggested the doctor was too involved with the patient and needed to stand back a bit. The doctor said she saw herself as a counselling doctor.

Dr. K.   It sounds as if the leader was inhibited by knowing about the doctor's personal life.

Doctor P.   It was difficult to get into what was happening between the doctor and the patient in the room and away from blaming this absent partner, on whom we seemed to spend so much useless, fruitless effort.

Dr. A.   Was anyone interested in why she was having dyspareunia, and what was going on there?

Doctor P.   I did on two or three occasions say, "Let's talk about what this patient is complaining of"; but then it was difficult to get them to focus on the pain in her sexual life.

Dr. Tunnadine   The leader's difficulty was that she didn't want to get on to the doctor's personal life because that's dangerous, for some reason that is not very clear to me. There seemed to be a fear that her doctoring was being interfered with because of her identification with the patient's problem. But if she had been the sort of person who could say, "Look, I know a thing or two about what it's like to be in this position", she might have been the best doctor the patient could possibly find. Somehow the group, or you, were so anxious about this doctor presenting herself that you couldn't find a way of relating it to her doctoring blindness. The trouble was that this doctor didn't use her knowledge of what it is like to be a deserted woman in a clinical and useful way. She somehow identified with the patient, which is not a clinical thing to do.

Dr. Main   How many people in fact know that this doctor is separated from her husband?

Doctor P.   I would suspect most of them, but I don't know. Maybe I should have brought it out.

Dr. Tunnadine   Well no, I wouldn't say that.

Dr. Main   There was some reference to this, that she was too involved. The question is, should it have been brought out? What do people think?

Dr. C.   If you commented, "It's easy to identify oneself with this situation", that is perhaps even more threatening, even though you're not actually saying she *is* identifying.

Dr. Main   Well, you are. You're saying, "I'm frightened to say it".

Dr. C.   It doesn't really help, though, does it?

Dr. N.   In our research we are *always* talking about the doctor/patient relationship and then only look really at the contribution the patient has made. In our groups, and in this group too, we shy off ourselves; but we are a part of the relationship.

Dr. Main   A decisive part.

Dr. N.   We are a coloured mirror, that adds our own tones.

Dr. C.   And we can use that. The group could perhaps realise that she was using this. You felt that she was identifying with it, and therefore. . .

Dr. Tunnadine   I think she was. I think what happened was that it went down the line, as these things always do; but because the doctor was so paralysed by her own inner feelings, she couldn't be sensible with the patient; and because the group was so paralysed by this doctor, they couldn't be sensible about that either. The fact was that, whether the doctor was divorced, married or on the game, she identified with the patient instead of thinking what was going on. It interfered with her work to that extent.

Dr. Main   The question is what to do about it. The doctor is not at her best, because she has personal problems of her own. — Would it be all right to say, "We all know that Doctor So-and-so can't be at her best with this because of personal reasons of her own. . ?"

Dr. Tunnadine   I feel not. It is personal.

Dr. Main   It brings the truth out: it has that merit. I'll shoot anybody who says that, though! It's highly personal, it's the doctor's private life. What you *can* do is point out what this doctor is *not* doing with this patient: not using her brains, swallowing the whole thing hook, line and sinker, not seeing the cruelty in this patient — 'Because I suffer, you bloody must!' This is real cruelty, sado-masochism — this story of awfulness. This could be pointed out without any reference at all to the doctor's personal life, with her working ego, her professional ego. You could talk about what the doctor was doing in this relationship. The doctor is there listening and she obviously loves stories of suffering and trouble. You know there are some suffering doctors; there are anxiety doctors, depressing doctors — they are keen on depression. Very few joy doctors, very few fun doctors. As you know, there are an awful lot of death doctors, especially dead baby doctors. But sex doctors. . . not so common. What's this doctor contributing?

Doctor P.   I did try to look at what the doctor was doing and feeling in that situation. But then, having said that, I couldn't follow it up. It seemed to be the right lingo, but we still couldn't do it with the doctor and patient.

Dr. Main   What about telling it to the group instead of working hard like that? You didn't know what was going on much. You were doing your best. Why not get the group to do your thinking for you? Say, "I wonder what's going on between the doctor and the patient?" Or, "What sort of doctor has the patient got?" — It gets the group to think.

Dr. Tunnadine   The leader was in a spot because she knew that she was identifying with the patient, and it was the doctor's private life. . .

Dr. Main   But she won't let the group work. She wasn't a good group leader at that point, not a bad consultant. She didn't help the group to work.

Dr. A.   The group might have acted the same way if she said, "Look at this — why is this doctor behaving this way?"

Dr. Main   The leader has got to stop that, to free the group to do some work.

Dr. A.   But the group might also have felt nervous for this doctor if they knew of her trouble.

Dr. Main   It doesn't matter. Her work as a doctor is what matters and the group should discuss what sort of work she is doing.

Doctor P.   There was an effort on the part of the men to suggest that the boyfriend might have — might not be as bad as all that. Then that sort of got lost in the patient's despair.

Dr. Main   Couldn't you have used that in the group?

Dr. Tunnadine   Yes, this is what I would have liked to have seen.

Dr. Main   ". . . Isn't it interesting, all the men are for the man and all the women are for the woman. War, this, isn't it! Are we being had for a sucker by this patient? Is this doctor in fact doing to us what the patient did to her? . . ." All sorts of possibilities. My main point is that the leader has somehow to work with that *group*, not with that case. It doesn't matter if you don't understand the case, it doesn't matter *at all*. What does matter is that the group should be made to work on it.

Dr. Tunnadine   But it was difficult for the leader, because of her own identification that she didn't want, at any cost, anything about this doctor's private life. That is what removed her leadership skills just as surely as the patient, being so close to home, removed the doctor's therapeutic skills. This is something I would like to go into because we've got time here.

Dr. Main   Well, the patient dies, but the poor doctor just lost her husband last night. Nevertheless, the coroner would say, "The patient died because of your incompetence".

Dr. Tunnadine   It would be very good for the doctor, in the long run, if she could use her painful experiences and actually not identify with her patients but know a bit more about them. But that was difficult in the group. They couldn't see it as a positive thing. They were all protecting her against — she's clearly revealing herself, it seems to me, and that's the real trouble. The doctor put you in this position, didn't she?

Dr. S.   By presenting that case.

Dr. Main   It doesn't matter. The doctor will get a lot out of facing this woman's sado-masochism. There are no excuses for a doctor for not being a doctor.

Dr. Q.   So as a leader you should try and get it back to the patient's feelings.

Dr. Tunnadine   It comes back to what Dr. N. was saying about how to focus on the fact that there are two people in the room and what is going on between them? — and it is not always that easy to know how to do this. I thought the thing about the women picking up one side of the case and the men the other would have been one way.

Dr. Main   I think I would have said, "What sort of doctor has this patient got — what sort of *doctor?*"

Dr. Tunnadine   One doctor had a go at it, didn't he?

Doctor P.   Yes, he did.

Dr. Tunnadine   It was hot for everybody.

Dr. Main   'Emotionally involved' is a step towards 'What sort of doctor?'

Doctor P.   He actually said, "Are you a doctor at all?"

Dr. Main   Well, she has been a doctor: a sweet doctor, a nice doctor. . .

Dr. Tunnadine   She said, "I was being a counselling doctor", which was being absolutely accurate.

Doctor P.   And all this sympathy without really any attempt to *understand.*

Dr. Main   A doctor who won't think about the problem but just sympathises with it.

Dr. Tunnadine   What about this word 'counselling?' — You haven't had a go at that for about five years.

Dr. Main   I've given it up! *(Laughter).*

Dr. Tunnadine   It's no good giving it up with this leader, because she was grumbling about the doctor/patient relation last week, saying she didn't know what it was all about.

Doctor P.   No, I didn't say that. I said it was a talisman word.

Dr. Tunnadine   That's right — like 'counselling'. But it isn't counselling, what we do, is it? At least, it's not counselling as it is known.

Dr. Main   No.

Dr. C.   It's very frightening what people call counselling today.

Dr. Main   I think it's called 'doctoring'.

Dr. Tunnadine   If that doctor really felt, in that situation, that she had to be a counselling doctor, then the burdens of her own experience would be much greater for her than if she was just there to think, wouldn't they? This whole idea of giving counsel puts the burden on us to know about it and it sounds as though she was a sucker for it on this occasion.

Dr. Main   I think our Institute should be called the Institute of Psychosexual Doctoring.

Dr. Q.   Is that a way it could be put back to her, then, that counselling is stopping and thinking about what is going on there?

Doctor P.   I don't know. I don't worry too much about putting all the blame on the word 'counselling'. Some of the definitions of the word 'counselling' are actually very good. The one they quote in the College of General Practitioners preventive psychiatry booklet, I think is a super definition. And it seems to contain a lot of what we do; not *all* of what we try and do.

Dr. N.   If you worry too much about the semantics of words, you get away from the message.

Doctor P.   I am interested that you picked up so quickly this sado-masochism, and I'm not so sure that I really quite felt this in the patient.

Dr. Main   She tortured the doctor.

Doctor P.   — and the boyfriend, too. I thought you were actually talking about her insisting on it always being painful on intercourse. But 'torture the doctor' is the same thing, I suppose.

Dr. Main   Well, let counselling thrive. *(Laughter).* — It's a misquotation of Lear. You know the original quotation? — "Let copulation thrive!" *(Laughter).*

B.   SEXUALISING THE INTERVIEW — A DEFENCE

Sexual feelings between the doctor and the patient are not uncommon in this work, and the anxiety they produce in the doctor often leads to conscious or unconscious denial of the feelings and difficulties. This denial hinders the work with the patient and needs to be recognised and explored in the training seminar. The leader's task is to help the group to do this.

1. In the first example, the doctor is only too conscious of the sexuality in the consultation, but the leader finds the presentation threatening and is not able to explore in the group the existence of the sexuality. In the leaders workshop, Dr. Main introduces the idea of sexuality as a defence mechanism used by the patient.

2, 3, 4. In these other three examples, neither the doctor nor the group were fully aware of the sexual content of the consultation.

Sexualising the interview — a defence: 1.

Leader Doctor P.

The case was described by a trainee G.P. who is rather older than many trainees as he was a hospital medical registrar for a time before changing to general practice. He is an amusing raconteur, who used to turn every case into a little drama and kept the group all laughing with his impersonations.

The patient was a 37-year-old woman who came complaining of heavy periods. He described how she was an attractive brunette, flirtatious in manner, how he had slightly flirted back and it all seemed all right and controlled. He felt he should examine her, and she agreed, but then to his dismay, instead of going behind the screen to the couch, she dropped the trousers and pants she was wearing just where she stood by the desk. This was somehow provocative and embarrassing.

He did examine her without any difficulty, but as she was getting dressed, she burst out that she no longer liked making love with her husband. She started to cry and continued sobbing as she came and sat down at the desk. He felt overwhelmed by her distress, and when she said, "Please hold me, I feel so awful", he put an arm round her.

She came back again two weeks later and again wept, but not so violently, and this time the doctor tried to face her with what was going on. At first she pretended not to understand, but then she did say, "You mean, when I asked you to hold me?". He had found this difficult and embarrassing, but on the other hand he was relieved that it was out in the open.

Doctor P.   The group were very admiring of his courage, I think partly in presenting it. One of the group was very good at trying to stick at how the patient was making him feel as she made other men feel; she did seem to have got the hang of the fact that this might be one of the things that this woman did to men, that she had this rather hysterical sort of sexiness which almost enveloped people — at least, that was the feeling which came out after it had been discussed a bit. I have written in my notes, "The doctor washed into sexiness". I don't quite know what I meant by this, but it was how we felt after we'd talked about this woman for a bit. Another member of this group tried hard to get at the doctor's personal feelings about it, and how turned on he had been by this woman, which frightened me as a leader. I didn't feel the man's personal feelings were very relevant. . .

Dr. Main   But juicy!

Doctor P.   The whole thing was a bit juicy. The group got a bit giggly and the doctor said yes, he found her attractive. I did two things and I'm sure there are better ways of doing it but I'd better come clean and be honest. First of all I quoted to the group something that a colleague says to her medical students about, 'If you're examining a man and he gets an erection, what do you do? How do you cope with it? Are you so embarrassed that you can't cope or do you say, "How nice to see that it all works properly"?' I think I was trying to get the thing back on to a way to discuss these difficult feelings, a professional way. The other thing I did was a thing I have never done before: I used the word 'transference', in a desperate attempt to see what was happening as a professional happening. I said, "If you get involved in this work you will find patients become attached to you. I suppose this is what the analysts might call transference". The group didn't like that much and I didn't like it much either. I think I used that word in order to somehow look at the emotions as a clinical event.

Dr. Main   Can you tell us more about the group — over that. discussion?

Doctor P.   There was this giggliness; a lot of anxiety. There was a bit of a split in the group between those who wanted to explore the doctor's personal feelings about the patient and how excited he had been by her, and one or two of the group who were trying to see this as a reflection of the patient.

Dr. Main   How did the leader handle that?

Doctor P.   By flying away and using these ploys to try and see the doctor's reaction as a professional reaction rather than a personal reaction.

Dr. Main   Let's discuss it. This is very interesting.

Dr. Tunnadine   Mmm, very.

Dr. S.   It seems you didn't quite *say*, "It seems this case has made the group excited and a bit giggly".

Doctor P. No, I didn't.

Dr. S. In the way the doctor didn't say, "What's going on?" to his patient, did he?

Doctor P. He did in the second visit by the patient. He did say just that; faced her with it.

Dr. Tunnadine All the group, including the leader, must have been infected to some extent by the excitement and the anxiety and all of this about this transaction.

Dr. Main Yes, one doctor almost asked him if he'd had an erection. That's what she meant.

Doctor P. Yes, that was the psychiatrist who is always trying to make it more personal.

Dr. Main Personal therapy.

Doctor P. Yes.

Dr. Tunnadine It seems on the face of it, that you chose to calm the anxiety, as if to say, 'Let's have none of this personal excitement', in the same way, incidentally, that the doctor has done with the patient at the first visit. The other alternative would have been to do as Dr. S. suggested, that is to open it up and say, "Let's have a look at the doctor/patient relationship in this context; what is this all about?"

Mrs. R. But surely he was presenting the problem because this was a problem to him and therefore he was wanting them to look at it and why she should provoke him, so it's a bit difficult to get away from.

Dr. Main But why was he bothered about it, do you think?

Mrs. R. I should think anyone would be.

Dr. Main It's jolly nice being excited by a woman, believe me. So why was he bothered about it?

Mrs. R. It's unprofessional.

Dr. Main His problem was that he couldn't get on with his work, otherwise it would be pleasant. The group didn't talk about how difficult it is for the doctor to stand sexual excitement within himself and how difficult to stand sexual excitement with the patient.

Dr. Tunnadine He coped with it pretty well, it seems to me.

Dr. Main I'm nagging your colleague. What about if we go round the group and tell me this afternoon about the state of your sexual organs at the moment. How useful would that be? You see, it's got nothing to do with what we're meeting here for. The poor chap couldn't get on with his work. I'm surprised that you didn't latch on to this. Here's a woman patient and a male doctor and somehow he can't do any work. That's what is going on. I wouldn't say she excited him so much as *castrated* him as a doctor.

Doctor P.   Is that what happened in the group — that we stopped working?

Dr. Main   That's what I think. The woman put sex into the middle so the doctor couldn't think about her resistances to discussion of this problem, and the group were the same: they put sexual excitement right in the middle and the work stopped.

Doctor P.   Except in a funny way, you know, when she'd been discussed it seemed to clarify it for me. I felt that her sexiness was able to be seen as the way this person coped with things, which sort of took the giggliness away. I think the group did do some work on it; maybe they could have done more and better.

Dr. Main   How about going further? Sexiness is the way the woman copes with it, but you could say sexiness is the way this woman resists *any* investigation of herself. She hit the doctor with her sexuality like a club to beat him down. It was the use of femininity as a club, like a penis, and the doctor was brow-beaten as a doctor. Do you see what I am trying to get at? The group got into the sexual excitement, it didn't get into this woman's bitchiness with the doctor, the way she robbed him of his doctorhood. Suppose he had spotted this, I wonder what he would have done?

Dr. Tunnadine   It sounds as though by the second session he was feeling in better shape.

Dr. G.   Yes, he was wanting to face her a bit with what was going on.

Dr. Main   But not how she was destroying him. She must do this with other people.

Dr. G.   I was very interested when you were leading up to this. You presented him as a doctor who had been a bit superficial in his presentations beforehand and yet somehow something had allowed him to present a case where he was very vulnerable.

Dr. Main   I think it was because he was in trouble.

Doctor P.   He has changed enormously. In this case he was able to share feelings with us which he certainly couldn't have done before.

Dr. Tunnadine   I think you must be very pleased with him and I would too, but the fact is that you were also put in the position of feeling very protective — 'Let's calm all this down'.

Doctor P.   Yes, I did.

Dr. Tunnadine   It may be that your need to protect him was also a sign of his anxieties about the group and how much he felt he was expected to expose himself: 'Must we all drop our trousers straight away without the shelter of a screen?' It sounds as though you said: "We're here to work", and then it was all right, and I think that relieved them.

Dr. Main   After all, you're not there to cure the case. What you might have done more with was the fact that work had stopped. It was jolly interesting and juicy — it nearly stopped *us!* We got some of that here. It's just a bloody awful patient. The best way to avoid sex and having to look at your difficulties is to be sexy.

2.

Leader Doctor Z.

This case was described by a young trainee G.P. at great length. He launched into a long and involved story. He was not sure if the problem was physical or psychological and he wanted to air it with the group.

The patient was a lady who had frequent dyspnoeic attacks and he had seen her several times in the last few weeks. He had been out to her house several times when she had called him, but when he got there she was all right again. However, when he wasn't speaking to her she got breathless again. He went into great detail about all the investigations he had done.

The last time she asked him to visit he said, "No, you're all right. You can come into the surgery". "Shall I be all right?" "Yes, you'll be fine". When this lady came into the surgery eventually, she said: "Well, doctor, you've always been asking me what is the matter with me and now I'll tell you". She proceeded to tell him that she got these attacks of dyspnoea when sexual intercourse was mentioned or attempted. She then went on to describe her feelings when her husband told her she was unattractive and not feminine, and how she felt she was not feminine.

Doctor Z.   The doctor presented this and said, "Do you think this is a psychosexual problem? What do I do now?" The group said they certainly thought it was a psychosomatic problem and they had quite a discussion about physical as opposed to psychological causes. They decided that it was definitely a psychosomatic problem, but in fact this lady's real problem was with her femininity. This woman had been collecting most of the doctors in this practice and getting them to come and see her, but had now fixed upon this particular doctor. Every time he had visited he would say, "Is there anything you want to tell me?" and she had always said "No". This time the doctor had called her bluff and said, "You can come and see me", and this somehow made her tell him a bit more of her problem and what she was really worried about. In a way this was precisely what the doctor had done to the group, because he kept us on tenterhooks for ages while was was describing the various signs and symptoms before he came out with the problems with intercourse and her image of her own femininity.

We talked about that for a bit. I felt this was how this doctor/patient relationship with this woman was being acted out in the group. He kept us waiting for so long like this woman had kept him waiting for so long before she gave him a bit more. Even then we didn't have a great deal to digest because she was only going to give him so much. . .

Dr. Main   What comments?

Dr. I.   Was it a question of having to spin things out because it was a small group?

Doctor Z. I don't think so. It could have been.

Dr. I. I don't know if it was intentional.

Doctor Z. I felt it was much more that this woman had strung him along and he was going to do the same with us; perhaps not intentionally, but that was how it came out, because she had taken up a lot of his time and he did the same with us as a group.

Dr. Q. How did the group feel? Were they angry?

Doctor Z. More surprised. Slightly bored, actually. I think they were all wondering what he was on about. He addressed his comments about the details of the tests he had done to the other G.P.s in the group, assuming that I knew nothing of these things.

Dr. F. He was really asking for reassurance, then, because he had done a pretty naughty thing as a G.P. with someone who said they were breathless, saying, "You come in and see me": that's a little bit transgressing the rules, isn't it?

Doctor Z. He had been out several times to her.

Dr. F. But he transgressed a bit

Dr. Main When did she get the dyspnoea? Under what circumstances?

Doctor Z. Usually when intercourse was suggested.

Dr. Main Then he went to see her.

Dr. F. On his white stallion. *(Laughter).*

Doctor Z. Not the last time.

Dr. Main He went to see her when she had dyspnoea because intercourse was mentioned.

Doctor Z. He didn't find this out until after. I think he was a bit anxious about this lady.

Dr. Main But was it discussed?

Doctor Z. Yes, we discussed this quite a lot.

Dr. Main I think it was something to do with sex, actually.

Doctor Z. We talked about this too, that this lady had in fact set her eyes on him; she had picked him out of the rest of the practice.

Dr. Main That was mentioned?

Doctor Z. Yes.

Dr. Main Did the group discuss this?

Doctor Z.   Yes, they did.

Dr. Main   How was it, the discussion about that?

Doctor Z.   They reassured him that he had not done such a naughty thing. Did we get down to the sexual side? I don't know if we did, actually. We got down to the fact that she had picked him out of all the others, and why was this?

Dr. Main   And did you discuss why?

Doctor Z.   I think they decided that perhaps it was because he had asked her these things.

Dr. Main   He's quite a good-looking chap, isn't he?

Doctor Z.   Moderately, yes.

Dr. Main   Panic is there, isn't it?

Doctor Z.   Yes. I don't know if it was sexual panic or because he had done a naughty things as a G.P., as Dr. F. suggested. There was panic there, all right.

Dr. Main   He suddenly realised, too late, what it was all about, I would have thought. It's only a guess.

Doctor Z.   You might be right.

Dr. I.   Or was he deliberately trying to calm the panic that she was in because she phones him in a panic each time.

Doctor Z.   I think he felt worried that he had brought her in to the surgery, as was suggested.

Dr. F.   That is a trifle worrying, and he wanted reassurance on that point. He was still stuck in this dilemma of physical versus psychological, wasn't he? A little bit of him was still worried that she would have some strange paroxysmal dyspnoea and would drop dead en route to the surgery. He hadn't convinced himself 100%.

Dr. Main   My feeling is a bit different. — If this woman threw her arms round his neck, would he be thinking, 'Let me see now, is this something psychosomatic?' *(Laughter).*

Dr. Z.   I have just remembered that she did actually say to him: "Do you think I am good-looking?"

Dr. Main   I am not in any way surprised. And what did he say? — "Oh yes, rather ..."

Doctor Z.   Yes, I think so.

Dr. Main I think if he had done a vaginal examination, it wouldn't have been a professional one. The thing here is that this is a frightened doctor, but did the group get it out in the open? It's a flirtatious patient and he is frightened.

Dr. F. Was he frightened to go to her home, do you think, the third time?

Dr. Main Let's get it clear: did the doctor think that was going on, or not?

Doctor Z. I don't think so. I am not sure. I don't think it was ever brought out in the open.

Dr. Main The leader didn't bring it out in the open?

Doctor Z. No, I didn't. I made a few hints, like, 'Why has she picked on you?' sort of thing — 'Perhaps she finds you more attractive than the others'.

Dr. J. This is very difficult, isn't it? Because the doctor himself is feeling not only threatened by the woman but possibly rather attracted to her too.

Dr. Main Frightened by his own wishes, yes.

Dr. J. And you mustn't discuss it, or you can't discuss it.

Dr. Main I don't see why you shouldn't. This is the important thing, instead of this so-called reassurance which we can't give. Why can't his colleagues help him? Certainly occasionally a doctor is attracted towards his patient, and here is a good example. Why was he attracted to the patient? Because she is an attractive woman and a bit flirtatious and he didn't get into his professional thinking — 'How interesting, I have a flirtatious patient!'

Dr. E. 'And it worries me . . . '

Dr. Main 'And it worries me' was his first reaction, instead of thinking, 'What an interesting patient!'

Dr. I. But did it come out that this was part of his anxiety when he asked her to come to the surgery because he was afraid of going to her house?

Doctor Z. No, not really.

Dr. Main The group could have spotted this and the leader could have helped them.

Dr. J. I still think it is very threatening, because this is not the only woman patient he has on his list.

Dr. Main   That is why it should be brought out into the open and turned into a professional matter. But the doctor slipped up a bit, and doctors do sometimes. But they can recover themselves if they are willing to see: 'Here is a flirtatious patient. How interesting! I wonder what it is about?' And they can then start discussing with the patient.

Dr. J.   Yes. This is the meaning of his perpetually looking at the other G.P.s, who happened to be men, of course.

Doctor Z.   That's right.

Dr. J.   'Does this happen to you?' sort of look . . .

Doctor Z.   I remember, he was quite surprised when he reported her question, about 'did he find her attractive?'

Dr. Main   Let's get back to the task of the leader.

Dr. I.   Yes, I was wondering if the leader was surprised as well.

Doctor Z.   Yes I was, actually.

Dr. I.   I was expecting you to say that the patient had dropped dead on the way to the surgery.

Dr. Main   I think the leader was a bit disapproving of all this because she latched on to this man's own disapproval of his own conduct.

Doctor Z.   I expect I was half-aware, but in fact I didn't bring it out.

Dr. Main   It was frightening, and that is why there was this attempt at reassurance. Reassurance means the doctor can't stand it. Or if the leader starts reassuring it means the leader can't stand it — 'No need to worry!' *(Laughter).*

Doctor Z.   I don't think it was deliberate. I don't think I had really fully taken the point about the sexiness.

Dr. Main   But you should have done.

3.

Leader Doctor S.

A doctor who does a special family planning clinic in his practice talked about a young, newly married patient, pretty, blonde, who came for the pill. While he was doing a routine vaginal examination she said, "Could you tell me where my clitoris is?" He said that it seemed fairly easy to show her and afterwards as she put her clothes on she said she didn't feel she was getting all the feelings with sex that she should do. She used to get some contractions when she was young and masturbated, and thought she ought to get it when she makes love. At the end she asked if she could come again with her husband.

The doctor said: "When they came they held hands together while I talked to them and I felt like a kind of teacher again, talking about 'were their expectations a bit too high since they had only been married a short while and perhaps they were going at it a bit too much'. At the end of it this pleasant girl said, 'I feel much better about it now. Thank you very much, doctor'. . . ".

Doctor S.   I don't remember much about the group discussion, but I felt pleased that it seemed to be a suitable case that had been dealt with quite sensitively, and I sort of congratulated him.

Dr. Tunnadine   I think he was frightened out of his wits and got cold feet. Sexy girl. . . Ran away from it badly after starting off well.

Doctor S.   Yes. There was a point when somebody said: "Why did you let the husband come?" And somebody else said: "Perhaps you wanted him there as a chaperone". I forgot that bit. He did say, "Yes, I do like to have someone else around".

Dr. Tunnadine   The group had no opportunity to look at the seductiveness of this patient and the difficulty for the doctor and his need to bring up reinforcements. What a wonderful story: five weeks married . . . But the bit that is missing is that she knew how to do it ten years ago, as I heard the case.

Doctor S.   I didn't hear it like that. I heard it just as a girl who had great expectations, but was rather disappointed and needed to talk it over to find out what it was about.

Dr. Tunnadine — but was told, "Don't have such expectations". In the same way as you and the group apparently told the doctor: 'Very good so far'.

Dr. I. But why did the patient need to come and talk about it? She's not dim, is she?

Dr. Main She didn't know where it was.

Dr. V. She wanted *him* to point it out.

Dr. I. Yes. And she was still up on the couch.

Dr. Tunnadine It was very hot stuff. I think the doctor did do pretty well with it and reported very honestly that in effect, although he might not have seen it in those terms, he got cold feet and brought in the husband and calmed them all down. My fed-upness is that it somehow went down the line and we all agreed that he was very sensitive and the opportunity to look at the hot potato side of was missed simply because the leader found herself saying, "I think you did very well".

Dr. Main The group didn't understand or discuss much about the patient or the doctor's technique. It was as though you were saying, 'It was nice, we're not going to criticise you'. There is something about this doctor which requires the leader to respond in this way, and perhaps the group too.

Doctor S. Mm, I think it's his bashfulness.

Dr. I. It didn't come through that he felt anxious when she asked him to show her her clitoris when she was up on the couch. He must have been worried sick.

Doctor S. I'm not sure you see. He's nervous about presenting cases in this group, but back at the ranch he was doing some good work without realizing it.

Dr. Main The girl said it wasn't as much fun as she thought it was going to be and she was told, 'Well, your expectations are too high, dear'.

Dr. I. — 'You are having it off too often'.

Dr. Main Yes. So, 'Don't be distressed, don't feel the way you are feeling, feel the way I would like you to feel'. I don't know what the trouble with the woman was. Wasn't enjoying what? What's her complaint about?

Dr. Tunnadine What she said in much more attractive terms was: 'These men are not nearly as good as my finger any day'.

Dr. Main   That's right. The good thing about masturbation is that you get a better class of partner. I think this is what she was saying.

Dr. Tunnadine   I think so; which is not very nice for a nice but frightened doctor doing his best.

Dr. Main   There are a number of things missing. The particular thing I wonder about is that you could have asked the group what was going on between the doctor and the patient. Ask them to inquire into the doctor/patient relation. It's been a discussion of patients' and doctors' techniques, but not the doctor/patient relation. So what do you think was going on between this patient and this doctor?

Mrs. R.   A lot of sexy seductiveness.

Dr. Tunnadine   Making it very difficult for him to be a doctor.

Dr. I.   But that didn't come out. He didn't express any of it at all.

Dr. Tunnadine   No. And I'm not at all surprised that he then found himself bringing in the husband and saying, 'Don't ask too much of me'.

Dr. Main   A lot was going on. The other thing which could have been discussed which I like to bring up in a seminar is: what sort of hot potato was this? What's the woman like? What sort of person? What is she doing there? What does she look like, what does she sound like, what is your feeling about her, what's it like to be with her? I think this might have opened it up. Nobody seems to know what is going on between these two. You can't discuss the doctor's technique unless you know what is going on between the patient and the doctor.

Dr. I.   Unless it was too frightening, because he found her attractive.

Dr. Main   There you *are* discussing the doctor/patient relation. Maybe the group could have got at that. My impression is she's a good-looking girl.

Dr. Tunnadine   Oh yes, I think we've all got this blonde bombshell picture.

Dr. Main   Yes, and she's really come to say: 'Look, I'm very disappointed with my husband'. And the doctor said, 'Well, don't expect too much'. The other thing is, perhaps they have indulged in it too much. What is too much? Is there such a thing as too much?

Dr. Tunnadine   The fact is that the leader, who is normally very interested in why partners are brought in, didn't explore this, but just said, 'very good'.

Dr. Main   The other thing is to be in a group where there is praise and say: "What good do you think that is going to do?", and draw attention to the fact that they are not criticising or commenting.

Dr. Tunnadine   And yet the leader couldn't open it up either.

Dr. Main   That woman is certainly too passionate for her doctor, and he told her so.

Dr. I.   But he didn't tell the group so.

Dr. Main   The group didn't spot it.

Doctor S.   There was the atmosphere that he stayed very professional as the doctor *(Laughter)*.

Dr. I.   He could still have admitted his feelings about it.

Dr. Tunnadine   But he did report that he'd actually thought about it. He'd thought: 'I'm being a teacher'. So it wasn't bad, was it?

Doctor S.   I thought in a sense it deserved a lot of praise compared with so much work that we hear about.

Dr. Tunnadine   But deserved, therefore, a little bit more of a look at the spot he was in.

Dr. Main   Yes, praise is useless. They are not there to be praised, they are there to learn; and he didn't learn much from it.

4.

Leader Doctor A.

The case was of a 59-year-old woman who came to the doctor, a G.P. who had recently joined a partnership of three others. She asked if he could give her something to calm her husband down, as

*he was always chasing her about and making sexual advances. The
doctor must have made some encouraging remark, because she went
on to tell him how it had been difficult at first: it had taken them
eighteen months to consummate the marriage. She felt this was
because her mother had warned her to be careful with men who did
bad things to you. Later she had learnt to enjoy it, but after her
mother died she had stopped enjoying it, although she still allowed it
every now and then.*

*The doctor tried to say that this was rather sad, and the patient
said: "Do you think I am too old?" Later in the interview she asked
whether she ought to be discussing this with someone as young as he
was: "You are a young man, with a young family, new to the
practice". He reassured her that if this was something she was
worried about, then it was all right to discuss it with a professional
doctor. He felt quite hopeful that he could help her.*

Doctor A. The group felt a bit despondent about the chances of
helping someone of this age, but did discuss the effect of her
mother, and although it seemed a hopeless sort of case the doctor
remained hopeful. After some prodding from me they began to
look at what sort of husband this was who went on trying, and
maybe she did manage to give him some encouragement. Perhaps
she was rather ambivalent about it. I had to poke them into
looking at what had gone on between the doctor and the patient,
and they seemed to think the remarks about his age were a ruse to
divert the doctor's attention from her sexuality.

Dr. S. It seemed as if the presenting doctor saw the
doctor/patient relation as, 'I am young and she is old'; but he
didn't conceptualise it as that. He must have been feeling
something about, 'Maybe she thinks she is too old for sex and I
am young and sexy': a certain amount of discomfort in that
revelation. But he could only report the facts. He couldn't
actually talk about his feelings.

Dr. Main It wasn't discussed much.

Dr. Tunnadine The leader had to prod them into it.

Dr. Main Did she prod them about this funny age remark?

Doctor A. Yes. They did think this doctor was in a difficulty.

Dr. Main No — did they discuss what the woman *meant?*

Doctor A. Yes they did. They said, 'This woman is using a diverting tactic of the doctor's age, hopefully for the doctor to say that they shouldn't be discussing it'.

Dr. S. I don't think that is right, you see. I think they just thought that up as an answer.

Mrs. R. I thought he was quite professional in the way he said it was a professional encounter.

Dr. Main He wasn't getting at the anxiety, as Dr. S. is pointing out.

Dr. S. I am not suggesting he should say so, but just be aware that he was some kind of young person who has all the fun and sex nowadays and is envied by older people.

Dr. Tunnadine It's interesting how we all heard this differently. I heard that despite her 59 years she was disturbingly seductive in that remark, and he said, 'Yes, this is a *professional* interview'.

Dr. Main She was excited at this doctor.

Dr. Tunnadine She set him up for it in lots of ways.

Dr. Main Dr. S. can smell the excitement about it.

Dr. S. Yes, I can. I haven't quite got it right, but I was aware that there was some bit of excitement in that communication.

Doctor A. Somebody in the group said: "This is a man/woman relationship now rather than a doctor/patient relation".

Dr. S. You kept that sexy bit quiet, didn't you? *(Laughter).*

Dr. Main The doctor ran away from it. He couldn't stand the excitement.

Dr. Tunnadine It was very difficult for him and he was carefully professional, but she was a very seductive and powerful patient. What impressed me was that the group did in fact get round to drawing a parallel between the doctor/patient and the husband/patient — not the one that I would draw, but they did work on that. It seemed to be rather good, really.

Dr. Main I am sorry they didn't acknowledge the woman's sexuality. They ran away from it.

Mrs. R. Someone did pick this up, in fact.

Dr. C. They said, 'Why did he continue to try?', or something.

Doctor A. Yes, they did say that. They started off by saying that she tried to avoid sex altogether. Then they came round in the end to the fact that she was a person who was sad that she wasn't enjoying it and something in her really did want to get back to enjoying it.

Dr. S. And kept men going.

Dr. Main — 'But it's not right that I should be enjoying this. . .'

Doctor A. She was ambivalent about it.

Dr. Main The question is, could the leader have done more to help the group discuss it?

Doctor A. I wish they could have got on to the doctor/patient relationship without my having to say anything, because I think it's time I didn't have to say that.

Dr. Main Of course it's time they should! The trouble is, they have difficulty discussing the sexuality of their patients.

Doctor A. It was mentioned, but it wasn't very thoroughly discussed. Somebody said: "Here we are now with a man/woman relationship", but the doctor very quickly tried to turn it into a doctor/patient relationship because he didn't like it being a man/woman relationship: that made him feel awkward.

Dr. Tunnadine In a funny way I felt that the leader had to do something like it, because she had a poke at the doctor/patient relation and the sexuality; and then she said that it somehow didn't bear much fruit. So she then decided to draw attention to the patient/husband relationship, as though she thought, 'Let's get this safe again' or something.

Dr. Main What recommendations would any of us here make to a doctor who is faced with a sexual situation? Does he run away from it, or discuss it? I suppose the task of the leader would be to point out to the group that it was not discussing how to handle sexual doctor/patient relations.

Dr. A. I suppose I do find it a bit difficult to draw attention to this and discuss it.

Dr. Main Offer it to the group.

Dr. Tunnadine That is the most difficult thing — a young man with a seductive older woman patient — an embarrassing difficulty. . .

Dr. Main — Or, the old man and the young seductive woman.

Dr. Tunnadine All right, that's the other one. It's one of the most important things, if they can find some way of making this into a clinical event. There must be skills for it; I don't know what.

Doctor A.   I didn't really draw as much attention to that as I could have done.

Dr. Tunnadine   You had a go at it. You are looking at the bad side of them. It was quite a brave case for a doctor to bring after three terms. That's the good news, I would have thought.

Dr. C.   It's a compliment that the doctor comes and brings it. One of my doctors just stays away, because he can't face it.

Dr. Main   What's the relation between this doctor discussing things with the group and the kind of leadership they have got? Does this leader dominate the discussion, for example?

Dr. S.   No. She leaves them free to do a lot of talking.

Dr. Tunnadine   And then pulls them away at a certain stage.

Dr. S.   And pokes them! *(Laughter).*

Dr. Main   But not very often.

Doctor A.   But I hear other people's doctors, in younger groups than mine, making really perceptive remarks without having to be poked to do it.

Dr. F.   You did express the anxiety that maybe you had spoon-fed them about the particular aspect of looking at the doctor/patient relationship, and that has become your role in the process.

Doctor A.   To say, "Look here, get on with the work". And then they begin rather reluctantly to start looking at what was happening.

Dr. Main   Is it possible, if you let them alone for a bit longer, they would come round to it?

Doctor A.   I don't know. I don't think I have ever let them go the whole discussion without making a remark.

Dr. S.   It's quite a difficult concept for people to get hold of; it's part of this unlearning and then learning a new thing. I think you do have to poke them.

Dr. Tunnadine   And it wouldn't be surprising in this particular case if they would prefer to stay longer; because it is very dodgy stuff, hot stuff, and they would rather discuss anything than that.

Dr. Main   The   leader   didn't   discuss   the   doctor/patient relationship except in rather generalised terms.

Dr. Tunnadine   Rather professional terms.

Dr. Main   Remote terms. Instead of saying, 'How about the doctor/patient relation?', say, 'How about the sexual remarks this woman made to the doctor?'

Doctor A.   I suppose really I rather fled away from it as well because I feel it is a rather difficult thing to deal with.

Dr. Main   Sex is.

Doctor A.   Rather a difficult part of it.

Dr. Tunnadine   But a particularly important part of it for this work. I think something about our discussion is a clue to it, because somehow we were concerned with the doctor's sexuality and it is nothing to do with the doctor's sexuality, as far as I can see. I think he presented it because it felt like that to him, which makes it more difficult to look at. It was the 59-year-old who was doing it all actually and the doctor presented it as if he was uneasy about his own response.

Dr. S.   He admitted to feeling awkward, didn't he? But it really didn't get interpreted.

Dr. Main   The young doctor can't imagine that a 59-year-old woman's sexual life could still be dominated by ardent wishes on the one hand and a disapproving mother on the other. A 59-year-old woman dominated by her mother!

Doctor A.   The group discussed that quite a bit: how could it be possible?

Dr. Main   And he will see the patient again, won't he?

Doctor A.   Yes.

A further case of hidden sexuality in the interview, where the doctor is a younger woman and the patient an older man, is discussed in II A 5.

C

C. MORE DEFENCES

A multiplicity of defences are used by patients as a protection against anxiety and as a flight from pain and difficulty. Sexuality, as illustrated in the previous chapter, is one of these. Defences are also employed in many ways by doctors and groups. Some of the varied faces of these defences are mirrored in the following digests.

1. HISTORICAL DEFENCE.
2. DEFENCE BY LABELLING, EXAMINING, QUOTING THE SEMINAR.
3. DEFENSIVE LABELLING AGAIN.
The first three digests in this chapter are concerned with a few of the many defences put up by doctors. They include taking a history, giving things labels and doing physical examinations. Others are mentioned elsewhere in the text.

4. ANYTHING IS EASIER THAN TALKING ABOUT SEX — DEAD BABIES.
5. ANYTHING IS EASIER THAN TALKING ABOUT SEX — CANCER.
The last two digests tackle the way in which both doctors and patients can sometimes find it easier to talk about the most painful and distressing subjects, such as death and dying, rather than face the intimacy and embarrassment of talking about sex.

1. Historical defence

Leader Doctor S.

A leader brought this difficulty of a doctor who always presented cases with a long history.

Doctor S.   We had been round the room to see what work there was to do, so I took the next case in order. The doctor presented a patient with a very long rambling history and everyone started to look a bit confused. I interrupted the doctor and said, "I think this patient is giving you too much information so that you cannot look at what is happening in the here and now". She did manage to bring it back to what the patient was doing to her. It had all been about mothers and grandmothers.

Dr. Q.   This dismay at the reference to the grandmother — was that taken up?

Doctor S.   I think I said, "That's irrelevant, isn't it? The patient is with this doctor. What went on a century ago doesn't matter, does it?" — and then she sort of looks at me as though she is squashed and I feel I've squashed her.

Dr. A.   And you feel terrible.

Doctor S.   I feel that it's not helping her really to go away crushed. She doesn't understand why I said it was irrelevant.

Dr. Tunnadine   Well, that's her fault.

Dr. Q.   You need to put it back to her — "Why ask that question? What is your feeling behind it?"

Doctor S.   Sometimes I've done that and she will say, "Well, I thought perhaps the grandmother would have had an effect on the mother and this may be having an effect on her". You know, all the mothers and fathers bit which we've learned to —

Dr. Tunnadine   How about letting the group get at her, then?

Dr. Main   Or, to pick up another thing: when people use a defence like that — the *historic defence* — it's because there has been some moment of difficulty between the doctor and the patient, and the best thing the doctor could do to get out of the difficulty is to say, "Tell me more about your mother and father". The history-taking occurs at a moment of tension. It's very nice to be able to pin-point the moment when these tensions arise; then you can really get at the anxiety between the doctor and the patient.

Dr. Q.   So this is what we need to bring out as a leader?

Dr. Main   It's not always easy to do, though. If a doctor starts defending, it's not because they are a good doctor or a bad doctor, it's because *something has gone on* to make the doctor that way. You might as well talk about the weather as talk about the grandmother — it's some sort of retreat from a painful situation which the doctor doesn't understand or is too difficult.

Dr. Tunnadine   Presumably if this doctor was making this comment about somebody else's case it was because she had got stuck at that point in listening to the case.

Dr. Main   If we could go back to that moment when she got stuck, wouldn't it be nice to be able to examine it — scientifically, not "That's good, that's bad" — and look at what happened and see what the problem was.

Dr. Q.   Then she wouldn't be squashed; she would be learning.

2. Defence by labelling, examining, quoting the seminar

Leader Doctor L.

A doctor began to tell his group about a patient who had come in that morning in a distressed state because her boyfriend had just told her he wanted to be a homosexual. In response to the opening, "tell me about yourself", the patient had given a very long story about getting married young to a man who only wanted anal intercourse, and then being told by her second husband that she had made him impotent.

Doctor L.   I felt this was rather beefy stuff for a young group. In response to the story the group began to talk about the patient and finally labelled her "a castrating female". Having found a label the group seemed happier.

Dr. Main   Once they have got a label, that is the end of all thought, so that's another defence. You know how an anxious woman with a hot kid thinks, 'My God, suppose they are dying!' The doctor comes and says, "It's measles", and the woman says, "Ah, I see . . ." It makes an enormous difference to the whole anxiety situation if you can put a label on things. This labelling defence could have been remarked on by the leader, because you saw it. You saw how comfortable they felt afterwards. — What was the patient's complaint?

Doctor L.   "I don't want my boyfriend to be homosexual".

Dr. Tunnadine   At some stage, I think, you said that he did a vaginal examination, or some such crazy carry-on.

Dr. C.   He didn't know what else to do, and she did have a coil in.

Dr. Main   When you don't know what to do, that is the trick: get them up on the couch!

Dr. Tunnadine   The funny thing is that although it seems premature and unthinking, it wasn't a bad bit of intuitive doctoring, because it sounds as if the woman was saying: 'What's wrong with me that I drive people away?'

Dr. Main   So was she asking what the matter was with her, or simply that she wanted to keep her boyfriend? — 'My boyfriend says he is leaving because he wants to become a homosexual. Please help me'. And he gives her a vaginal examination. What an odd thing!

Doctor L.   In the case presentation he said that when she finished the story he didn't know what to do. He thought about the seminar and that the first thing I would ask was about a vaginal examination. So he said, 'Hop on the couch'.

Dr. Main   You might have pointed out that when you are in trouble there are various things you can do to get out of the trouble. One is to take a history and we've just seen another one: put the patient on the couch, because that is another way of dodging the problem. Another is to say, 'What is the seminar going to do?' You don't have to go on thinking about the problem really; you just turn to magic. This was a frightened defence against the immediate situation which must have been very frightening for him. I don't know why it was so frightening for him, but it was, and the group didn't really inquire into what was so frightening for him. They wanted to kind of comfort him.

Doctor L.   They certainly wanted to comfort him, particularly at the beginning.

Dr. S.   You didn't want to be so beefy, and I thought this was a seminar about psychosexual problems, which are likely to be beefy, aren't they?

Dr. Tunnadine   Well, some are more beefy than others. Not many of our psychosexual problems are women who pick men who prefer the rectum; because that is what the patient has got, isn't it? Never mind what bad luck she has had, she's a funny picker, isn't she? It's a bit off our beat, I would have thought.

Mrs. R.   Then her other man can't keep going, any how.

Doctor L.   Yes, the second husband said she made him impotent. There is a power in this woman. This was discussed — that this woman was a powerful woman — but I don't know that it helped us all that much.

Dr. I.   They didn't help him to understand what he was looking for, which was a diagnosis of what she was really complaining of.

Dr. Main   Was the conclusion that she was a powerful woman generally accepted?

Doctor L.   Yes.

Dr. Main   The evidence being?

Doctor L.   Well, I think they went back to this castrating woman thing.

Dr. Main   Yes, but I wondered what the evidence was for it, that was all. Is there any evidence?

Doctor L.   Well, she was supposed to have made the husband impotent.

Dr. P.   That's what he said.

Doctor L.   Her interpretation was that she had driven the first husband away.

Dr. Main   That's the anal chap. He was a really strong man.

Doctor L.   I don't know about him being a strong man, but certainly she felt he had run away from her. Now this third man . . .

Dr. Main   Who wanted to be a homosexual. A very powerful woman. It's not evidence, is it, that she's castrating? It's evidence that she picks up weak men but she is frightened of strong ones.

Dr. I.   She frightened this doctor.

Dr. Main   I don't think she did frighten this doctor. The *problem* frightened the doctor: he never looked at it.

Dr. I.   So perhaps she is frightened of being weak.

Dr. Main   The sign that the doctor was frightened was that he rushed into the vaginal examination and didn't look at the problem; but what was the problem frightening him?

Doctor L.   I don't think he knew what the problem was.

Dr. Main   I don't either.

Doctor L.   He said he'd never had this experience before.

Dr. I.   He didn't even attempt to find out what the problem was.

Dr. P.   I think it's something to do with the woman being a victim, that somehow whatever you do for her it's going to be wrong.

Doctor L.   You feel that again this woman has been made a victim by his vaginal examination — is that what you mean?

Dr. P.   I suppose so, but somehow he was being . . .

Dr. S.   Too forceful, or . . .

Dr. Tunnadine   I haven't heard what the doctor felt. We know he felt some panic which needn't necessarily be fear.

Dr. Main   There's been a fair amount of talk about what kind of woman this is — is she castrating or not? — and I'm going to get hooked on the same thing: is she really a castrator, or is she a chooser of weak males, or what? We don't have any evidence for this, but the group also got hooked on what kind of patient is this? and is she a castrator? and so on. But they didn't work out what the hell was going on between this doctor and this patient who came and complained about her men going off, and what the doctor did with it, and why he did what he did, and what he felt about it, and what he was doing with her, and what she was doing with him . . . I don't know. The group wasn't able to examine this side of it clearly, was it? Was she presenting herself as a victim, or not? We don't know. What was she doing with that doctor, what was she trying to get from him, how was she using him, how was he using her? I don't really know this. Once you start studying the patient you are lost.

Dr. B.   She herself came out with a long, long history, didn't she? — because I was surprised in a way that she told him that her boyfriend said the night before that he was going off and was going to be homosexual. The doctor said something about, 'Tell me about yourself', and then there was this long screed about all her sexual experiences. I don't know whether he had expected that, but she went back over the whole of her sexual history.

Dr. Main   Did the doctor initiate that?

Dr. B.   Yes. He said, "Tell me about yourself".

Dr. Main   It's better than listening, isn't it — asking questions?

Dr. Tunnadine   And got what — a tale of woe or an exciting sexy story? Or both at the same time?

Dr. Main   Was the woman distressed when she came to him? Apparently she was distressed; she came to the doctor and said, "My boyfriend is leaving me". Not, "There is something wrong with me".

Dr. P.   When given the option to start somewhere, she chose to start way back at the beginning.

Dr. Main   I know, but the question is: who had achieved that? The doctor said, "Tell me about yourself", that is, he took the attention away from the distress and said, "Tell me about the history", and she gave it to him. If he had shut up and let her have her head then that wouldn't have happened. I think he would have had to examine the events of last night or the relationship in the present.

Doctor L.   It's so obvious when Doctor Main points it out that she escaped from what happened last night, but how to get the group to look at this?

Dr. Main   Why not show the group the comfort that labels bring? They end all thought. 'We've got the whole thing taped — a castrating woman — we needn't bother any more, needn't discuss anything with her, needn't work with her: she's a castrating woman and that's that. The anxieties of dealing with *that* patient by *that* doctor *that* night is a different order altogether. It's interesting how the group uses its defences against thinking. I once wrote a very good paper — well, it wasn't a very good paper, but it had a good title, the title was the best thing about it, it was called, "Knowledge, Learning and Freedom from Thought". It was a discussion of how the possession of knowledge saves you from the burden of thinking. You don't have to think, you just *know*; and then you don't have to stick with the situation, be ignorant and flounder around and do your own thinking. Once you have got knowledge in, then you are all right. The group is at present at the stage of grabbing at knowledge — 'Ah, it's due to this. That's what it's called'. This is our traditional medical training.

Dr. Tunnadine Castration anxiety — that's something I've read somewhere!

Dr. Main Go on, say another big word!

3. Defensive labelling again

Leader Doctors J. & E.

In a fairly new group a doctor was talking about a patient who came to the surgery with a red eye. She had a nine-month-old baby and the doctor's first impression was that she looked different; she looked huge. They had a discussion about the sore eye, but the doctor was conscious all the time of the patient's changed appearance and he was trying to get round to discussing it with her. He said things like, "Everything back to normal?" and the woman said, "More or less". Finally, he said: "What about contraception?" and she said, "I am thinking about the Pill". This gave him the opportunity to mention her weight and at this the patient burst into tears and said everything was awful: they hadn't had sex since the baby. At this the doctor became very active and gave her instructions about diet and how she should talk to her husband and communicate more. He said that he felt very sympathetic and really wanted to help this woman.

Doctor J. The group talked about post-natal depression, about sex and pregnancy, and about reasons for the weight gain. I tried to point out the change in the doctor before and after the tears: the gentle listening doctor who became an active instructing doctor in the face of the distress. Some of the group felt that this was perfectly reasonable: 'When someone is in a state like that, you tell them what to do'.

Dr. Main   It sounds as if it was discussed in terms of good and bad, rather than 'What was going on between the doctor and the patient?'. I was impressed by the fact that they started to talk about post-natal depression; what that is, I don't know. There are a lot of sad women about and labelling them ends all thinking, because once you have got a good name for it, all thinking ends. So I noticed a flight from the difficulties by using that term. It satisfied them. The other flight was the doctor, understandably in the tradition of his own prescriptive medicine, telling the patient what to do. The doctor didn't understand the problem; was faced with this sad woman who was fat and unhappy sexually. This is what we all do when we don't know how to deal with it: we get certain, and leave the problem. I would have thought there was a chance to point this out.

Doctor J.   Yes. There was such a contrast for the doctor before the tears and after the tears. He had been a very quiet, understanding doctor who had been prepared to let the patient say things or not say things. He knew the patient wasn't talking about being fat, but he was prepared to wait. Then after the feelings were exposed, he did take fright and started giving directions. I think the group were clearly on to it and showed him — well, they needed a bit of prodding — but they recognised that it was the pain that had made him do this.

Dr. Main   You were able to face the group with the idea that the doctor's behaviour was because of the inability to face the problem?

Dr. Tunnadine   The interesting thing about the doctoring to me was that the doctor knew what he wanted to talk about as soon as the woman came into the room, and pussyfooted about it so much, as though he was feeling, 'Can I get away without talking about this weight?'

Doctor J.   — And when the pain of the problem was revealed, he was overwhelmed by it.

Dr. Tunnadine   Of course. That was the point, wasn't it! It sounds as though the group were discussing it well enough, but the leaders' technique. . . — they keep saying they prod, but they don't really say how they do it, or how they got the group away from this theoretical stuff.

Doctor E. You asked a direct question about the feelings involved when this woman burst into tears.

Doctor J. I said, "Can you say what response you felt when she burst into tears?" I think he said that he felt overwhelming sadness for her.

Doctor E. I said something like, "Isn't it interesting that this doctor changed at that point in that consultation? Can we discuss what sort of doctor he was *before* and what happened *afterwards* and what was the reason for the change?"

Dr. Main That's a good bit of group leadership. You draw attention to something they were on the point of recognising. You pointed it out there and asked them to think about it. They took up odd positions after that, like, "I think it was quite right", which is not the same as discussing; but they got round to the change. It was something to do with the doctor's distress. I would have thought the change was because the doctor didn't know what the hell was going on. The route out of ignorance is to pretend to know what to do. The case is not understood and I wouldn't have expected the doctor to have understood the case in a general practitioner consultation, where the woman came in presenting her eye. I think the doctor did very well to get anywhere near the fact of the woman's distress and then — "Aah!" — he took flight: understandably in a busy surgery. Doctors do take flight, but groups shouldn't be allowed to.

Dr. P. Would it have been possible for the leader to say at this point, "We are not here to say it is good or bad; we are trying to *understand?*" Did you say, "Why did the doctor act in this way and what did it mean to the patient?"

Dr. Main It was inevitable because of the doctor's fears. It wasn't good or bad. It was a defensive manoeuvre: understandable.

4. Anything is easier than talking about sex — dead babies

Leader Doctor A.

A family planning doctor said she wanted to talk about a patient with a very sad background. Her trouble was that she did not want to make love, and this had started after her baby had died. It had been born prematurely and was taken into the special care baby unit where she was watching it one day and she saw it stop breathing. She told the nurse, who said she thought it was all right but she would send for the doctor, but the doctor didn't come for twenty minutes and the mother knew the baby was dead. It was made worse by the fact that the husband had left just before the baby stopped breathing. She was deserted at her time of need. Afterwards the editor of a woman's magazine heard about it and wrote it up, so it became something of a cause célèbre.*

The doctor felt terribly sad, almost like crying, but gave the patient her pills and arranged for her to come back again. At the next visit the doctor tried to open the subject up, to discuss the grief and anger at the hospital and the husband, but the patient denied this. The next time she came to the clinic she firmly told the nurse that she didn't want to see the doctor, who felt rejected and guilty, not having helped the patient as she should have done.

Doctor A.   I had great difficulty making the group discuss the doctor/patient relationship, because when this was finished all the group could discuss was: 'What should you do if people have dead babies? Why did the hospital not say they were sorry? Why did the report on the hospital not identify the neglect?' They went off at a tangent.

Dr. Main   Why would they do that?

Doctor A.   I tried to point out to them that it was such a painful business altogether and that we were so depressed and miserable afterwards, it was better talking about all these general things than looking at what was actually happening. Although I said that several times — I counted six times — they were still talking about generalisations and all sorts of other things.

Dr. B.   It was much too painful.

Dr. Main   Interesting point. Obviously you went back and back to it — your timing was not right. I wouldn't know what the right time was. You should time an interpretation at the time when they can accept it. As you know — not too early and not too late!

Doctor A. I obviously did it at the wrong time.

Dr. Main Yes, but how do you find out the right time? It's really a very difficult matter. Let them have their defence for a certain time. You can't just kick it down as soon as it arises unless the underlying pain is mentioned. Telling them they are running away won't do. You see a man running away and say, "You're running away from something", and he says, "Yeah", and keeps on running!

Doctor A. It was actually because the group felt very depressed and miserable after they had heard this story. They felt like crying too, as the doctor had done.

Dr. Main Well, thank God the leader had no feelings!

Doctor A. Well, it was a dreadful feeling. It was a terrible report.

Dr. Main What about the leader, though?

Doctor A. I felt depressed as well. I thought, 'What a terrible story!' I could understand why the group were all sitting there looking depressed and miserable.

Dr. B. But were you able to say it? Did you say, "We're all caught up in this terrible mood of depression"?

Doctor A. I think somebody else said it. They also bolstered the doctor, but she felt she had hardly been able to do anything because she had been so depressed herself by it. The group tried to say to her, 'Just sitting and listening to the woman and sympathising and being there allowed her to pour all this stuff out; and that was useful'. I suppose in a way they were running away from saying something hard to the doctor about how she could have used the situation.

Dr. B. Perhaps it wasn't the right moment. Next time she would be fit to cope with the patient. Perhaps the grief was too great to be able to do more than just sit and listen.

Dr. Main I don't hear too much grief in this story.

Dr. B. There was a tremendous lot of anger. But that was hidden, wasn't it?

Dr. Main   The point was that the woman wasn't showing grief.

Dr. B.   The doctor was. The doctor was showing the grief the woman should have been feeling.

Dr. P.   The doctor was feeling blamed because she was medical.

Dr. Q.   Ashamed for the medical system.

Dr. Main   Did the group have a go at this at all? Surely when they heard this story they thought: 'What an awful set-up!' That's the message the woman wants to convey. She took this to the doctor, who brought it to the group, and the leader brings it to us; but the group seem to have discussed grief rather than how angry they were on behalf of this patient. Tell us a bit more about the group.

Doctor A.   The group discussed how the patient was rejecting the doctor as she did the husband. They also discussed what they felt was the patient's guilt at not making more efforts to get help for the baby. They felt the patient was still blaming the husband for not being there at the crucial moment; although the patient denied this. There was some anger in the group against the patient for not letting the doctor help her. The magazine story she didn't want written hadn't helped.

Dr. Main   Hang on a second. What's wrong with this patient? What is she complaining of?

Doctor A.   Loss of libido.

Dr. Main   Well, when people have just lost a baby, they don't complain of loss of libido. It's a funny complaint.

Doctor A.   Sorry, I haven't told you something.

Dr. Main   I think so.

Doctor A.   After she'd had the baby, she then conceived again, not very long after, and had another baby.

Dr. Main   So this death occurred a long time ago. We're talking as if it happened yesterday. Did anyone get the impression it was a recent death?

All   Yes.

Dr. Main   If we listen to the story, she said: 'Look, something has died of neglect and it was the callous doctors and nurses who didn't take any notice, but let it happen'. How long ago was this?

Doctor A.   About three years ago.

Dr. Main   You see — so what is it, this story? The woman's got loss of libido, there's that story. But it's interesting that we don't use our brains in this business. We're all suckers.

Dr. G.   May I ask what put you on to that?

Dr. Main   The material: that something was dead out of neglect. The other thing was that she was complaining of loss of libido after the death of a baby. I don't believe it. We have lost sight of this woman's complaint altogether in some story or other. The patient has been neglected and is dying of neglect. The other business about the publicity given to it: that's the official story and that's what you're supposed to talk about. You must talk about that because people like to hear about it.

Doctor A.   And the doctor feels a failure because she can't go on discussing the patient's problems.

Dr. Main   The patient is fed up with the damn problem. She says so, doesn't she, very clearly? The group was affected by all this. Did the group cotton on to the fact that this death had happened quite a long time ago?

Doctor A.   I think they knew that, because the woman obviously did have intercourse again after the death of the baby. She conceived this other baby, but from the minute she conceived this other baby she wouldn't have intercourse in case something damaged this other baby, and she had not wanted it at all since the delivery.

Dr. Main   It wouldn't have stopped a keen woman. There's something wrong with her.

Doctor A.   We were all assuming it was because she was still very angry.

Dr. Main   Suppose we go back to the doctor. The doctor will not defend her. She will insist on this publicity and won't defend her from being a *cause célèbre*. She won't let her tell her own story.

Dr. P.   The patient is only valued for the sake of the story.

Dr. Main   There's a marvellous double offence here. First of all, it's easy to talk about death; much more easy than to talk about sex, which is the difficulty in this case. 'Let's have a good chat about dead babies — keep off the track'. The second offence is the generalisation.

Doctor A.   They talked about how awful hospitals are.

Dr. Main   The poor woman's shyness in talking about sex is apparent, isn't it? But was missed by the doctor and the group. They lost sight of the fact that she came complaining about loss of libido. They took their eye off the ball.

5. Anything is easier than talking about sex — cancer

Leader Doctor I.

In an early group the case presented was a very sad one of a woman with a carcinoma of the lung and secondaries. The patient was complaining of loss of libido. It was a heart-rending story and very long and it seemed the doctor would never stop. The patient had lost weight and has not got long to live and the doctor went on and on about the symptoms, and how he wished her could help her get her libido back in these last few months.

Doctor I.   Finally I said: "Perhaps the loss of libido is secondary to the main problem, as she'd had a ghastly history".

Dr. Main   What did you say that for?

Doctor I.   Well, he'd gone on for about half-an-hour and I was conscious of this being a fairly new group; and the problem as it was presented, the loss of libido, appeared to be just a secondary thing. The doctor was so concerned with the patient, the patient's father, the mother who was in a mental home and her sister who had asthma and nearly died.

Dr. Main   So you let him go on.

Doctor I.   I did. I kept thinking: 'I must stop him! but I don't know how to!'

Dr. Main   Well, at the sister's asthma, you could have said: "Has this got anything to do with the case?" But as it was an early group, you wanted to let it run on.

Doctor I.   I was in two minds.

Dr. S.   How did the rest of the group react?

Doctor I.   They were quite interested, but eventually we did get back to this loss of libido. The husband was very protective of her and scared stiff. The doctor is now seeing the patient on her own but he is also attending a foursome group at the hospice: the patient and the husband and the doctor from the hospice and himself.

Dr. Main   And the foursome was about death, or sex?

Doctor I.   About death. The sex bit only comes when he sees her on his own. The doctor is feeling in need of help because he's not quite sure how to help her to regain her libido. The group discussed how she felt about her own body because she'd lost weight and she feels this is also a loss of femininity. But every time I attempted to ask people what they felt was going on, it was all very cut and dried. I asked him how he felt himself. He's very sorry for this woman. In fact, another member of the group got a little aggressive in that she said, "Isn't he getting too personally involved?" So there was a little discussion on whether one gets personally involved with patients or whether this is a professional involvement. I don't think they came to any conclusions about that. It did seem to go on for a long time and when I once again said, "Perhaps we'll see how she is", one of the others piped up with the fact, "Well, we don't know much about the husband".

Dr. Main   Oh my God!

Doctor I.   So it started all over again. I felt very useless from a point of view of trying to keep it on the problem of the doctor/patient relations as far as the sex problem is concerned, and getting all tied up with this large story of death and, 'She is going to die soon — will she get her libido back in time?'

Dr. N.   Was she wanting her libido for herself, or was she wanting it for her husband?

Doctor I.   She wanted it back for herself.

Dr. Main   Wants to have some fun before she dies.

Dr. N.   That didn't come over clearly to me. I had the feeling she was being pressured by her husband.

Doctor I.   No. In fact, if anything he isn't pressurising her.

Dr. B.   He should be.

Doctor I.   Whereas she felt she was being rejected by him.

Dr. Main   What did the group do?

Doctor I.   All of them participated. They all said something, at which I felt relieved, but it didn't seem to be much of a case to get going on.

Dr. Main   It's very interesting about this sister who has asthma and nearly died! — Absolutely irrelevant, but it's a form of flight.

Dr. Q.   The group didn't want to look at it, or maybe they didn't want to work and it was easier to talk about these other things.

Dr. Main   The question is, how was the leader to draw attention to this in an early group? The flight from the problem, which is not death but sex. The last patient used the death of a baby as a defence, but this doctor is putting cancer up. Doesn't want to talk about sex, but cancer. After all, she's not a human being, she's a cancer case! Cancer cases aren't allowed to have lust or anything like that, or wish to be loved.

Doctor I.   It was a long time before the doctor mentioned sex at all, and I wondered, 'When are we going to get on to the sexual problem?' He felt he had to give all the background, which went on and on.

Dr. Q.   There's relief, though, that they verbalised their feelings to a certain extent, in an early group.

Doctor I.   There were a lot of questions, of course, about the cancer rather than the sex problem, although someone did suggest that she was feeling less of a woman because she had stopped having her periods as well, and was getting thin.

Dr. Main   She needed reassurance that she was a woman.

Dr. N.   What is it about cancer that puts this woman off her sex life?

Dr. P.   You said she was thin and didn't feel she was a woman and wanted to be reassured — was there actually some evidence for that?

Doctor I.   The doctor said he felt this coming from the husband: he felt rejecting of the woman because of her cancer, because she was thin.

Dr. Main   She wasn't being loved because she had cancer.

Doctor I.   He was trying.

Dr. P.   This was coming through the woman — presumably the doctor hadn't seen the husband.

Doctor I.   Yes, he had seen the husband.

Dr. P.   So the woman felt she was rejected by the husband.

Dr. Main   Cancer she could stand, but not this withdrawal of her husband. She wanted a fate worse than death.

Dr. G.   And the interesting thing is that in a foursome to discuss the ending of her life, sex can't be mentioned.

Dr. Main   The business of living isn't allowed to be discussed; only the business of dying.

Dr. B.   There is no reason why in a foursome they shouldn't talk about living, too.

Dr. G.   I am just saying that they don't, the doctor can only do this on a one-to-one.

Dr. B.   Maybe the doctor could bring this up.

Doctor I.   They have raised the fact in the foursome group, that the husband doesn't feel affectionate towards his wife and does want to be close to her, but I don't know how far it's . . .

Dr. Main   That's a bit decent, that talk.

Dr. G.   Arms around the shoulders.

Dr. S.   I think the problem was: 'I feel rejected'.

Dr. Q.   The group were rejecting it, and the doctor was.

Dr. S.   Yes, and you didn't want the presenting doctor to feel rejected.

Doctor I.   No, I didn't.

Dr. Q.   But if you'd said it to the group as a whole, their anxieties and the way they were going away from the problem, it wouldn't actually be attacking the doctor who was presenting it.

Doctor I.   I said: "You must be feeling under pressure to get a result in such a short time", and she said, yes, she was.

Dr. Main   How much time is there?

Doctor I.   Well, she's got secondaries now, although at the moment she's feeling reasonably fit; but the implication was, it's not long.

Dr. Q. So they dismissed it.

Dr. Main   She's got a lot of goodbyes to say, but she hasn't said goodbye to her sex life yet. It is a great delight and it's very important. Is she dead as a woman? There's all sorts of things like that. I would have thought that this woman is in a hurry, and this doctor is in a hurry. These sexy things need to be discussed, but cancer and death are getting in the way.

D.   SMOKE SCREENS

The title of this chapter is taken from the text, where it occurs in two of the three digests. These are rather longer than normal and show the leaders struggling to discover the hidden emotions behind the presented material.

1. ANGER HIDDEN BY SADNESS.

The patient presents the history to the doctor as one of sadness, which made the doctor feel very sad, and it was difficult for the group to see behind this to the hidden anger.

2. THE MUDDLED PATIENT.

The placating doctor has difficulty coping with a patient who was in a muddle, unable to help her express her anger and thus unable to relieve her depression and sadness. This muddle was carried through to the group and the leader.

3. THE LOVER WHO DOES NOT CAUSE DYSPAREUNIA.

Both patient and doctor appear to hide behind a smoke screen of facts, so that the exciting part of the woman was missed, not only by the doctor but also by the group.

1. Anger hidden by sadness

Leader Doctor L.

A patient came to see his young female GP several times with abdominal pain, which was diagnosed as spastic colon. Eventually he said he was worried because he was losing interest and ability in sex. Two years before he had married a nurse, several years older than himself, who already had two children of her own. They had lived together for several years before the marriage and sex had been very frequent and satisfactory. His wife was very keen for them to have a child together, especially as he had no child of his own. The man said, "It's a terrible situation and the most terrible thing about it is that the more she wants a child the less I am able to perform. I am a very busy man. I come home at 12 at night, sit in the train thinking, 'It's going to be tonight. I know I'm not going to be able to manage it', and then I sit downstairs watching the television wondering and worrying. The trouble is, you see, I can only actually manage it occasionally. I must admit that it is during the time of her ovulation, but even so it's very disappointing. She has said, "Of course, if I knew it was going to be like this I'm not sure I would have married you. Perhaps we should separate".'

The doctor went on to say how sad this patient had made her feel. As the patient was leaving the room, he said, "We have been seeing a clinical psychologist who says we have a mother/son relationship, which has made us very angry". This made the doctor feel that she should offer to see the wife as well, but the patient didn't want this.

Doctor L. This is a doctor with a lot of natural talent and empathy with her patients. During the discussion the group agreed it would be useful to see the couple together, but I tried to use the opportunity to discuss this question of sending for the spouse and to point out its uselessness. I felt a bit 'teachy'.

Dr. S. I wonder if the group could really understand the point that you were making in that 'teachy' way.

Dr. Main You just *wonder* — you have no opinion?

Dr. S. I have heard you talk about systems more than once and it made clear to me that having a couple is a different *system* to having one patient. I think it is something which had to be put into words like that, maybe again and again.

Dr. Main   Better than work, isn't it?

Dr. S.   I'm not sure: she hasn't told us.

Dr. Main   And the light that throws on the doctor/patient relation? It swallows the case.

Dr. S.   There was something about how it might be a defence for the doctor to have the other person come.

Dr. Main   Might be? Come on! — do you think it *was* in this case, or not?

Dr. A.   The doctor was so depressed, she hadn't even made another appointment for him, had she?

Doctor L.   Yes, she had.

Dr. A.   I thought she'd sort of dismissed him, but she hadn't.

Dr. Main   This teaching business. . . A funny thing happened. Here is a group supposed to be discussing a case and they finish up with this interesting problem about sending for the spouse — well off the case by now. Then the leader went up this blind alley as well and talked about the general principle of husbands and wives. Very knowledgeable stuff. It's a lovely defence against the problems of the moment with this doctor and this patient, isn't it? It seems to me that you got away from the work, and who can blame you for that?

Dr. A.   It was such a miserable situation. It was so painful and horrid with this doctor sitting there feeling so sorry and having no idea what to do.

Dr. Main   The only way with these husbands and wives is to find out; and you find out case by case by case. In this particular case it was fairly clear what happened between the doctor and the patient, I thought. Do you remember what the report was?

Dr. I.   She kept on saying she was sad.

Dr. Main   The doctor was sad and thought it would be easier if she brought the wife in; and so she said, "What about bringing your wife?" And what did he say?

Dr. S.   "We've been to a psychologist".

Dr. Main   And she thought the psychologist must have got somewhere, so she changed her mind. You call that technique? *(Laughter)* It's nothing to do with technique.

Dr. S.   The patient didn't want the wife to come, did he?

Dr. Main   He made that quite clear. I would have thought the group would have seen that he was saying, "I've tried this wife lark and I don't want my wife here. You're another one too". The man attacked her, didn't he?

Dr. S.   I think he couched it in his rather seductive way, so that she didn't realise she was being attacked.

Dr. Main   It wasn't aggressive, it was sadistic. He slid in the knife, didn't he?

Dr. I.   One way of saying, "That's useless".

Dr. B.   Wasn't his anger with his wife coming out to the doctor?

Dr. Main   Do you want me to tell you? — Come on!

Dr. I.   I couldn't believe the sadness. I think this doctor is annoyed. 'Sad' doesn't seem appropriate. I would have felt angry.

Doctor L.   I did suggest at one stage that there must be some angry feelings. The group took this up and realised that *they* were feeling quite angry with the woman and that maybe this was something that the man was feeling; that it was not only despair and needing to be loved, but also a sense of anger: the sense that this man has a great need to be told that he is good and that love — as opposed to being a sort of stud — was enormously important to him.

Dr. F.   You didn't get on to the good sex at the beginning: four or five times a night. And then. . .

Dr. Main   And then terribly sad. Isn't it interesting how the group didn't get on to this? Let's identify the other things that they didn't discuss.

Dr. I.   The fact that the doctor veered off because as soon as she felt she wasn't getting anywhere her answer was, "Let's get in the wife"; which was irrelevant. And off they went on this other tangent.

Dr. Main   Because she felt. . .

Dr. I.   She wasn't getting anywhere.

Dr. Main   Overwhelmed by sadness.

Dr. I.   I can't go along with the sadness.

Dr. Main   But where's the evidence there is any anger?

Doctor L.   There was the business about, "If you can't make me pregnant, I think we will have to separate. You must have a child, you are younger than me".

Mrs. R. It's a pity he can't produce his own.

Dr. Main He was kind about that.

Dr. B. He was furious.

Dr. Main That's another thing the group didn't pick up.

Dr. I. There must have been a lot of anger coming out and all she picked up was sadness.

Dr. Main She demands, "Either we are going to have a child or not". But he does have intercourse with her.

Dr. B. When she's ovulating.

Dr. Main Not discussed. What's it all about?

Dr. I. And he can't manage it at other times.

Dr. Main She said, "I want a child, otherwise we part", so he has intercourse when she ovulated. It must be marvellous for him, doing what he is told, but nobody picked it up.

Dr. B. They didn't look at the chain that seemed to have developed since they married.

Dr. Main Did they get onto this business of his life as a slave?

Doctor L. No.

Dr. Main It's amazing they didn't. I think the group leader might have pointed out the funny things about this.

Doctor L. Yes.

Dr. Main Ogden Nash said, "The friends of the born nurse are always feeling worse". The nurse has to have a baby to look after. The only other thing about this that the group didn't pick up at all was the fact that this chap did slap the doctor right in the face when she suggested, "Bring this nurse in".

Dr. I. So he has got some gumption, hasn't he?

Dr. Main It wasn't open enough. It was sadism rather than aggressiveness. If he'd said, "Not on your bloody life!" you would know there is nothing wrong with him; he could go home! *(Laughter)*

Dr. B. He wouldn't act like a slave if he'd said that.

Dr. Main There's something about this doctor that the group didn't pick up. In this doctor/patient relation, the doctor has got more and more sad.

Doctor L.   It's almost as if the man had blinded the doctor, deliberately putting her off the scent.

Dr. F.   There is something very sadistic about going to a psychologist for a long time and then using a tummy-ache as an entrée to the doctor, followed by a "by the way. . ." Making the doctor feel she had been clever and done some work, but then more or less saying a lot of other people have been there before. It's not a nice way of doing it.

Dr. Main   Bloody useless, yes. — What brings the patient, now? Come on!

Dr. B.   His wife had said something.

Dr. Main   '. . . I am going to leave you unless you do something about this'. I would have thought he had come to please his wife. He is an absolute bastard: a furious patient, I would have thought. That is only my guess. How is it that the leader didn't get on to this?

Doctor L.   We did get on to 'How did the doctor feel when he said they had gone to the psychologist for such a long time?'; and the answer was, she felt overwhelmed because it must be such a massive problem.

Dr. Main   Let's take this up. We should all forget about, 'how did the doctor feel?': it's a silly question. It doesn't matter a bugger how the doctor feels. What does matter is, 'How did it happen?' She's overwhelmed. It's an incomplete sentence: by whom?

Dr. S.   He made her.

Dr. Main   Yes.

Dr. S.   In some kind of subtle, seductive way that she didn't take it as a slap in the face. She took it as, 'How sad, it must be a huge problem'.

Dr. Main   The group didn't get it, either. There is something about this doctor's presentation which paralysed them all.

Doctor L.   I think the paralysis came from the patient.

Dr. Main   No question about it: he's only presenting sweetness and light and the doctor seems to have done this with the group. Nastiness mustn't be mentioned.

Dr. B.   The patient made it seem as though the doctor was not in command of the situation, didn't he?

Dr. Main   It's a sweet story of suffering. — How did the leader fall for it?

Dr. B.   I still think there was something in this man, this patient, that made everybody take fright from looking at him and going off into husbands and wives, and the group who wanted to discuss that to get away from the difficulty in that transaction.

Dr. A.   I can't understand how it was that the doctor didn't feel anger. Sometimes doctors feel anger but don't admit it; but when they report it to the group, you find the group's angry and you wonder why. It somehow comes through the doctor without the doctor acknowledging it. — But that didn't happen here. Somehow all the anger was negated and even the group weren't angry.

Dr. Main   The man's wish to have a child was not discussed. All sorts of things. Why he married an older woman — all this. . . What is it about this doctor who presents this paragon of virtue, this man, and the group doesn't see it; and the leader doesn't see it?

Doctor L.   The idea was put to her that the man might not want to have his own child, and she said, "No, that's not so: there's no evidence".

Dr. Main   He was not impotent when it was demanded of him.

Doctor L.   Not when she is fertile.

Dr. Main   That's not intercourse. He is just doing what he is told.

Doctor L.   Yes.

Dr. Main   He doesn't enjoy his wife any more.

Doctor L.   The group got on to that. They were aware that they weren't sharing happiness, they were just trying to make a child; or that his wife wasn't being happy or enjoying sex, she was just wanting to become pregnant. They were well aware of this change between before and after.

Dr. Main   You didn't talk in terms of anger or annoyance.

Doctor L.   There's a difficulty about the anger. At one moment I said, "Aren't we aware of this woman? How do we feel? We haven't mentioned anger".

Dr. Main   Very good point.

Doctor L.   I do remember that I was the first one to use the word 'anger'. Everybody looked at it, and then they went off on to the relationship not being so good, and the man's need to be loved.

Dr. Main   He hates women and puts them in their place. He does with his wife; did it with the doctor. But he does it by being *weak*.

Doctor L.   Yes. You mean, if he'd come in and said, "I am feeling very angry", of course we would have all got in touch with the anger quite quickly.

Dr. Main   The best way to make the world suffer and feel guilty for 2000 years is to get yourself crucified. It's a very cruel thing to do.

Dr. S.   But he was presented in a way that we feel he reacted cruelly to his bossy nurse wife; that that is his way of handling powerful women.

Dr. Main   Yes. — Go on strike.

Dr. S.   I suppose he could be helped to see that?

Dr. Main   Don't forget he did marry a woman with an already established family. I think the psychologist was not far out.

Dr. I.   He started by evoking sympathy, anyway. He sits on the train late at night chewing his finger nails: 'Am I going to manage to achieve it tonight?' — Poor little thing!

Dr. Main   The doctor reported vividly about the man's sadness and the leader swallowed that hook, line and sinker.

Dr. F.   You slipped in about the word 'anger', but somehow as though it was a very indiscreet and rude word.

Doctor L.   Yes, I felt I was talking out of turn.

Dr. Main   You were being nasty.

Doctor L.   Yes, it's quite true.

Dr. F.   But if the doctor says she feels terribly sad, we do have an awful tendency to respect sadness.

Dr. Main   Better than that — she's got empathy, that terrible thing. Empathy means that you mindlessly go on with the patient's pain and don't think. You suffer with the patient — empathos.

Dr. I.   Or fall for it hook, line and sinker.

2. The muddled patient, depressed and unable to express her anger

Leader Doctors E & J.

Doctor E.   At this meeting my group spent about an hour talking about a case which left me feeling that I had been grappling with cotton wool. I didn't feel there was any depth or anything to get hold of. . .

The leader then went on to describe the case which the doctor had presented. The patient was a woman for whom intercourse had been difficult and painful from the beginning. She had managed to have a baby, but sexually things were no better afterwards. The doctor saw her in general practice and gave a vivid account of the way this patient was sometimes bright, cheerful and very smartly turned out, but sometimes appeared very depressed and dowdy. It was a presentation typical of general practice, with a number of contacts with the patient, both at home and in the surgery, described in some detail. When she was doing a vaginal examination the doctor said, smiling, "This isn't really pain, it's tension, isn't it?"

Dr. Main   Thank you. You have given an account of the doctor/patient relationship but not of the leader/group relationship.

Doctor E.   At the end of the presentation, I felt, 'I don't really know what is going on under this woman's behaviour'. I could see one or two cracks in the crust, but I had no idea what was underneath it. I felt the only thing to do was to guide the group back to what was happening between the doctor and the patient.

Dr. Main   But the group didn't take this up?

Doctor E.   Not really. They had a little go and then backed off again. There was one moment when we discovered that the patient was frightened and anxious and rather ambivalent about things and this had affected the doctor, who didn't quite know what to do. She seemed to be pussy-footing, not wanting to disturb the patient for reasons she couldn't quite put her finger on. I kept saying, "All right, how could the doctor have used that?" One of the group said, "I don't know what you mean". So

I said, "All I was thinking of was just saying to the patient something like, 'I notice you are very frightened about this'," and this person said, "Oh, I dismissed that. I thought of it". I asked why and she said, "It hits the nail right on the head". *(Laughter)* That was fairly typical of the group work. It was very frustrating.

Dr. P.   The leader's dilemma seems to be how to get the group to work when she doesn't quite know what she is wanting them to work towards. It is easier in a way if you have got a few clever ideas up your own sleeve and can sort of poke them where you want them to go.

Dr. Main   *(laughing)* Rape as model won't do! *(Laughter)*

Dr. Tunnadine   The case was a muddle. I don't know how the muddle that the group was in and the muddle that *you* were in can be related to the case, because it wasn't a simple question of picking up sides, which it ought to have been with a patient like that. The doctor made her view of the patient very clear to the group: when she is made up and happy she is nice; and when she is depressed she is awful. There is a kind of crazy patient who does swing, or who at least appears to swing; although possibly it is more a question of putting on a mask. It seems to be that sort of case. The doctor appears to have fallen into the trap according to the mood of the moment. You are usually very good at getting on to that in the group, drawing attention to what is going on. But something stopped you, I think. Perhaps there were reasons why you felt you had to be gentle with that doctor at that moment.

Dr. P.   I think it's actually the material which is all about being too young and not wanting to be a great big grown woman yet. Does this reflect the doctor's feeling about this work, and not being sure if she is able to do it?

Dr. Tunnadine   Even Dr. E. sees this as a frightened little girl rather than a furious post partum disappointed woman.

Doctor E.   That other bit of the woman did come out quite a lot in the group. There were different views about her. One was that she is a very manipulative, very powerful, very determined woman. It came over not as a direct understanding of the woman so much as the group's reflection of how it felt to be with her. There was also one member of the group who said, in contrast to the others, "I feel very sorry for her".

Dr. Tunnadine It seems that the doctor is a sucker for her; visiting her at home for little good reason, in great shape when she can be that sort of doctor, but somehow running away when things got unpleasant. The clinical fact is that the woman is in a mess and mucks the doctor about. What I don't understand is that Dr. E. somehow feels she should have done better as a leader and that it was an unsatisfactory discussion.

Doctor E. Not better. I suppose I'm always like this: I wanted to know what was underneath this woman. I wanted to be there.

Dr. Main But you can't find out what was wrong with that woman. All you can do is study the doctor/patient relation.

Doctor J. There was a very important moment which you did pick up about: — "Oh, so you *did* do an examination?" The doctor reported that the woman had appeared very ill at ease, and she had said to her, "This isn't really pain, this is tension, isn't it?"

Dr. Main And she said that with a grin.

Doctor E. Yes. This was one of those cracks in the crust that I was trying to get them to look at more.

Dr. Main But there seems to me something that the doctor is not wanting to hear. The doctor seems to be interested in one thing — to have bowls of roses round the place, pot pourri or something — everything smelling nice. Smiles. . .

Doctor E. Can I recall another bit on that tack? One of the group said something about the husband should be able to give her good feelings about sex, or the doctor ought to be able to. We got around to saying, "How can you possibly give this woman good feelings about sex when she has got *bad* feelings and they haven't even been looked at?" I remember saying that and just being stuck there. They were thinking that perhaps somebody could tell her that really sex is awfully nice — that would work!

Dr. Main Can I make a general remark? — When there is confusion it is about love and hatred. When you are confused you don't know whether to be loving or hating. Your defences are confusion, you throw up a smoke-screen. As in naval warfare, when you don't know what to do you throw up a smoke-screen and retire behind it. It's not just naval manoeuvres: it's naval war. A smoke-screen is usually some sort of defence against aggressiveness. The thing I miss about this is what a bloody awful woman this is: her hatred, her hostility, her rages. We have to talk about suffering, pain and sadness and all sorts of lovely things.

Doctor E.   No, we didn't talk about sadness; only once.

Dr. Main   The group mentioned it and I haven't heard anything that strikes me that this patient is a human being: like the people in this room. When you look around and take it honestly, people are pretty horrible at times. The doctor is sweet and attends to the patient. She smiles on her, visits her home. I think the whole thing stinks of good will or something awful like that.

Doctor E.   I think you are probably right, but I don't honestly think that I was sitting thinking, "I must maintain the good will".

Dr. Main   But you *were* talking about pain and suffering.

Dr. Tunnadine   She talked about manipulation as well.

Dr. Main   But in the very first encounter between the doctor and the patient, the patient was up and off. She stormed out, didn't she? — Her relationship with the doctor seemed to me to be absolutely filled with venom at that point.

Dr. Z.   And it was later in the relationship, too.

Dr. Main   You think so too?

Dr. Z.   Yes, definitely.

Dr. Main   Well, why didn't you *say so,* then! (Laughter)

Dr. Z.   That's right. I think she is frightening this doctor and making her be a nice woman.

Dr. Main   I think the doctor is afraid of the patient's rage.

Dr. Z.   I am sure she is. So would I be.

Doctor E.   Yes, but this wasn't left out. The group did bring it up. They said so several times. One person in the group got quite uptight, saying, "I wouldn't stand for all this from this woman".

Dr. Main   I see. So it was quite plain that here is a *placating* doctor who wants the patient's good will and works for that and has to shut out everything else. No wonder the patient gets so depressed and sad. I am surprised it wasn't brought out —

maybe it was brought out clearly in the group, but I didn't hear it.

Dr. Tunnadine   It is a difficult patient for anybody.

Dr. Main   But we are here to look at the handling of the group's discussion of this doctor's work.

Dr. I.   I can't quite get this bit about the grin, when she examined her; what it meant. That seems to be an odd bit in all the rest of it.

Doctor E.   It was an odd bit.

Dr. I.   Did she imply that the patient grinned? I thought the patient was colluding and she was also grinning, as much as to say, "No, it isn't really painful, but let's keep the pretence going!" And then it didn't sort of follow on like that.

Dr. Main   I thought the grin was to convey the fact, 'I can't stand any trouble with you. I don't want any trouble with your vagina. It really is only tension, isn't it?' This is what I thought: this doctor's fear of the patient.

Dr. I.   It didn't follow through. It was a little bit all on its own.

Dr. Main   The patient is complaining and the doctor couldn't stand it and said, "It's only tension, isn't it?", and talked the patient into saying it was only tension. Suppose she hadn't talked the patient into it. I wonder what the patient would have said, if the doctor had allowed her to grumble a bit.

Doctor E.   Having got the answer, "Yes it *is* tension", that was the end.

Dr. Tunnadine   It sounded to me like a real defensive bit of patter, but it wasn't even in a vacuum: it was in response to a real communication by the patient. The patient actually *said something* for once.

Dr. I.   Yes, that's right. I thought, "Aha — we are now going to hear!"

Doctor E.   The patient was tightening up, and she was about to examine her, so in that sense it was a communication.

Dr. I.   It wasn't developed.

Dr. Tunnadine   I am impressed to hear Dr. E. apologising for what I thought sounded like quite a good group discussion, given that the case is a muddled one.

D

Dr. Main The group discussion seems to have been about the muddle and this woman's — this *poor* woman's — rages.

Dr. Tunnadine They at least had a go at what she was doing with the doctor. They were on the sort of track I would hope they would be on in their second year, weren't they?

Dr. I. Yes, but I wonder if the impression being given is that we are all nice doctors and we don't get angry.

Dr. Tunnadine That's what I am afraid of.

Doctor E. We have got one super doctor in our group who gets angry very easily! *(Laughter)*

Dr. Tunnadine Everyone needs one.

Doctor E. She doesn't let us get away with those bits. It isn't all a sweetness and light group.

3. Hidden excitement of the lover who does not cause dyspareunia

Leader Doctor F.

The patient was a social worker who came asking for a termination, but who had also complained of deep pelvic pain with her fiancé but not with her black lover. She gave a long, complicated history with a great flood of words during which she said that if the baby was not going to be black she would make it up with her fiancé and pass it off as his. She also volunteered the fact that she thought she might break with her fiancé because he thought he was a woman. When the doctor tried to discuss this the patient said "she had worked through all that" with her social work colleagues and did not need to talk about it.

    The group were rather silent after listening to this and eventually the leader said, "Let's forget about the patient's problem, we are not going to attempt to solve this whole battery of stuff. Let's just look at this doctor's technique". The group did then comment on the doctor's listening technique and her passivity, but also on there being something rather unrealistic about the story. Then still more history came out, including frequent referrals to specialists.

Doctor F.   What emerged gradually was that the group were saying to her, 'It is all right to groan about some people. This woman has got awful problems. She is probably going to end up having a hysterectomy at a premature age — maybe; we can't tell, we don't have enough information. But she possibly isn't really suitable for brief treatment by you. In this context you have a protective rôle, preventing her from being over-investigated. You are allowed to make decisions not to take people on; you are allowed to groan about them; you are allowed to think you don't want anything more to do with them'. So it was focussing on this doctor's inability to do anything but be totally tolerant, just sitting there and taking it all. She admitted that she had found it very helpful to say that she had felt negative.

Dr. S.   The group were critical because she wasn't reporting honestly. She was editing out her bad feelings.

Doctor F.   Yes, she hadn't said how negative she felt.

Dr. E.   Did it really keep her away, all this volume of talk? It seemed to contain quite a lot of feeling.

Doctor F.   I don't think she had any idea about the patient's feelings about the pregnancy or termination at all.

Dr. I.   But then the group hadn't got much idea about the doctor's feelings, either. You let us know what you felt.

Dr. Main   Can you extend your idea a bit, because it does tell you about the patient. The doctor's manner of presenting was — how can I describe it? — she was hiding behind the patient. The doctor presented a smoke-screen — not about herself: she just talked about the patient, so it does tell you about the patient; but there is some funny identification of the doctor *with* the patient. The doctor's manner is in that way similar to the patient's. She puts up a smoke-screen and is hiding behind it.

Dr. I.   Both of them seem to be giving a story as though they are not there.

Dr. Main   Yes. The patient gives a smoke-screen of facts.

Doctor F.   But you see, this doctor has done this before. I would read more into it about this individual patient if this doctor weren't *always* doing this smoke-screen.

Dr. Main That may be so, but the value of that comment for that group, and for that doctor, is to see that there are patients who do this as well as doctors who do it. There is Dr. E's point — what does it tell you about the patient? I think it tells you quite a lot.

Dr. P. But the bit that seems to have been helpful to the leader is that you think this doctor is presenting this sort of patient all the time because of some problems for *her*; that this is the sort of patient which she is deciding to bring to the group.

Doctor F. Yes.

Dr. Main It's quite possible.

Doctor F. Incredibly complicated. . . vast volumes of words, or time, or work or something — and no clear representation of what goes on between the doctor and the patient. What seems to be hidden more than anything is the doctor's feelings about the patient. O.K., you can say it is a reflection of what the patient is doing, but I think it is more a reflection of . . .

Dr. Main — It's characteristic of this doctor.

Doctor F. Yes. That is what the group is getting so frustrated about.

Dr. Main One of the rules of naval warfare, if you are under guns and don't know what to do, is put out smoke and hide behind it, because then you are safe. This doctor is doing the same with the group. She's got a lot of feeling and daren't talk about it.

Dr. Tunnadine My phantasy about the identification is that it was a very interesting case about a social worker who was going to abort her interests in black men; and what that says about the doctor's attitudes to psychosexual medicine in a purely practical, doctoring kind of way, I think, are very interesting. After all, she's had to learn about sex and she's saying to this group, "I'm a good virtuous social-worker-type doctor and we don't want to talk about that other stuff".

Dr. Main I'm slightly uneasy about it coming into group therapy.

Doctor F. I could see that there was a thin line over which we could easily fall, where it could become, 'Let's have a look at this poor doctor's problems', as it were.

Dr. V.   Isn't that what she's been doing to the group? She's been bringing her patients for help for *herself*, hasn't she?

Doctor F.   I think she has been. I think she's been bringing her most difficult, chronic, awful stuff to the group; presenting it and taking a great deal of the group's time and energy; and getting very little back, really.

Dr. Main   It doesn't matter a damn if she brings her own personal needs.

Dr. V.   But isn't that why she's been making other members of the group feel uneasy?

Dr. Main   That's one way of looking at it. After all, that group is not there to cure this doctor. I don't give a damn about what her personal problems are. What matters is, what was she doing with her *patient*? It's her doctoring we are concerned with and you can only examine the doctoring in detail one case at a time. I thought you did very well with this particular case because it *was* studied. You took a sample of this doctor. All you have got to do is take a sample of this doctor, examine it and it will improve her doctoring.

Dr. Tunnadine   I thought that was marvellous, but I suspect they got therapeutic afterwards; because this doctor presents her doctoring in terms of martyrdom, which is extremely irritating. That is why by the end of it they were saying, "It's all right, dear, you don't have to be marvellous!", patting her on the head; which is where it got lost again.

Doctor F.   Almost that she is a universal doormat, if you like.

Dr. Tunnadine   Yes — which is exasperating.

Dr. Main   We haven't heard a lot about what went on; but I think the group were doing a bit of that, too. — Let's put it to *this* group. Anyone got any ideas about this fling with this black man?

Dr. Tunnadine   It's the best news I've had! *(Laughter)*

Dr. Main   I would like to hear more about it! The doctor just said, "Yes, and next?" *(Laughter)* So did the group. There is a real inhibition about discussing this. It would have been a useful opportunity for you or the group to draw this doctor's attention to the fact that she had failed at that point to take up the patient's excitement and what it was about. One can guess it — that she was fed up with this fiancé: it was a remark of fed-upness, or revenge, or whatever. The other was the excitement of the black man.

Dr. Tunnadine   — who didn't give her dyspareunia. . .

Dr. Main   I know: that was the good thing about him. There is nothing more exciting in a love affair than that they didn't get the usual symptoms! What a summary for a romance that would be! That's the level it is going at. There is nothing about excitement and the group accepted the doctor's acceptance of the woman's hiding this part of herself. The study of the individual patient is important; the study of the individual detail of the encounter is important. It is minute by minute. Why did the doctor not take it up? What was it about the doctor? What was it about the patient? What was going on at the time that it was just passed by? They were good interesting clinical facts about there being no pain.

Doctor F.   In fact, she said more than no pain; she actually used the word "elation" in relation to the lover.

Dr. Tunnadine   We could question Dr. F. on getting the discussion going by saying, "Let us concentrate on the doctor's technique and nothing else"; by going that far away from the patient's element of it.

Doctor F.   They didn't actually do that, because they brought it back and said, "What we have been presented with is much more to do with the patient in the way that she has kept the doctor out". They did look at that in some length. They were also talking about, "Isn't it interesting that you didn't even think of examining this woman? — Here she is complaining of an early pregnancy that needs confirmation, and pelvic pain; and you are going to refer her for a surgical procedure and it didn't even occur to you to examine her".

Dr. Main   The only criticism I have about that — and it's not a major criticism — is that it's not so much about the doctor's *technique* as about the doctor's *style*, general style. Technique after all consists of what you do in detail, bit by bit, minute by minute. For example: sure the doctor didn't do an examination, but at what point did she fail? When in the interview? What was it at that time which was going on between her and the patient which led to that not being done?

Doctor F.   The generalities arise, I think, from this doctor's complete inability to give us details about her technique.

Dr. Main   I don't know what other people think, but — on this business about her fiancé. He thinks he's a woman. . . Yawn. — No-one is interested in that? — I think it's a very exciting communication. What did the doctor do with it? Why did she handle it the way she did? There are bits that you could pick out. The doctor writes it down conscientiously and says, "Yes. Have you got a headache?"

Doctor F.   She didn't actually, to be fair to her. What she said was, "You are presenting me with this amazing information. It sounds quite out of the ordinary to me, yet you seem to be competely unmoved by it".

Dr. Main   The scorn of this woman shows and the doctor didn't discuss it.

Dr. Tunnadine   I remember it differently, actually, as you just happened to pick on that detail. I recall it as one of the things that the doctor *did* have a go at and the patient said, "No, I'm a social worker: we understand all these things. I don't wish to discuss that".

Doctor F.   She said, "I've talked this through with some of the colleagues and I have come to terms with that".

Dr. Main   I don't think it's very interesting whether this chap is a pansy or not. What is interesting is this woman's scorn, and that was in the room.

Dr. Tunnadine   Yes, that's right. I thought the black man got very short shrift, too. 'Elation!' — goodbye! The group didn't discuss that either.

Dr. E.   There seemed to be a point at which you decided this is the sort of woman who puts up smoke-screens, or keeps you away from her feelings, as if that is the diagnosis. What is missing for me is, why? What is she hiding? What is it specifically that is behind that? This group can be content with labelling her: 'You are the sort of person who presents me with all this amazing stuff and sits there looking calm. What is it all about?' The woman doesn't *know* what it is all about in those sort of terms.

Doctor F.   Yes, I can see that, but the sort of labelling by the group — 'Well, this is a very complicated awful problem and no-one is going to get anywhere near this woman's feelings' — was really an attempt to look at the fact that the doctor had been dishonest about the awfulness and chronicity, and that made a difference to the way she presented it. It wasn't so much an attempt to dismiss the woman, but it was an attempt to reinforce the fact that the doctor was allowed to groan.

Dr. Main   I don't think the group was working so well as all that. I don't think this group is, either. Let's have another look at something else. This woman said she wanted an abortion because it would be a black baby. If it hadn't been a black baby she would have said nothing about it and landed it on her boyfriend. No-one said a thing about this. They have got no feelings about it. — Well, I have!

Doctor F.   I did interject sarcastically at some point, something like, "As we all know, if the baby is black, then the logical thing is to terminate the pregnancy". They did have a think about, 'What on earth is all this?'

Dr. Main   What does it show? The doctor didn't handle it, so far as I can make out.

Doctor F.   No.

Dr. Main   Well, why not?   The patient didn't handle it either. — What is going on? What does it show?

Dr. P.   It seemed to be a terrific collusiveness between the doctor and the patient, that everything that the patient was trying to pretend that she didn't feel — she was a social worker, she didn't have moral ideas about it — somehow the doctor had to go along with this all the time as though, if she were to challenge the patient, she wouldn't be doing right by her.

Doctor F.   The way they described that was that this doctor has had to be totally tolerant with this patient.

Dr. Main   But look again — tolerant of what? Tolerant of detail; one detail after another, such as the business about the black baby, such as her fiancé being a woman — these are the details that *shouldn't* be tolerated. They should be picked up; some interest shown in them. What do they tell you? What does the doctor feel? It would have been worthwhile, I think, to have discussed these details: what the doctor did with each particular detail, and why.

Dr. S.   Like what the doctor felt when she said, 'I would have cheated my fiancé and not batted an eyelid'.

Dr. Main   Well, you know damn well what the doctor felt.

Dr. S.   Well we don't.

Dr. Main   We do: we just know the doctor is concealing it.

Doctor F.   Yes. She's concealed it totally. She has not made any comment.

Dr. Main   And the group concealed it too.

Doctor F.   No, the group didn't, you see. They said they thought that was all terrible.

Dr. S.   Presumably her feelings about this patient were so very negative — that she could be such a cheat and despise her fiancé as she does — that she just couldn't face her own negative feelings.

Dr. P.   I thought when you said, "being a cheat", you were actually talking about the doctor! I think that is what the group find difficult to cope with.

Dr. Main   Being extra sensitive, I have come to the conclusion that this woman's relationship with her fiancé was not perfect! I think her sexual life might have a few little flaws in it. — Not discussed, not mentioned.

Dr. Tunnadine   The other thing that wasn't discussed was this detail about the doctor trying to have a go at some challenge, and the patient saying, "I am not going to discuss that. I know all about it", and the anger or the resentment or the helplessness of the doctor in the face of it wasn't overtly discussed.

Doctor F.   They said the patient was simply able to wipe the floor with her.

Dr. Tunnadine   Yes. Strong words.

Doctor F.   They *were* strong words. It was at that point that I started to get really worried that we were looking at the Inadequate Doctor aspect of this, instead of how this patient had achieved that.

Dr. L.   Having said all that about the doctor, we are still dealing with an incredibly powerful patient who has set the whole thing up. The doctor had fallen for the whole set-up.

Doctor F. Yes, actually someone pointed out that she was not the first doctor to have gone along with this patient's wishes. She'd had all sorts of operations and investigations 'down there'.

Dr. Main Something wrong with the genitals. . .

Doctor F. Yes, that's right.

Dr. Main I'm not so sure that this patient is so difficult. She *is* frigid — we can see that all right — and the fact that she gives nothing out to her doctor is typical of frigid people.

Dr. L. Is she not very controlling and powerful?

Dr. Main And with her fiancé and her own feelings — sure. But this could be picked up.

Dr. I. But she is having difficulty coming out with her real symptoms.

Dr. Main She doesn't have access to her own feelings; nor, in the same way, to her sexual feelings. I would have thought this could have been seen.

Dr. L. I thought there was something from the presenting doctor, a sort of protest at being controlled.

Doctor F. She certainly communicated it. I fully sympathised with a previous doctor who hypnotised her when she was sixteen! It seemed to be one way of dealing with her, like an anaesthetic, really.

Dr. Tunnadine I heard a different view. Given that we know this doctor is in the habit of being a martyred, social-worker-type doctor, thinking that if you give time and accept everything it is all right, I heard the patient say, "I don't want all this social work stuff". She seems to be screaming out from beginning to end, "Examine my sexuality, examine my sexuality!" It's the liveliness in the patient that I am missing and I think that *is* the doctor's fault, because you tell us that she never wants to know about that. She wants to sit there and be accepting and suffering.

Dr. Main The general advice of, "It's all right to be angry with your patients" is fine, but what is required is an increasing courage on the doctor's part.

Doctor F. Something I missed out is that this patient always seems to get her doctors into a muddle and her notes are full of a feeling that she is persecuted by hospitals and doctors.

Dr. Main — and anyway she has got a sore finger! *(Laughter)*

Doctor F. And incredibly apologetic letters from everyone who has been involved with her.

Dr. Tunnadine Yes, but you see that is what this patient offers, and that is what this doctor likes, because she is that sort of doctor. I picked up a different side: this patient is complaining of being in pain with a poor little 'woman' and with a great big black penis she is 'elated'. That is the muddle about the ordinary psychosomatic stuff which was completely missed by the doctor and we too are all caught up with the social work side of it. The patient kept on saying, "I don't want to think about that, I have come to terms with all that. Look at my bloody vagina and the fact that it is in pain when it is not being fucked good' — if you will pardon the expression — 'It is happy when it is'.

Dr. Main Now look, let's keep this clean! *(Laughter)* Let's talk about generalising!

Dr. Tunnadine That is what happened, I think; except for my rude interventions. This is what I missed.

Dr. Main I would go for this woman's frigidity myself and discuss it in terms of this presentation. I believe this woman has one or two sexual difficulties. The doctor didn't examine that. I wouldn't care about the physical examination — that was so obvious. The doctor could have seen surely that the patient is putting her off sexual topics and the doctor was in collusion in keeping off them.

Doctor F. I'm not sure how much she did see that, really.

Dr. Main The group didn't see it either.

E. EARLY DIFFICULTIES FOR DOCTORS — failure to consummate their work?

Some of the early difficulties for individual doctors, both with their patients and in the group, are illustrated in this short chapter. It is perhaps no accident that three of the digests are concerned with cases of non-consummation. At the beginning of training doctors often appear to present cases which express their unconscious feeling that they have not consummated, or got to grips with, their own work in this field.

The idea that the case material presented by the members may be an unconscious expression of the feeling of the group at that stage of training is explored further in the book's final chapter, "Unconscious material 'going down the line'" (III F 7 & 8).

1. ADMITTING THEY DON'T KNOW.
2. GETTING TO THE DOCTOR/PATIENT RELATIONSHIP.
3. THE ABSENCE OF PHANTASIES.
4. A NEW USE OF THE S.T.D. CLINIC.

1. Admitting they don't know

Leader Doctor I.

During the first meeting of a new group, one of the doctors had been rather aggressively confident, seeming to have answers and comments on everything.

Dr. Main What's this doctor's job?

Doctor I. G.P. Actually, he's a trainee.

Dr. Main He's come to teach.

Doctor I. Yes. But right at the end of the seminar he talked about a diabetic patient who was impotent. At that point one of the other doctors in the group walked out! I thought, "Oh!" — She didn't say a thing about where she was going.

Dr. Main That's not a thought! What did you do?

Doctor I. She came back a minute later with the latest copy of the B.M.J. to show us. She promptly read out a little piece saying 50% of diabetics do have impotence.

Dr. Main But why, we don't know. What's the level of impotence in the general population? As a G.P., what would you say?

Dr. N. Do you want me to guess? — No idea.

Dr. Q. No-one does. It would be impossible to find out.

Doctor I. The patient gets morning erections, so I said, "Did that make him feel pleased, or was there some sort of feeling when he said that?" "No, no". His wife is under a psychiatrist, but runs a successful business of her own. At the end of the story we were all feeling quite sorry for the chap and not too fond of the wife because she was rejecting and getting very angry. The doctor had thought of one or two things he might do to try to help, but got no backing from his trainer G.P.; so at the end he did nothing, and felt he had rather let the patient down. At least he was able to say that he hadn't achieved very much whereas prior to this, in the group, he had been someone who seemed to know all the answers.

Dr. Main Plucked up his courage. — That is a group event. The leader can observe that, as a step.

Doctor I. Yes, to say, "I've let this man down".

Dr. S. But you wouldn't comment on it at this very first meeting?

Dr. Main Never — good God, no!

Dr. S. I do that now, in term 4/5. It is enough just to notice it at this stage.

Dr. Main Progress is what matters: what he'll report from now on. Something about the atmosphere you created allowed him to report, although he was a bit of a know-all earlier on.

Doctor I. Yes, I felt pleased that he brought up something which, in a sense, was his failure.

Dr. Main I know, but the thing is that the doctor showed that he could report failures, and he will get a bashing on them, although he'd been bashing other people about before. — Well, thank you very much.

Doctor I. I hope they all turn up next time.

Dr. Main There's the hostess reaction! I hope the ones who are no good *don't* turn up!

2. Getting to the doctor/patient relationship: the teacher taught

Leader Doctor I.

The patient was a newly qualified primary school teacher who had not been able to consummate her marriage. She had been discussed several times in the group.

Doctor I. On this occasion the doctor seemed very sad and depressed about the patient. She told us how her parents were both secondary school teachers and had always belittled her, and how they had led her to believe that having a baby was simply ghastly. . .

Dr. Main How do you know her parents did that?

Doctor I. She explained to the doctor how much she was afraid of having a baby when it was first discussed —

Dr. Main Don't tell us about the patient. Tell us about how the doctor behaved to the group. What did the doctor tell the group?

Doctor I. The doctor told the group that she had felt obliged to explain the details of labour to this patient because she was obviously so afraid of having a baby.

Dr. Main What was the doctor's presentation to the group like? Was it about the patient or was it about the transaction, the encounter?

Doctor I. I was giving you a bit of background about the patient.

Dr. Main I want to hear about what the *doctor* said to the *group*.

Doctor I. You just want to hear about the doctor. Well. . . — you don't want to hear about the background of the patient?

Dr. Main To hell with the patient — I am just wondering if the doctor presented the patient or the transaction.

Doctor I. She presents the transaction very well.

Dr. Main Oh well, let's hear it.

Doctor I. She's about the only one who does. She described the patient coming in and sitting down and she was rather irritated about it because she had told the patient to come back at a special time, but instead she had come in the middle of a busy surgery. When we discussed whether she was actually feeling annoyed, she said No, she was really feeling more sad than annoyed. I said, "You must have been feeling irritated with this patient", and she said No, it was really more sadness about this young girl who is a new teacher and not been married that long and they have still not managed to consummate their marriage. She was very descriptive of the girl and of the husband who had come on one occasion and we tried to discuss the feelings of the doctor as far as this patient was concerned. But she still maintained that she just felt very sad.

Dr. Main But what work was done? Did she discuss that at all?

Doctor I. In the group?

Dr. Main No, I mean with the patient. Why is it that the doctor felt sad rather than angry? — That's not much to do with work.

Doctor I. She was trying to get the patient to understand she was putting things off. In fact, the time before when she had produced this patient, she had been very pleased because she'd actually got the patient to examine herself, which she'd never done before, to use tampons; whereas this time she was apparently back at square one. She was messing about with her pills, which meant she was having great bleeding and therefore couldn't attempt intercourse, and the whole thing seemed to be getting more depressing.

Dr. Main How did the group discuss the doctor's presentation?

Doctor I. They discussed the feelings of the doctor and the irritation that they also felt she ought to be feeling; but somehow the doctor seemed to manage to get across this feeling of sadness rather than irritation about what I felt was an irritating patient who just wouldn't co-operate and do anything. But there was quite a lot of discussion amongst those who were there.

Dr. Main About what?

Doctor I. About what else they felt she could have done; how they felt that she could have been more positive with the patient.

Dr. Main Do you remember any of the ideas?

Doctor I. I can never remember precisely what people said. The doctor herself is quite descriptive and remembers quite clearly words that she says and the replies that the patient makes, which is unfortunate in as far as I can't recall them myself.

Dr. K. This doctor's technique seems to be to attack the defences without being able to use it. She doesn't appear to comment or interpret, it's more —

Doctor I. I don't know that she interprets very well, although she does manage to get them to explain how they feel about it.

Dr. Main Not with this case.

Doctor I. The patient has felt very belittled by her own parents and conveyed this; but at the same time she asked her how she felt about her husband and she is feeling very irritated with her husband because there are times now, she said, that she wants him to go ahead, but she can't take the initative herself. The doctor said, "Why can't you do just that?" and she said, "I just can't bring myself to initiate it or to ask him to get on with it". Again one has this impasse of 'Can't you do this?'; 'No, I can't';

or 'Yes I have, but it's no good'.

Dr. Main   The doctor is telling the patient what to do and the patient is saying, "No, I can't"; and the doctor says, "Well, you've got to try harder" and there is a funny kind of teachy atmosphere between the doctor and the patient. The patient is young and is accustomed to being instructed by her parents; and the doctor seems to be doing the same thing. The doctor instructing the patient seems to be a product of this particular patient, and the doctor falls into the trap. *That* is the doctor/patient relation, whereas what the doctor *feels* is *not* the doctor/patient relation. The fact that the doctor is either irritated or sad is unimportant. What is the patient doing with the doctor? It would seem to me to be: making the doctor teach her.

Doctor I.   Yes, and blocking it all the time.

Dr. Main   But the doctor didn't draw attention to that fact, that the patient *wants* to be told. There was a very good clue for this because the patient did say, "I wish my husband would take the initiative" — making the doctor take the initiative — but the doctor didn't interpret in any way that what the patient wanted done was being enacted there in the consulting room. The patient wanted the doctor to take the initiative and like an idiot the doctor did, instead of interpreting that this girl doesn't want to give anything away, doesn't want to open out, wants the other person to do the probing, or advising — and didn't discuss that phenomenon with the patient. But the group didn't spot this, did they?

Doctor I.   No. I didn't, either.

Dr. Main   The doctor must be frustrated because she doesn't see it. She is teaching and teaching.

Doctor I.   Yes, but I got irritated too, because —

Dr. Main   It's a non-consummation. With a non-consummation case you want only those who can consummate! You can bet your life that if you have a case of non-consummation, you will end up with a disappointed doctor. Don't you think so — the first session or two?

Doctor I.   Yes.

Dr. Main   It's a sign of non-consummation that the doctor feels frustrated, or whatever.

Doctor I. Yes, but she wouldn't agree to that: she wouldn't agree to feeling irritated and frustrated. — *I* was feeling irritated and frustrated.

Dr. Main Mmm. She's only got sweet feelings like sadness.

Doctor I. Yes.

Dr. Main Lovely doctor!

Doctor I. Yes, she is rather! *(Laughter)*

Dr. Main The rest of the group were frustrated, too. They had cottoned on to it.

Doctor I. They said they felt sad, too: I think partly because the doctor has tried so hard for so long. We have heard about this case on several occasions and each time we have felt, "Aah, at last!. . ." And she actually said that when the patient came in she thought, "Aah, perhaps everything is going to be all right. One day she is going to walk in and look quite different". But this hasn't happened; so we all feel that all this effort has been brought to nothing.

Dr. Main But there hasn't been any effort; except teaching.

Doctor I. Yes, although she did remark that, having taught her about what goes on in labour. . .

Dr. Main 'Come here, my child, to the blackboard!. . . — A. . . B. . . C. . .'

Doctor I. But she did say that isn't her usual technique. She doesn't normally tell people. . .

Dr. Main That's fine. — 'What is this person doing to me? She's teaching the two times table'.

Doctor I. Yes, I should have pointed that out, because it is unusual for her to do that.

Dr. Main It tells you something about the patient; and the patient knows nothing about these things. She's a dumb-bell. She's never seen anything in magazines or newspapers and has to be told all about sex by this kind, clever doctor. It's nonsense, isn't it? The doctor has fallen for it. And she is a very young patient, and child-like, I suppose. . .

Doctor I. She's a new teacher; doesn't like teaching.

Dr. Main That's what I thought.

Doctor I. Doesn't like the school; can't come to the meetings because it would be getting into the school's bad books if she misses any more sessions; she wants a good reference so she can move to another one; and so on. It's all sort of depressing.

2. The absence of phantasies

Leader Doctor S.

The patient was a girl with hair right over her face who wept all the time during her first two visits to the doctor and refused to be examined. At the end of the second interview the doctor said that she would have to examine her next time because she did not like giving her the Pill without examining her. At the third visit she did get on the couch, but there was a lot of vaginismus. However, the doctor suggested the patient should examine herself, which she did.

Dr. A. Did the group discuss why the girl had become more co-operative and what actually happened when she did the vaginal examination and what was the meaning of it?

Doctor S. Yes, they did a bit.

Dr. A. They didn't just say, "That's great".

Doctor S. No, they didn't. They said things like, "You kept to the point, didn't you, that it was her difficulty in revealing herself to the doctor or to her fiancé". I thought they conceptualised what had happened pretty well.

Dr. Main I couldn't understand why it was a good thing, that's all.

Doctor S. Well, it was a way of understanding what went on between the doctor and the patient and I thought that when they begin to know what is happening in the doctor/patient relation
—

Dr. Main I'm sorry, I just didn't get that. Maybe I missed it, that they discussed the doctor/patient relation in this case.

Doctor S. I probably didn't say it. I was trying to be brief. It was an on-going patient. She had told us before that this girl had made her angry by her silence and the group had said, "Why do you feel angry?" and she said, "I feel so helpless and I can't bear it when people can't talk, so I tried to make her laugh and she laughed through her tears". We got quite a lot about the feelings between this doctor and this girl patient. She'd noted that this time she walked in quite differently and sat down and said Yes, she would like to be examined this time.

Dr. Main I didn't understand why the examination was a good thing, though. Everyone seemed very pleased about the vaginal examination. It's a kind of hobby that some people might go in for, but what's the point of it?

Doctor S. I think the doctor was trying to help her to find out that she wasn't too small.

Dr. Main Not too small for vaginal examination, that's all — I can see that.

Doctor S. Not too small for vaginal examination, not too small for herself.

Dr. Main What's the good of vaginal examination, that's what I want to know? It seems to be an O.K. thing in this group.

Doctor S. Somehow helping this girl to grow up and not be frightened any more of sexuality.

Dr. Main — of vaginal examinations. . .

Doctor S. Well, of her smallness and immaturity.

Dr. Main I'm teasing. . . — of her smallness and immaturity or vaginal examinations?

Doctor S. And the sexual feelings.

Dr. Main No, never mentioned. That's a dirty subject — don't bring that into it.

Doctor S. It was mentioned a bit: the boyfriend being fed-up and she wanted to get a better time with him. It was mentioned a bit.

Dr. Main There is something missing about this. This was about vaginal examination being a good thing. The discussion of why she was having difficulties — I didn't hear it. I am a bit critical of these vaginal examinations being mechanical and being a good thing when really it doesn't matter, so long as the woman understands what is going on inside her. As a matter of fact I was a bit fed-up with this group being so pleased that the vaginal examination had occurred, rather than thinking, "What the hell is going on with this doctor and this patient? Why can't they discuss sex? What is the matter with the girl?" It doesn't matter what is wrong so long as you do the vaginal examination. The mechanical business is all right — but what about the rest of it? Maybe other people got a different impression, but this is what I got. I missed the discussion about the girl's feelings.

Dr. Q. I thought the group got excited about the girl being able to accept her sexuality by touching herself, because in actual fact there was no vaginal examination at all.

Dr. I. The girl said that she's not small, is she?

Dr. Main It's fine not being so small, or big or whatever — but what is it fine for?

Dr. Q. Well, maybe I was assuming these feelings were discussed.

Doctor S. They were. The girl finds it very hard to speak, so Dr. X. said, "You've got your finger in — if you had to choose between nice and nasty, what would you say?", and the girl smiled and said, "Nice". I think there was then further silence, and then Dr. X. said, "What do you think about the size of it? Small or large?" and she said, "I'm not small, am I?". . . — It was a sort of moment of truth.

Dr. Main The doctor is asking questions — nice or nasty, big or small, blue or pink? If you ask any question, you get an answer. There was nothing revealed by the patient. This is what I'm missing.

Dr. A. Did the girl understand what the smallness meant for her as a person? Did the group discuss what the smallness actually meant?

Dr. Main The doctor assumed she was small and the patient never said a word. The doctor asked, "Is it small or big?" and then the doctor thought, 'She might be bothered about being nice or nasty', so she asked her that question. — There isn't anything coming from the patient. Do you see what I mean?

Doctor S. I do see what you mean. The patient is so inhibited and so shy that it is really quite an achievement for the doctor to have stuck this out and invited her back and, finally, the last time she said more or less, "I am fed up with this. I will give you two packets of pills and don't come until February". — Quite cross with her. The group were quite cross with *her* for being cross with the girl and thought it unproductive. I thought she did very well, myself, and I'm going to remain proud of her! *(Laughter)*

Dr. Main   Pushing this girl to behave herself worked quite well; but nobody discussed that. Why shouldn't Dr. X. get fed-up with the girl? Why is that bad? The group can't stand doctors laying down the law, or getting fed-up a bit. The boyfriend is fed-up, the doctor is fed-up — the doctor wouldn't stand it and threatened the woman and she behaved herself: got up on the couch.

Doctor S.   But still had vaginismus. The doctor then encouraged her to find out something for herself. O.K., she may not have found out much about her sexuality, but she found out about the possibility of it.

Dr. Main   Mmm. She knows she's got a vagina and she's a woman. But she knew that before.

Doctor S.   And can move on now a bit.

Dr. L.   I thought the joy of the group was that she had this girl who never stopped crying and never said anything; she persevered with her and then on this occasion. . . I thought that was where the group got their lift.

Doctor S.   It wasn't anything about history, or grandmothers, or abortions.

Dr. Main   But what about the group? I am bothered about this group getting the idea that that's a good thing. The vaginal examination itself is meant to be a psychosexual examination — that is, to reveal something about the woman's sexuality: to get at the truth, which is what this thing is about. The group, I'm afraid, will learn that this is an anatomical examination. There are *experts* on human anatomy who are frigid — it doesn't help. The feelings are missing. I wouldn't like that group to go away thinking that that was good business. I would like them to go away feeling that this woman's sexuality was studied and her phantasies were produced and the doctor understood them; and if that is so, it doesn't matter whether an examination occurred or not. This is what I am missing.

Dr. Q. This was a beginning of a breakthrough for this doctor, wasn't it? — this first self-examination revealed in this way. Although you feel that we didn't get at all the feelings in the patient and are only touching the surface, if you like, anatomically — you can't do it all at once, can you?

Doctor S. No.

Dr. Q. From the doctor's *or* the patient's point of view.

Doctor S. And no-one suggested to the doctor that this was a good thing to do. She thought it out for herself.

Dr. Main I would have thought the leader really should have drawn attention to the absence of phantasies.

Doctor S. If the girl says, "I'm not small", what's that if it isn't a phantasy?

Dr. Main It's not a phantasy. It's the doctor's phantasy that the girl thought she was small.

Dr. I. Well, the implication is, if she says, "I'm not after all" and looks surprised, that she did think she was small.

Dr. Main The doctor said, "Is it big or small?"

Doctor S. The girl said, "I'm not small, am I?" — so that is expressing that she *thought* she was small.

Dr. Main As you reported it, it was an answer to the doctor's question. I criticise the leader for not pointing out the shortage of phantasy material.

Doctor S. Well, obviously a little bit more went on than I remembered to say.

Dr. Main What is she small *for*?

Dr. Q. Is that moving too fast for this doctor? The next time with the patient would have been better.

Dr. Main Not with this patient!

Dr. Q. I feel sometimes you can go too fast.

Dr. Main This doctor was really too fast with the examination. She should have examined the patient and said, "What is the trouble about this? What do you think is going to happen?" and explore those phantasies.

Doctor S. With that sort of patient you can't really say anything; she's so shy and inhibited.

Dr. Tunnadine   I don't entirely agree with Dr. Main, but where I do agree with him is — by the end of that group, when everyone felt relieved and pleased, did the doctor *know* why her doings had made this patient better? Do we even know why it was relieving to the patient? There wasn't much discussion of how it worked. It was just congratulations as you reported it. But it had worked. I think that Dr. Main is right that there were quite a lot of hints in that afternoon's material that they are anxious about phantasies.

Dr. Main   Let's look at the phantasy that the whole thing is dirty, which hasn't been tackled. I don't see what they were so pleased about. I am bothered that you are pleased that a vaginal examination has been done, because that's not a feat at all. I think it would be a pity if they acquired the idea that doing a vaginal examination was an O.K. thing.

Doctor S.   They certainly were picking it up that doing it in a certain way was very useful. There's no doubt that it was. I think I probably haven't given you the evidence. I don't know if it was the doctor who said, or someone in the group, "She thinks she is small and young and she's now decided not to stay like that". Those were the sort of remarks which came out which I thought were probably right about this girl.

Dr. Main   It might be right, but it's not confirmed and we don't know if the patient is any better.

Doctor S.   The patient may not be fully fledged as a sexual woman yet, but she has certainly moved on a stage from a shy, crying, weeping girl with her hair over her face. We've all met them, haven't we? — impossible to work with.

Dr. Tunnadine   Absolutely right. I don't agree with Dr. Main about whether she is better because it sounds to me as though something good went on there, but the fact is that it was not this doctor's step-by-step questioning vaginal examination which transformed this girl into the sort of person who could open her mouth in more ways than one — it was what went on *before*. The doctor said, "Go away!" and the group said that was a bad thing to do and was unproductive. In fact it was productive and allowed the girl to come back and let the doctor do these things to her.

Doctor S.   It sort of came out that she got irritated with the girl, but she tried to say, "Look, I will be there if you want to come back and use me". I think I'm probably not putting it across very well. It's very difficult, isn't it? I appreciated her report and I felt I knew what she was saying, but it's difficult for me to give it to you in the same way, even though it was only two days ago.

Dr. N. I have a vague feeling about this group, and maybe it's coming from the leader, that there is difficulty in accepting the agrressive side of people's natures as being of any use.

Doctor S. That does come from me, I expect, yes.

Dr. A. She was aggressive to the patient and the patient came back.

Dr. Main She was criticised for it.

Dr. Tunnadine From this patient, have the group learned that she got better because of the right finger tricks?

Dr. N. You're a bit early yet in talking about her having got better. She might just be able to open her vagina a bit, but we don't know what use she is going to be able to make of it in the future.

4. A new use of the S.T.D. clinic

Leader Doctor C.

This short extract is taken from the beginning of a transcript dealing with other subjects. However, it is included to show that patients unable to consummate their marriages seek help in different ways. A woman came to a venereologist complaining of a vaginal discharge. She was on the pill and said she had made love a few times. When he came to examine her he found an intact hymen. When she got dressed he said, "You told me you were making love, but I don't think you have, have you?" She said, "No, doctor, but a friend of mine told me that if you came to the VD department they always pass that instrument and that would get rid of the hymen quickly. I've tried to make love a couple of times, but my boyfriend couldn't get in and he was getting a bit impatient, so I thought I'd better do something about it".

Doctor C.   The group had quite a laugh and discussed it — a new use of S.T.D. clinics. But this doctor had handled it very sensitively.

Dr. K.   Had this doctor presented a case before?

Doctor C.   Only one before, some time ago.

Dr. K.   I wasn't sure if he was producing the case of the virgin because he was a virgin in the work. Maybe he was saying, "I'm a beginner".

Doctor C.   That was my feeling a little bit.

Dr. J.   How far do the cases which they present reflect their own feelings?

Dr. S.   You get over your virginity by having someone rather roughly and deceitfully penetrating you or something.

Dr. Tunnadine   I think that's right. The only question I'm interested in is the leader's area of interest. You seem to be pleased that he had been able to present a second case after being silent for some time. But I didn't actually pick up that he'd learned what was going on between him and the patient except that it was good and he wasn't frightened any more. Maybe that's just because you didn't report it here.

Dr. Main   But he didn't really report anything about his work.

Doctor C.   There wasn't a lot of doctor/patient relationship in it. We really were discussing his feeling with the patient and how he felt rueful and a bit cheated that she hadn't been honest with him; but he had been able to discuss it openly.

Dr. Tunnadine   I think that is what I was puzzling after, really.

Doctor C.   It also opened up the difficulty of examining virgins, which is something that the Asian doctors in my group are sometimes hesitant about. It was only a short case.

SECTION TWO

THE GROUP

AND

PSYCHOSEXUAL WORK

A. THE WORK OF EARLY GROUPS

When a new group of doctors start in a seminar the work is often characteristic. Although each seminar is unique, and the case material is different, the requirements of training and the concerns of the leader can be remarkably similar.

In this chapter I have selected digests in which the work of some early groups is discussed, and where the leaders face typical problems.

1. PATIENT (AND DOCTOR?) NOT WANTING TO BE EXAMINED.
Here we again see a possibility that the case material may express some unconscious doubts in the doctor, this time about having her work examined.

2. HOW DO YOU GET AWAY FROM THE PHYSICAL?
It is very common, indeed almost universal in new groups, for doctors to find it easier to talk about pathology and physical problems rather than about feelings.

3. GETTING BEYOND THE QUESTIONING TECHNIQUE.
4. QUESTION AND ANSWER.
These two digests are concerned with the questioning technique used by doctors with their patients, as well as in the group.

5. DOCTOR AND GROUP HAVING DIFFICULTY FACING SEXUAL PROBLEMS.
Finally there is again the difficulty for the group of facing up to the subject of sexuality. The leaders discuss how to help doctors in an early group to develop a professional attitude to sexually difficult material.

1. Patient (and doctor?) not wanting to be examined

Leader Doctor I.

At the first meeting of a new group a doctor reported a patient who refused to agree to a vaginal examination. She had been on the pill for several years. The doctor felt that her refusal must mean she had a problem, but the patient denied this.

Dr. Main   What did the patient complain of? What did she come for?

Doctor I.   A repeat pill prescription. As far as the patient is concerned she has no problems: 'Everything is fine, thank you very much'. Yes, she enjoys sex. So I put that to the group and asked whether other doctors had had patients who refused to be examined.

Dr. Main   Oooh — into generalisations!

Dr. G.   Desperate leader. . . 'Let's get them all in. Let's get them all talking the first time. . .

Doctor I.   '. . .while I think of something to say to the doctor involved'.

Dr. Main   What about saying something different but sticking with the case?

Doctor I.   Such as?

Dr. G.   Like Dr. Main has been saying: "What is this patient complaining of?"

Dr. A.   Did she say why this was a problem? She must have had a clue from the patient in order to say, "This is a problem".

Doctor I.   This patient has refused to be examined. The patient isn't complaining.

Dr. G.   So who has a problem?

Dr. Main   "What went on between this doctor and the patient?" is another thing you can ask the group. Good example of a doctor/patient relationship, isn't it?

Dr. G.   An impossible case of a non-case.

Dr. Main   There's a technical problem for the doctor. The doctor wanted to do a vaginal examination and that's *proper* medicine.

Doctor I.   I asked her what she was intending to do and she said she had explained all her reasons to the patient, again on an intellectual level, as to why she should do a vaginal examination and her patient still refused. She hummed and ha'ed as to whether to refuse the pill, which a couple of them said they would do. I said, "Use blackmail?", and they said, "Yes, use blackmail"; but she felt that all that would happen then is the patient would go and find another doctor who *would* give her the pill, so she may as well stick with it.

Dr. Main   On the surface this patient is being very awkward, but we don't know why. The doctor didn't discuss with the patient the awkwardness and what it was about.

Doctor I.   We did suggest that it might be useful, if she comes up again and still wants her to have a vaginal examination, to ask her why, what the real reasons are.

Dr. Main   That was your point of view?

Doctor I.   I made that point.

Dr. Main   How did the group discuss the case in general?

Doctor I.   They just sat there until I said, "Is there anyone else who has had a patient who has refused to have a vaginal examination?"

Dr. Main   So you ran away from that patient and didn't discuss it?

Doctor I.   Well, we didn't get very far.

Dr. P.   And yet there is such a lot going on between that patient and that doctor, isn't there? — Vast amounts of anger and control.

Dr. Main   If the leader doesn't keep her eye on the ball, the group never will.

Dr. C.   It tells us something about the doctor, too, that she's feeling so resistant.

Dr. Main   The patient should be examined — is that not right?

Dr. C.   Yes.

Dr. Main   Well then, the doctor is within her rights to say, "Look, I want to examine you".

Dr. G.   Why?

Dr. Main   It is this doctor's practice to examine patients, and she has come up against one who doesn't want to be examined. That's a phenomenon that needs understanding — not fighting, but understanding. Did the group attempt to understand it?

Doctor I. One of them said that some people did feel that this was a violation and didn't want to be touched.

Dr. Main That's a guess. Did the group discuss what the woman and the doctor were doing together?

Doctor I. No.

Dr. S. Did the doctor, for instance, say that it made her angry, the patient that wouldn't give in?

Doctor I. No.

Dr. Main The question is, is it right at the first session to start talking about the doctor's feelings? — most improper, medically. Don't forget, *we're* pretty sophisticated about the fact that doctors might have feelings. The general standard is that they should keep their feelings out of it and get on with their doctoring. That's the routine teaching.

Dr. S. Yes, but don't you start the way you mean to go on?

Dr. Main I would have thought that six months was a reasonable time at which to start making remarks of that sort. You've got to face it, they will report traditionally. You don't just say, "Hey, stop being who you are and where you are!" Point out that not much was mentioned of what went on between the doctor and the patient. But most people do just bring patients' stories to start with, using traditional methods.

Dr. S. Yes I know, but. . .

Dr. Q. Surely there's no reason why the doctor couldn't put it back to the patient why she didn't want a vaginal examination?

Doctor I. I suggested she might try that the next time the patient comes in; but that came from me, not from anyone in the group.

Dr. C. I think they're a jolly good group when I think of my first session.

Dr. Main If you're just going to be nice, you'd better get out and leave this seminar!

Dr. C. Isn't it helpful, right at the beginning, to get the group to contribute, even if they don't contribute very effectively? In that very first new group when they all feel a bit vulnerable, I would have thought that one would aim to let them go away feeling fairly comfortable and thinking, "I want to come again".

Dr. S.   They might, if they just talked, go away thinking, "Oh, we just talked". . .

Dr. C.   The leader *was* putting in suggestions and feelings.

Dr. P.   Did the reporting doctor tell you anything about the patient?

Doctor I.   Yes, a very efficient, competent woman; independent, got a good job, married to a civil servant; aged about 26.

Dr. Main   So it was a living picture?

Doctor I.   Yes, she gave quite a good picture.

Dr. G.   It was interesting, wasn't it, that what the doctor did was to project on to the woman, 'She won't allow *me* to examine her', which was the very right and proper medical thing, and therefore she must have a problem. Not that she doesn't fancy being examined by someone who has been unpleasant, and all that sort of thing.

Doctor I.   She presented her because it was a transfer from another clinic. She had already been on the pill for two years and had never been examined and the doctor's attitude was, 'Ah, I shall!'

Dr. G.   So she wasn't actually looking at the woman, she was just going to show what a clever doctor she was.

Dr. P.   That's right. The other thing I remember a leader saying so clearly once was: "People aren't difficult on purpose". I would have thought, at the beginning of a group, it might be worth looking at why this patient was difficult.

Dr. Main   No prizes, but the other thing is: why did the doctor present this case? — 'I refuse to be examined'.

Doctor I.   Yes, I hadn't thought of that.

Dr. Main   No, well you didn't hold your seminar on a Wednesday afternoon with bags of time. That doctor may well leave the group if you push too hard. She is not sure how much she wishes her work to be examined.

2. How do you get away from the physical?

Leader Doctor N.

In a fairly new group a venereologist presented a patient who had been sent to her because of deep pain on intercourse. This had started suddenly after being married for three years. The patient had already seen her GP and a gynaecologist, who could find nothing wrong.

Doctor N.   The husband was pushed off to the other side of the screen for his examination. The woman was led in and put up in stirrups, which is the standard way they examine people in this particular department. The examination was easy and uneventful. Swabs were taken and looked at in the department straight away. Nothing was found and then they were sent off for culture, just in case. The lady was told to dress and come into the office where our reporting doctor thought it would be nice to have a quiet word with her about what was going on. She asked, "Is there anything else you would like to know?". "Yes, would you have a word with my husband?" "Certainly", said our doctor, and the wife went out and sent the husband in. By this time the husband had also been cleared. The doctor went outside and said, "Wouldn't you like to come in as well?", and the patient said, "No, thank you". She was sitting outside with her mother. The husband came in by himself. He seemed to think there wasn't very much to this. He was co-operative; he would do as he was told; if he was wanted, that was O.K. His wife was O.K.? — Fine, pleased to hear it. They were given an appointment to come back in a fortnight's time, when the doctor thought she would make an appointment for the woman to be seen by herself and have a chance to talk.

   The group spent some time discussing the fact that the mother had come to the clinic, and there was also a lot of talk about pathology and possible physical causes for the pain. Then the group wanted to know why the patient had sent her husband in: what was the doctor supposed to do to the husband? Various scenarios were worked out for this: that the husband was to be told something — maybe he had had an affair of which he had to be cleansed. I said, "This is fine; we can write plays about this,

E

but we can really only work with the evidence. What evidence have we got as to why this woman sent her husband in?" Nobody could see any evidence, thank God, because neither could I! I noticed that she had sent him in and said, "What does it tell us about the patient? I don't know why she sent him in, but what sort of patient have we got here?" People said "anxious, concerned, worried" — all this sort of thing. No-one would say what I wanted them to say, which was that she was a manipulative, strong woman and that she had not only sent the husband in, but she had been through the GP, through the gynaecologist down to the V.D. Department. At the end of the case I said, "And what really happened during the vaginal examination?", and she said, "Nothing, really. She just got up into the stirrups — she didn't mind". I said, "I didn't think any woman didn't mind" — a fairly provocative thing to say, but I felt the group wanted a bit of a lead about this.

Dr. I. Did the group pick up this remark?

Doctor N. Yes, they all agreed. One of the GPs there said "trussed up like a chicken" and they talked about this and what it was like.

Dr. S. Apparently this patient didn't mind.

Doctor N. No. This is it: I think we got down to this bit of control.

Dr. L. It was safe and clinical, do you mean?

Doctor N. Well, she showed no emotion, kept herself controlled. She bore everything.

Mrs. R. Did you point that out to the group?

Doctor N. I think the group got that point.

Dr. A. The pain she was describing on intercourse never got talked about. When she sat down with the doctor afterwards, the real thing that she had come about was pain on intercourse, and it was never talked about.

Doctor N. It was the old reassurance; but the doctor wasn't unaware of that, which is the reason she has asked her to come back again, to give her a chance to talk about it. If one took into account the fact that it was a busy clinic, I don't think she'd done too badly.

Dr. A. Did the group discuss her feelings with the patient? The patient said, "Please see my husband". Did the doctor feel pushed about?

Doctor N.   Yes, she did; she felt she had been manipulated. She wasn't sure what the husband was there for. She didn't know why she should talk to the husband, and that was why she went out and asked the patient if she would like to come back in, but the patient said, "No, it's between you two".

Dr. Tunnadine   It sounds a bit like any case where the patient is a mystery or the case is a mystery. The talk was more about that and it was difficult to talk about the doctor and her work — which was not a lot, was it?

Doctor N.   There was quite a lot of talk about the use of the V.D. Department as a dumping ground, and how she couldn't understand why, when the Hospital has a Department of Sexology, she had been referred to her. A bit of resentment that she was being made a fool of by a silly gynaecologist who had referred her.

Dr. I.   And perhaps she felt a bit deflated because, having seen the husband and nothing transpired, it would make her feel, "What have I done?".

Mrs. R.   But she never actually picked up the point that this patient was complaining of dyspareunia. This was never picked up during the whole time.

Dr. A.   She wasn't able to use the fact that the patient had not felt anything during the examination.

Dr. Tunnadine   It was the doctor who said, "Now let's talk: you're perfectly all right". In other words, 'Shut up!' and we now hear at the end of this consultation that the doctor said, "I would like to talk to you", and the patient said, "No, thank you!" So next time she is going to talk to her again — she'll be lucky! I don't know what this doctor, towards whom Dr. N. sounds rather protective or something, was doing to the group by bringing such a non-bit of work. This was the difficult thing. These are the things from the leadership point of view which I would like to understand. Somehow this innocent doctor set the group up a bit, and her own work, or non-work, which she's not to be blamed for, really slipped away.

Doctor N.   Non-work, in a way. . . I think she's puzzled by it and you've got to give her credit for that, haven't you?

Dr. P. But did the group really cope with the doctor's fury about being used and being set up, because that is how she brought the case to the group: all this anger about being somehow manipulated by her colleagues which seems to me to have got in the way of any real work. She was irritated at being asked to do yet something else: 'I told her she was all right and now I've got to talk to the husband'. It is strange to agree to see a man when you don't know what it is you've got to say to him.

Doctor N. Very powerful patient.

Dr. P. Very powerful.

Dr. S. — who retreats to mother. We get the feeling that the doctor was supposed to tick the man off, don't we?

Dr. Tunnadine I think this is right, but what Dr. N. was trying to get at is that this patient, who you saw as powerful, made mincemeat of this doctor; whoever else she had made mincemeat of over the years, she made mincemeat of the doctor and the doctor must have felt pretty inadequate. You had a go at getting the group to look at that, but somehow they couldn't: they were protective towards the doctor, or thought she just had a nasty patient or something.

Dr. G. Or was it — I had a feeling of panic creeping in with the leader: something like, 'We've got to see the true path!'

Doctor N. The difficulty was to get them off the pathology, you see. They got stuck on pathology and genital herpes and so on.

Dr. Tunnadine It sounds as though the patient had to see it as physical. That would be one way of drawing attention to this. But somehow I think you're right: this doctor's irritation made it very difficult for the group to criticise what she'd been doing. Somehow the leader was put in a spot by this sweet little doctor, or sweet little patient, or whoever it was. You were aware that there was something nasty going on.

Doctor N. Yes, I was also very much aware that this had a lot of loose ends. It was a working consultation and good, because it was real life: the way you pick things up in your surgery when you don't have an hour's interview. This woman had come in with another problem, wearing a different hat, but the doctor had picked up something and there were a lot of loose ends which no-one could solve; but she had come along to present that. It made it very difficult to talk about the case as such, because she had been dealing with clinical pathology. That was what the patient was there for, but the doctor was aware that something was underlying this. It was basically the stuff that the Institute is made of, isn't it — the way people present with these disguised presentations and visiting cards? I felt it was a worthwhile case for her to bring, but our discussion was unsatisfactory.

Mrs. R. Surely, as a leader one has to show the group that one can do work with someone like that? It doesn't have to be a nice consultation: they can reasonably quickly pick up something which this doctor didn't appear to do. Although she'd picked up that the patient needed some help, she really didn't work with her at all, apart from the clinical side. The actual problem was not worked with at all.

Dr. A. But the patient stopped the doctor by her attitude and, through the doctor, stopped the group working, and made the group discuss all the clinical things instead of what was actually happening with the patient.

Dr. Tunnadine I don't think the group had much of a go at this doctor's inadequacies, and the leader somehow, despite his protectiveness, got impatient at the end.

Doctor N. I was looking at it, as far as I'm conscious anyway, in comparison to last week when we had a nice case of something coming out of a genital examination — and here was a case when we had got nothing out of it.

Dr. Tunnadine It was Dr. N. declaring his terms, which I like.

Doctor N. I said, "You did the vaginal examination of her as a venereologist. You examined her as part of an infected birth canal rather than as an organ of pleasure, which is a different way of looking at it". — A bit of teaching, you see. . .

Dr. Tunnadine The other level to look at is: what is the doctor doing? Did she present a case in which she knew she had done badly?

Dr. P. I think she's not sure whether a venereologist wants to be associated with this work, or not. 'I'm a venereologist and I put people's feet up in stirrups', and it's very difficult to be a different sort of doctor. Perhaps she is not sure that she wants to do it.

Dr. Tunnadine She must have known she has not done very good work. After all, she presents a patient whom other people have tried to reassure, but they have failed; and the doctor now does nothing more than that herself. 'Would you like to talk to me?' — but doesn't give her the chance to talk, but says, 'I, too, think you're all right'. And so the patient says, 'No thanks. I came here specially to talk to you, but I don't want to talk to you any longer', and gets back to mummy. Very unsatisfactory, and the doctor must have known it: brought it to the group but somehow didn't get much help.

3. Getting beyond the questioning technique

Leader Doctor I.

A group had been meeting for nearly a year when one of the doctors presented a case for the first time. The leader felt pleased, as she was a shy general practitioner, a quiet person who said little, but seemed to be a nice, kind doctor. The patient was a woman who said she felt depressed and, when asked if her sex life was all right, said, "It's funny you should mention that: I am having problems". The doctor then asked a lot of questions, but did not seem to get very far, and as it was a busy surgery she made an appointment to see the patient again the following week.

Doctor I. As a result we had quite a lot of discussion from all the others to say, 'How old is she?' and 'What is her grandmother doing?' and so on; a whole lot of questions to each of which she said, "I don't know; I didn't have time. I don't know; I didn't get that from her". I merely said, "We seem to be doing the same thing: asking a lot of questions and getting nowhere, which is much the same as you were with your patient". I then turned to the next one. . . I feel protective about this doctor.

Dr. Main   You are talking about the group behaviour. They asked a lot of questions. It might be worthwhile at that point bringing it back to the clinical situations that they know and saying, "You see the value of asking questions? I think you might be doing this to your patients and getting nowhere".

Doctor I.   Actually she denied it.

Dr. Main   No, I'm not talking about *her*, but the rest of the group. You made your remark quite pointed about her. It's landing a lot of focus on her. The other thing to do is to find out what the group is doing. They are asking questions: "The doctor didn't get anywhere asking her questions. How did you get on with yours? Again nowhere. I think that is what you, the askers, must be doing clinically as well. That is how you are tackling this problem".

Doctor I.   In fact she did deny that she spent all her time asking questions.

Dr. Main   It's the others I'm talking about.

Doctor I.   Yes, I agree. I feel a little bit protective as this is her first case.

Dr. Main   I'm not talking about *her*.

Doctor I.   No. Push it on to the others.

Dr. Main   I'm talking about the mode of discussion, not the presenting doctor. They are just showing the usual medical practice and it's no use. You can show it's no use. Get them away from this questioning technique on to the *listening* one.

Doctor I.   And there was quite a lot of asking.

Dr. Main   The other thing you can do with this, and maybe you can do it on another occasion, is to point out what is behind the question. They have some phantasy behind it. You know what it's like: they say, "I think it might be Oedipus complex. How old was her father when she was born?" They ask a silly question like this, which apparently has no meaning at all — but you should get at the thought behind it.

Doctor I.   Yes, I am bad at that.

Dr. Main   It is a difficult thing to do. — 'Can you say what it is you would like to know? What thoughts you have that you want to settle? . . .' Ask the questioner to answer the question and they will tell you. What I am talking about here is a lovely example to push this group on from the questioning technique.

Doctor I.   Which they do tend still to do. It didn't last very long, that one. I felt somehow protective towards her, because I didn't want her not to present. We then went on. . .

Dr. E.   Can I just ask you what you are protecting her *from*?

Doctor I.   I didn't want her to feel uncomfortable, because I was aware of feeling critical myself. She had come and reported a lot of questions about this, that and the other, maybe to try and get from the patient what her particular problem was. Although she'd said she'd got a sexual problem, she didn't really get down to the nitty gritty.

Dr. Main   Dr. I., you made a big mistake there — you answered the question! *(Laughter)*.

Dr. E.   I was hoping she wouldn't flick it back to me, because I couldn't think what was behind it! I was annoyed with Dr. I. for saying she was feeling protective.

Dr. Main   Why did she want to protect the doctor? — Come on, what's your thought?

Dr. E.   She'd done such a tentative, unsatisfying piece of work, and also I guess she'd been pretty uncomfortable with the patient, hadn't she? and the leader didn't want her criticised for it. I am annoyed with you for not looking at it more.

Doctor I.   Yes, I did feel protective, I suppose in order to help her next time and help her to feel more confident about producing a case.

Dr. E.   I am still very dissatisfied with the fact that this poor woman has produced her case, which didn't get very far, and she's been more or less patted on the head and told, "Try again next time".

Dr. Tunnadine   I don't know. I think Dr. I. slipped in a clever bit of leadership which you then jumped upon. That is to say, she had a clever thought — 'This group is doing the same as the doctor is' — and let it go at this. The result, as far as I can see, was a stunned silence; after which you then felt protective towards this doctor, knowing that you had bashed her good. Dr. Main suggested a slight modification of your observation, but it *was* a bit of leadership.

Doctor I.   Yes, I think perhaps I brought it to an end more quickly, partly because I didn't want her to feel embarrassed at not having more to produce.

Dr. Tunnadine   But I thought you reported that you had done rather a good thing for once by thinking, 'Very interesting, the group are doing the same as the doctor'. I thought that was what you presented to us; and then it backfired.

Dr. Main   Your job is with the group, not this doctor, and the group is asking questions. Why not address the group about their bloody questions?

Dr. Tunnadine   She did.

Dr. Main   She ticked them off for doing so.

Dr. Tunnadine   Well, I disagree with you.

Doctor I.   I said to the group, "Isn't it interesting that you are doing the same as the doctor did this morning: asking a lot of questions".

Dr. Tunnadine   That's right.

Dr. Main   And that's bad — that's the implication.

Dr. Tunnadine   Ah, well. . .

Dr. Main   I am suggesting that you should examine the phenomenon. They are asking questions because they have got thoughts.

Dr. Tunnadine   Yes, that I would agree with.

Doctor I.   That I should have done.

Dr. Main   Even my colleague on my left has thoughts behind this question.

Dr. Tunnadine   Yes, and my thoughts are that in her good intentions of clever leadership, she knew she had actually bashed her and then became protective towards her.

Doctor I.   Yes.

Dr. Main   I think the best thing you could do is leave her alone and start making comments about the group's behaviour.

4. Question and answer technique in a vasectomy counselling session.

Leader Doctor Q.

Doctor Q.   The first case presented by my group, which is still fairly new, was about an Irish teacher who had a very unhappy marriage. There was a lot of history about her Catholic upbringing and how unhappy she was in her marriage and how she hated sex. The group discussion seemd to be mainly about the phantasies that the patient had about her parents and her husband: all background things. It was all rather vague.

Dr. Main   They didn't discuss the consultation, the encounter?

Doctor Q.   Not really. Just the patient.

Dr. Main   Go on.

The leader then described the next case which presented in a vasectomy counselling clinic:-

Dr. Q.   It seemed to be a perfectly average sort of case: a husband and wife came in requesting a vasectomy and there didn't seem to be anything unusual about it in any way. She went through the form asking various questions and filling in the various bits, and got to the question about intercourse and ascertained that they were quite happy. I am not sure who answered that question, or whether they both did. At any rate, she felt satisfied that there was nothing to worry about: they were a suitable couple for vasectomy. So they signed the forms and made the arrangements for the appointment for the operation.

It was at this point, when the doctor was about to shake hands, that the wife burst out and said, "I have got to be truthful, haven't I? I want to be honest, I must be honest with you", in a very agitated way. She burst out that she had never enjoyed sex, at which my presenting doctor felt absolutely floored. The husband turned to his wife angrily and said, "Why didn't you say anything before about that? When you said sex was all right I naturally didn't say anything about it". The main feeling that the presenting doctor picked up was a very distressed wife and a very angry husband, and it seemed to paralyze the doctor into not being able to think coherently. She thought, "I have signed everything, organised it and now it's all gone wrong. What am I going to do?" She said to them, "Would you like to sit down and talk about this?" and they said, "No no — vasectomy is the thing. We have talked about it and discussed it and we want to go ahead". She said, "I just let them go out and I feel dreadful about it. I don't know what to do".

There was silence in the group for quite a while. Then someone said, "You don't have to agree to anything. Why didn't you give them an appointment to come back and talk about it again?" She said, "I just don't know". Very great distress. The majority of the group felt this distress of the doctor, that she had done something or arranged for something to be done which she was unhappy about, and was quite unable to do anything about because she wasn't going to see them again and felt she couldn't contact them. I think it paralysed me as well, because I can't remember making any sensible comment, except trying to look at what was going on between them: how strong the feelings were and the doctor not able to use that. I think the presenting doctor was left in no doubt that the group felt she should have asked to see the couple again, or torn up the form, or something. I think perhaps we all learnt how strong the feelings are that come from patients to doctors and affect their way of working.

Pause

Dr. Main   Any more cases, or was that the end of the group?
Doctor Q.   We had two more.
Dr. Main   What shall we do — discuss those? . . . Let's stop here and see what we can do. We have got half a group so far, the first half. What do people think?

Pause

Dr. A.   It's obviously paralysed all of us as well as paralysed the doctor and paralysed the wife into not telling the truth.
Dr. N.   The group seems to be in a very uncritical phase at the moment. It doesn't seem to take up the cases and discuss things very much at all: very little discussion seems to have gone on.

Dr. Main   Very little about the doctor/patient relation. Like all early groups, they are still discussing patients rather than the doctor's work. With the first case they went on have lovely phantasies and playing violins about the possibilities of what might have happened in Ireland. It's an interesting place because there is a lot of clover around, fairies and pixies and all this imaginary stuff about this Irish woman. There was no discussion really of the clinical features, or the relationship with this husband, or the relationship with this doctor. But this is an early seminar still. In the second one, they didn't discuss what the patients and the doctor did together, and how it was that the doctor was very tactful and didn't ask very much about "Everything all right sexually? Bowels all right?" — that sort of rapid filling of a questionnaire. No query about what the doctor was doing with the patients. I think it's just an early group: they don't know each other yet. They are not comfortable enough with each other to discuss each other.

Doctor Q.   Perhaps I have not presented that second one in the correct light, because there was a lot of feeling in the group.

Dr. Main   They ticked the doctor off — but that is not discussing the work.

Doctor Q.   Well, understanding that the patient has affected the doctor in her normal way of working, because she is an extremely able doctor and she just couldn't go on with this patient and discuss the distress or use the husband's anger.

Dr. Main   The detail of the patient/doctor encounter really wasn't worked out. It was only after the patient burst out in anger that the doctor realised and was dumbfounded that this had happened, and ran away; and the group was dumbfounded and we were dumbfounded. It's easy to be critical about it, but what was going on before that to produce this last-minute situation?

Doctor Q.   I did try and bring it out.

Dr. Main   I don't mean *you* — get the group to discuss it.

Doctor Q.   Certainly there was a lot of discussion about whether one should have forms at all and how you get the answer you expect.

Dr. Main   They discussed that?

Doctor Q.   Yes. But in a way that was a bit of criticism of this doctor for using a form; but you have to, as they have to be filled in at the end of a consultation. Nothing had come out of the consultation and then I suppose the patient realised that the doctor was signing the form and if she didn't get it out now she never would — and the outburst came.

Dr. P.   She hasn't actually told you anything about that consultation. We don't know anything about how the couple sat, or how they looked at each other. It's easy to put it all down on the form, but actually she hasn't reported on the patients.

Doctor Q.   She kept reassuring us all the way through — 'I felt quite happy about all this; there is nothing spectacular to tell you'.

Dr. P.   There is always something to tell about what goes on between two people, and she hasn't told you, and the group doesn't seem to want to know.

Doctor Q.   I didn't bring that out, it's true.

Dr. Main   It sounds like the questioning technique used by the doctor to gain information; and when the doctor had the information and was ready to fill the form in, the patient hadn't said what the patient came to say.

Dr. Y.   I wondered if it was just the form, or something to do with the patient. This was a sort of last-ditch cry.

Dr. Main   Yes, I know, but produced by a doctor who hadn't given her a chance to say it earlier.

Dr. J.   I think the doctor was very angry about it. I think she felt that she had mismanaged it and she was bringing her anger to the group. I am not sure that they told her. She said what she felt about it, but I don't know that they recognised. . .

Dr. Main   I think that is right. I think she said, "I did something terrible. Please give me a good hiding". And they said "Right" and let her have it.

Dr. J.   She wanted to do that to the patients, didn't she?

Dr. Main   But in the group she wanted to be beaten up and they let her have it.

Dr. Tunnadine   I think that she didn't get it — that is what interests me. The group was paralysed by anger and pussyfooted about. They did not give this doctor the bashing she asked for.

Dr. Main   I thought they did.

Dr. D.   Why didn't they inquire into exactly how she had asked about their sexual relationship? They let her off completely, it seemed to me, just because she was so angry or distressed with herself, and felt that it was all irrevocable.

Dr. Tunnadine   — and responded to it by saying, "There there, dear", as I understood it.

Dr. Main   Did they let her off the hook?

Doctor Q.   No. You're going to ask me now, I suppose, to be specific and say what they said, and I don't remember; but I did have the feeling that we all felt she shouldn't have agreed to the vasectomy, and didn't really help her in her distress.

Dr. Main   She knew that all along.

Doctor Q.   Yes, but I don't think there was, "There there, don't worry about it".

Dr. Tunnadine   Well, I beg your pardon!

Doctor Q.   I think it illustrated how strong some patients can be and how they can manipulate.

Dr. Main   And it shows what a bloody awful group this is — when the doctor says, "I did very badly, I should have got this out before", the group says, "Yes, well, in our opinion you should have done this before and you did very badly with the patients" — repeating exactly what the doctor had said. The group didn't work on it. But *how* we don't know: *how* did this doctor do bad work? They didn't examine the doctor/patient relationship, it seems to me.

Dr. Tunnadine   I am suggesting that the doctor's flaw was being paralysed by anger.

Dr. Main   It is early days for these people. They are simply talking about patients and feeling inferior. That doctor didn't see that the difficulty was the product of what went on in the consulting room. She didn't report even what was going on under her nose — didn't discuss it: what the man was like, what the woman was like, how they were together, and so on. She just said everything was all right to sign the form. It isn't easy.

Dr. Tunnadine   I don't see that case as you do, evidently. I see it as a very nice illustration of the way people can so skilfully, on a vasectomy counselling decision, hide the real feelings which you can't attribute to bad doctoring but to bad patienting, if you like. If there was any bad doctoring at all, it was the fact that the doctor was so paralysed by the rage and the last-minute thing, and by them saying, "No, we will not sit down and talk", that she flapped. That was all. It sounds all right.

Dr. Main   The interesting thing is that the doctor took the answers at face value.

Dr. Tunnadine   Yes.

Dr. Main   At the end she found that the face value things weren't good enough. Ask a silly question and you'll get a silly answer.

Dr. Y.   That patient has been doing it to that husband for years, hasn't she? — so I'm not very surprised that she did it so skilfully to the doctor.

Dr. Main   And this chap is fed up and said, "Right, I'll show you. I'll have this vasectomy and see if *that* will do you a lot of good".

Dr. P.   So if perhaps somebody in the group could have seen the doctor's need to be bashed for what it was, then they could have stopped and actually looked at your idea about why it had to be last-minute; and then could have got on with it. The doctor's need to be bashed was in a sense what paralysed them.

Dr. Main   My phantasy about this man is that he is a shit and he said, "No, we've finished the form and that is it. No more discussion". Whose initiative was the vasectomy? Do you remember?

Doctor Q.   No.

Dr. Tunnadine   What impresses me about the case is that the doctor felt it was her fault. Not only does she think it's her fault, but *you* think it is her fault, too. She felt that nothing could be done about it. It's not true that nothing could be done about it: she could have torn up the form. Anyway, the patient may not turn up for the operation, since they are obviously going to go home and have a row!

5. Doctor and group have difficulty facing sexual problems

Leader Doctors J. & E.

A young woman GP talked about a man of 60 who ultimately told her he was under-sexed. It was a very complicated story and later his wife came to the doctor complaining that he was watching blue video films and asking her to do "impossible things". The doctor decided that in the future she would only see the couple together.

Doctor J.   The group had some difficulty discussing this case and there was a lot of discomfort and long silences. Someone suggested that she had decided to see them together so that she had a chaperone with this patient. My feeling was that it was a rather grotesque and difficult case for an early group.

Later the same doctor told the group about a man in his eighties who was planning to re-marry and was hoping that sex would be all right.

Doctor J.   I remember saying, "You don't report it with nearly so much anxiety as the first case: I wonder why?" She said, "He was an entirely different man".

Dr. Main   It seems that this early group has some difficulty facing up to sexual problems.

Dr. I.   I felt the anxiety was more, 'We are not quite sure what sort of case to bring. . . What about this?' Then they bring up something extraordinary.

Dr. Y.   I think the first case was much more frightening. That was the sort of feeling that came over.

Dr. Tunnadine   The group was extraordinary: even in this room we believe that it's an extraordinary case. It didn't seem to me to be a particularly extraordinary case. I have about two a week like that: frightened old chaps with bossy complaining wives who turn to video — and what else should they do?

Dr. Main   It was the doctor's anxiety.

Dr. Tunnadine   That's right. That's what I mean. It was very powerful; you brought it to us too. Everyone seemed terrified of it.

Doctor J. I'm not quite sure what the frightening content was. We didn't really know very much about the bizarre things going on, but the doctor was embarrassed and uncomfortable.

Dr. Main Yes.

Doctor J. We picked that up. We couldn't exactly say why it was she was embarrassed, unless it was that she was embarrassed by the fact that a 60-year-old person should want to be sexual; and I think I assumed that that was part of her embarrassment.

Dr. Tunnadine But it was wrong, wasn't it? because she came back at the end and said 82-year-old men were normal. Do you see what I mean?

Doctor J. Yes, that's quite true.

Dr. Main I think myself something frightened that doctor; and I think I know what it was, too. — Go on, tell us.

Doctor J. Sexual ideas.

Dr. Main Yes, what sort of sexual thing? — Come on!

Doctor J. The man having sexual ideas, male sexual ideas.

Dr. Main What sort of sexual ideas?

Doctor J. Bad, wicked.

Dr. Main Tell us about them. You haven't said a thing about them. *You* are frightened too! *Tell us!*

Doctor J. She didn't report them.

Dr. Main I know she didn't. . . That's why — because you didn't go into it. This is the difficulty.

Doctor J. She was asked. She couldn't tell us. She couldn't really ask the man.

Dr. Main She did say he'd seen this video. It's this video which is the exciting thing.

Doctor J. I'm so sorry, I think I've got that wrong. I don't think she reported the video at the very first stage. It only subsequently came out when. . .

Dr. Main That's the point I'm trying to make. The video was frightening and frightened her off.

Doctor E. It ties in with the account which she gave of the wife coming and being terribly angry. The wife kept saying that there were these things he'd seen, but the doctor presenting said, "She didn't tell me, and I didn't like to ask her what kind of things".

Dr. Main   That's my whole point.

Doctor J.   . . . 'He sees the videos and he wants me to do all the things he sees in the videos'. — They couldn't really mention them.

Dr. Main   "No-one seems to want to talk about these perverse activities in the video". — I could have said that in *this* group.

Dr. Q.   Is that because the leader was paralysed by the silence too, or frightened of it?

Dr. Main   The doctor was; the group was; the leader was. But the leader's job is to keep her head and see that this is the embarrassing thing.

Dr. I.   But isn't this again part of a new group that is frightened that what we are here to discuss is spicey, nasty bits of video — that aspect of sex — rather than the problems of the doctor/patient relation.

Dr. Main   All right: but the point is we have to have a professional attitude to anything which happens, and the professional attitude is that the doctor is frightened.

Dr. I.   Yes, but it seems as though we've heard before that new groups bring up bizarre things.

Dr. Main   It didn't matter very much this chap going to the video. What is wrong with this chap?

Dr. I.   I think the fear of the group is the sort of thing we are here to discuss, rather than 'we are here to discuss the doctor/patient relationship'.

Dr. Main   What is wrong with this chap?

Dr. I.   What, the doctor?

Dr. Main   No, this chap. Do you remember what the man's complaint was?

Dr. Tunnadine   Under-sexed.

Dr. Main   Yes, that was his problem.

Dr. I.   I had forgotten that.

Dr. Tunnadine   And incidentally, the wife comes along and says, "Ought I to approve of these awful things he picks up from the video?" I don't know that I agree with you that the group are paralysed by the naughty bits. I thought the group were paralysed because it was such an awful, blind, frightened, defensive bit of report.

Dr. Main The doctor is afraid to talk about it.

Dr. Tunnadine That's right. How to free that? — that is the question.

Dr. A. The doctor wasn't afraid to see an 82-year-old man without his wife; and yet she wouldn't see the 60-year-old man without his wife.

Dr. Y. It's not the overt sexual person she is frightened of, is it?

Dr. Main But this doctor did nothing; and she might have told you about why she hadn't done anything. It's an early group, it's their first case: she doesn't know how to begin.

Dr. Y. It's a bit tough on her. She's feeling a bit new and raw, and she gets a patient in the same state.

Dr. S. She only felt inadequate with *that* patient. She didn't feel inadequate with the 82-year-old.

Dr. Tunnadine I think that doctor got something out of the discussion. It's hard to identify it but it sounds as though, by the end, she at least was reflecting on whether it was just old people she couldn't deal with.

Dr. Main She couldn't ask this man what his trouble was.

Dr. I. But she was obviously trying to refute the idea that she had been merely frightened by an old man. It was the sex bit that she felt so inadequate about, or the video bit, rather.

Dr. Main The man who confessed to her that he had taken to videos.

Dr. I. He didn't say that, did he?

Dr. Main That's what I am trying to establish.

Doctor J. The first time that the video came into the story was when his wife came in.

Dr. Main That's what I thought.

Doctor J. He goes to videos and he comes back asking to do this.

Dr. Tunnadine And the doctor, in pure commonsense everyday ethical terms — I thought doing quite well there — said to his wife, "I am not going to discuss your husband behind his back", or something.

Doctor J.   There was a suggestion of some sort of masturbatory experiences with the video.

Dr. Main   And the GP was frightened that the man was going to use her in the same way, and said, "If you want to masturbate, do it in front of your wife". Was that not discussed in the group, then?

Doctor J.   Yes.

Dr. Main   The doctor's fear of the man using her for sexual purposes?

Doctor J.   Not so specifically: the doctor's fear of this sexual man.

Dr. Main   But the doctor's fear was about the man using her for sexual application.

Doctor J.   It wasn't initially quite so spelt out as that, because she didn't know very much. She didn't ask the man an awful lot. She didn't know about the videos in the first interview. One of the bad moments for me was when I said to her: "How did it feel when you were with this man at the original interview?" and she wouldn't answer. She went back and told me about the interview; and I said it again: "How did you feel?" and she couldn't say that she was terrified.

Dr. Main   If you thought she was terrified you should have said so.

Doctor J.   I think the other people did, actually, when I prompted them. I said, "How did you feel?" and she couldn't say and then, as far as I remember, they came in and said, "You were very upset about it and embarrassed".

Dr. Tunnadine   I feel more and more that "How did you feel?" is a very direct remark, which somehow sounds so personal and is not very helpful to someone who doesn't know what you are talking about. I'm puzzling after other sorts of remarks: "What was the effect of the patient on the doctor?" is more neutral and kind of shared, isn't it?

Dr. Main   Or to put it in the other context: "What does the group think the doctor would feel?"

Dr. Y.   "It must have been very difficult for you", or something.

Dr. Tunnadine   The Balint jargon was "a dose of Dr. What?", wasn't it? "How do we define the dose of the doctor?" — it is somehow more neutral.

Dr. Main   It's a matter of technique. If you address your remark *to the doctor*, you make it highly personal: "Look what you are doing"; or "I think you are doing so and so". Or it can be said to the group: "What does the group think the doctor was doing?". It's a different thing because it makes the group do some work and doesn't put the doctor right in the limelight, more or less in the accused box.

Dr. Tunnadine   Even that puts rather an emphasis on the doctor and her behaviour, rather than the effect the patient has on her. It is a bit phoney when a doctor is always blind with every patient to say that this particular patient did it; but it is what we are there to study.

Doctor J.   Or: "What was the patient making the doctor do?"

Dr. Main   I'm afraid I use: "What was going on between these two?"

B. GROUP EXCITEMENT

One of the things the leader has to recognise is group excitement, often shown by the members breaking into pairs and all talking at once.

1. EXCITEMENT AND DENIAL OF PAIN.
In this extract the excitement seemed to come from the patient's and the doctor's denial of pain, which the *group* could see and appreciate.

2. FEMALE CIRCUMCISION.
Exciting clinical material threatened to stop the doctor listening to the patient or the group studying the patient's dilemma.

3. INCEST.
The main problems for the leader in this complicated digest seem to have come from her failure to bring the group excitement out into the open.

1. Excitement and denial of pain

Leader Doctor Q.

A couple came together to see their doctor and to ask for help because the husband had become impotent. The doctor gave a very rosy picture of a happy, loving pair. They sat holding hands and frequently smiled at each other and joked. They told her how romantic their sex life had always been, with soft lights and music. His impotence seemed to have started after he had been told by the doctor's partner that he had high blood pressure. He was not on any treatment, just regular checks, but the possibility of treatment in the future to reduce the risk of a stroke had been discussed.

Doctor Q. Despite the fact that the doctor gave rather a flat, factual account, the group immediately started to discuss it, with everyone talking at once and breaking up to talk to their neighbours. They couldn't understand how there could be so much laughter and fun now, if their love life had suddenly come to a stop. I felt confused and the presenting doctor appeared to feel attacked in some way.

Dr. J. I'm struck by the flat description and in spite of the lovey dovey it came over as boring, although the group became animated.

Dr. Main What do you make of it?

Dr. J. That during the presentation by the doctor to the group, there was a great deal of evasion and suppression of feeling; no real understanding of what was happening. But the group became aware of it. They didn't know quite what it was — they knew there was something there which they were trying to discover, but couldn't reach.

Doctor Q. That was when the presenting doctor became angry.

Dr. Tunnadine I agree with you, but I saw it differently, that the group did understand a sight more about this very interesting case than this doctor, who took it at face value and couldn't understand it and got no feel of the fear that sex might give him a stroke or something.

Dr. Main I don't think we have had the truth about the presentation. I'll tell you why I think so and I am the bearer of glad news actually as well. The phenomenon that baffled you about the group — everyone trying to talk at once and later on in pairs — this is the glad news — these are the classic signs of a group that is so excited it can't contain itself, the group breaks up and people wet themselves all over the place. There were signs of great excitement: that is why I don't believe you about the flatness of this presentation. That group is very excited by this presentation, and didn't know what to do with it; that's what held up the group discussion. But in telling us about the presentation I got no measure of what was so exciting for the group.

Doctor Q.   I am thinking of the case at this point. The picture that I got was: 'I can't understand why they were laughing and joking and being so affectionate when they've had this super sex life for so long'. Then the group were all talking at once.

Dr. Main   Here is a man and a woman who have been together for a long time, the man's become impotent, then there is a burst of giggling about what a splendid sex life they had before that. I don't really believe that this couple did this. Maybe the doctor reported it in this way, but the attention is taken right away from their present pain. Did the doctor present it that way?

Doctor Q.   She said she asked them what it had been like before.

Dr. Main   I see. That was the trouble: she couldn't stand the pain, instead of asking what the trouble was now. It's a very old trick of going into the past and dodging the present; taking the history.

Dr. E.   She was angry because the group wouldn't swallow her pretty picture. Is that right?

Doctor Q.   I think that was her anger, but I wanted to get it back to the fact that she must be picking it up from the patients. They were angry that this had happened.

Mrs. R.   Why were you wanting to protect this doctor at the same time?

Doctor Q.   They were quite critical, I felt.

Dr. Tunnadine   I say again that they were right to be, if your report is anything to go by.

Dr. Main   It makes sense to me now with hindsight. If you had been able to say: "There is a great deal of excitement here in this room. People are breaking up and that is why everyone is talking at once" — that is one of the rare occasions when you draw attention to a group phenomenon in a semi-interpretative way, to get some sort of order. But what is the excitement about? I think it is, if we are right so far, because the doctor ran away from the pain and we don't believe the patients are happy. The doctor went into the past happiness because she couldn't stand the present pain. Something like this. Does it make any sense? — because the group attacked the doctor for not dealing with the pain. They said, "We don't believe in this happiness" and went on to attack the doctor. They had no sympathy with the doctor's unhappiness and why she couldn't face the pain.

Doctor Q. She ended her presentation by saying: "I am wondering if I am missing an organic thing", which is how we got on to that.

Dr. Main Yes, but she didn't even look at the present pain. That is what I am trying to say.

Dr. Tunnadine Yet the doctor got angry with the group, who knew what the patients were feeling, but she insisted on denying it.

Dr. Main I don't think the doctor should be attacked for denying it

Dr. Tunnadine Nor do I.

Dr. Main The doctor didn't see it. There must be some reason for that. Was it so awful?

Dr. E. There must be some reason too why we haven't quite understood why the group got so excited, and attacked this particular doctor.

Dr. Main I think they got excited at the denial of the pain.

Dr. E. Is that so exciting for a group, though — that someone has denied pain? I don't quite understand that. I am wondering if there is something about this doctor that they have spotted.

Dr. Tunnadine Frustration that they can see what the doctor is missing, and the doctor won't have it.

Dr. E. Or maybe something has dropped into their laps. They wanted to attack this woman for some reason for a while, and isn't it nice to be able to see exactly what they can attack her for?

Dr. Main   She got attacked for her denial. She got attacked for her flight from the pain. She did it straight away, apparently. She said: 'What was it like before? Let's not look on the black side, but the bright side'. She couldn't stand the pain. No-one had any feeling for her.

Dr. Tunnadine   That's right. Terrible for her. Worse for the leader, I think.

Dr. K.   It's somehow very wrapped up in candlelight and roses, isn't it? Sex is not really mentioned; it was romance.

Dr. Main   It was all very good, it was all very good — let's have no nonsense about trouble. It used to be splendid. Roses.

Doctor Q.   Yes, that's one of the things she said — I remember now — 'Roses!' *(Laughter)*

2. Female Circumcision

Leader Doctor S.

The patient was an African woman who sat down and said, "You will be terribly shocked, doctor. I have been circumcised". The patient had already told the story to another doctor in the practice. It had been done when the patient visited her grandmother as a child without her mother, who did not want her to have it done.

Doctor S.   There was a sort of deathly hush in the group and I noticed myself feeling absolutely shocked about the dilemma of this woman, who was unloading her own anger and shock on this doctor, having done it before to the other doctor in the practice. The group discovered that she was complaining of not enjoying intercourse, and getting pain. They asked if the doctor had examined her, and she said, "No, I didn't; my partner had done that already and I was trying to get away from the horror of it". There was then a general discussion about female circumcision and what it involved. One man in the group felt that the doctor should be trying to get her to accept that this was part of her African culture, but the others were horrified by him and felt that was going back to the Middle Ages.

Dr. I.   Actually, he wasn't saying, "Let's say it's a good thing". He was saying, "How do we help this woman accept it?"

Dr. Tunnadine   And it is possible that he was speaking for another bit of the patient, who did as her grandmother said.

Doctor S.   She was only seven: she couldn't help it, as it were.

Dr. I.   You can't put the clock back for that child — the woman.

Dr. Main   Hang on a second! There are an awful lot of people against female circumcision, and an awful lot of people for it. Which are right?

Dr. I.   I don't think he was saying that, was he?

Dr. Main   No, I'm just saying, let's not take sides; let's stick to the clinical material. The woman came to the doctor and said, "I am ashamed to say this but I have been circumcised".

Doctor S.   " — and you will be shocked, doctor"; and she was.

Dr. Main   Is the patient shocked? Or is the patient simply aware that the doctor would be shocked, that she won't be accepted by this doctor because. . .

Dr. Tunnadine   What she said was that *she* was ashamed.

Dr. Main   The thing about female circumcision in that particular country is that the women want it. It's a sign of maturity to be circumcised and if you are not circumcised you beg for it. 'When am I old enough? I am old enough *now*'. there is an argument for it and that's why it's difficult to overcome; because the women want it — not all women, of course. This girl of seven says, "My mother was away and my grandmother and I got together, and my mother was angry when she got back". But we don't know if this woman is tribally ashamed or tribally proud. We don't know, so we have to keep an open mind about this. . . — Suppose the doctor's attitude to this had been, 'Oh yes, and is the female circumcision the trouble? It doesn't strike me as being the trouble'. If we get hooked on this we are lost.

Doctor S.   I thought the doctor's shock was just her picking up the shock from the patient and that. . .

Dr. Main   No, she was shocked before she ever saw the patient.

Dr. I.   The patient has lived with it since she was seven. She's not going to be suddenly shocked at twenty.

Doctor S.   Well, now that she's married and made love, and all the pain. . .

Dr. Main   Yes, but is it the result of that? I know some women who haven't been circumcised who have pain, too.

Dr. S.   Yes, right.

Dr. Tunnadine   Nevertheless, we come back to the doctor's work; coming to this patient new; set up with the shock. The group did to some extent get over this protective 'How awful for you, dear!' that the doctor was seduced into. They began to talking about working with the patient's rage, but missed out the fact that if she is circumcised she needs to learn to enjoy her vagina even more than other women.

Doctor S.   That's what she talked about to the patient.

Dr. Tunnadine   So that was all right. Your dilemma was as a leader about this picking up sides and the argument in the group.

Dr. Main   Hang on — the group showed all their prejudices. They feel circumcision is terrible. They don't know about the woman.

Doctor S.   There is no doubt that the woman felt damaged and that she is not going to get enough pleasure now, because *they* did it to her.

Dr. Main   That's the doctor's theory, but the woman didn't *say* that. The woman said, "You will be shocked that I am circumcised". Circumcision is a sign of motherhood for a little girl and we don't know that it was so awful for the woman. We do know that they are not having a sexual life. We do know that the doctor did not examine the woman. The doctor landed the whole thing on the circumcision and stopped the seminar thinking. . . — I don't think this woman is bothered about circumcision. I think she is bothered about sex.

Dr. Tunnadine   She may be apologetic and testing out each new doctor about her African-ness and primitiveness, because people do that too, don't they?

Dr. I.   Yes, because the attitude was, "I suppose you will be another doctor who will be shocked".

Dr. Tunnadine   The breaking up of the group suggests to me some sort of battle of the sexes: an aggressive male and female battle.

Dr. Main   The leader at this point might have taken an interest in the group. "What an excited group this is! What an exciting topic!" — Once you get this kind of thing they will go on about morality and excitement and so on and the cruelty involved in circumcision. Some years ago there was a huge debate in the BMJ about male circumcision, about cancer and Jews and Gentiles and all this stuff. The correspondence went on for months, arguments for and against. It was the biggest correspondence the BMJ has had in my lifetime, and eventually it was proposed by one person that, before people put forward their argument, they should declare whether *they* were circumcised or not. It was quite clear that all the people who produced arguments for circumcision had been circumcised and those who argued against it had not been. They thought that theirs was best; and eventually they put an end to all this by printing a memorable letter. It said, "Dear Sir, There is a destiny that shapes our ends, rough-hew them as we will!" *(Laughter)* If you want a good debate you just have to use the topic of circumcision. So there is something very exciting about this and it showed in the group. It affected this doctor and the group might have discussed how it affected the doctor, because the doctor was thrown off course. There was no examination. Wouldn't you have thought that would be one of the first responses? — It was worth asking the group to discuss that.

Doctor S.   They did.

Dr. Main   What did they conclude?

Doctor S.   Well, they said, "We are all having phantasies about how awful it is. If only you had looked you might not have found that it was so bad".

Dr. Main   Or was worse. — We don't know.

Doctor S.   Right. Then somebody said, "Like if you are a doctor dealing with wounds or something, you are supposed to touch them, so the patient doesn't feel she is untouchable. That would be another reason for examining her: so she could stand it".

Dr. Tunnadine   I can't resist saying that it sounds as though they think they have come to your group to learn to be witch doctors!

Mrs. R. It's anxiety about dealing with something which was unknown.

Dr. Main They said, "You should have examined her, because not examining her showed that she was untouchable". But no-one was examining the doctor/patient relation and the doctor's concern.

Dr. Tunnadine — and how the patient set her up.

Dr. Main No-one bothered about the doctor and why the doctor didn't examine her and what was going on — what the patient was doing. The patient seemed to me to want to shock the doctor.

Dr. Tunnadine It was good that they had a go at the doctor not examining. But they didn't notice the patient's part in it. Tell us how you dealt with the breaking-up of the group.

Doctor S. I think I made some comment like, "Everyone is talking among themselves. Let's get back to the task in hand", or some comment like that. I don't think I dealt with the provocative male doctor.

Dr. Main I suspect that his remark was a sensible one. He said something about, "You have got to help this woman get accustomed to it", and then he was attacked because he wasn't shocked enough and he should have been shocked by it instead of finding out about the woman. The excitement that put the doctor off was never even tackled.

3. Incest

Leader Doctor I.

Doctor I. The next case was given by a general practitioner who brings a lot of cases, but she does give a very, very long story; mark you, her stories are usually very exciting and this one was.

The story was of a young woman who had been under psychiatric care because of incest with her father, an uncle and, more recently, her brother as well. She came complaining of a sore vagina and was very upset and worried that her father might find out what she was saying. Her boyfriend was a drug addict. The doctor felt distraught and that she had been put in an impossible situation by the patient: not allowed to tell the psychiatrist and not feeling competent to deal with the problem.

Doctor I.   The group felt excited and very concerned for the doctor, and offered a lot of support and reassurance: "She has come to *you*, so why do you think you are no better than the psychiatrist?" I threw in this bit about, "Are we reassuring the doctor?" and did she feel she was being manipulated? I shouldn't have said that, but nevertheless one of the others jumped in and said, "Wait a minute — what about this patient doing this to all these various people? Whatever sort of a person is she, that not only has she had all this terrible history, but . . ?". There was quite a bit of discussion. Every time I said anything, I got the feeling I was saying, "What are you bothered about? It is not all *that* bad". I didn't actually *say* that, but I felt from their reaction that it was the implication: "You are listening to it. The patient walked out and felt better. It is *you* who feels so ghastly". This was discussed in the group to quite a large extent. Nevertheless, reassurance or no, the doctor obviously didn't feel particularly reassured at the end of it. I didn't know how to do it without making it appear. . . not exactly *derogatory* to the doctor, but belittling her anxieties.

Dr. Tunnadine   There was a little phrase that Michael Balint used quite often about the dog, in Sherlock Holmes, who didn't bark in the night. To me there is a dog not barking very loudly in this report about something that used to be called a 'presenting symptom', I think. . .

Doctor I.   Yes. — We did get back to the sore vagina.

Dr. Tunnadine   You did, did you? Was it clear that the doctor got sucked into all the rest of the stuff?

Doctor I.   We did get back to the sore vagina, but I must admit that the story overtook the sore vagina.

Dr. Tunnadine   As it did with the patient evidently, you see.

Doctor I. Yes. The doctor who said, "What about this patient — what is she doing to everybody?": she said, "She has actually come complaining of a sore vagina".

Dr. Tunnadine It isn't clear whether the doctor knew all about this patient before, being in general practice.

Doctor I. Yes, she did. It was her patient. But she had been referred back from her partner with this complaint.

Dr. Tunnadine Was it in that living consultation that the patient diverted into the past?

Doctor I. Yes. The patient was sent to this doctor because of the sore vagina, and out came all this horrific past which had not been told to anybody before.

Dr. Tunnadine Did the group get round to this?

Doctor I. There was a lot of waffle about how useless psychiatrists are because they hadn't got all this story, the background, which the G.P. felt must be very relevant.

Dr. Main What background?

Doctor I. Three lots of incest and the boyfriend a drug addict. It was all so exciting.

Dr. S. She seduced the doctor into thinking, "You are the marvellous doctor. You are going to help me. All the rest are bad". — Powerful. . .

Dr. Main What do people think?

Doctor I. Yes, one of the others picked up the fact that she was powerful because of what she has done to everybody. There must be something about her to make all these things happen.

Dr. Main How did the discussion go on?

Doctor I. I think there was quite a bit of confusion because they got bogged down with the fact of the psychiatrist not knowing: the doctor being faced with this dilemma of having to keep this secret, and being so unsure of herself that really the sore vagina was lost sight of. It was picked up but not held on to.

Dr. Tunnadine They were talking about whether G.P.s or psychiatrists are better, rather than that this patient had offloaded to the doctor what to her was a shameful, exciting secret.

Doctor I. That came out: the fact of what the patient was doing, telling her all these things. In fact, it was an even longer history of violence with the father. She was so ashamed of what had happened, and the only time he'd shown her any kindness was when he'd had intercourse with her. He had come into her bed one night and fondled her and been kind and warm and loving, when at other times he had been very violent and unpleasant. So there was quite a bit of, "Can she possibly say that this ghastly experience was something she had enjoyed?" — Again, it was getting away from the sore vagina.

Dr. Tunnadine I don't think it is. I think this is what the patient was talking about metaphorically, her sore vagina. She was saying, "I am an awful woman. I am a seducer of relatives. You should be shocked by me. Nobody must know, on pain of death". It sounds as though the discussion was on the right track, but the link between the living doctor/patient relation wasn't really made.

Doctor I. Yes. I tried once or twice to get it back to the sore vagina. I think probably because of the excitement, there was a lot of input — lots of people talking, all tending to go on their own. . .

Dr. Main Did you point that out?

Doctor I. I mentioned the excitement at one point.

Dr. Main In the room? — How everyone was very excited and wanted to talk about it?

Doctor I. Yes. But I felt it waffled badly and I couldn't draw the strings together.

Dr. Main You didn't say, "Isn't this lovely! Isn't this exciting! Isn't it sexy! — Nothing as good as this, is there?"

Doctor I. I think I felt irritated. Why does she have to bring such a —

Dr. Main I am talking about the discussion. The group members were excited?

Doctor I. Yes.

Dr. Main That was worth pointing out: how exciting it is and what a sexy business, isn't it? — Getting it quite clear that the discussion is being impeded by the excitement.

Dr. J. Like the presenting doctor's suffering.

F

Dr. Main   The group was excited by this business of the incest. They were all chatting at once about it and when the group breaks up like that, it is almost always due to some excitement.

Doctor I.   Yes, and I felt I wanted to dampen it down, but it seemed as though whenever I passed a remark, it was belittling her very great anxiety.

Dr. Main   I mean, leave the doctor alone and discuss the *group*. Here is an occasion when it is essential to make remarks about the group's behaviour. It is not often so. You have to stop this general chat and realise they are all excited and bursting with excitement instead of doing some thinking. It is quite important to leave the patient, leave the presenting doctor alone, and discuss the group's behaviour.

Dr. Tunnadine   You wouldn't add: "I wonder where it has come from?"

Dr. Main   No. On a number of occasions I have said, "Isn't this juicy! Isn't it exciting! Incest is better than politics, isn't it?" — I make remarks like this to make it clear that they are all chatting because it's frightfully exciting.

Doctor I.   Yes, I felt it had got out of hand and I had the feeling I ought to dampen it all down.

Dr. Main   That is why I am suggesting that remark. It needs some sort of insight to stop the group. One of the doctors in the discussion went on to say something about the way this patient had upset the doctor. There is nothing like suffering for upsetting people. Was it taken up?

Doctor I.   It tended to be more in the form of reassurance: "Look what she is doing to you: so she has passed her anxiety on to you. Why are you feeling so awful? — She has gone home feeling much better. . ." Again this tended to belittle or undermine this doctor, who was very upset and concerned. One could feel it coming through. She said, "You should have seen how awful she looked". She felt she hadn't said enough to convince us what a terrible situation she was in. It was almost, 'It's not as bad as all that'. 'But it is!'. 'No, no'.

Dr. Main   It was a good example of reassurance in action and the effect of it.

Doctor I.   Yes. I did say, "Here we are — reassuring her!"

Dr. Main No — "The value of reassurance: is it working? . . . 'Now do you feel better, doctor?' And the doctor says, 'No'. — *That's* the value of reassurance!" — It's in action in front of their eyes. They would stop it and start thinking about what the patient is doing with the doctor.

Dr. E. Did you mention — I can't remember whether you did or not — whether there was any examination? If there wasn't, was that looked at?

Dr. Main Can we put that — instead of a question — say, "This doctor notices no mention of . . ."

Dr. E. I am slightly hesitant. . .

Dr. Main You noticed that no mention has been made of a vaginal examination. That is a good observation.

Doctor I. She felt too much had come out for an examination to be done at the time. She had been examined by the partner, who had done nothing and referred her to the presenting doctor; but so much came out that she didn't get that far.

Dr. Main Come on, tell us.

Dr. E. You can't examine a vagina like that, can you?

Dr. Main Why not?

Dr. E. It's full of stuff that you don't really want to look at. It is wild and exciting and full of all sorts of things.

Dr. Main Of course the patient is dead keen to be examined. All she is doing is talking about rape and stuff like that.

Doctor I. The group didn't pick this up, either.

Dr. Tunnadine I was talking about this really, when I was talking about the dog barking in the night. I was meaning that saying 'dogs that don't bark in the night' is a good leadership trick, if you notice it. It would be a way to open up this area. The vagina and the vaginal examination were missing and, as you said, it is not surprising with a patient like this who says: "I want you to tell me how polluted it is — don't you dare look at me!"

Dr. E. Except — 'That's what I've brought in the door'.

Dr. Tunnadine Precisely.

Dr. Main I think what I would have used is the Sore Finger technique.

Dr. Tunnadine What do you mean?

Dr. Main   My mother wanted to send me to bed. I wasn't ready, it was too early — and anyhow I've got a sore finger! Examine the vagina? — No, I've got a sore finger. Here is the doctor weeping, more or less.

Doctor I.   Yes, and I felt very conscious of not reassuring her when it appeared that was what she was asking for.

Dr. Tunnadine   I noticed this offloading phenomenon, which was quite good, it seemed to me. They picked up something about that, didn't they? It's just that it didn't help the doctor very much. They got on to the fact that this doctor had been a sucker for this patient quite well, I thought.

Doctor I.   Yes, they were on to her manipulating.

Dr. Tunnadine   But not how the doctor might have spotted it and used it; but rather that she should be comforted for it, rather as the patient had got herself comforted.

Doctor I.   Yes. She didn't want to carry on with this. It was almost as if she was asking the group, 'I don't have to carry on with this, do I? What can I do with it?'

Dr. E.   It is this awful bit about, 'Aren't patients difficult?' You point out what the patient has done and how awful it makes you feel, and you say, 'What a rotten patient that was!'

Doctor I.   I think she does tend to carry the patient's anxieties.

Dr. Main   She loves to hear about this woman's complaints. . . — "That's all right. How many times? Right! — Now about your vagina: let's get on the couch". — The girl was putting her off that moment.

Doctor I.   I don't think that was picked up.

Dr. Tunnadine   Or it may be, "No wonder you don't feel very good about that part of yourself". She is a beginner doctor. You felt you were not dealing with the reassurance bit very well. Is it that you draw attention to what this group is doing without any follow-up so that they are stimulated to think? Is that what you are saying?

Doctor I.   Yes. I am trying not to teach and I have this awful feeling that if I then say *why* I have made the observation, I am back into the teaching.

Dr. Tunnadine   I think this "I wonder why. . ?" is quite a good brief phrase to tack on to the end of these things, don't you?

Dr. Main I would do it slightly differently: saying to the reassuring doctor, "Let's see if it's working, Dr. X. — Are you feeling better?" She is bound to say, "No" and then you can say, "Well, *that's* the value of reassurance — it doesn't work!" Isn't it interesting that the patient's complaint has never been attended to? This stuff has got in the way. It sounds like a huge defence by the patient.

Doctor I. In fact, I am doing what she is doing, because I thought about this doctor all the week, thinking, 'What else could I have done?' and I am sure this is probably what she has been doing, too. It is unusual for me. I felt very concerned for her. All I tended to do was to undermine her all the time.

Dr. Tunnadine What do you think you'd done? — I don't buy that.

Doctor I. I was belittling her anxiety and she *was* anxious.

Dr. Main I wonder what about. This patient had been to see a psychiatrist. . . Had intercourse with her father. . .

Doctor I. Her father, and also she had a close relationship with her brother.

Dr. Main In other words, another incestuous relationship.

Doctor I. She has now cut off relationships with her brother, who was her only close friend, from what I can see. She went to live with an aunt, and promptly had intercourse with her uncle.

Dr. Main Poor little soul! *(Laughter).*

Doctor I. And so it went on.

Dr. Main She broke it up with her aunt there. — That wasn't nice of her.

Dr. Tunnadine I think she must have been tired that day!

Dr. Main If *she's* broken up, it's quite clear who started it.

Doctor I. Yes, but you see I was doing that — what you are doing now. "Poor soul, she's unloaded all this on to you"; which gave the impression of "What is the doctor whingeing on about? It's not that bad. You can go home. You don't have to worry about it all week, until she comes again". One of her worries was that the patient might become dependent. The patient phoned the following day to confirm the appointment.

Dr. Tunnadine If I was the doctor, I would be more worried about my husband! — That's the missing side.

Dr. Main   One of the things that is worrying the doctor is that the patient swore her to secrecy.

Dr. Tunnadine   That's right. It's ridiculous — there's no way you can agree not to tell the psychiatrist.

Dr. Main   I think the father probably said, "Don't tell your mother".

Dr. Tunnadine   She has got the doctor believing that this is really a terrible secret she has got, instead of an interesting one.

Dr. J.   But the leader is worried that she denied the doctor's anxieties in the same way you would be worried if you denied a patient's anxieties. That is what worries you at the moment.

Doctor I.   I suppose in a sense, it is like reassuring, isn't it? The patient has unloaded to you. How do you think the patient went out?

Dr. Tunnadine   It is possible it went down the line. The doctor found herself saying, in the face of all this, "It's all right. It's not so terrible"; and she brought it to you and you found yourself somehow having to do this "It's not so terrible". And the patient was really wanting her to say, "Please respect how terrible it is for me and help me get better".

C. GENERALISATIONS

The tendency for a doctor, the group or even the leader to generalise as a defence is so common that it warrants this separate chapter, although examples have occurred in previous digests.

The first two extracts are very short, but the third one is a long record of the leaders trying to make sense of a presentation which was full of speculation by the doctor and the group, but short on facts about the precise doctor/patient relationship.

1. SEX AND THE ELDERLY.

2. HOW DO YOU END CONSULTATIONS?

3. PATIENT'S NEEDS GOT LOST

1. Sex and the elderly

Leader Doctor J.

In an early group a doctor talked about an older patient who was having difficulty with sex. After she had finished presenting the case, there was an awkward silence.

Doctor J.   The silence was broken by one of the doctors saying that she thought this case was extremely difficult, because it involved an older person; and when older people talk about their sexuality it reminds all of us doctors of our parents' sexuality and therefore it is difficult to talk about. She went on a little bit about this, so I said, "You are talking about two things: one is a personal one, and one is sexuality in older people. Could we talk about what we felt about sexuality in older people?" There was a bit of discussion, but it quickly petered out and the group went on to the next case.

Dr. N.   I thought the group got down to case-solving, getting stuck solving the case, instead of looking at what was going on under their noses.

Dr. Tunnadine   Even that took a while, didn't it, because there was this kind of crazy thing — 'What can we do? I know, let's discuss our views on sex in the elderly', or something like that. The leader reported it very honestly. You must have felt frantic at that point. I am not quite sure why.

Dr. Main   I would agree that the leader led the group into a general defence away from the case: the defence of generalisations — 'Let's not talk about *this* business; let's talk about *general* problems of dealing with the elderly'; taking the action nicely away from the case: no more case study. The question is: why did the leader do it?

Doctor J.   Well, I'll tell you why: because this doctor had on the first occasion talked about her anxiety with something — I can't remember what it was — but this second time she said, "If I ever meet a patient of 60 who is talking about his sexual problems, I am so concerned about it because it could be my parents, and of course I don't feel very comfortable. None of us feel very comfortable about talking about our parents' sex lives." And I didn't want her to talk about her problems with her parents' sexuality. That's the second time she has brought her own problems.

Dr. Main Can we put it another way? — She brought her own problems about that, and then you led it away from that into discussion on general problems of sex with the elderly: this kind of empty stuff. You said why you did so — out of anxiety about this doctor — but the doctor herself was making a generalisation. She wasn't discussing the case at all. She talked about, 'The problems are such and such with older patients'. She was making an observation that perhaps the doctor, in this particular case, was put off by the fact that this man was so old. But there was no time to examine that, whether it was true or not: the doctor didn't give any response to it; nor did the group take it up. This doctor was saying that was how she would feel *always*, but the question was: did this doctor feel that in this particular instance? What was going on between this doctor and this patient? There was that chance of going further and examining the doctor/patient relation, but you fled from it into generalisations. I think you fled from it because *you* are afraid, as was the doctor, of discussing the general embarrassment of an early group in facing sexual problems.

2. How do you end consultations?

Leader Doctor P.

Towards the end of a seminar, one of the doctors suddenly said, "I want to know how you finish these interviews. If you are not going to give them a prescription, and if you are not going to give them advice, what do you do? I like to end my interviews on an optimistic note".

Doctor P. I felt she was sort of talking about the group, bless her heart; that she was a bit cross, or wasn't getting the goods, or something.

Dr. Main ". . . How do you finish these interviews with patients? — Just write it down for me, will you, please?" . . . It's the same thing. She wants a prescription about that, and I suppose a reasonable technique would be, "What patient are you talking about?" — have an instance of it, rather than let the generalisation defence go on.

Doctor P. I am a bit concerned about that particular doctor. I suppose it was that she was asking for the goods, and I was saying, "Those goods aren't on offer". But I didn't feel I did it quite as well as that. She is going abroad for three months now.

Dr. Q. Your worry is that she will not come back as a result?

Doctor P. Yes. After that she then did two little follow-ups. Perhaps I should just tell you those, if we are talking about this.

Dr. Main Hang on — are there any views about how you dealt with that point?

Dr. J. You said something rather odd, I thought: "This doctor, bless her. . ." — do you usually talk about members of your group in that rather patronising way?

Doctor P. It is a bit patronising, I suppose.

Dr. Main Yes, she usually does — or she usually doesn't. The point is, she *did* in this case. So what do you think?

Dr. Y. She's treating her like she treats her patients.

Dr. Main We don't know.

Dr. Y. She gave her a bit of care and concern.

Dr. Main I don't know. — Contempt? Care and concern?

Dr. J. She was very junior. She has just come up to your form, and you were rather careful of her.

Doctor P. Yes, I do think rather like that. She's only presented two cases. I think I feel that she's junior in the work compared to some of the other people who seem to be doing pretty well.

Dr. F. She's also expressing her terrible anxiety about ending a consultation without giving someone a boost or something positive and going away feeling good. That is very primitive, to need any sort of consultation to end that way. It is worrying.

Dr. Tunnadine What interests me is that the leader hears it in this way. The doctor says she wants to be given something, and

Dr. P. feels she ought to give her something, and is worried about it. It doesn't have to be this way at all. She may be saying, "I want more". That's not a complaint; that's enthusiasm.

Dr. Main She's also saying, "I always like to end my consultations on an optimistic note and I don't know how to stop'. 'I don't know how to stop' means that she's already aware of a kind of funny, routine, unthinking bit of behaviour that she needs to review. She offers a general point: "I like to give *all* my patients. . ." — she can't discuss an individual patient. I think I would have been inclined to say, "I don't believe you unless you produce a case".

Doctor P. I think what I did was say "Let's see as each case comes up". I tried to do that, but I think she would have felt more cher— . . . here we go again: I was going to say 'cherished', but I somehow feel, if I could have said to her, "Let's look at it with *your* cases", then she would have felt encouraged.

Dr. Main That's what happened, because doctors do this, and there are various reasons why they do.

Dr. F. But it is her need to cherish the patient which she is bringing to you, and her concept of cherishing . . .

Dr. Main Look into her cases and you'll find she's not cherishing.

Dr. Y. But Dr. P. linked it in with something to do with her being the person who wouldn't let another patient be angry.

Dr. F. Yes, that's what I mean by cherishing. She can't be angry with people, or let people be angry with her. She has to appease, particularly at the end.

Dr. Main "Have a food parcel — I'm really very nice!" *(Laughter)*.

Dr. Tunnadine I don't feel bothered that this young doctor, at this stage of her career, still thinks her job as a doctor is to give people things. That is something you will train out of her. What I am bothered about is that Dr. P. is left feeling *she* should have given her something. That's the crazy thing. You don't like her being hungry? I would have thought it was good.

Dr. Y. Isn't the leader just picking up her feelings?

Dr. Tunnadine Yes, that is why she has brought it here. She feels she reacted intuitively, or motherly, or something, and is dissatisfied with herself.

Dr. Main   That group didn't give that doctor everything she wants, did it? How terrible! It isn't the group who should adapt; it's the doctor's trouble which should be looked at.

Dr. Q.   Would it have been in order to have explored her feelings on it, put it back to her why she felt the need to ask how to end?

Dr. Main   No. With one specified case, yes. It's no use discussing generalised problems like that: "Don't know what you mean. Let's have a case. . ." Never, never, never discuss general issues — "my usual practice is. . ." — all this stuff is meaningless.

Dr. Q.   I meant, it might bring her anxiety out.

Dr. Main   No. On a case it will come out. That's the only way to see it.

Dr. Tunnadine   And yet this group here is, on the whole, concerned about individual doctors and their anxieties. We don't seem to be able to help it, and we have to learn not to. It's not what we are there for as trainers. We shouldn't be concerned with the development of individual doctors at a personal level. This doctor landed you briefly with her own personal anxieties and I think it is good you did resist it. You may not have resisted very skilfully by saying, "I always do this", but you resisted the temptation to say, "Is your heart aching because you are leaving your mother?", or something like that.

Dr. Main   Generalisation is always a defence, and very often a defence against active incidents. Can I give you an example? — I will make one up. I had a row with my wife this morning and I come here this afternoon and say, "What do you think about a row between husbands and wives?" Something stimulated this remark, and something stimulated this doctor to ask *that* question at *that* seminar. It's not, "Reviewing my total general experience I notice that. . ." It's not that. Something happened to her that day, that morning.

Dr. Q.   So the thing to do would be to just ask her to talk about it?

Dr. Main   — "Give us an example. . ." It is never, I repeat *never*, worthwhile discussing general points.

3. Patient's sexual needs got lost

Leader Doctor G.

A patient went to her general practitioner because she had become pregnant with an I.U.D. The doctor arranged a private termination, and subsequently re-fitted her with a coil. The anxieties that the doctor brought to the group were that she felt she could never get cross with this woman, and always ended up doing what the patient wanted. The doctor had worries about the way the woman was bringing up her two children, who were always brought to the surgery and seemed uncontrollable, and also there were inconsistencies in the patient's story. Her husband, who was in the army, was presented as an ogre who demanded sex unreasonably whenever he was at home. The patient often went home to Ireland, seemed to have lots of money and was now divorcing her husband.

Doctor G.   When she had finished telling her story, one of the doctors said, "You may do what she wants, but I don't get the impression that you like her much". So they got into quite a good discussion on the doctor/patient relation. I don't think I did much work. I just made one or two noises occasionally, but I felt that the group was working on this very well. The doctor's feeling of impotence with this woman really came over: the way the woman manipulated her all the time and wouldn't allow her ever to look at any kind of reasons why she wanted the termination, what her relationship was, what her feelings were. One of the doctors made the suggestion, "You've talked about the husband being away, yet she always needs contraception, she always has money — do you think she's on the game?" The doctor said yes, she really felt she was and that these children were at risk and she didn't know what to do. They really got down to how the doctor was being rather forebearing and kind and thinking she'd better give her what she wanted; and also her anger at the woman which she just couldn't express. I think they seemed to work quite well at that. As I say, I'm not really conscious of my doing much at all in the way of interventions.

Dr. Main   You did a lot just by sitting and keeping your mouth shut.

Doctor G. It's very difficult for me.

Dr. Main It's a positive thing. . . Well, thank you very much. Let's hear what people think.

Dr. P. It seems that somehow this group has got to the stage where the doctor can tell a bit about the doctoring which is going on; and there's a true ring about it, about the doctor's difficulties with the patient, which the doctor was able to show the group. The antagonism of the doctor, which she wasn't able to express, was picked up by the group. In other words, the doctor was a bit vulnerable. I am impressed by that because it seems it can't happen in my group. Something about the doctor sitting there not doing much, the leader sitting there not doing much, allowed the reporting doctor to expose herself and be discussed without being destroyed.

Dr. Main The doctor didn't do very much. She said she did what the patient required and the group discussed this, but she didn't do very much for the patient, I thought, and the group *didn't* discuss that.

Doctor G. The group came out with a few ideas about how she might be able to break down the patient's wall, and her determination only to talk about the contraceptive problem. It was a question of whether it would be possible to discuss with her what her feelings were about more children, as she seemed quite determined not to have any more. Could the doctor have got to the patient's feelings that way?

Dr. Main But that's speculation about what the doctor *might* do, not examination of what the doctor *did* do. Did anyone get a clear idea of what the doctor did?

Doctor G. The doctor did what the patient wanted.

Dr. Main I know, but what was it?

Mrs. R. Put the I.U.D. back.

Dr. Main I know, but the human transaction wasn't described. The doctor began very well, didn't she?

Doctor G. I haven't reported it very well. She brought in a whole lot of things like how this woman will bring these children who are very disturbing and wreck the place.

Dr. Main But those are general remarks.

Dr. N. It seems that the doctor couldn't discuss what was really worrying her most of all. She couldn't discuss with the patient her fears about the children.

Doctor G.   No she couldn't, because she had the children there.

Dr. Tunnadine   I thought that was the interesting thing. The *non sequitur* in this story which woke me up a bit amongst all this stuff about doctor's feelings, was, the doctor was angry with this woman because she thinks she's on the game. . .

Doctor G.   No, she's angry with the woman because of her treatment of the children.

Dr. Tunnadine   That's right. In other words, the woman's sexual needs are totally missing as far as I can see: not considered by anybody.

Dr. S.   I don't think she came with a complaint, actually. She came to manipulate this doctor.

Dr. Tunnadine   Well, she didn't, actually. She came saying, "I've had sex and got into trouble again", but somehow, like so many people who put children and attitudes to children in front of everything, her sexual needs got lost.

Dr. Main   The doctor contended this, though, and was against the sexuality, and actually attacked it. The woman asked for an I.U.D. and the doctor said, "Aren't you getting divorced — what do you want an I.U.D. for?"

Dr. Tunnadine   That's right — of all times she should most need an I.U.D! That was what was missing, to my mind: the doctor's anger was seen, but not the doctor's anti-sexuality or the way the patient evoked this in her.

Dr. Main   The group didn't pick that up.

Doctor G.   Yes they did. They asked if it was her own feeling of dislike, that this woman might be on the game and so on; but she said No, it was her fear particularly for the little girl and what she might be exposed to.

Dr. Tunnadine   It seems to me that the emphasis is on the doctor's difficulties, or the patient's difficulties, rather than what is going on between them.

Dr. Main   I don't think this doctor dislikes this patient because of the children, or because she's on the game, but because of something which went on in the room.

Doctor G.   She says it's this patient's manipulation of her.

Dr. Main   For example? . . . — the example is not here.

Doctor G.   Well — "Can you tell me why you want an abortion? How do you feel about it?" The doctor was concerned, because she was Irish and she thought she would feel guilty about it.

Dr. Main   We all know the Irish — they're all the same! *(ironically)*

Doctor G.   The group said, "This is your anxiety, isn't it? You don't know anything about what the patient feels". She said, "Yes, that's the problem. I don't know what this patient feels. I just can't get at it".

Dr. Main   Not with that technique. But the group didn't take this up. The generalisations were all that were presented: the safe stuff. Not what was going on in the room between the patient and the doctor, but the safe stuff: like, "She's Irish — you know, that place across the water. Another thing is, she's got children. She's got money". Not a word about what is going on in the room. "She's very difficult" — that sort of general remark. How did the group acquire details?

Dr. Tunnadine   In a general practice, where they do know so much about their patients, it is more difficult to focus on the one encounter.

Dr. Main   Yes, this is typical medical reporting and one can't expect a mature form of reporting, such as one gets at the end of a year of our kind of training. I think we should at least be alert to the generalising nature of the report.

Dr. Tunnadine   If Dr. N. had been there, he would have said: "Look, I'm interested in what was going on in the room', or something like that. That would be his style of saying, "I've had enough of all this".

Dr. Main   I'm not too sure about that tone of voice, but I think he would say something like that!

Doctor G.   Yes, in the discussion they were pinpointing what she had reported on the two occasions when she had seen her recently, and why she felt as she did.

Dr. Main   But what is going on? I don't know. Have you any idea?

Dr. P.   I think there was a lot of dishonesty going on, because the doctor was sitting there thinking, 'I think you're on the game', without actually being able to say it; while the patient was thinking, 'I'm damned if I'm going to let the doctor know anything about my sex life! I just want an I.U.D.'

Doctor G. What she was really presenting was her difficulty in doing work with this patient.

Dr. Main And the patient's difficulty in doing work with this doctor.

Dr. N. It sounded to me as though you had an intimidated doctor here, who was being manipulated and controlled by the patient, who was having to do what the patient said, and who knew all the time there were other things going on, but she didn't dare to raise them. She didn't dare raise her thoughts about the woman being on the game and the problems with the kids. They were too threatening. This woman might have come down very heavily on this doctor if she suggested these sort of things.

Dr. Main With that doctor, yes. This doctor didn't say, "Oh, you're making a lot of money these days". This doctor wasn't an earthy doctor. This is a different style of coping with it. Moralistic. . .

Dr. Tunnadine The point is that we don't know whether it's the patient's unease about the sexuality, or the doctor's unease, that makes it all into 'protecting the children' stuff. The fact is, *that* question is the one which was somehow missed in the discussion. That is the one clinical question we don't know the answer to yet. From the leader's point of view, she was so pleased to have this lively discussion about anything that she really wanted to sit back. There was something about the case, I think, which you too couldn't get impatient with, wasn't there?

Doctor G. Yes. Obviously I could see the flaws in it and so on, but the group were doing quite a lot of work on it.

Dr. A. There was something which wasn't mentioned. I thought the original complaint was that the husband came home and made her have sex hundreds of times.

Doctor G. That was in the past. She's leaving him now.

Dr. A. I wondered why that wasn't brought up in the discussion.

Dr. Main She wasn't going to examine her, because she'd got a lot of money. . . 'Can't have that — she was on the game'. — I don't know what the evidence is for her being on the game.

Dr. Tunnadine   As far as I can see, she only has sex once every few months and gets pregnant every time.

Doctor G.   No, I'm sorry — I've given you a completely different story. O.K., she was married ten years ago. The doctor has never seen the husband.

Dr. Tunnadine   And nor has the woman, and I think this is what she's complaining about!

Doctor G.   She's left him. She doesn't want to see him again. She's got another relationship, though she's not going to get married to him. But she must have contraception.

Dr. Tunnadine   But all I'm saying is, she's in difficulty with the sexuality. But it was not the way the doctor saw it: the doctor thought her sexuality was wicked and must be stopped.

Dr. Main   Anyhow, she has money. . .

Doctor G.   No, I'm sorry — it didn't seem to come over like this at all.

Dr. Main   The fact that there are *no* facts is the interesting thing.

Dr. H.   The doctor was more anxious about the children than the woman's sexuality.

Doctor G.   The doctor's anxiety was that she could not work with this woman's problem because of the block.

Dr. Main   Whose block — the doctor's?

Doctor G.   The patient's.

Dr. N.   I don't know. I think the doctor had a complete block. There was something moralistic about this doctor, I felt: 'Girls on the game deserve what they get'.

Doctor G.   No, I don't think it was that. O.K., she came over saying something like. . . — I didn't feel she was moralistic. I feel she accepted that she was probably on the game. She was anxious about how she couldn't doctor with this patient; she couldn't be a professional doctor.

Dr. Tunnadine   It seems to me that the discussion was more to do with the doctor's feelings, or the doctor's difficulties, rather than the precise detail of how this patient at that moment evoked them. This was about the doctor's difficulty, because the doctor didn't bring up the doctor/patient relation. The doctor's *feelings* are not the doctor/patient relation: the doctor/patient relation is some little thing which is just happening at the moment, isn't it?

Dr. H. Didn't the patient come feeling rather guilty and defensive? I thought that was why the doctor felt so paralysed by the front with which the patient was presenting.

Dr. Tunnadine The question is: how on that occasion did the patient put the doctor in that spot? Or was the doctor blind in that spot? We don't know.

Dr. Main We are in danger ourselves of speculation. The doctor discussed general points which weren't germane to the interview. I don't care whether this woman is on the game or not. Did it come up in the interview? No: it's just part of the doctor's thinking. But there wasn't any detail of what the patient said, or how the doctor responded, that will lead us to understand the difficulties.

Dr. Tunnadine I suppose if one were really looking for 'A' levels: because the *patient* put up a block to discussing her feelings with the doctor, the doctor had to speculate, and the group did the same.

Doctor G. I think the doctor was saying that this was a patient she had seen over ten years, and still can't get to know her. There was an interesting little bit which came up: after the abortion, the doctor came face to face with this woman in the supermarket. The woman turned away and went down another aisle. She thought that was a bit odd. She noticed she was with a man, but didn't take in who it was. The woman turned up in the surgery that evening to see her, wanting an I.U.D. fitted. The doctor had said how she'd really been quite hurt at being cut or not acknowledged, and when the woman had come in the evening, the doctor couldn't say to her, "Oh, didn't I see you in the shop?"

Dr. Tunnadine This reinforces my feeling that the doctor has you defending her in her view that she has got an awkward patient. We all defend the patient here; you defend the doctor, and it's that phenomenon, it seems to me, which is missing in the group discussion. You haven't got the patient to treat; you've only got the doctor to help — unblock, if you like — and that seems to be missing.

Dr. Main We go on and on with this, because this is general gossip about the patient. What the hell went on in that clinical

room? What was the clinical event? There was general chat about
'She must be on the game — has got money — Ireland' — all
irrelevant. This is something that doctors do in an early group —
'I've had a patient for over 24 years; funny family, you know,
always bad with their chest' — general stuff. It's irrelevant to the
study of the clinical event, but it's how doctors discuss cases;
because it's too naked to discuss oneself in action. It's dangerous
to underestimate the difficulties doctors have in presenting these
things, but they never will, unless they are pushed. I would be
worried about this group getting into the habit of presenting
generalised gossip about people. The fact that the doctor saw the
patient in the supermarket is all juicy — but so what!

Doctor G.   I thought it showed the doctor's difficulty in facing
the woman.

Dr. Main   That sort of thing doesn't describe the precise minute
in the consulting room when a difficulty arose.

Dr. Tunnadine   The doctor, it seems to me, was saying to the
group: "Look how hard I've tried over the years"; and so the
group sympathises with this. But what the doctor was actually
saying was, "Look, I'm blind, and I'm still blind after ten years. I
don't know how to deal with a woman who blocks me like this".
After all, that's what she was there for: to learn to do better. Was
she helped, do you think? She was reinforced in her view that
she'd got an awkward patient. But that's not the same thing.

Dr. Main   The doctor's technique wasn't looked at. How fast do
you go with an early group? It might have been useful to have
pointed out about the generalisation.

Dr. P.   The other thing about this patient is that it has been going
on for ten years, and we're not really entirely sure which, of many
consultations, we're actually discussing.

Doctor G.   The consultations which were discussed were the last
two or three about this termination and the demand to have an
I.U.D.

Dr. P.   But it was well over three weeks ago, so it might perhaps
have been helpful to say, "Next time you meet her, tell us exactly
what happens", or something like this; to help them to focus their
ideas and help the doctor to focus.

Dr. Main   Maybe we should pinpoint our aims a bit more instead of talking about studies of the doctor/patient relation. Perhaps we should say 'studies about the doctor/patient relation in specifically clinical events'.

Dr. P.   It's a terrible phrase that, isn't it? It's becoming a sort of bogey, this doctor/patient relationship. We say it when we can't think of anything else to say.

Dr. Main   I *can't* think of anything else to say!

Dr. P.   I know. It resounds in my head until I don't know what it means, almost.

Dr. Main   It's very difficult to know what it means. The doctor/patient relation here was one of — what? Mutual distrust? Uneasiness? Struggle. . ?

Dr. P.   Annoyance — because the other one won't actually listen to what they're trying to say.

Dr. Main   Which one are you talking about — both?

Dr. P.   Yes.

Dr. Main   Strained, insincere. . . limited communication on both sides.

Dr. P.   I think of what Dr. N. said about this frightened doctor: she is terrified she is going to have a battered child, and that is a very frightening thing when you're in practice.

Dr. Main   Well, that's fine. But what is she going to do clinically with the woman?

Dr. Tunnadine   We hear a lot in this story about how blocking the patient is and what is forgotten is that she keeps coming back and back, looking for something presumably that she hasn't found yet.

Dr. Main   I would still like to know what happened the last time she came.

Dr. L.   When you say, "comes back and back" — this is to a G.P., isn't it? It needn't necessarily be -

Doctor G.   Yes, she's seen her over many years.

Dr. L.   I feel it's this doctor who is more concerned about this patient than the patient about her own sexuality.

Dr. Main   Very good point. We've fallen into the trap — the doctor's trap. The doctor wanted to make this a psychosexual case. Is there any evidence that the patient wanted help?

Doctor G.   No. This is what the doctor was presenting. The patient had come saying, "I want so and so, and if you won't give it to me I can get it somewhere else".

Dr. S.   It wasn't a request for help really, was it?

Doctor G.   I think the doctor felt there was a whole lot here that she should be working with, and the patient wasn't giving her any opportunity.

Dr. Main   She wasn't the patient really for this kind of doctor. She didn't want a doctor with psychosexual interests.

Mrs. R.   Or did she want to produce a case for the group?

Doctor G.   I think she wanted to show a case which she was in difficulties with. I don't think she was trying to make a case.

Dr. Main   It was a bit like that, wasn't it? The atmosphere was a bit, "I think you've got a psychosexual problem. I've decided that, so come on — talk about it!" "I haven't got a problem". "Yes, you have". — That sort of struggle. The doctor had to present a case, or something or other. Does she feel obliged to do this sort of thing?

Dr. L.   Isn't that again speculation? — because we don't know whether the doctor thought she'd got a psychosexual problem.

Dr. Main   That's true. But the doctor was complaining that the patient was not complaining.

Dr. S.   Did the group pick that up? I think we've taken a long time to come to it.

Dr. Main   Well, we'd better stop because of time. Thank you very much.

SECTION THREE

THE LEADER AND GROUP

IN

PSYCHOSEXUAL TRAINING

A. BEGINNINGS

The way a group is started can affect its atmosphere and eventually its success or failure. The idea of starting a seminar in a particular area often comes from one or two keen doctors. Others may be recruited by means of a circular letter or 'trawl', and those who are interested may be interviewed by the leader or leaders.

The question sometimes arises as to whether there should be one leader or two. It is then necessary to ask: is this a technical choice? a political decision? or are there elements of personal rivalry?

The selection of those who would be suitable for training is a complicated task. The digests consider some special problems in this area: the leader's 'favourite'; the rôle of a personal interview; the importance of group members being actively engaged in relevant clinical work; and the situation of the keen leader with a group which is so small that it is only marginally viable.

1. STARTING A GROUP (i) & (ii).

2. ONE LEADER OR TWO (i), (ii), (iii) & (iv)

3. SELECTION FOR TRAINING — (i) BEWARE TEACHER'S PET.
       (ii) THE INTERVIEW.
       (iii) IS THE DOCTOR WORKING IN THE FIELD?   a. the eye doctor
             b. the genetic counselling doctor

4. SELECTION AND THE SMALL GROUP

1. Starting a group (i)

Leader Doctors E. & J.

Doctor E.   This is not about a group, but only about setting up a group. Is that valid?

Dr. Main   Yes, of course.

Doctor J.   This is a group that may be coming into being in S———shire. Dr. X, who did two terms in another group some time ago, is very keen to start a group in this area, and she has canvassed some general practitioners and found a certain amount of enthusiasm.

Dr. Main   You've got an organiser there.

Doctor J.   Yes. She has talked to the Director of Training about it.

Dr. Main   So she is looking for a group and a leader?

Doctor J.   Yes. We have agreed a letter that we have sent to every family planning doctor, and via the Family Practitioner Committe to general practitioners in the area.

Dr. Main   Can you tell us about the letter? Roughly what does it say?

Doctor J.   It says that a training seminar will take place fortnightly, it gives the place and time and says that it is designed to train doctors interested in work with psychosexual problems. It also says that doctors who apply must be seeing patients with these problems.

Dr. Main   Does it say anything about what happens in seminars? I am wondering if you give them any idea of what goes on.

Doctor J.   I think it said something like: 'The training is based on discussion of case material'.

Dr. Main   So how many doctors will it go out to?

Doctor J.   I expect two or three hundred.

Dr. Main   There are some figures that are known about this and it is similar at the Tavistock Clinic and the Cassel Hospital. Out of 100 letters you get 30 replies, and of these about 12 will start, and at the end of the first year you will have about five or six per cent. You will get a group from it. Can I just ask: you said fortnightly

— why? Why not twice a week?

Doctor E.   Because we can't afford more time than fortnightly.

Dr. Main   You'll get paid for it.

Doctor E.   It's not that.

Dr. Main   Proper seminars are once a week. Once a fortnight is half training. I am not joking. This business of once a fortnight is serious: the gap between cases means that people can't report their cases more than once a term.

Dr. Q.   How is it we all do it once a fortnight, then?

Dr. Main   That's what I want to know. This has grown into an unthinking practice. It grew out of a fear that leaders wouldn't be popular if they asked for once a week. My feeling is that instead of encouraging people to join a seminar, *discourage* them from joining. Keep them all out if you can, and those who won't be kept out will be the ones worth training. It is better to find this out at the beginning, because you are wasting your time and sabotaging the work if you are anxious to keep people.

Doctor E.   We are doing our best to discourage them at the moment.

Dr. Main   Just get people who are mad keen, that's all. You need people who are crazy about the work, like you.

Doctor E.   We have been rather anxious that we may have three leaders, because Dr. X has been so very helpful with the organization.

Dr. F.   Are you frightened that she is going to become the third leader?

Doctor E.   Yes. It did seem necessary to clear the air about this and say, 'Look, there is a boundary here and you can't do both. . .', but it was difficult because she will have had more experience than the others.

Doctor J.   We did point out that this would only be a basic seminar.

Dr. Main   I know her. I wouldn't worry about her. I don't think she wants to be a leader at all. She wants to come and bring cases. I wouldn't worry about her at all. She is crazy keen.

Dr. Q.   It's nice to have one member who knows a bit about what it is like, anyway.

Dr. Main No, she's too far ahead of the others. I absolutely disagree with you. Horrible to have one person who will drag the others along faster than they can go. I once threw two people out of a seminar because they were too advanced for the rest. They were doing super work and making the rest feel uncomfortable; shaming them a bit, being a bit too clever. They are now the Director of Training and Chairman of the Panel in this Institute.

Dr. Q. So you are saying that this doctor who set this group up shouldn't really be in it?

Dr. Main Well, she is keen; but she will have to be watched, because she may shame the others who are beginners. I like the way this is being set up. You are being asked for as leaders: that is the right way round. The trouble is, there is only one person doing the asking. If there were twelve asking, you would be sure you would get off the ground easily.

Dr. K. I know someone in B——— who might be interested.

Doctor J. That's about 70 miles, isn't it? — Too far.

Dr. Main What's wrong with 70 miles? People have come from Scotland and Wales to London every *week*. Don't exclude on the ground of distance at all. Can we take this question of once a week seriously?

Doctor E. It might be possible.

Dr. Main If you have a decent group of eight to ten people meeting six times a term only, how many times are you going to be able to follow a single case through? Logistically it is much better to have them once a week; people are fresh and remember much better.

Dr. Z. What about the financial side?

Dr. Main Finance is all right. Work it out. It is very little per member if you have a healthy group. Once a fortnight you don't get such a healthy group. People get a bit bored with the long wait; it's a minor interest in their lives, minor not only in terms of time but in terms of enthusiasm. You capture them and get them going. Suppose someone was dead keen: if you offer them once a fortnight, it's not much.

Dr. Z. What about the length of time — would you still go on for the two years?

Dr. Main Yes. It's much easier for everybody. Easier for the leader, too.

Dr. Q. And not so terrible if you don't come to one: from the group's point of view, you haven't missed so much.

Dr. Main They don't miss it if it's once a week. Once a fortnight they do.

Dr. Z. They'll be twice as good.

Dr. Main Yes, they will be. A change will occur after about 18 months in the thinking of all people if it's a reasonable training, whether it's once a week or once a fortnight. But the depth that they go in the change is greater if it's once a week.

Starting a group (ii)

Leader Doctors B. & K.

Doctor B. This is a new group which is a mixture of doctors and nurses. We also put out a trawl and had ten replies. We didn't interview anybody because I think they were all known to Dr. K. Two of the nurses had been in Dr. K's group before, and I think she felt they would be suitable in a group of doctors: they were sort of promoted.

Dr. Tunnadine Or demoted if they had done two years already *(Laughter).*

Doctor B. The other doctors are all new to the group.

Dr. Main But they are known personally?

Doctor B. Yes, at least to Dr. K.; and I know who they are.

Dr. Main You took Dr. K's word for it.

Doctor B. Yes, I think she was so grateful that there were people who wanted to come and be in a group that they were accepted, as it were!

Dr. Main Do you hear this? Isn't it interesting!

Doctor B. It never occurred to me to interview them except that we did know they were working in the field.

Dr. Main No, I am talking about the atmosphere between the leader and the people who come. The leader is grateful to them for coming; *they* should be grateful to the *leader*. You see the difference? It's an atmosphere which is very different to that when you are a reluctant leader willing to bow to the needs of the people's pressure for training. — Do you give them sugared cakes? *(Laughter)*.

Doctor K. I did know them all, because they all work in family planning clinics, apart from two.

Dr. Main My point is that the need of the leaders for trainees means a kind of anxiety, and the whole conduct of the seminar will be coloured. Why do you want them at all?

Doctor B. I rather feel I have been given them.

Dr. Main By whom?

Doctor B. By Doctor K! *(Laughter)*. I think you want them because you see yourself retiring and nobody else to do the work. Is that true?

Doctor K. There may be an element of that. There is also the element that when you read other family planning doctors' notes you feel, 'Oh my God, they need training!'

Dr. Main But do they *want* it?

Doctor K. Yes, this group do want it, I think. They are aware. They feel a need.

Dr. Main We know the leader wants it: 'There are some people out there who need treatment; shall we go and get them?'

Doctor B. Certainly the one doctor who comes from my home area has been asking for some time for a seminar, because she has become more involved in the work.

Dr. Main I am not questioning that. I am querying the leader's need: not acceding to the trainees' need for training so much as to Dr. K's need for people to be trained.

Doctor K. Always there is this factor, that you have one or two who really want it, and one wants to form a group for them.

Dr. Main But what a bully you are! — I didn't know that!

Doctor K. I'm a terrible bully! How do you form a group unless you have a group?

Dr. Main The whole point is, it's a bit evangelistic.

Doctor K.   Yes.

Doctor B.   Doctor K did say you wouldn't approve because they weren't hammering on the door! *(Laughter).*

Dr. Main   It's not approval: it's the effect of this on the work of the group. We'll watch it as the weeks go by.

2. One leader or two (i)

Leader Doctors P. & D.

Doctor P reported the steps she had taken to set up a group in the city of W---. She had decided to do this with a colleague, Doctor D, who knew the city well. They felt that it would be easier for them to start the group together rather than for either of them to do it alone. There had not been a group in the city for a long time, and several doctors had shown an interest in the training. The two doctors met and decided that for both of them the most important thing was that the group should work well, and that they could be fairly fluid about the way in which the co-leadership would be arranged. Doctor P then described a number of interviews with the doctors who were interested in joining the seminar. The workshop discussion continued:

Dr. N.   Can you just tell me: you wanted to get into this big tough city and so you turned to Doctor D. Can you say what she had got to do with it?

Doctor P.   She is a member of the Institute and an experienced leader. She does a lot of work in the city and is well known by the general practitioners, community health department and the university. She is a very good link between these people and will help to bridge the gap. The group is going to be financed jointly by the post-graduate general practitioner fund and the community health training fund.

Dr. Main   The co-leadership is not a technical decision, then, but a political one?

Doctor P.   I think it was mainly political, but there are probably things we can learn from each other and I think, provided we can watch what is going on, it could be productive.

Dr. S.   Isn't it just that you both want to lead the group?

Doctor P.   I suppose we do.

Dr. Main   You shouldn't ask silly questions when you know quite well what the answer is.

Dr. S.   It seems to me that is how it is.

Dr. Main   Of course.

Dr. N.   It's two people standing on the brink — 'We'll both jump together'.

Dr. Main   Yes.

Dr. S.   And neither wants to let the other one do it alone.

Dr. N.   It seems that the two of you somehow gave each other confidence to go ahead and do it.

Doctor P.   It was something like that.

Dr. Main   The important thing is that it wasn't a technical decision. Co-leadership is where two people are speaking the same thing at the same time, so there cannot be any such thing as co-leadership. The group has got two leaders.

Doctor P.   Don't you believe it — I think we've got about five! *(Laughter)*.

———————

Three weeks later these leaders again discussed their group which was now rather too large.

Doctor D.   There's no question that we have absolutely the wrong number at the moment: too large for one and not quite enough for two healthy groups.

Dr. Tunnadine   It looks like eight in one group and nine in the other. This is as many as most people have, although I agree it is better to have more.

Dr. Main *(to the leaders)*   You know the people . . . Do you think they are going to stay, or not?

Doctor D. We think they are going to stay and this is why we must split; and they are also people who seem to have quite a lot of experience and they don't have any hesitation in talking.

Dr. Main Each of you will have your own groups, too. The technique of co-leadership isn't something which has been well worked out: it seems to be a dog's dinner, by and large.

Doctor D. It has not been a dog's dinner with the two of us, so far. On our two occasions I think it has been extremely productive and interesting. We would like to explore some time how much you think it makes a group more rebellious and become a more cohesive group ready to rebel against two powerful leaders, just because there are two of you there.

Dr. N. Divide and rule, you mean!

Dr. Main There's no such thing as co-leadership. It's not 'co-' at all. It's *double* leadership. You are bound to always agree, aren't you, on all this?

Doctor P. The only problem about having two groups is if the numbers fall a lot. Perhaps if they were held at the same time, they could be joined if the numbers were very low?

Dr. Main But in a group, individuals form a relationship with each other and with the leader. Different groups differ in character, but each forms into an organic whole. All sorts of inexact words like 'gel' are used. Having a change prevents that development which is essential if the group is to work.

Subsequently two groups were formed, and on the only occasion when an attempt was made to amalgamate them this was strenuously resisted by the group members.

2. One leader or two (ii)

Leader Doctors J. & E.

Dual leadership was discussed again when a group was being set up in D---shire.

Doctor J.   We had been thinking it would be nice for Doctor E and me to lead a group together.

Dr. Main   Who decided that?

Doctor J.   I think Doctor Tunnadine suggested it.

Doctor E.   I am interested in learning how to lead a group.

Dr. Main   You have never seen a leader at work, of course! *(Laughter)*.

Doctor E.   I wasn't intending to watch a leader at work. I was hoping to *be* watched — that was the point; and we have discussed how we can use the fact of having two of us there in a positive way. Obviously there will also be disadvantages.

Dr. Q.   Doctor J has had previous experience of leading a group?

Doctor E.   Yes. We are not equal in that sense at all. Doctor J has had quite a lot of experience.

Doctor J.   But we are still both learning.

Dr. Main   You will learn to the end of your days. About co-leadership . . . — Speaking in unison, at the same time?

Doctor J.   We have thought about this, and we thought we would take it in turns, either week by week, or term by term.

Dr. Main   Rival leadership. It is bound to be.

Doctor E.   We really want to do this; but afterwards you can come back to us and say what a bad idea you think it was.

Dr. Main   No.

Doctor E.   Our idea is that one of us will lead the group and try to keep an eye on the doctor/patient relationship; and the other one will stand back further, watching the leader leading, so that she can hopefully take in the whole thing. We thought that might be a more positive way of using the two of us, rather than one sitting around doing nothing special.

Dr. F.   Could you say what that means?

Doctor E.   We didn't think it would work if both of us tried to lead at the same time, with both of us jumping in when we felt like it. So we thought that we would start off by agreeing that one of us would lead it and the other one would try and keep quiet or come in when invited. Then this idea developed a bit more into watching the one who was leading and sharing that afterwards.

G

Dr. F. I think it's very fascinating.

Dr. Main Drop the word 'co-'. Find another word. The word 'co-' is a bit pious. There are two different people there, two different leaders.

Dr. Z. Two different points of view, too.

Dr. Main Of course.

Dr. Z. This is probably the strength of it, having done it myself. You can almost have your own leader doctor workshop afterwards: that is the positive thing about it. At least, this is what we found.

Dr. Main An honest co-leader workshop afterwards is a bit dangerous. Physical assault should be banned. Underneath all the agreements and so on there are quite a lot of disagreements sometimes.

Dr. Z. But if you can in fact come out with it, it's surely better, isn't it?

Dr. Q. Is there a danger that the group will side with one or the other leader?

Dr. Z. It didn't happen when we did it.

Dr. Main If the leaders stick to the task, it doesn't matter.

Dr. Q. I am wondering how the leaders would feel in that situation. One might get the feeling that 'I'm not as good as she is'. Does that happen?

Dr. Z. We didn't find that it did.

Dr. Main I'm sorry Doctor Tunnadine isn't here, because I think she would agree with you: she is my co-leader. We don't have to agree with each other, that's the point.

Doctor J. Wouldn't it be confusing for a new group, to have two leaders who were disagreeing with each other?

Dr. Main Well maybe, I'm not so sure. If there is disagreement, it is better out in the open *if it's about the task*. It really is important that it should only be about the task, not about the case.

Doctor J. I think we were a bit worried that if we started saying, "well, I don't quite agree with you", it would upset the group and we didn't want to do that.

Dr. Main Well, the last time I was here, Doctor Tunnadine and

I disagreed.

Doctor J.   Yes, we noticed! *(Laughter)*.

Dr. Main   What harm did it do?

Doctor J.   None here.

Dr. Main   Well, she was wrong, anyway! *(Laughter)*.

Doctor J.   With a new group of people who are testing the water and finding out whether they like this work, you need to go very carefully. They are coming to see if this is something they want to do and a way that they want to think, and to confront them with two leaders who are in open disagreement would be very confusing.

Doctor E.   Like everyone else we will also be tempted to solve the case instead of sticking to the leadership task and this would obviously be wrong for the group. We hope that if we do disagree about something that happens in the group, we can bring it back next time and talk to the group about it.

Dr. Main   The really important thing is to know when you disagree, because to hide disagreements means that they pile up.

Dr. Z.   Oh yes, you've got to have it out — I know from experience.

Dr. Main   It's best out in the open.

Doctor J.   It is difficult to know one's self, but we think we will be able to talk about things that we disagree about.

This group continued with both leaders for two years, but subsequently the leaders chose to lead alone.

The work of these two leaders in action together is discussed further in III F 8.

2. One leader or two (iii)

Leader Doctors K. & B.

A group which was led by two leaders, Dr. K. and Dr. B., was subsequently discussed as follows:-

Dr. J.   I felt this report was incomplete. The leaders didn't talk about the conversation they had together afterwards. We talked about rivalry, but it seems to me the benefit of having two leaders might be that each might potentially criticise the other's work.

Dr. Main   Frequently, yes! *(Laughter).*

Doctor K.   We didn't *not* talk about it on purpose: we just haven't seen each other. I think we would have done.

Doctor B.   I'm *sure* we would have done.

Mrs. R.   It's also very threatening, isn't it? — I think you've expressed it already, that you felt slightly threatened by this.

Dr. Main   Suppose we turn Dr. J's exhortation into an observation. You notice that there has not been reported any account of what these co-leaders talked about afterwards. — That's what you meant?

Dr. J.   Yes.

Dr. Main   The next thing is, I wonder why? Don't you?

Dr. I.   We've already said it is a threatening situation, isn't it? It's easier to say things here because it's safe, with the rest of us here.

Dr. Tunnadine   It's like getting rid of the partners of the patients — if two sweet people have got nothing but nice things to say to each other, you do find yourself wanting to send one out.

Dr. Main   What about those two co-leaders — how do they get on? — Easy topic, isn't it?

Dr. I.   One has said that she felt threatened. She mentions it in a nice safe group, because the other one can't get up and hit her! *(Laughter)*

Dr. Tunnadine   I know these two very well: they love each other — that's what the difficulty is for them.

Doctor B.   If I am being honest, I hadn't realised Dr. K. was going to come in on that group at all; and you said, "I am going to come so I know them in case you are away". I think it's a good idea for you to know them; but it's better for one of us to take them, and only if something arose would the other one come in. What I am really doing is pushing you out, isn't it?

Doctor K. Well, you have said to me in the past that you didn't feel put down if I was there; and I suppose I took that too literally.

Doctor B. I don't feel put down, but I realise I wonder how you think I am doing.

Dr. Main It's quite clear that you are in full agreement! *(Laughter)*

Dr. Tunnadine She didn't actually say she felt put down. She said she didn't feel good enough in your company; and I think that may be sheer phantasy, but . . .

Dr. Main Dr. K. is frighteningly competent.

Dr. Tunnadine Perhaps not *frighteningly* competent but, if one is her junior, then it is not easy in this situation.

Dr. Main She is the grand old lady of . . . *(Laughter)*

Dr. Tunnadine I say again, quite seriously, if these two hated each other, it would be easy.

Dr. Main Well, they do. They love each other as leaders.

Dr. Tunnadine Well, they do; and they interfere with each other's work, like everybody else.

Doctor B. I certainly feel the deputy to you, as it were.

Dr. Main — and it's not nice for you in that group.

Doctor K. Unfortunately one of the doctors turned to me, didn't she, and asked me something?

Doctor B. That's right: and that's bound to happen.

Dr. Main What did you say to them — "Get the hell out of it!" *(Laughter)*

Dr. Tunnadine As you can see, I've deliberately stirred this, because I know that these two have a good relationship that will survive whatever happens; but it seems to be so important for anybody getting into this co-leadership situation to have this aired, because it is very difficult. Not that it's good or bad, but it is important.

Dr. Main Absolutely, it is essential. The group suffers otherwise.

Dr. S. There are leaders who would not touch this with a bargepole. I wouldn't get into that situation. My trainee leader remained a definite trainee.

Dr. Tunnadine With my trainee, it didn't work at all, did it? — *(To Dr. P.)* You didn't feel able to contribute when I was there.

Dr. P. That's right, but I've grown up now!

Dr. Tunnadine I tried hard; it wasn't because we didn't work well together at other levels, just a bloody difficult situation. We didn't do it well, did we? — we wasted opportunities, or something.

Dr. Q. Why does it arise that we have two co-leaders at all? — because you are wasting two skilled people on one group.

Dr. Main It's the area of generals chasing around for troops. This is what has happened here. Instead of having an honest quarrel — 'I wanted this group': '*I* wanted it' — we have, 'Let's join forces and be sweet'. There is a certain amount of genuine sweetness, actually.

Dr. Q. I think it must be difficult for a group to try and relate to two people.

Dr. Main It's never technique; it's a political decision.

Dr. Q. I know, but I am going one step further: they are just starting, so they can do something about it now.

Dr. P. Are you saying there is nothing to be gained *ever* from co-leadership? Are you determined to kill them all off at this stage?

Dr. Main No. An individual leader is very often hypocritical inside himself. Two people not only have their own individual hypocrisies but they have hypocrisies between each other. This word 'co-' is awful: it means they have to agree instead of quarrelling openly; and it can become a problem. I haven't done a great deal of study of co-leader problems. I have done some, and from the study I have done it is not encouraging.

Dr. Tunnadine We have more here and we can study it some more.

Dr. Main Let's not pretend it's a technique.

Dr. Tunnadine   Alternatively, perhaps we can find a technique for it. That's the other way of looking at it; but we shan't unless we talk about it honestly and openly, so we hear how it works. This is the point.

Dr. Main   Yes. Let's see what happens and learn from it.

Dr. I.   It's like being a parent, isn't it?

Dr. Tunnadine   That's right.

2. One leader or two (iv)

Leader Doctor A.

The leader of this group had previously shared in co-leadership. She reported her new group soon after it started (see Leading an early group) *and the discussion continued:-*

Dr. Tunnadine   I thought for a second meeting this group was going like a train.

Dr. Main   I think so too. The other thing that she is telling us is that it's better to be on your own than with a co-leader.

Dr. Tunnadine   I missed that.

Dr. S.   She hasn't said it, has she?

Dr. Main   She's more comfortable.

Doctor A.   I was more comfortable with the fact that I decided that I was going to interview all the people, and I was going to decide. . .

Dr. Main   Your technique in the group is freer. It's very clear to me that you were easy with it.

Dr. Tunnadine   I think so. — 'I thought to myself, was I going to do this or was I going to do that?' — as though you had time to make your mind up.

Doctor A.   I didn't think that in the group, but I did think in the beginning: "I am going to decide how I am going to do this interview"; because, as I told you before, my co-leader had decided to have someone in the group who I didn't want.

Dr. Tunnadine I begin to think there is another twist to it. Maybe it isn't so much that one is *freer* not having big sister beside you, but that you have bloody well got to get on and do your own thinking.

Dr. Main What strikes me about this business is that you lay down the ground rules very clearly: 'I am not here to sort out your problems; we are here to discuss the doctor/patient relation', and so on: the ground rules really are quite clear.

Doctor A. I feel there is a subtler way of saying these things.

Dr. Main All we can judge by are the results. I think the results are very good.

3. Selection for training (i) Beware the teacher's pet

Leader Doctor Y.

Doctor Y. I could introduce my group. Where would you like me to begin?

Dr. Main Well, I think, begin at the beginning, then go on to the middle and then stop at the end!

Doctor Y. The beginning, if you like, was the last leaders' workshop when I was firmly told not to advertise; but in the end I did, by sending out a letter to about 200 doctors, and I got about two dozen replies.

Dr. Main There is certainly no harm in advertising to let your presence be known. That's all you're doing. It's passive advertising and you leave it at that. You got 24 replies out of about 200. How many came to the group?

Doctor Y. Eight came the first time. We are now up to ten with possibly two more joining us who can't come at the moment because of work commitments. Most of the people who have come forward are general practitioners. Two have been in practice quite a long time, but the others have not long finished their GP training. I get a feel of much more interest among these young doctors than there would have been a few years ago. Certainly two of the group have been influenced by sitting in with a member of this Institute.

Dr. Q. As students, you mean?

Doctor Y. Yes.

Dr. Main So their interest came from early contact as students?

Doctor Y. The attitudes of the students are changing.

Dr. Main It's interesting that these people are inspired by their teacher rather than hard-headed thinking about the experience they've had. On the whole, that has been the main reason why people came to these seminars before. They've found the need from their own experience. These people haven't found that. They're not old enough yet.

Doctor Y. Can it not be that the teachers told them where to come?

Dr. Main I'm trying to sort out the difference in the keenness, the different styles and motives for it. These people don't know how important it is except from their teacher; whereas people who have found out from their own professional lives and experience that they are so incomplete have a different sort of interest.

Doctor Y. I don't know. I feel very differently about this group than I have with previous ones. I feel much more that they start where the last group left off. I have one health visitor and one trainee psychiatrist doing a lot of work in child guidance.

Dr. Main It will be interesting to see what happens to these people who are working in a different setting. Did you select them or use any criteria?

Doctor Y. In a rather backhanded sort of way. One or two who answered the letter asked for more information, and then I contacted the ones who did not turn up to the first session, and encouraged them or not, depending on the sort of response that I got. One was a man who had just started in general practice and I asked what his reasons were for joining and he couldn't really give me any. I said, did he meet the problems in general practice? and he said no. So I didn't encourage him.

Dr. Tunnadine   The trainee psychiatrist is presumably not doing psychosexual work unless she lays it on herself.

Dr. Y.   No. But she has done her family planning training and seems very interested.

Dr. Tunnadine   But she is not now seeing patients who would expect examinations. It wouldn't be appropriate in a child guidance clinic. They'll be getting marital problems rather than psychosexual problems.

Dr. Main   They won't be doing body doctoring.

Dr. Tunnadine   No.

Doctor Y.   Well, I would quarrel with that a bit.

Dr. Tunnadine   The patients will not expect to be examined by her. They don't go for that, do they?

Doctor Y.   No.

Dr. Tunnadine   I'm not against it, because I think it's interesting.

Dr. Main   I think it's very good for the psychiatrist. But is it any good for the seminar?

Dr. Tunnadine   When we have discussed mixed groups before, we didn't say that people should not be mixed. But Doctor Main pointed out that if you are faced with a mixed group, you have to make a positive, overt virtue of it, and study the different settings rather than pretending they are all doing the same thing.

Dr. N.   There was that group that got definitely split into the professionals and the non-professionals.

Dr. Main   But people don't listen to this. We do not learn from history. It will be interesting to see what happens to the psychiatrist. If people are not in the field, they will be like flies on the wall, watchers, and have a passive, non-responsible kind of position, because they won't be exposing their work of a similar kind to their colleagues. We'll see what happens.

Doctor Y.   I must say that we've had some very helpful insightful comments from the psychiatrist.

Dr. Main   You'll get plenty.

Doctor Y.   I'm willing to bet that this will go on and we'll start talking about vaginal examinations, too.

Dr. Main   And the health visitor — is she in the field?

Dr. Y.   She came because she had met so many clients who had presented sexual problems to her and she had wanted to refer them, but the patients hadn't wanted to be referred. There is a feeling that she is overwhelmed.

Dr. Main   And she sees a different kind of case to the case who comes to the doctor. The important thing is to get the difference clear, not only with her but with her colleagues, so that they don't mix up their techniques. Otherwise you just get the health visitor turning into a mini-doctor and the doctor turning into a mini-health visitor. There's a mix-up of this sort. If it's geared to the task, it's fine. How often have they met?

Doctor Y.   They've met three times. Nobody has fallen by the wayside yet, except perhaps one GP who is trying to do it as well as being on-call, and this may be impossible. He may not be able to cope with it. I think the psychiatrist might leave because of a shortage of material for herself. I think she's sophisticated enough to say that. The health visitor might decide that the material is too different.

Dr. Main   You think it is those people who will leave, not the general practitioners? You should lay your bets now, because you can check on them in a year's time!

Dr. Tunnadine   Can I pull your leg and be really nasty? Suppose this psychiatrist doesn't leave, because she sounds pretty good to me as a psychiatrist, and if she doesn't bring material but continues to make good psychiatric observations — what will be the impact on the value systems of the group?

Dr. Main   Never answer questions! *(Laughter)*.

Dr. Tunnadine   But that wasn't a question, was it?

Dr. Main   Of course it wasn't.

Dr. Tunnadine   I shall be interested to see.

Doctor Y.   I'm afraid I would be sorry as a leader to see her go because I think she'll be helpful.

Dr. Tunnadine   And who's leading this group, and it's about what? I know it's second-rate compared with child guidance! *((ironically)*. You think she's going to be useful to you! You don't think there's going to be any question about her talents being better than yours?

Dr. Main   Yes. You will look upon her for good ideas, when she is really there to learn.

Doctor Y.   Can't one do both?

Dr. Main   It seems that you need her and you want her. There is nothing wrong with giving things a try. If you fall flat on your face, then you might learn something. If you find you walk on air, then you will learn something from that.

Doctor Y.   I'm going to take you up on this. *She* came to *me* — I didn't suggest it. She is not the sort of person I would have thought of. Now I can't turn round to her and say: "I'm not sure whether you should come, because I think you might have something to say and this might clog up the situation from your learning point of view". I would have thought that was just something I'd got to acknowledge and bear in the back of my mind, isn't it?

Dr. Tunnadine   What does she want? Does she want to learn? — this is what isn't very clear to me.

Doctor Y.   I've just got to find out. In the case she did present I was surprised by the way she tackled it, which is not the way she tackles her other work.

Dr. Main   What does she want to learn for? She's not in the field, so what does she want to learn for?

Doctor Y.   She would say that she wants to be able to cope with patients who present psychosexual problems, because she finds it difficult.

Dr. Main   The question is, should this psychosexual work be done in a child guidance setting? Should you pervert a child guidance doctor to do this work when there are probably not very many in that area of the country? Should that doctor not have said, 'Let me send this patient to someone else who does this work?' Or was her work with the woman an integral part of helping this child?

Doctor Y.   I think it was.

Dr. C.   One ENT lecturer found she was doing her psychosexual work in the ENT clinic. If you can relate it to the work you are doing, the patient is going to be better.

Dr. Main   If it's relevant to the ENT clinic, why not? If it's relevant to the child guidance clinic, why not? But it shouldn't be changing the clinic because of some mission; that's all I'm saying.

Dr. B. GPs frequently refer psychosexual patients to psychiatrists because they don't know where else to send them. I would have thought it would be ideal training for a psychiatrist.

Mrs. R. Can you mix your training, though? This trainee doctor is presumably already being trained under some other system. Can you then bring another system in at the same time?

Dr. Q. Why not?

Dr. Tunnadine I have some anxieties about the leader's need for the psychiatrist and her talent. I don't think it's going to be any good to you, the group or anybody if that is the reason why she is there. It's putting pressure on her to make perceptive analytic remarks; it's putting pressure on you as a leader; and it's pressure on the group to think that is what they are there to train for, and they are not.

Doctor Y. Can I not *hope* that she stays there, rather than needing her to stay?

Dr. Tunnadine You hope that she stays, that is, you see her as an asset rather than an unusually difficult trainee, someone with particularly difficult learning needs.

Dr. N. It makes life very much easier if there are just one or two people in the group who leaven it a bit.

Dr. Tunnadine It depends what you leaven it with.

Dr. Main It's the leader's attitude.

Dr. Tunnadine Yes. If she's any good, and it sounds as if she's very good . . .

Doctor Y. So I've got to say: "Right, I can't have anyone in this field because I know you, and I might welcome you too much?"

Dr. Main No, it's an important statement. You've been very honest about it, you've said she's a kind of teacher's pet. Let's see what happens to her. Time will show.

Doctor Y. I recognise that she stood in that position before she ever began. I know I've got to watch it.

Postscript: *After one year the health visitor left to continue on a general counselling course which she found more helpful. The psychiatrist continued for the whole two years and went on to an advanced group, but is now working in family planning and well woman clinics.*

3. Selection for training (ii) The interview

Leader Doctor A.

Doctor A.   With my new group I was determined that I was going to interview them all beforehand, so they would know what they were in for, and I would know what they were expecting. I telephoned them all. The first two really had no intention of doing anything about it at all. The third was a young GP who had intended to come, but he was overwhelmed with rebuilding his premises or something. Then I phoned a woman and from the minute I said 'Hello' to her, she took complete charge of the telephone interview. I found that she was a single-handed urban GP who did one session a week in the psychiatric department of the local hospital. I did actually manage to arrange an appointment to see her but she had finished the conversation and said 'goodbye' before I had the chance to say 'goodbye'. I thought, "Oh goodness, I hope she doesn't come, or something happens so I don't have to have her — she'll take the thing over!" At the interview she sat down and I said, "I wonder why you want to do this sort of work?"; and she got up and wandered over to the window and looked out telling me as she went how well she did this kind of thing in her own practice — she was very sensitive to patients' problems. She finished by saying, "You know, I'm very well qualified to do this sort of work as my husband and I had sexual problems, but we've sorted them out now. What about you, Dr. A.? — Is your marriage really happy?" So here was I getting into a muddle between personal and professional matters. I should have picked it up and said, "Whether our marriages are happy or not is irrelevant to our professional work". But I was just sort of flabbergasted, and I was a bit pleased because by that time she had almost talked herself out of coming; so I just didn't say anything at all. Finally she rounded off the interview and said, "I will let you know" and walked out. She telephoned later to say that as she was single-handed, she really had too much to do and couldn't manage it; so I heaved a very big sigh of relief that I didn't have to cope with her. I don't know what I would have done.

Dr. N.   Well, you didn't have to cope with her, did you?

Doctor A.   No, she coped with herself.

Dr. N.   No, I mean it *was* an interview and you didn't have to accept her.

Doctor A.   It would have been difficult to tell that sort of woman, "No".

Dr. N.   So why do we have interviews?

Dr. I.   Perhaps you did it in a more subtle way.

Doctor A.   I said virtually nothing at all at the interview, which lasted about a quarter of an hour. I just said the odd word.

Dr. I.   You weren't encouraging, were you?

Doctor A.   No, I wasn't.

Dr. S.   If she had let you know on the phone that she was coming, what would you have done then? — had her?

Doctor A.   I don't know what I would have done.

Dr. Tunnadine   This is the point, isn't it? You quite rightly say if you have an interview it is for a reason; and the leader didn't want her, because. . .

Dr. S.   She felt she was coming to teach.

Dr. Tunnadine   Yes.

Dr. N.   And she was coming for personal problems.

Dr. Tunnadine   Right. And because she is coming for personal problems, the leader found herself having to deal with her like that: she couldn't say whatever you would say if you were an interviewer, because she felt like a therapist. But I take your point: what do you do *instead?* That's the question, because we are all going to have this type of person.

Dr. N.   If I had felt as strongly against the woman as you do, I wouldn't have had her. It's easier to say goodbye to her now than have her as a member of the group and have to suffer her week after week. The thing is, was she really suitable for a group? That's the main thing, isn't it, and there are a lot of things against that, as you have told us.

Doctor A.   No, I don't think she was suitable.

Dr. N.   So you've got to have the courage of your own convictions.

Doctor A.   She practically talked herself out of it and I could see her doing this; so I just sat quietly and hoped that she would finish the process off; which she did. She had almost done it by the time she had finished the interview, but she said, "I will let you know".

Dr. P.   There is something sad about it, too, isn't there, because this woman obviously had doubts about her ability or she wouldn't have even thought of coming; yet somehow it was so threatening to her that she had to become all teachy and could not allow you to do the work with her that you wanted to do at all.

Doctor A.   When I suggested that it was not a question of lectures but of bringing cases, I think I could see her backing off. She said, "I don't have very many cases. I'm very good at picking them up, but I've only had about four in the last year". So I felt she was a bit threatened by the fact that she might have to give cases and expose herself; and she was a part-time psychiatrist.

Dr. I.   I think one can say this is a threatening situation and she might find it difficult to be a member of the group; because she obviously would. I would have been tempted, if she only had four cases, to say, "What happened to all the others?" — I don't know if I would have actually said it.

Dr. Tunnadine   We're clearly all relieved by the result. It's just that she was fairly defended, or something, and ought you to have given her a chance?

Doctor A.   She said at the end of the interview, "I think I really just wanted to see another way of doing things"; as if to say, 'I wasn't really serious about wanting to do the work'.

Dr. S.   You couldn't say, "I don't think you are very serious about it, Dr. So-and-so". Do you say that in an interview?

Doctor A.   I didn't feel I needed to say anything, because I saw her talking herself out of it, and I wasn't going to talk her into it.

Dr. S.   No, but she didn't have an opportunity to say what her real feelings were, like if you'd said, 'It seems you feel a bit threatened by this', or something like that.

Dr. N. Do you want to get into treating this woman? This is really my criticism about the interviews. I think you handled it absolutely splendidly: you allowed her to talk herself out of it, which is the kindest and most fruitful way of dealing with it.

Doctor A. Yes, but when she got to the bit about my marriage, I didn't pick that up, as I should have, and said, "This work isn't really about. . ."

Dr. N. But the difficulty is that we all talk about these interviews, but very few people will lay down their guidelines as to when they pick people out. It is very difficult, isn't it, and maybe the interview isn't the best way of choosing people at all. The other way is to say, "You come and look at me for three months and I will look at you; and then we will make our minds up". Is that just dodging the interview or is it a different technique which ought to be respected?

Dr. Tunnadine It is difficult, because it's no good studying something that didn't happen. But I take your point very much. Suppose she *hadn't* talked herself out of it? Supposing she had rung up and said, "I've decided that you are worthy of my favours" — then where are you? How would you have said "No".

Doctor A. I would have felt a bit cheeky, somehow, to have said anything like that just in an interview.

Dr. S. It all finished with her not knowing that you, as it were, saw through her. I think it would have been better if it had been a more honest interaction.

Doctor A. In a way I think she did see this because she said, "I just really wanted to come and see how you did this sort of thing. Psychiatrists do it differently and I wondered how you do it".

Dr. N. If you were interviewing for any other job than for a member of your seminar: if you were a consultant interviewing a houseman for cardiology housemanship, you wouldn't feel a lot of embarrassment. You are only going to take one candidate; you have got to turn the rest down, haven't you? — and that isn't taken hard on either side. The person turning them down isn't saying they are no use for medicine, and neither does the chap who is being turned down feel he is being denied a living; but somehow what comes out of this is that it is not so much a professional as a personal interview. In the actual seminar we take great care to be interested only in the professional life; but at an interview this is more difficult.

3. Selection for training (iii) Is the doctor working in the field? — (a) the eye doctor

Leader Doctor Z.

Doctor Z reported that she had recently started a new group, but that over the first few meetings the numbers had fluctuated from ten to four. She had decided not to interview the doctors, but had suggested that they should come and see what it was like and stay if they wanted to. There were some family planning doctors, some general practitioners, and one doctor doing an ophthalmic job but planning eventually to work in general practice.

Dr. Main   The eye doctor is not presenting psychosexual cases?
Doctor Z.   She can't.
Dr. Main   Except winking, or something like that! *(Laughter).*
Doctor Z.   I think actually she has seen some cases before.
Dr. Main   There is no sense in that doctor going in for it.
Doctor Z.   Well, she seems awfully keen.
Dr. Main   That's why she should be thrown out.
Doctor Z.   She only came once, so I think she's thrown herself out. She may have come to keep her friend company.
Dr. Main   I was just thinking of the usual criteria for entry: they should know what the seminar is like, have some idea of what goes on, and be working in the field; and she fails on all those counts.
Doctor Z.   I don't know how long she is going to be working in that particular field. She is actually on a vocational training scheme, so the chances are she will be coming off that and doing

something else in three months time.

Dr. Main   Doesn't it sound to you as though we have got a keen leader who will admit anybody? Her methods of entry are that she puts her hand on them, and if they are warm they are in.

Doctor Z.   That's right.

Dr. Main   This is a way of ensuring disaster for the group.

Dr. Q.   Well I don't know. The interviewing method doesn't seem to have been totally successful.

Dr. Main   The idea is to have them in if they know what they are in for and, secondly, that they are working in the field.

Dr. Q.   I was just trying to put the point that of all the methods that we have, none of them seem to be perfect.

Doctor Z.   My idea was to let them in to the first seminar and let them see how it was done, by discussing cases. And I was being a bit lazy, too, because I didn't want to interview everybody.

Dr. Main   I am raising the question of how wise it is to let just anybody in. If they are warm, they are in: is this a good idea? Is there any sense at all in having people for whom the work is utterly irrelevant?

Doctor Z.   My eye doctor was actually quite good with her observations.

Dr. Main   On whom? On her own work?

Doctor Z.   No, they've hardly had any time at all yet.

Dr. Main   She can talk on other people's work of which she knows nothing and has no experience?

Doctor Z.   Maybe.

Dr. Main   I am pretty critical there.

Dr. I.   How soon was she going to do the GP traineeship?

Doctor Z.   I can't remember. This is an interim job for a short while. She is not actually in the field of eyes at all, just doing a six-month appointment.

Dr. Main   You must have been anxious to get this group going to have such low admission standards.

Doctor Z.   No, I suppose she caught me. She rang me up at home and I though, 'Oh, she's dead keen'. I thought keenness was more important — well no, not more important than anything else — but I thought it was an important factor.

Dr. Main I think you must be promiscuous — you just can't say no, can you!

Doctor Z. I allow people to opt out, perhaps.

Dr. Q. She wasn't wanting it for her own help?

Doctor Z. Not yet.

Dr. Main The point is, how realistically was this group formed and how genuine was the interest? You were left with only four people last time.

Doctor Z. Yes, as I say, of the others there were three who had said they were going to be on holiday, so I think honestly there are in fact seven who are genuine. They had specifically said: 'I will be away that particular day', so I think that was fair enough.

3. Selection for training (iii) Is the doctor working in the field? — (b) the genetic counselling doctor.

Leader Doctor G.

A fairly new group of doctors had been rather a 'roaming' group with some of the people who started in it moving off, and new people joining. The leader raised the question of a new doctor who was working in genetic counselling.

Dr. Main Can I just ask something about this doctor? Does she do any other work than genetic counselling?

Doctor G. No.

Dr. S. She doesn't really do vaginal examinations — or does she?

Doctor G. I don't think so.

Dr. Main Can we just hear a bit about where she works? Do the patients come or are they sent?

Doctor G. Some of them are request referrals: they can ask to go for counselling, but they have to come through their G.P.s or hospital departments. There are none who are going to walk in through the door.

Dr. Main Yes. — They don't come complaining of psychosexual symptoms?

Doctor G. No.

Dr. Main The question is, whether she should be in the group at all. You must have thought about it yourself?

Doctor G. Yes, I did wonder, and she said that what she really wanted was to have a chance to talk about the emotional difficulties people were presenting her with.

Dr. Main I can see that. There's no question about that. The other thing is that Dr. G. has got rather a small group and her selection system is not unbiassed.

Doctor G. Well, she was referred to me by Dr. Tunnadine.

Dr. S. This doctor might start doing some family planning clinics. You could make it a condition.

Mrs. R. But surely, amongst some of the patients who are going to see her, there will be some who have sexual problems, which are not being seen at the moment, perhaps.

Dr. Main But she's not in the psychosexual business, is she?

Dr. Tunnadine She is, however, in the doctor/patient relation business, with otherwise healthy people.

Dr. Main This is a one-off kind of doctor. The usual criteria for people coming into a group are: do they know the process of case reporting, and are they in the field? It's a bit doubtful whether this doctor is in the field or not. She is well aware of the group business, isn't she? She knows what's going to happen; but whether she is in the field or not is doubtful.

Dr. P. It's one of the fields our doctors have gone into after training and found the training immensely valuable. I agree that's the other way round.

Dr. Main That's true. Sweetness is very expensive.

Mrs. R. She's going to have to get another job.

Dr. Main If there is a mistake here, Dr. G. will pay and so will the group. That has to be faced. It is not just this doctor who is involved. Her wishes are admirable.

Dr. I. Does she see the patients on several occasions?

Doctor G. Yes.

Dr. Main It really is true. I don't know how to put this. There should be Danger notices — "Danger Keep Out". The way the group is formed will decide the future, and if you make mistakes in forming the group, by God you pay! You never stop paying.

Dr. I. Don't they usually go, the ones who aren't suitable?

Dr. Main No. It is no fun for me to say, "I told you so" in six months time. I am worried for Dr. G. on this. It will have consequences; of that I am sure. Whether the consequences will be good, bad or indifferent remains to be seen.

Dr. I. But if she seems unsuitable, surely you can turn round and say, after a few weeks, "I'm sorry, but I don't think it's suitable for you to continue in this group".

Dr. Main That's not a bad idea, because you then select on a basis of knowledge, instead of a hunch.

Doctor G. What I said was, she could come until the end of the term and that I wasn't certain what the outcome of *the group* might be. It might have to be re-formed, and that if she wanted to join that. . .

Dr. Tunnadine My own impression, and the reason I will take some of the responsibility, is that I think genetic counselling *is* in the field — at least as much as venereology.

Dr. Main Look, I agree. But there's no harm in taking on a three-month engagement; and I do recommend this way if you're in any doubt. Say, "Let's try it for three months and at the end of three months we'll talk; and if it's no good, either on your side or my side, then we may as well part with no hard feelings". Give it an honest try and then face the facts. There's no harm in examining the situation. It's not so difficult telling people to get out. — I don't want to go on at length about this. We'll see how it gets on.

4. Selection and the small group

Leader Doctor Q.

The leader was worried because the number of doctors in her group had fallen from eleven to six. The last doctor to pull out had been a G.P. trainee who had written to say his duty commitment had changed, so he couldn't come.

Doctor Q. Five of those six are extremely committed and good and want to continue. One of them did say recently, "You have talked about letting in new members if doctors wanted to join. I wanted to tell you that I like it as it is; we're working very well". As it was the end, I didn't take it up, but I felt perhaps he was saying he would be threatened by lots of people coming in. I am encouraged to hear that other small groups are working well. I felt a little angry, as I tried to select carefully, and I felt if it was to be worth anything, they have got to go on for two years, and I was putting myself out to do it for them. I felt they had got to make up their own minds what they wanted; so I was a little nettled when we went over this again at the beginning of this second term. And then I got this resignation letter.

Dr. P. Is this the beginning of just your second term?

Doctor Q. We're half way through the second term.

Dr. P. It's quite soon for one member to be saying so definitely, "Don't let's have any more strangers".

Dr. S. There are other people who could join you now, are there?

Doctor Q. Well, one could do this trawling, which I hate. There are G.P.s who have rung up and said they want to come; but when you go into it, they are not prepared to do anything and want it at their convenience.

Dr. Main How did these doctors get to know about this group?

Doctor Q. We did a day symposium. Yes, they were trawled for and we got a very mixed bag.

Dr. Main If they are trawled for, they are people who are not very keen.

Doctor Q. This is what I sensed at the beginning, and this was my anxiety.

Dr. Main　Keen leaders are not enough.

Doctor Q.　I don't know that I was keen, but I felt there was a need; but I wanted *them* to spell out the need, not me go fishing for it. I think this is what has annoyed me.

Dr. Main　Yes. It's better to have five who are keen than twenty-five who are not.

Doctor Q.　Yes, I think this is what I'm learning by coming up to this Workshop: that I'm not having very different problems from other people.

Dr. P.　My group has got very small now, but it's survived virtually to the end.

Dr. A.　Yes, our group went from twelve down to six, but it didn't happen suddenly. People moved house, went abroad, got pregnant, or that sort of thing; but it's still a good discussion group.

Dr. Main　My own feeling is that we worry too much about these things. The magical number, of course, is eight. It's the ideal number for discussion.

Doctor Q.　We only had three the last time. But in fact I thought we worked extremely well, at which I was surprised: not just cosy chat.

Dr. Main　Could we hear another aspect of this? Maybe I've talked nonsense in the past about numbers, but one thing I'm sure about is that if eight pay a certain sum of money, it will pay better than five paying the same sort of money.

Dr. C.　Ours don't pay.

Dr. Main　Oh? — Who's got the motive?

Doctor Q.　These particular five are extremely motivated. In fact one of them, who joined late, said, "I'm so glad I managed to get in. I hope I'm not too late, but I couldn't bear to wait two years before the next one".

Dr. H.　Don't you think the doctor who said, "I like the group as it is" might be anxious about the group folding up, rather than you getting extra people in?

Dr. Main　You think it might be?

Dr. H.　Mmm.

Dr. N. You started off by saying you selected them very carefully on the grounds which Dr. Main had pointed out, and a fat lot of good it seems to have done you! What are these wonderful grounds? Perhaps we ought to look at those. How did you select these people?

Doctor Q. I didn't select them. I tried to select the ones who were sent to me on a list. I tried to talk to them individually and explain how we worked for two years, so that there were no illusions that they would be taught. Several were from different cultural backgrounds where there is an expectation that on courses you are taught things. In fact, four of them fell out straight away. Then I tried to select them again at the beginning of this term by saying, "Look, do you really want to continue? It is important, this commitment" — because I think it is important for them to make up their minds what they want.

Dr. N. That wasn't selecting them again, was it?

Doctor Q. I was trying to say, "If you want to drop out now, I would rather know now than later". . . make it easy for them. Because it is two-way, isn't it?

Dr. Tunnadine That's where I really begin to start wondering about things. Who do you think it was who was most anxious about whether they were committed or not at that particular moment? The leader felt she had to go and test them again. I don't think after one term most people would *know*, actually.

Dr. Main I would go easy about this other thing, too: that they should be in for two years. They are not. They can have whatever time they like; and how long it goes on will depend on *them*, rather than on the leader's decision. I don't mind my criteria being used. I'll tell you what they are: 1. They should know what they are in *for*; and 2. They should be working in the field.

Dr. Tunnadine And "they should be sane", you used to add! *(Laughter).*

Dr. Main I have given that one up!

Dr. Tunnadine I think that's right, in a way. We do agree that their personal problems are not the concern of the group.

Dr. Main If the leader has any doubts, my suggestion is that he says, "Come in and we'll discuss it after three months".

Dr. K. It seems to have been the letter from this G.P. which was the kind of crunch for you.

Doctor Q.   Well, *I'd* had to make a commitment and I didn't think it was unreasonable to expect colleagues to make a commitment.

Dr. P.   But they don't know at the end of one term really. I think it's very early to say, "Now you say you're to come for two years — or else". They don't really have a clue.

Doctor Q.   Not quite "or else".

Dr. N.   I think the fact that they were there the second term — they knew enough to know that they wanted to be there a second term — you've got to take it from there, haven't you?

Dr. Tunnadine   We're attacking Dr. Q. for this now and I think it's because she's got anxious about it.

Dr. Main   My guess is another one: there are some people who she *didn't want* to attend!

Dr. S.   But she did want this particular G.P. who dropped out. That's the upsetting thing, isn't it?

Doctor Q.   I think so; because the last time he was there, he had the most insight of all of them.

Dr. Main   So you wanted *him*. But what about the others?

Doctor Q.   Some of the others were very good, too.

Dr. Main   Which ones are you trying to push out?

Doctor Q.   I'm not really trying to push any of them out.

Dr. Tunnadine   But were you at the beginning of the term? is what we're saying.

Doctor Q.   Perhaps I'm a person who likes to know what my commitments are; and if I'm going to make an effort and go, at rather personal inconvenience to me, that they should come or feel sufficiently about it to let me know if they can't come.

Dr. S.   Can we understand why he opted out? We always feel that when they drop out it isn't for work. If they want to come they'll re-arrange their work.

Doctor Q.   As a trainee, his work commitments had been changed, which could mean anything.

Dr. S.   What do you really think? Why do you think he dropped out?

Doctor Q.   I don't really know, but I do think he's quite good.

He had been attacked in the group before, but he could stand up to it and didn't seem to be upset by it. — It might be a genuine reason. He didn't say what his work commitment was.

Dr. A. Has he had to go back into hospital as part of his training?

Doctor Q. Another trainee has dropped out for that — because he's moved his hospital — and wants to come back next year, when he's doing his G.P. part of his training.

Dr. Tunnadine So you're not in fact anxious that you let them bash him too hard. You're more anxious about being mucked about yourself.

Doctor Q. I suppose that's really it.

Dr. Tunnadine I don't know. I just wondered. . . You did just slip in that he was bashed the time before.

Doctor Q. The remaining members though, although very few, are working well. I was encouraged when I read this report and felt that perhaps it is worth going on for five or six keen members.

Dr. Tunnadine Dr. Main isn't going to say it, so I will: so what are you going to do about it, and what about letting the group take care of it? That's the next standard answer. How about them taking care of it? One of them messed it up for you: he said, "No". But he's only one out of six.

Dr. P. Did he actually say that to you *in the group*?

Doctor Q. He wrote a letter.

Dr. P. The chap who said he didn't want any more people joining the group?

Doctor Q. Oh, he just dropped it out as we were getting up to go: "By the way — ", or something like that, " — You did talk about whether we would agree to new members". I had asked them, if there were any new members, would they be happy for them to join, or not?

Dr. P. The other thing to do would be to take this back to the group and say, "It's a workable group at the moment with only five or six, *but* in the next few terms one or two may have to drop out, and it wouldn't be workable". This is the practical side of it, isn't it? "How do you feel about it?" — and let them. . . He might be the minority in the group. It would be easier to have one or two people in now than it would be at the end of the first year.

Dr. Main   The resignation letter is also really group property, because he resigned from the group, not from you. The private relation between you and this doctor does exist, but then, the relation of the group does too. I would have thought it was for the group to accept his resignation.

Doctor Q.   I do mean to bring it up, saying that this doctor has written saying he can't. . .

Dr. Main   Read the letter out. Let them respond which ever way they want to. It's a group event, it seems to me. I would like to come back to this other thing, which Dr. H. raised, about the man who said he didn't want any more people in, he liked the group as it was. I would just like to point out one thing about group dynamics: that a group is a group is a group; and it doesn't like any change — anyone leaving, anyone coming in. Groups do not like breaking up; they refuse to die; you can't kill them easily. It's very important that you see that they hate you if you stop; they hate you if you change things from once a fortnight to once a week — if *you* change it — they don't like people coming in and they don't like people leaving. People coming in will mean, "It's not our group any more" and it's the truth. They will start again with another person, and it will be a different group to the one they were accustomed to. So this is ordinary resistance to change, I would have thought. It shouldn't, however, deter the leader of the group from having keen recruits. They have rights as well. This must be discussed with the group. I know groups love this cosiness, but people need training. You can justify this. The main thing is resistance to change. I worry about that clinically, and what light that throws on his doctoring skills.

Dr. Tunnadine   The snag about the idea of getting the group to do the recruiting — which very often works very well — is that those who want to stay go out and bring in all kinds of rabble, don't they? *(General agreement).*

Dr. Main   Not very successful.

Dr. Tunnadine   No, on the whole. I rather like her asking permission as to whether she could have other people in, or not. It's five-to-one in favour.

Dr. N.   He made this remark at the very end — a going-out-of-the-surgery remark.

Dr. Tunnadine Absolutely, and the other five didn't, as far as I can see; and we don't know that that means.

Doctor Q. I suppose I should have sat down again and said, "Let's talk about it". But I think I'd had enough by then!

Dr. Tunnadine This is always the trouble with starting a new group. Do you wait until there are enough who will jolly well come to you, banging on the door; who will travel to Putney from Northern Ireland; or do you make the best of what you've got? I still don't think there's an answer to that, because in theory we would all wish to wait until there are enough. But then there is always the problem of what do you do with the four keen ones?

Dr. Main But should you recruit people who are not keen?

Dr. Tunnadine It's not so much a matter of recruiting as a matter of, you've got four who weren't recruited who are keen. How long do you delay them by saying, "I'm sorry, until I've got twelve who are keen, who will travel all the way to see me, you can't start".

Doctor Q. I suppose to put it back to the group that they're prepared to accept the pressure of only being small numbers and having to work perhaps twice as hard in bringing cases. . .

Dr. P. I don't think you'll find that they will mind being a small group.

Dr. N. Have they got enough work?

Doctor Q. One of them had loads of cases.

Dr. K. I just feel I want to make reassuring noises, as being a chronic small-groupie, that out of the other end of this chronic dilemma will come quite a few members of the Institute.

B. LEADERSHIP TECHNIQUE

After a short introduction taken from Dr. Main's Weekend talk, this chapter starts with digests which are primarily concerned with some common technical problems for the leader. How to move the doctors from talking about patients, problems and diagnoses to the more useful doctor/patient transaction? How fast can you go? How active should the leader be?

Some of the defences that have already been discussed, such as the historical defence and generalisations, are met again here. The focus of the chapter then shifts on to the leaders themselves, their individual styles of leadership and their reactions to particular group situations.

1. THE WORK TASK.

2. LEADING AN EARLY GROUP.

3. THE DOCTOR/PATIENT RELATIONSHIP: HOW SOON?

4. WHAT SORT OF LEADER? (i) & (ii).

5. THE LEADER AS MODEL.

6. THE ANXIOUS LEADER.

7. THE LEADER MUST NOT BE TOO CLEVER.

8. THE LEADER WHO *WAS* TOO CLEVER.

Leadership Technique

Extract from Weekend talk

Dr. Main   The transition from being a good clinical doctor to being a leader is never easy. Certain doctors who are extremely able at clinical work would never make leaders; similarly there are a few good leaders on whom I would not put much money as clinicians. We need to see the two tasks, treating a patient and leading a seminar, as different, distinct and requiring different skills. Although it is useful to have both, it is not the case that the two skills automatically go together. The leader who is essentially a keen clinician may be tempted to solve the patient's problem for the reporting doctor; that is certainly *not* the job of a leader.

Let us consider what will happen if he does. The presenting doctor will have the solution taken out of his hands and will not return to his patient with his own thought-through ideas, but with the ideas of the leader. Such a leader, concerned to listen to the patient's problem, will "train" the doctor to be increasingly dependent on *his* thinking. He is liable to produce a group of doctors who use the seminar not for the development of thoughtful personal skill, but dependently, as a source of consultative help in their daily lives; of other people's "good ideas", to be taken back and tried out. A group led in this way is not a source of provocation to the members' own thinking, where they may learn something of their own blind spots and of their own clinical assets which they should value, and of their liabilities which they should review. Thus a "case-solving" leader, listening to and thinking about patients' problems, inhibits the doctors' opportunity to review their own techniques; their own part in the doctor/patient transaction.

Doctors entering training for the first time, accustomed to the medical model of receptivity to authoritative instruction, expect such of their leader. There are various techniques for a leader to help a group out of their own wishes to be taught in dependent ways.

I am liable, if I hear too much about a patient rather than the doctor/patient interaction or the doctor's part in this, to yawn loudly; thus to indicate that I am not interested. I am interested in the group's case work behaviour; not in the case material, but in the clinical interventions. There are many such techniques; each leader must grow his own.

1. The work task

Leader Doctor V.

The case was of a woman who complained she wasn't interested in sex, who then went on to explain at length about her husband. He had a back injury and had not been able to work for years.

Doctor V.   The doctor gave this historical type of presentation, giving a lot of information that she'd obtained before and I interrupted her, because we weren't going to have time, and asked her if she could tell us actually how she felt when she was with the patient on this last occasion.

Dr. Main   Hang on a second! — Isn't that interesting?

Dr. F.   It sounds so easy!

Dr. Main   Your patient flooded the doctor with information and this doctor flooded *you* with information — and Dr. V. dealt with it in that way. . .

Doctor V.   Well, you know how bossy I am!

Dr. Main   You made an observation. There was no thinking, just facts, and you were going to waste time.

Doctor V.   Yes. A lot of other people all wanted to present their cases and we'd got to get through them fairly quickly; so there was pressure from the group as well, and I was expressing this. . .
— The doctor then went on to describe the patient's appearance. I thought, "Oh God!" and I said, "How did she make you feel?" She then said, "I just listened to her. She didn't make me feel anything".

Dr. Main   Same problem.

Doctor V. The group then asked if she had any children, and when told she had a daughter of seventeen they were very surprised, having got the impression that she was much younger. After some more general discussion someone said, "Do you think she could be menopausal?" This doctor is a gynaecologist, but it rather stunned the group as there was no evidence for this. It led to another general discussion about the menopause. Again I got fed up and said, "I don't think this discussion is helping us with this particular patient". I felt very directive and really shut them up. — Shall I stop there?

Dr. Main Yes, very good. What do people think?

Dr. S. It's as if they weren't producing thoughtful remarks and, instead of letting them struggle on and perhaps eventually directing them how to think, you said: "You are not doing it, so stop altogether!" *(Laughter)*

Doctor V. Yes, I felt guilty that I had cut them off before they had time to work out that they weren't doing any work. I was thinking afterwards of alternative ways I could have got them back.

Dr. F. You didn't just cut them off. You had done quite a lot of trying to get them back to something more realistic.

Dr. Tunnadine Yes, but failing. . . — I like your style. You had a couple of good goes. The next thing is: since it failed, what next? What's the thing about paying tribute to the defences? How to find out why they won't do what you want? It seems to me you did the right things, but they wouldn't play.

Dr. Main If you take W as being the work task, you set the group a work task and of course, who the hell likes work? The group erects all sorts of defences against W, the work task. The evasion of the work task occurs whenever the work runs into an anxiety area; and then you get defences. The defences here were fairly clear, weren't they? — There were evasive topics like 'Is she menopausal?' and 'How old is she?', all this getting away from the work task which you set quite clearly: the discussion of the clinical events or, if you'd rather, the discussion of the doctor/patient relation. That is the work task and any dodging of that you can notice with interest. But you also have to wonder *why* they are dodging. What is the anxiety they have run into which leads to this dodging? What is their difficulty? — I don't

H

know what their difficulty was. The presenting doctor was how old?

Doctor V.   Twenty-eight.

Dr. Main   Is she married? Does she have children?

Doctor V.   I've no idea.

Dr. Main   She is dealing with an older woman with sexual problems. It is not necessarily very easy for her; strange territory. The patient is a woman with a 17-year-old daughter. I don't know what it was, but the doctor would have her own anxieties. You didn't spot them. You noticed that she was keeping away from the event by taking refuge in a defensively long history.

Dr. J.   Actually the group did spot it a bit because there was all this business about, 'As old as that? I thought she must be younger'. They were vaguely aware of the age discrepancy. They didn't say it, but there was something going on.

Dr. Main   The point I am making is that the doctor gave a defensive account. Never got down to what the patient was like. Never got down to what she did with the patient.

Dr. Tunnadine   The leader had several goes. First she said, what it was like being with her. She gave a description of her. Then the leader had another go at what did it *feel* like; and the answer was something like 'nothing'.

Doctor V.   She said, "I just listened".

Dr. Main   I think you might have got the group to discuss, "Why do you think the doctor just listened?"

Dr. Tunnadine   That might have been a point, mightn't it?

Dr. Main   Somehow keep the group on the work task. When they start talking about things like how old she is, you could let it run for a bit and hope they will discover that it is useless. That is one way: to let them learn for themselves. You have to let it run for quite a time before an interruption by anyone would be acceptable. It is a defence and you have to let it run before you have the evidence to make a comment: 'I notice everyone is talking about the woman's age as if it was important' — that sort of remark invites them to have a go. But if they are very frightened they will run away and find another defence. Then you have to say, "What is it about this patient which makes it so difficult for us to discuss what went on between the doctor and the patient?" — Keep on thinking about what they are doing.

Dr. F.   You don't think the difficulty with the work task was that there were so many of them wanting to present cases?

Doctor V.   This group has been very active. They have all tended to bring a case every time.

Dr. F.   That could be a defence itself against doing any work.

Dr. E.   It could be what the leader expects of them. I didn't feel terribly comfortable listening to you talking about this group in action. Maybe you presented it differently from how it was, but they didn't sound as though they were allowed to run on for very long before they got whopped.

Doctor V.   I felt like that. That was what I was uneasy about. I did feel as though I kept on cracking the whip.

Dr. E.   What you were intending to do didn't come out quite right, did it?

Doctor V.   No. I got very dissatisfied with it.

Dr. P.   Can I ask how many G.P. trainees you have got in the group?

Doctor V.   Three.

Dr. P.   I wonder if it is difficult for you to value their work as independent doctors who have come to try to increase their skills rather than come to be taught. You have trainees yourself, don't you, in the practice, and I think it must be quite difficult to make this change in approach. The other thing I noticed was that they were in a terrible muddle about the patient's feelings. It sounded to me as though this woman's had a ghastly time. She's had to give up everything to look after some invalid husband who hasn't worked for years. It sounded quite horrific, really: it didn't sound at all adolescent that she might want a life of her own.

Dr. Main   The group is attempting to classify, aren't they? But they weren't discussing what went on. It was guessing.

Dr. F.   It was very much guessing. It swung from one to another, from adolescence to the menopause.

Doctor V.   It's almost as though they were plucking ideas out of the air.

Dr. Tunnadine   I think the group couldn't discuss it because, despite the leader's efforts to bully the doctor to tell you about it, the doctor is not capable of doing that. She was not capable of answering the question. They were on to the fact that this woman had been presented as younger than she was. They got completely lost in it, but it was quite an important clinical finding actually; and to get from that, which might have been useful, to theories about adolescence, or was she in fact a menopausal adolescent, was a pity. Something got lost which might have been useful.

Doctor V.   That's right. I felt very much I had just cut them off because I personally had got fed up with trying to get back all the time to what had happened between this patient and this doctor.

Dr. Main   You did say, "Let's go back to what happened between this doctor and this patient?" and then somebody said, "Do you think she is menopausal?" — this defensive thing. You might have picked this up and said, "Isn't it interesting how difficult it seems to be to get back to what went on? We have general discussions about the menopause, which is a safe general topic. What about the doctor and the patient? Isn't it difficult to talk about it? I wonder what the difficulty is. Let's hear some more". — Do you see what I mean? It's a demonstration of how difficult it is for them to discuss this because it is a hell of a change for them all to stop talking about patients and problems and diagnoses and cases and start talking about doctor/patient transactions. You are asking an awful lot that they should pick this up at once. Go on keeping at it and pointing out every time there is a deviation.

Dr. F.   I can't help feeling, though, that part of the leader's difficulty was all these extra presentations awaiting, as it were.

Dr. Tunnadine   I think it was, but I noticed Dr. V. turn over a page or two before she elected to present this case. That is to say —

Doctor V.   It wasn't the first one.

Dr. F.   Oh, I thought it *was* the first and you knew you'd got five more to go.

Doctor V.   No, this was getting towards the end. This was the third one we did, in fact.

Dr. P.   So you have picked this one out because you felt in particular difficulty with it.

Doctor V.   Yes.

Dr. Main She wants us to tick her off for having been impatient! But you are already doing that yourself.

Doctor V. I felt there must have been some other way that it could have been dealt with.

Dr. Main Sure.

Dr. Tunnadine You gave one way, Dr. Main, which is to say, "Isn't it difficult for us", but there are others, aren't there? Everyone has got their own style.

Dr. Main Another is saying, "Isn't it difficult for the doctor to report? We haven't heard anything about what the doctor did".

Dr. Tunnadine Yes, that's another way. Getting rougher. . .

Dr. Main No, it's *difficult* for the doctor to tell us. She's not very proud of it, or something. That doctor didn't reveal herself at all to the group, did she? It's worth pointing out.

Dr. F. I think it's very interesting how you did try and keep such tight control of it and interjected so frequently. Maybe it would have been more helpful to have let them run for longer; maybe they would have come back themselves. It was almost as though, when you pointed this out to them, in defiance they kept swinging back again, as if the dynamics were between you and them, that they weren't going to have it somehow; more than the difficulty of the work. Something like, 'We are not going to be organised in this way. . .'

Dr. Main I got the impression — and it is an impression — that the doctor wouldn't let them go on with it.

Doctor V. But the whole group did that as well, not just the presenting doctor.

Dr. Main I know. That is why I suggest something to draw the group's attention to the fact that here is a discussion about a patient which is a pack of lies. You can then start discussing the doctor's transactions.

Dr. F. But you did try, and you asked her what her reactions were; and she said she didn't feel anything at all, she just listened.

Dr. Main I wouldn't be bothered about that. Say — "What did you do?"

Dr. Tunnadine One suspects, of course, that all she did do was listen, since she was absolutely at sea.

Dr. Main   She doesn't know what to do, really.

Dr. Tunnadine   It isn't an easy case: the woman bursting out with loss of libido and then going to grouse about the husband. It's not the easiest thing. None of us much enjoy these, do we? How to get the group to discuss it is another matter, when they won't do as they are told. I would have thought, at this stage, the effect the patient had on the doctor with her complainingness or something might have been another way: "What has the patient done to the doctor?"

Dr. Main   'I liked the patient', or 'I didn't like the patient'. . . — What you are really asking is —

Dr. Tunnadine   — 'What did the patient do to you?' It is just a different emphasis, isn't it? Gentler. You all say hypocritical, but I think it is gentler for beginners because it's not quite such a personal attack.

Dr. Main   In a way the doctor's feelings are irrelevant. What does matter is, what were the doctor's responses? What was the doctor doing? If you say "What are the doctor's feelings?", it sounds as though you are putting the doctor on the spot.

Dr. Tunnadine   'What did the patient make you feel?' one could say, perhaps.

Dr. Main   And this doctor is very much up a gum tree, or frightened, or something. Of course, you have got all these other people helping the doctor fly away from the clinical events as well.

2. Leading an early group

Leader Doctor A.

The leader described a very early meeting of a new group. Four cases were presented.

The first case was of a man who came to a doctor's surgery complaining of spots on his penis. When the doctor examined him he could see nothing, but he gave the patient a course of antibiotics.

At the next visit the patient admitted that he had been impotent for five months. The doctor tested his urine, found it contained sugar and, after treatment of the diabetes, his impotence improved.

Doctor A.   I thought, "What on earth am I going to make of this?" so they had a bit of discussion about it and how interesting it was for diabetes to be presented in this way: it was unusual to present first as impotence. They had a discussion amongst themselves, not addressing the leader or the presenting doctor as they often do. The discussion didn't seem very profitable, so I said, "Let's actually look at the first interview. What happened in the first interview?" So they discussed this a bit: what the man felt like; that he felt shy and embarrassed. They asked if the doctor was embarrassed and shy himself, but he denied it and said he wasn't a bit embarrassed. They were surprised at this, because he had said that this man was about 52 years old, about as old as his father, so that the fact that he said he wasn't embarrassed seemed a bit strange if he was regarding this man as a son to a father. They noticed that he hadn't made anything of the fact that the man said he had spots but when he looked at him he hadn't got any. So then one of the group said to him, "Why didn't you ask him, 'Is sexual intercourse all right?'", and the doctor replied, "I wouldn't have dreamed of asking that on his first interview. If I had, he would have gone off and I would never have seen him again". Other people had a different opinion and thought he could have put it, not quite so directly, but say, "I wonder if everything else is all right?" Various suggestions were made as to what he could have said to him. In a way they did look at the doctor/patient relation but the fact that it ended up not really being a psychosexual problem made it a bit of an unsuitable case.

The second case was a woman who came and said openly that for the last five months she couldn't let her husband touch her at all; she couldn't let him kiss her or come near her. When they got into bed at night, she got to one side of the bed and he got to the other side, and he knew if he dared to stretch out and touch her she would reject him, so he had just stopped reaching out now. The doctor described her as a nice-looking motherly type, youngish. The patient said something had to be done, so the doctor changed her pill.

Doctor A. The group had a discussion about this: whether it was a good thing to change pills for libido and whether it really did make any difference. One doctor said it was terribly important to bring in the husband — "You have got to see what sort of chap he is before you can really understand the situation". There were all kinds of discussions and suggestions and I just wondered how long you were supposed to keep quiet as a group leader or try to get them working. In the end I said — I am not very subtle about it — "You haven't looked at what was happening between the doctor and the patient at all, have you? What was the patient doing to the doctor? What was the doctor doing to the patient?" So they did begin to think about this and began to suggest that perhaps the patient had made the doctor feel that she had got to do something, and she certainly had done something: she'd done what the patient wanted; done something active.

After some more talk it came out that the doctor had been sort of manipulated by the patient to give advice and change pills rather than actually sit down to look at what the patient was doing and how that might perhaps have affected her relationship with her husband. So I tried to get out of them that it might be that she was manipulating the husband and liked to be in control: she seemed to be in control of the doctor/patient interview, and she was in control of her husband, not letting him have intercourse, or controlling when he could have it. I found it very difficult to know what phrases to use and how to push them to look at it further. So in the end I probably did too much telling, although I tried very hard to get them to tell me.

The doctor who presented the third case had said earlier that it was sometimes better to listen than to give advice. The case was a man who had come asking for tranquillizers because his wife had left him. The doctor had listened a bit, but had then told him to go and have it out with the man his wife had gone off with.

Doctor A. This case was discussed in all sorts of ways, but they didn't start looking at the doctor/patient relationship till I poked them a bit; and then they did see that although this doctor had been very good at making this man talk, she had also done the same thing as the doctor she had previously criticised: giving him advice and so on. I tried to get them to see that in *this* doctor/patient relationship, this man was a mild, meek sort of man. From the description he was also a down-at-heel man: his hair was scruffy and he was rather badly dressed. In the relationship he had been almost the opposite of the other patient we had, where the determined woman had come in and was determined to make the doctor do as she wanted. This man did as he was told; tried to please his wife, and perhaps that was his problem.

The last patient came for a routine examination as she was on the pill. She didn't seem to be troubled by this, but just as the doctor was finishing the girl said, "I have got a problem with sex, because I am just not interested in it now. I used to love it, but since we got married I just don't seem to be very interested. Although we have it every night, I just wish he would get on with it and finish, just get it over with so we could get to sleep". The doctor went on to explain what a tiring day the girl had now, working full-time, travelling a long way to work, and then having to cook and clean when she got in.

Dr. A. After quite a long description of this girl's life the group said, "So what did you do?" and the doctor said, "Well, I told her now that she had got married there was a lot to do, she was tired and that it would be better to come in, sit down and have your dinner, and then have a nice little rest after and put your feet up; don't take things so quickly, and they will come out right in the end. Somebody asked her how she felt about the patient and she said she felt motherly.

Dr. Main What a mother! *(Laughter)*

Doctor A. Giving good advice.

Dr. Main She could have given her a hiding. Some mothers do!

Doctor A. Mother had actually been doing everything for this girl. They had been living together for two years before marriage. They had come home from work; mother had got dinner all ready and mother had done all the housework; and they had just come in, had their dinner and gone out and had fun. So now she was really missing her mother and I suppose she was looking to the doctor, in a way, to sort things out for her as her mother sorted out her problems at home.

Dr. Main   And usually the doctor is someone she will get advice from and be dependent on; and the doctor, like an idiot, fell for it instead of interpreting.

Doctor A.   That's right. I tried to get them to say that, but I couldn't get the group to say it.

Dr. Main   Whenever I don't know what the hell to do, I give advice.

Doctor A.   Just as we were coming to the end of that case, the doctor who had given the case about the man with the spots on his penis, said, "Now, doctor, what would you have done if you had been faced with this girl and this history and you had been in this doctor's position. Just exactly what would you have done?" So I said, "You are doing exactly to me what the patient did to the doctor: trying to get advice and help out of me. That didn't help the patient at all, to get advice and help. The help was that the patient was to think for herself why she had got herself into this situation; and so you lot have got to think for yourselves and you have to work things out for yourselves. It is not my job to tell you". I don't know whether he got a bit put down by that.

Dr. Main   Well, that's quite motherly! *(Laughter)*

Doctor A.   The rest of the doctors sniggered a bit at this.

Dr. Main   I always insist on my kids standing up for themselves! *(Laughter).* That's the end of the group, is it?

Doctor A.   Yes.

Dr. Tunnadine   Very lively for a meeting of beginners. I think it's very impressive, actually.

Dr. Main   I think it is, too.

Doctor A.   I couldn't get them to do what I wanted at all. *(Laughter)*

Dr. Main   What impressed me was that the group worked. The leader refused to tackle the cases, left it to the group. And you didn't attend to the cases or the doctor: you attended to the group, which is the right thing. I am amazed that they were talking amongst themselves.

Doctor A. This is not at all what happened with my other group.

Dr. Main We are not interested in the other group! *(Laughter)*

Doctor A. But it was different.

Dr. Main You mean, groups *differ?*

Doctor A. Well, there are more men than women — maybe that's why! *(Laughter)*

Dr. Tunnadine She told us in a very loud voice that people vary. It was fascinating, really good.

Dr. Main Any comments?

Dr. S. I don't know why you felt that the first case was not a psychosexual one. This poor man thought he had spots on his penis and wasn't able to say, "I am worried about having been impotent for months". He must have had some feelings about it and they didn't come out at all.

Doctor A. Yes, they did. He was very embarrassed about being examined, that did come across; and he obviously had difficulty in saying that he was impotent and blurted it out at the second meeting. One doctor paid tribute to this doctor by saying, "You have created such an atmosphere by caring for this patient and examining him the first time you saw him that he was able to open up on his second visit".

Dr. S. Whereupon you felt it was a suitable case. I really felt it was a suitable case, but you were in a panic because you thought, "Oh dear, I've got a physical case". That's what you reported.

Doctor A. Yes, I did think that to begin with; but then I realised that at the beginning of the case there was a psychosexual event when the doctor was afraid to say, "Are you having intercourse?", or giving him a lead-in, or saying, "Is there any further problem?", having seen there were no spots at all. He must have wondered why the man had come.

Dr. I. It seemed odd that he didn't actually air that.

Dr. Main The man was complaining of spots and what did the doctor do?

Dr. I. The first time he didn't say he was impotent; he said he'd got spots, and the doctor didn't say, "You haven't got spots, so what *is* the trouble?". He said, "I will give you a prescription".

Dr. Main Yes. The second time the man complained of impotence, and what did the doctor do?

Dr. I. Tested his urine, and the man came back completely cured — I couldn't believe it.

Dr. Main Yes, but the point is, the doctor didn't discuss the anxiety about this problem.

Dr. Tunnadine And denied it.

Dr. Main The doctor was telling this group, "Look, don't listen to this psychological junk". On the other hand, the doctor is quite right: everything should be examined, including the body. It would be an inefficient doctor who didn't do this. His only failing was that he didn't examine the man's psyche, but out of anxiety, surely. The group didn't pick this up?

Doctor A. They said to the doctor, "Were you not embarrassed about this situation?" and the doctor hotly denied it. But he obviously was embarrassed or he would have said something.

Dr. Tunnadine I thought one interesting little bit, when you directed their attention to the doctor/patient relation, in the case where the mother did everything, was this crazy remark, "Feels like a mother", as though that's a bit of our folklore. I saw that doctor not as motherly, but absolutely seduced by the hearts and flowers. You can call that a mother if you like — we know her mother has filled that need before — but a mother? that's not a doctor/patient relation, is it? It's one sort; but it doesn't define it very well.

Dr. Main The idea that mothering is a good thing is very common, isn't it?

Dr. B. It's a generalisation to say she felt like a mother because all mothers are different, aren't they?

Dr. P. You kept trying to make sense of what was going on in the doctor/patient relation, and yet really there was very little material about it because we don't have much reporting. My suspicion is that the information she got from her patient she got by asking questions and being told answers. It was almost as though you were trying to make interpretations about what was going on without enough facts to make them on.

Doctor A. She talked about her as a girl and she talked about a feeling that she wanted to help her.

Dr. Tunnadine The case material was pretty clear, wasn't it? The trouble with her sex life was that she didn't feel like a girl when she was being like a mother.

Dr. Main Yes, when mother was busy doing the cooking she was all right.

Dr. Tunnadine So the doctor's response as a "mother" was quite in the wrong direction — you know, be more of a domestic lady, put your feet up. — If she'd told her to go down to the disco. . !

Dr. Main When you're not married, that's the time to have it.

Dr. Tunnadine The leader's difficulty in getting at what she wants does not seem to me to be well-founded, because I thought for a second meeting it was going like a train.

3. The doctor/patient relationship: how soon?

Leader Doctor B. (Leader Doctor K. present)

A new mixed group of doctors and nurses started with a case presented by one of the nurses who had done some previous seminar training. The patient had come to a family planning clinic for some sheaths, but had implied that they only used very few. The nurse picked this up and gave the patient an opportunity to talk about their infrequent intercourse, her general unhappiness and the fact that she was drinking a lot of alcohol.

Doctor B. The nurse's main worry was, "Is she really asking for help or am I interfering?" The group immediately began to discuss the alcohol problem and whether or not she should have liver function tests done. It was necessary for me to point out that everyone was shying away from the distress of the patient on to something safe and medical. It then became clear that the patient had also been seen by one of the doctors who was present in the group, but at the time this doctor had not felt there was anything wrong with the patient. The patient agreed to see the nurse again in three months.

The next patient was also complaining of infrequent intercourse, but there was also a long history of marital problems. The doctor had given some general advice, and had suggested she might see the husband, but he had refused to come to see her.

Doctor B. One of the experienced nurses then said, "I have learnt in these seminars that the one who is complaining is the patient". The doctor seemed to find it difficult to crystallise what the patient was complaining about. Someone asked if she knew whether the patient had ever enjoyed sex; but she didn't know. After further discussion someone suggested that the patient seemed very angry, and I thought, "Ah, perhaps we are beginning to cotton on to the fact that her anger is making her withhold any interest in sex". We discussed the confusion that this patient was making us all feel, and perhaps she herself was in a state of confusion and anger.

The last case was reported by one of the other nurses who was very anxious about a young girl who had come to the clinic distressed because she had made love for the first time without really wanting to. She was not worried about the fear of pregnancy because her boyfriend could arrange a termination if it became necessary. The nurse felt that the distress was because she had gone against everything she believed and had been brought up to believe.

Doctor B. Various people in the group found it difficult to understand that she wasn't worried about whether she wanted a termination or didn't want one, but that it was the fact of having lost her virginity that was really worrying her. The discussion went on to generalisations like "Do people really feel like that nowadays?" and "I thought many young people didn't worry about that".

Dr. Main But others do. *(Laughter)*

Doctor B. That's right. A sort of useless discussion, and I said, "Perhaps we ought to look at why she was so distressed", and I said to the nurse, "Do you think it was because she had actually enjoyed it?". The nurse said she was sure it wasn't, but it hadn't occurred to her that it might be. The nurse had said to her, "Were you actually raped?" and she said, "Well, I suppose I could have done more to stop him", or something like that.

Dr. Main   That's the end of the meeting?

Doctor B.   Yes.

Dr. Main   Let's discuss it.

Doctor B.   My feeling was that we had stumbled through as a first meeting of a group who didn't know each other when they started. I couldn't say there was much group feeling about it, but I didn't feel depressed about it.

Dr. Tunnadine   It raised the important leadership issue of how soon, if it is ever too soon, to stick to the doctor/patient or nurse/patient relationship. It was very interesting: you tried to say, "What were the nurse's feelings?" and she told you in her very first words: she felt like a meddler. It's very easy to do case-solving. I think all we are there for is to direct their interest to the nurse/patient relation or the doctor/patient relation; we're not there to do anything else at all. And yet you felt that it was somehow too soon to expect them to do that. — It's a technical thing.

Dr. Main   What happened thereafter was that there was an immediate generalisation of defences. — "One always feels this with all one's patients". Another nurse said, "It's always difficult: you feel like an intruder". There was a general rush away from the case and into the nurse's anxiety. How far it came from the patient is another matter. The patient wasn't studied then.

Dr. Tunnadine   She did say, "I can cope, thank you very much", and therefore the nurse felt an intruder. What I am meaning to say about the leader is how soon, having understood it, one should bully them about, "What are the emotional feelings?". It's never too soon, to my mind. That's all you are there to be interested in — why you felt like a meddler, for example.

Dr. Main   One of the nurses very early on used a word I liked very much indeed. I felt like adopting it in future and abolishing the other words like 'consultation'. This nurse talked about an 'encounter'. It's a marvellous word, isn't it, for a viewpoint about what happened? The nurse said this and yet later on all we hear about is bloody patients.

Dr. Tunnadine   That's right. That's what I feel.

Dr. Main   Not encounters. . .

Dr. I.   Aren't some of the generalisations a bit of reassurance amongst themselves; saying 'This is our first time and let's be general for a bit?'

Dr. Main   Yes, it's a defence and let's not just tear defences down. Unless the anxiety is tackled you have no right to tear the defence away.

Dr. I.   No, perhaps one should let it ride.

Dr. Main   No, I don't think let it ride; but find out why they are doing it. This woman brought up a difficult topic: the intrusion. All this generalisation stuff dodges the issue: what was going on between that nurse and that patient?

Dr. Tunnadine   Obviously she had made the nurse feel like an intruder. Obviously she's an experienced nurse and really it was a marvellous case for the first case in a group. This nurse actually presenting her difficulty with the patient, rather than just the patient: a pretty unusual start to a first group, by somebody who knows that is what you are there for. And yet somehow this group felt that it's too early to have all this Balint stuff, or something.

Dr. Main   *(Ironically)* It's pretty obvious that this patient was very keen to come and see this nurse, isn't it? She said it, didn't she? So you've got a clue about what is going on between her and her boyfriend — she backs away from any intimacy. There was an interesting point in the discussion about whether the girl herself had anything to do with the rarity of the intercourse.

Doctor B.   The difficulty was to keep on bringing them back to the point. I felt I was going to talk too much and I was hoping someone in the group might say that.

Dr. Tunnadine   Some awful people like me who talk too much, and Dr. N. here, declare their terms early, lay down the ground rules and say, "We are here to talk about the nurse/patient relationship". I'm not saying one way is right and one wrong.

Dr. Main   There is a very big problem here, which is the *pace*. How fast should one be? It differs, of course, between one individual and another, and between one group and another, but

I know that some leaders are very impatient to get the group on and doing better: "Good God, after two terms they don't know so and so!" Not all groups can go fast and not all groups who do go fast necessarily do the thinking. Let's take an imaginary doctor who has got dyed-in-the-wool habits of consultation and finds it very difficult to part with these. . . — it will take months and months. This is the kind of doctor you tend to bash at and the end result is a bashed-at doctor, who either vomits the lot and leaves the group, or 'I wish I was like you' and doesn't learn anything from it. Instead of thinking it out for himself he is well-taught, and that is a terrible thing to be. It's very difficult and people differ an awful lot — the slow movers that I have got drive me up the wall. They almost conspire together to hold the rest of the group back. It's very difficult when you have a group like that and we should think of groups as slow-moving or fast-moving and get people in the right sort of group. God help the leader who wants them to "do well!"

Dr. Q.   I thought your group went well. I thought you did do the right things, but you are obviously unhappy.

Doctor B.   I felt fairly neutral. I thought, "It's an interesting group" and felt hopeful to the point that I thought it would be interesting to see how it went next time. I wasn't depressed about it, but dissatisfied with how I had handled it, yes.

Dr. Main   As I heard it, they were discussing the problems out there and weren't discussing what happened between the doctor and the patient.

Dr. Q.   That's bound to happen, isn't it, in the first group? It's terrifying to open your mouth and gradually you work towards it.

Dr. E.   The nurses had to struggle a bit even though they had had more experience. They seemed to do a lot of reassuring.

Doctor B.   I didn't notice any difficulty between the doctors and nurses in the group, actually.

Dr. P.   This is what I missed. You've got experienced nurses, totally inexperienced doctors, and there must have been some feelings about this. But nothing came over at all.

Dr. Q.   Well, the nurse picked up one problem where the doctor hadn't.

Dr. Q.   And yet we didn't get any feeling of this in the group.

Doctor B.   I didn't detect any doctor/nurse type feeling.

Dr. E.   The nurse kept asking if it was all right in the meddling bit. I know that was also how the patient was making her feel, but I wondered if *she* was saying to the group, "Is it all right? Can I do this?"

Doctor B.   I got the feeling she would have done just the same if it had been an all-nurses group.

Dr. J.   How did you discover that this patient had been seen by two members of the same group?

Doctor B.   The nurse said so. She said, "She had been into you, hadn't she?" to the doctor; and *she* said, "Yes, I didn't realise there was anything wrong". . .something like that.

Dr. J.   As much as to say, 'It's all right; you weren't meddling with my patient. As far as I'm concerned, it's all right'.

Doctor B.   No, a bit more as though the nurse had ferreted something out that wasn't really very much in need of being looked at.

Dr. Tunnadine   In other words, she said, "Yes, you *are* meddling; which interpreted means, 'Yes, I can't stand that you are better at this work'. She was, and bringing a case of a doctor she knew was going to be there — and saying so, bless her heart!

Doctor B.   I don't know if she knew she was going to be there.

Dr. Tunnadine   Oh, I see. She reported it just the same.

Dr. Main   I think she got on very well. She was saying to the doctor, "You missed that case, didn't you?"

Dr. Tunnadine   That's right. I think she was saying that and she was perfectly entitled to.

Mrs. R.   "And I am going to work alongside you. . ."

Dr. I.   Did the doctors know that they were all green at it, whereas the nurses were experienced?

Doctor B.   No, perhaps the doctors didn't all realise it.

Dr. S.   I thought you said they introduced themselves.

Doctor B.   Yes, when we were introducing ourselves we said if we had been in a seminar before.

Dr. P.   It is interesting that she chooses a case which shows that she had experience.

Dr. Tunnadine   It doesn't sound to me as if it was too much of a problem in this group, the nurse/doctor bit. But I would have been more anxious about their flying away and not looking at the doctor/ or nurse/patient relation yet. It puts the leader in the position of being tempted to case-solve, doesn't it?

Dr. Main   Yes, the jigsaw-puzzling of the case.

Dr. Tunnadine   We all do it. It's very difficult not to, so early in the group.

Doctor B.   I think I said at one time, "What's going on?" or something like that, and there was a long hush.

Dr. Main   So there should be.

Doctor B.   Yes, but I don't think it was what was going on that broke the hush. It was again about something else.

Dr. K.   There was quite a long discussion about how to create the atmosphere where people could talk to you, that was a sort of general . . .

Dr. Tunnadine   To say, "What's going on?" — is that helpful?

Dr. Main   A very important general topic!

Dr. Tunnadine   Seriously, it's as though we've all got this cult in this room that to be quiet is good — and God knows, I am not a very good example of that — but "What is going on?". . . — how can anyone who has come to a first group know what you mean? I think some sort of Dr. N. remark like, "Why did this patient make this nurse feel like that?" at least puts them on the track of what you are on about, doesn't it? You always go on about this, Dr. N., you are letting me down today.

Dr. N.   I am practising being quiet today; it's a new term resolution. *(Laughter)* There are two things in these new groups which occur to me as I have listened today. We've been worrying about pace, as if sometimes things are too advanced for the group to talk about. But you may never get an opportunity to talk about a case like that again; and I think you can increase the group's knowledge by actually talking about the things that they produce. The other thing is, we are so dyed-in-the-wool, all of us lot; we have been doing it for so long we have forgotten what it is really like to be a new member. We're all talking a different language and mustn't expect them to pick this up straight away. After all, they've had, some of these doctors, fifteen years or certainly ten years of medical-type training. They come in to show off, don't they, with their histories and diagnoses?

Mrs. R. And the older doctors have got more to get rid of before they can assimilate something of what you're trying to do.

Dr. Main But you can query the technique. For instance, the doctor who asks questions could be asked, "How did your questions go? Was it useful?" This can start him thinking about his technique without telling him, "That's wrong, this is right". Get him to think about it. It's the doctor's technique we are concerned with, not the cases.

Doctor B. We did do a bit of that when the doctor had been kept off finding out anything about sex. I said something like, "You are asking questions and only getting answers which are not true answers, she is so defended about it". I think it was Dr. K. who said, "Perhaps you could say to her, 'You seem to find this a difficult area to talk about', instead of questioning her".

Dr. Main You can cover the same point by saying, "This patient seemed to have difficulty in talking about sex" and the doctor will say, "Yes". You could then say, "What about discussing that with the patient?" That is, they find it under their noses. The question is whether they use it or not.

Dr. N. Basically I think the leader's job is to give a lead to these people, not to sit back and expect it all to drop out of heaven.

4. What sort of leader? (i)

Further extract from Weekend talk

Dr. Main The leader/group relation and the conduct of the leader make all the difference in those areas of the mind where training is occurring. The kind of phenomena disturbing the leader/group relation are things like dependency, or the leader may have favourites, or they may be striving for favouritism with him. The members may be subservient, showing slavish submission and adoration and idealisation. Dr. Tunnadine has written about the hostess reaction: the leader's anxiety to look after the members, or wanting to be popular; the leader as an oracle. The leader as a policewoman is another thing which groups sometimes push the leader into; the unwanted leader; competition with the leader; and of course the group's need to be taught by the leader and the leader's need to know everything and be the expert. These are all disturbances.

What is a leader anyway? It's someone who is very sophisticated about group power and who has some idea what the work task is; someone who works with his colleagues and points out deviation from the work task. He may not be much of a doctor himself, but he can see where people go wrong; can suggest, "What about trying this?", and then the individual can go on practising and improving his own technique and developing his own style. There's something in that position like a kind of paid coach. Remember, a coach is an employee and has to be paid; not a boss, but a kind of expert; so it's a funny sort of relationship. The coach usually respects the boss, who is, say, a golfer who is trying to get some information, trying to get some skill and better technique into his golf swing; and he is respected by the coach.

The leader can make a big difference to the whole culture of the group by how far he really does respect the doctors, how far he is really interested in them, or alternatively how far he wants to be a kind of parent or mother to the group. Many of us feel protective towards the group: when you come to think of the savagery inside the group, perhaps this is not surprising. On the other hand, the coach, if he's any good, should be honest — that is not just to say, "That's a very nice swing" when he knows damn well it isn't a very nice swing. He should be quite concerned to tell the whole truth. Neither is it good enough just to say, "What a terrible golf swing!": you've got to be concerned about why the swing is bad, and to say, "Why not try so and so?". You get a small improvement and the details of the improvement occur later. It's a matter of time and I think you're all aware of this and make some attempt at doing it. However, the golf coach doesn't ask the man anything about his private life; isn't concerned about whether the man is ill-tempered or nice; only concerned with the one business — what his golf swing is like.

That is to say, the leader protects the reporting doctor from intrusions into his privacy by the group, watching the group report the relationship and getting the group to discuss the doctoring and not the person. He is tactful about those private things, doesn't approach them, but is not in any way tactful about professional behaviour. He must be honest about that: not nasty, but mercilessly honest.

The other thing a good coach does is when the trainee does make a good golf swing, he points that out and says, "That's excellent!" — that is, he pays tribute to the good things and isn't only looking for the errors.

What sort of leader? (ii)

Leader Doctor N.

A group was at the end of the first year of training and a doctor presented a patient who had not been able to consummate her marriage. She was described as looking very young, with her hair in plaits. They had a disastrous honeymoon in the Isle of Man and she had been seasick, so they couldn't consummate their marriage then. They had now lived in their own house for six months, but went to her mother for supper every night of the week except on Fridays when they went to the cinema. At the weekend they stayed with one or other set of parents.

When the doctor first discussed this patient in the group it was pointed out that she had not done a vaginal examination. So next time she did examine her and found to her surprise that it was quite easy, although she felt the patient had not got much insight into her problem from the examination. However, the next week the husband came in to thank the doctor and say that they could now have intercourse easily.

Doctor N. The main discussion in the group was about whether we should expect patients to be grateful or whether it is in fact better that they own it for themselves and chuck the doctor out.

Dr. A. Did you have to intervene a lot to keep the group discussing?

Doctor N. No.

Dr. A. They discussed with each other?

Doctor N. Yes. The only thing I can remember bringing in was this bit about gratitude of patients and how important it is that one does in fact break off this — whatever word you care to use — transference, or relationship — when they leave. They should stand on their own feet and the doctor should not expect gratitude. We digressed from the case to talk about general principles, in a way.

Dr. Q. We don't really know what that girl felt about her consummation.

Doctor N. No.

Dr. Q. Outwardly she had grown up and become a woman, but there was no indication of what that meant.

Doctor N. Not really.

Dr. Q. And yet the *husband* came along — because he hadn't been a part of it at all, had he?

Doctor N. He came along with her to the first interview to complain of non-consummation.

Dr. Main It doesn't matter — we are not here to discuss cases.

Dr. Q. No, but I was interested to know what was going on between the doctor and the patient. At the time of the examination nothing came out, apparently.

Dr. Main I am bringing it back to the purpose of this Workshop. You could be saying, "Funny thing this group didn't discuss this or take this point up" — it would then become a discussion of what we are met here for: not to discuss patients but to discuss *groups* and particularly the leadership of them. You were really making an observation that this group was not taking this matter up. It tells us what? — something about the level of sophistication of the group.

Dr. Q. I don't know. It seems to be all glossed over.

Dr. Main You think the group leader should have drawn attention to that?

Dr. I. How far should the group leader be making suggestions?

Doctor N. I said to the group that we really had to acknowledge the doctor's success, but we weren't going to give her 100% because we don't understand what has happened. We discussed the fact that we didn't get any understanding because this patient didn't give any feedback at all. The doctor had left the seminar armed with this bit about doing a vaginal examination. She confessed this, and one could see this becoming the hierarchical vaginal examination, part of Institute policy — which I think we have all tried to get away from.

Dr. I. But the group didn't seem to pick up the fact that she was doing it because she felt she *ought* to be doing it rather than because it seemed to be the right time to do it with that particular patient.

Dr. Q. I wonder if it had anything to do with the outcome anyway.

Dr. Y. The husband seems to have got the message at least.

Dr. Main Dr. N. has given us an example of his technique when he drew the group's attention to the fact that the doctor should be congratulated because of the relative success of this treatment, but they couldn't give 100% because we didn't know what the woman had experienced. The leader did that. The leader was quite right to draw attention to that, but was it a good technique to do it that way, or are there any other techniques that occur to anyone here?

Dr. I. I suppose one could ask the group what they felt about the doctor's ability.

Dr. Main Mmm. Or that no-one has discussed this other thing and have people got any ideas about it? — throw it to the group. My guess is that the group had some vague awareness of what the leader was saying. There was a lack of utter conviction about the case. The group must have felt it.

Dr. I. I suppose really one should try and get the group to say this rather than say it yourself.

Dr. Main Or draw attention to the problem.

Dr. S. That was a difficult moment, wasn't it? The group didn't know why it worked and so it's uncomfortable for them. Maybe the leader could have kept them there.

Dr. Main   Dr. N. reported that they discussed that quite a lot.

Mrs. R.   The leader rather shut them up by saying, "We haven't understood this", and moved on to the next case.

Doctor N.   No, not quite like that. I said, "Can we understand why?" and the outcome of that was that we didn't understand why; but we tried. People gave their theories, made up their scenarios about it, about the doctor giving her permission by examining her and becoming a mother figure, and all the rest of it. I haven't told you the case as a whole because it's far too long, and this girl had been unable to use tampons, but her sister had come along and said —

Mrs. R.   That's not really what I was worried about. — I'm not getting at the *case*, but I was getting at you as a leader. The way you recounted to us was that you said this was not 100%. . .

Doctor N.   We did have a talk about what it meant, but no-one could quite come up with what it had meant to that woman. So we didn't fully understand it, so full marks weren't to be allotted.

Dr. Q.   He didn't want her to go away with the idea that she had got a success and that was all that mattered.

Dr. Main   I don't see it that way. I agree that it is an important point. I see it as the leader's technique. The doctor reporting this case somehow conveyed to the group that the woman hadn't had any satisfaction from it. Although she didn't *report* it, the doctor was aware of that. The leader drew the group's attention to it. The question is: should he then wait for the group to go ahead, or should be go ahead of them? Was the timing right? My guess is that he is pointing out something that they all knew. That's not being too far ahead of them. He might have been miles ahead, but it didn't sound like it to me. It therefore wouldn't be seen as, 'I must learn to be clever like that'; or 'My word, I must do my duty next time and do the same as him'; but rather, 'Yes, it's a bit of commonsense, isn't it?' — the best area of the mind to educate. It didn't sound bossy or too clever. What I'm getting at is: what kind of leader is this? In the discussion here I think he showed himself. He didn't, for instance, discuss any group dynamics; he didn't give great reports on the way they talked to each other; he didn't give any kind of sociographical evidence at all; he didn't talk about the dilemmas of a leader. — What did he talk about?

Mrs. R.   What happened.

Dr. Main   No, he didn't talk about what happened.

Mrs. R.   The cases.

Dr. Main   Cases. — That's the kind of leader he is: interested in cases. Let's just have a look at this. What are the results of this leader's interest in cases? — Oh, come on!

Dr. I.   I don't know that he was just interested in cases. He described what else went on.

Dr. Main   All I heard was cases, cases, cases; a little bit about other things. I know a bit more about the Isle of Man than I did!

Dr. I.   Yes, although the description of the doctors was before you came in.

Dr. Main   I see.

Dr. S.   They don't come out with "The doctor/patient relationship was such and such" very much, do they?

Doctor N.   They discuss what they think the relationship is, and I often use Dr. Main's technique and ask, "What sort of doctor did this patient get?" We discussed how she was a hard-working doctor, putting forward ideas. . . cooking doctor, household management doctor and all this sort of stuff — and there is a rejected doctor.

Dr. Main   But I think this is right, that there was more discussion about the patient and what the patient was doing and how the patient could be understood than there was about the transactions between the doctor and the patient.

Dr. S.   Yes. I was trying to think how people in the third term could report anything other than what the patient said and did. What you're saying is that they ought by now to be getting on to talking about how they felt, and then what is going on in the group.

Doctor N.   I think the leader has to try and get them to do this from the word go. I don't think you can say, "This term we will only listen to histories, and next term we will start thinking about what the doctor/patient relation is, and in the third term we will think about the various dynamics in this group. I think you have to start off the way you want to go on. They won't understand it for the first term or the second term or maybe even the third term. But you must get them talking about the doctor/patient relationships, or thinking about a vaginal examination in a different sort of way than the gynaecological way, and there is no reason why you shouldn't start talking like that right from the beginning. It means more to them as they go on. But you've got to sow the seed some time.

Dr. Main Here is a leader who lays down the ground rules and that is it. They follow the ground rules and don't seem to have any difficulty with them. He's not insisting on them any more.

Doctor N. I speak much less than I used to.

Dr. Q. Because you have laid your rules down, so they can get on with it now.

Doctor N. Yes.

Dr. Main From the report this group is going well.

Doctor N. Yes, I thought it was good. They started off when I was late and didn't wait for me, which I thought was marvellous.

Dr. Main So laying down ground rules hasn't made them leader-dependent. It's a terrific change, isn't it? We are taught to talk about patients and findings from the patients. For the doctors to talk about *themselves* and their feelings is quite an innovation. — And then there is the doctor/patient relation, which is not the doctor's feelings, nor the patient's feelings: it's quite different. 'What are these two doing? What is going on?' You don't understand a marriage by knowing the wife's feelings and the husband's feelings. There is something additional going on: what they are doing with each other, the way they are using each other — it's these sort of things. The way the relationship is always changing and fluctuating is the *real* doctor/patient relation. — Thinking about that, what would you say these doctors were doing with these patients, by and large?

Dr. S. Certainly not reporting their own feelings.

Dr. Main Trying to understand them, aren't they?

Dr. S. Whether they are noticing the interaction, we don't know.

Dr. I. Well, they did. The one who did the vaginal examination felt it was a non-event.

Dr. Main But not for the husband.

Dr. I.   And that again was expressed the following week, when the husband came back. So something must have happened, even though no-one knew what it was.

Dr. Q.   That wasn't taken up, was it? The doctor didn't explore the husband's need to come back and say something.

Doctor N.   No, the doctor was very pleased — that's the point, you see — the doctor was very pleased to have a success and she accepted the thanks from the husband and noted that the wife didn't give her any thanks, and that is as far as she took it.

Dr. Main   We have a vivid picture of the kind of man, have we, and the kind of woman? — We really don't! We don't know what kind of man this is, we don't know what kind of woman, but let's not worry about it!

Dr. Q.   That's what I am saying. Is it right not to worry and just accept the gratitude and pass on? Should one really try and wonder why this husband has come back?

Dr. Main   What does it tell you?

Dr. Q.   We don't know. It's just his visiting card.

Dr. Main   What sort of husband is he? — Had to have the doctor do it for him. He comes back and thanks the friend. He's an insistent, dominant chap, isn't he? — No, he is not! There is something about this and it's not just to be taken at face value. If she has that kind of husband, that poor woman is not going to enjoy life very much.

Dr. Q.   But it was stopped then, the doctor stopped it all then; because technically they were better.

Dr. Main   Yes. What I am saying is that the description of the person, as well as the distress of the person, is a bit thin still. Do *you* get an impression of this woman and this man?

Doctor N.   I think that came out before you came in — about the girl with plaits being young and immature.

Dr. S.   — and prepared to keep going to mother for supper and so on.

Doctor N.   Yes.

Dr. Main   He's a fine chap, that. He's a good man.

Dr. S.   But the girl is making him like that; and she gave the doctor the brush-off. The doctor, as you reported it, must have felt a bit disappointed.

Doctor N.   I think she was, yes.

Dr. S.   But she didn't interpret that back, or help that woman to see that she is really rather a bitch.

Dr. Main   Mother's girl.

Dr. S.   Yes. So the girl hasn't really advanced, has she?

Dr. Main   How often did they go to the cinema?

Doctor N.   Every Friday. That is the only free night they have.

Dr. Main   Married one day a week! *(Laughter)*

5. The leader as model

Leader Doctor E.

A leader doctor talked about a meeting of her group where one case had been discussed fully for about an hour, and then there did not appear to be much more work. She waited quietly and eventually the group began to ask each other about one or two patients who had been discussed previously; but they again fell silent. Then someone tried to discuss a depressed relative, but the leader realised this was not a sexual problem nor a professional encounter.

Doctor E.   Finally we did have a useful offering with which we ended the afternoon. One of our newer doctors said, "I have a woman in the family planning clinic. She was about 40; she looked worn out. She got up on the couch and I was examining her to do a smear. She cringed away and said it was very painful. The doctor said, "And I felt: be careful here!" She waited and said to the woman, "How is it with sex?" The woman looked very tearful and said there hadn't been any sex for some time. Then she said, "I suppose there are other people like me?" The doctor said, "My instinct was to reassure her". She said something like, "Yes, there are, but it's still a problem, isn't it?"; and waited a bit. The woman then said that she really thought she would like to do something about it. The doctor, who was only a locum at that clinic, suggested she see one of the doctors who is trained in this work. So in a sense, it fizzled out; but what she described beautifully was the moment when she thought, "Oi, watch it! — I just can't run on. This has stopped being family planning: this is important"

Dr. Tunnadine From the leadership point of view, the interesting thing is that there was only one case on offer, so it was allowed to run for an hour.

Doctor E. It was a new case. There was a lot of material.

Dr. S. That last doctor did have a case, a very appropriate case, but didn't evidently think of it as something she would talk about. I noticed that the leader waited rather quietly and then other things came; and that doctor waited while she was with her patient who wasn't having any sex, and then she said a bit more. As if, the leader can do it, and so can the doctor with *her* case.

Dr. Tunnadine I am interested in the leader's dilemma of how to get people to present cases. I thought that was really what the report was about. It sounded to me as though you managed very well really, and impressively *not* having ones which weren't appropriate.

Dr. Main I think I go along with Dr. S. in noticing that the leader chose to keep quiet and something happened. So often it seems that you must have something great and this is an awful burden for someone who hasn't got great things to present: like this woman with the smear. How to help the members to have the courage to present what is there? You don't have to have olympic standards before you open your mouth. This is what I like about this way of handling it: just wait. . .

Dr. V. I felt that you made them feel that they had to search desperately to try and find something to talk about, because there was the gap.

Dr. Main She waited.

Dr. V. But it made them feel that they'd got to find something.

Dr. Main My point is that it made them feel, 'That's all right, to present that small thing'.

Dr. V. Yes, but they offered various things, didn't they? To some of them, you said, "Yes, we'll take that, we'll look at that".

Dr. Main   You and I are in disagreement about this. Let's get this clear. You see this technique as *pressure* on the group. You might be right. I don't see it that way. I see it as an invitation — 'anything will do'. I see it as *permissiveness* to talk about even small things; but you think it's pressure. You might be right. I don't know.

Dr. V.   Perhaps it depends on how experienced the group are.

Dr. Main   We need a comment from Dr. E. about this.

Doctor E.   It didn't feel particularly pressured. What I was feeling was, "I know there is stuff there of some sort". There were certain offerings which were not suitable, but I was really delighted with what came up in the end: that doctor talking about that moment when she had felt the red lights go on.

Dr. Main   Quite often I have people who say, "I have a case but I am not ready to present it", or "I haven't worked it out", or "I haven't prepared it"; as if only excellent work will do. It's very difficult to get away from this. Some will start on a case: "I first saw this case last June and I have seen them 147 times since! *(Laughter)* Whereas your last case was a lovely example of a simple situation, of the first time: there was nothing much, but it could be examined in detail, and the doctor/patient relationship was quite clear. How to create an atmosphere where the *little* things are permissible and right? — You obviously did it by waiting.

Dr. Tunnadine   She did, *but* I am going back to my original nag and say: how much was the fact that a one-hour case was allowed? Does that set the standard for the group? What is permissible afterwards?

Dr. Main   How many cases do you do in a seminar usually? *(addressed to all).*

Dr. S.   Two or three.

Dr. Tunnadine   I would say, three or four, ideally.

Dr. Main   I would like to say six; but it is often one. But I want to criticise this. If we think about how these doctors are working, they don't have hours at a time for their cases: they have to look at short bits of information and work fast. Shouldn't we be doing the same?

Dr. V.   This would encourage people to present a single encounter, because you do feel, if you've got to present something which is going to be *impressive*. . .

Dr. Main   We should be discussing issues of rapid sensitive psychosexual medicine, *not* prolonged psychotherapy. The danger is that we are teaching something if we have cases which go on for an hour at a time. *Mea culpa, mea maxima culpa! (Laughter).* Nonetheless, there is something about this business of working with short bits.

Dr. Tunnadine   Of course, you can only work with what you've got, and I suspect that if Dr. E. had had five people waiting she might have cut the other one shorter anyway.

Doctor E.   Or the effect on that doctor would have been to make her select a bit, wouldn't it? Knowing that you are the only one to present, you include all the little trimmings. If she'd known she'd got twenty minutes, she'd have thought, "Which bit of work will I discuss?"

Dr. Main   Let's take it back to the patient. What do you do with a patient who says, "Well now, doctor, this all began 35 years ago", and goes on with every year and tells you about every day. — What do you do? Do you accept it? *(General reply of 'No').* Well, how about a model of what you do in such a situation? You are inclined to think, 'For God's sake, come to the point!', because we know that this 35-year-old account is a defence against coming to the point which actually happened last week. We can do something like that with our own cases. When people delay in coming to the point, I say, "Don't bother about the whole report. Tell us about the last session". "But I can't tell you about the last session unless you understand about. . ." "All right, to understand the last session, give us enough to understand it". They never present unless there is something in their minds of the moment.

Doctor E.   Often we never get to it because we tolerate all this stuff. That is why some of the cases are so incredibly dissatisfying. You have worked and worked and haven't got to the nub at all.

Dr. Main   That's right.

Dr. S.   When there are a lot of people offering, I feel that each individual hasn't had enough.

Dr. Main   That's true; but that's true in clinical practice and that is why I think we should make sure that each person never gets enough. They get a certain amount and that is life, and they have to make do with it. No-one is ever fully satisfied.

Dr. S.   But isn't it better to do one thing properly than ten inadquately?

Dr. Main   It's a good point.

Dr. Tunnadine   The question is: what is 'properly' in our work? I suppose 'properly' in our training is to make the best possible use of the six minutes with the patient. That is the best work: not to turn out experts. So the 'proper' thing would be to get the most out of what is going on between the doctor and the patient, like your marvellous last case.

Dr. Main   Let's go to this business of satisfying people. There are various ways of feeding babies: one way is to give them everything they need, and at the first sign of needing, give them some more. You will turn out fat babies who are overweight; very content, but passive; who don't do anything for themselves. They don't need to; they are well looked after. The other way is to give them enough, but not any more than that: enough to keep them questing for food so they are active and demanding and working for it; and as they grow older they reach out for it. They are not passive, contented people: they are active little foragers. We need foragers, who forage for their own thoughts, and work, rather than come to the seminar and get thoroughly contented.

Dr. V.   Should we in fact be sending people away still going on thinking about. . .

Dr. Main   Appetised, yes.

Dr. V.   So they go on working at their ideas themselves. . .

Dr. Main   They should be given as little as they can do with; but they should get *something*.

Dr. V.   It's rather like walking a tightrope. . .

6. The anxious leader with a small group

Leader Doctor I.

Following the presentation of a group with only five doctors present, including the leader, the following discussion took place in the leaders workshop:

Dr. Main   What do you think about the group itself and the leader's position in the group? Any ideas about that?

Dr. K.   The leader is allowing the group to work on it and didn't say much.

Dr. Main   It seems to be a very matey group and friendly and they like talking about the doctor's feelings. It's a nice club where they comfort each other and give each other advice and tips on how to treat the patient. They try out the tips one week and then report back to see whether the tips have worked or not. I wouldn't say it is a hard-working group. — Am I right?

Doctor I.   Yes, I think you're right. It's very friendly.

Dr. Main   It's a small group and if you ask them to work it's a very difficult situation, to take the burden of producing cases and working away at them. The numbers make a rather anxious leader who makes sure that the group survives. The whole thing means you pull your punches a bit and the work ethic tends to be weakened by this small number. Of course, if they are decent enough to produce a case, you can't really take it apart fully. The effect of any kind of criticism is to make us retreat for a bit and digest it. It's painful to be criticised and you need a week or two to recover from this, and they haven't got time to have a week or two, because there would be no cases to discuss. I am very interested in these small groups, because there are quite a number of people who are struggling away with them.

Doctor I.   There are three more doctors who may want to join.

Dr. Main   I know, but it affects you and the whole atmosphere. It's matey and supporting, giving each other tips rather than criticisms; besides which, if you have double the number, you have double the amount of brains in the room, twice as many ideas. There is a conspiracy of friendliness.

Doctor I.   Yes, there is. I don't know how you overcome that.

Dr. Main   Don't have a small group. Pack it in. Find another group.

Doctor I.   But you can't, half way through. You've got to complete the year.

Dr. Main   Well, you think you've got another three: that's seven. . . — There was a chance right at the beginning of this group, where the leader told us she only had four people; and she asked who had work, and there was one follow-up and a possible new one — and she thought, "Oh, heavens!" That was the situation of the leader. Should it be shared with the group — "Oh, heavens!" — or should you take responsibility?

Doctor I.   I did say at that point, "Well, we can only work if we have got cases"; and in fact someone produced a third case at the end.

Dr. Main   That's a bit teachy itself. Suppose you said, "What can we do?" — because they really are only four people and they share with you the anxieties: it's depressing for them. Any modification of technique should be out in the open with them, because it is difficult for them. They know as well as you do that one case and a follow-up is not going to last them very long. It's not good enough; not what they have come for. The misery of having four, I think, should be shared with them, and the recruiting of other people should be their job. If you said, "Unless some more people come, I am packing it in", I bet you would have some more people by Christmas.

Doctor I.   In fact that anxiety was expressed by one of them at the very end, by saying, "What has happened to these other two?"

Dr. Main   Yes, they are just as worried. But if *you* worry about it, they needn't. — I would stop worrying about it and let them. It's their group, isn't it? — not yours. It's in bad shape with four people. What are *they* going to do about it? Put it back to them. You could say, "Unless the numbers increase, I am pushing off!" — I once did that to a group and it doubled within three weeks.

Doctor I.   Yes. You've got a different reputation than me! *(Laughter)*.

Dr. Main   They want to survive. It's not your fault. It's their misery and plight.

Dr. E.   Is it inevitable that they are feeling that way, or could they be enjoying the rather matey atmosphere and not particularly *wanting* to have new people in and to have to work harder. Your tactic, I suppose, will blow it one way or the other.

Dr. Main   Yes. It's this sense of being part of a club and being nice to each other. How to get the work going is a very difficult problem for a small group.

Dr. K.   I said to my group last time I was there, because the numbers have gone down, "It looks as though this group is going to pack up", and they immediately said, "Perhaps we can find somebody else".

Dr. Main   Groups should be chasing leaders, not the other way round.

Doctor I.   I will try.

Dr. Main   Dr. E's point is, if they get very matey, they won't want anybody else.

Dr. E.   That's what I meant. I was questioning the assumption that they necessarily felt miserable about only being four.

Dr. Main   If you make them work, they are miserable.

Doctor I.   It does become difficult when there are so few cases to present.

Dr. Q.   The other side of the coin is that, in a small group, the shy doctor is enabled to come into it slowly at his own pace. With a big group, he may think, "Oh, this case, I can't present it, it's not a proper case"; whereas if it is a small group and he is desperate, he thinks, "Perhaps I will just mention this thing and see if it's any good". That is what I felt happened with one of my doctors.

7. The leader must not be too clever

The following extract from a leaders' Weekend meeting further explores the problem of the leader who is too clever.

Dr. Main   The model of being 'super' is a dreadful one for doctoring, especially in this work. A 'super' doctor is one who knows; who does not listen and puzzle about patients; is not a co-equal partner with them in ignorance; will not work *with* patients but will tell them; will know better and will think for, rather than with, them; will ask questions of them.

Our task as doctors is to help the patient find things out for himself; the leader's task is to help the doctors in the group find out things for themselves. Thus a 'super' leader provides a very bad model for doctors in training, however tempting for the inexperienced leader. Trainees always and inevitably try to emulate the leader; however unwittingly, they will identify with, and model themselves upon him to some extent. If a leader can offer a model of one who listens, thinks and puzzles, offering his own ideas tentatively, checking and re-checking their truth, relevance and effectiveness, seminar members may acquire and recognise the effectiveness of such a non-directive, non-clever approach to their patients.

Another reason why the leader must avoid being too impressive is that his group may become adoring, silent — and soon fed up! In this group (at the conference) everyone may begin to feel inferior because this speaker has been laying down ideals which we all inevitably fail to emulate. We may all do our best, but life is not perfect — perhaps it, and we, should be! Meanwhile we all have to face the pain of uncertainty which leads all doctors to seek defences in 'objectivity'.

The leader's job is not to listen to the case material but to listen to the doctors. He is concerned with training the latter, not with curing the former. His main interest should be in what the doctor has done; how he reports this; how he thinks with his patient; why he intervened as he did, with what tactless and unthinking responses, blind spots and omissions. What anxieties were evoked in him by the patient? Did he act upon these or think about them? How sensitive was he to what was going on — in the patient and in himself? These are the things the leader should be listening for and thinking about, though not necessarily talking about.

But life is not easy for the leader. He has an additional task. He must be concerned not only with his own understanding of the doctor/patient relationship, but with the group's understanding of this. In other words, he must attend not only to the reporting doctor and how he is getting on with his patient, but with the group's responses, behaviour, feelings and thinking; and act so as to free them to think and respond relevantly.

The group will not be challenged to think if the leader thinks for them and pre-empts discussion. It is better for him to leave the group to conduct the discussion, reserving his own remarks until every doctor in the group has had an opportunity to offer his contribution. When the group has exhausted its own ideas, the leader may seek to help the group to think further: about the reporting doctor's understanding and handling of the case. His remarks should aim to illumine the clinical events not only for the presenting doctor but also for the other group members.

8. The leader who *was* too clever

Leader Doctors B. & K.

The following short extract is a rare example of an honest report of a leader who found herself being too clever:

   A case where a girl of twenty was very upset about losing her virginity had been discussed in a new group.

Doctor K.   There was quite an interesting little bit. I said, "We are talking about this girl as though she is fourteen, and she's actually twenty", and one of the G.P.s jumped in and said, "It's not actually compulsory to have sex nowadays". So then I got all defensive and said, "Well, she's internalised her parental influences — at any rate, she is not a rebel: more of a daughter than a lover".

Doctor B.   And as the group broke up one doctor said, "I wish *I* could say clever things like, 'She's internalised her... *(Laughter).* It sounds so much better like that!' I felt they were recognising Dr. K. as the leader and not me, and I felt rather put down by this. I thought also that she saw it was on a more scientific and less anecdotal level.

Dr. N.   Or were they taking the mickey out of you — you were just wrapping it all up in jargon?

Doctor B.   I don't think so, actually.

Dr. Main   The doctor was so much impressed by Dr. K.'s clever remarks that she learned what a clever doctor Dr. K. is — and nothing about the internalisation! That's the effect of it: to learn 'What a clever lecturer this is!' — and that's all.

C. SOME PROBLEMS FOR THE LEADER

Several ideas that have already arisen in the book — silence in groups, depressed and aggressive groups — are further explored in this chapter from the leader's point of view; as well as the disruption that can be caused when a doctor's personal problems interfere with the primary training task of developing the professional ego by study of the doctor/patient relationship.

1. THE SILENT GROUP.
Three possible reasons for silence in a small group of nurses are discussed: the size of the group, the group atmosphere, and the members' possible perception that cases need to be clever and high-powered. The leader took full responsibility for the silence, blaming it only on the small numbers. (Compare the leader who took responsibility for group anger, III D 3).

2. ANOTHER SILENT GROUP.
How long should the leader let the silence continue?

3. GROUP DEPRESSION.
Silence is seen as a sign of repressed feelings about the difficult nature of the work. The non-aggressive leader was unable to help the group air their anger and relieve their depression.

4. GROUP AGGRESSION.
The careful use of group interpretation to remove difficulties that stop the group working is discussed.

5. THE DISRUPTIVE MEMBER.
This discussion returns to the idea, introduced in the first chapter of the book, that concern about the personal problems of an individual doctor detracts from the central idea that the work task is training the doctor's professional work by the study of the doctor/patient relationship.

1. The leader and the silent group

Leader Doctor B.

A doctor who was leading a nurses' group had difficulties when no-one had any cases to present.

Doctor B. Nobody seemed able to find anything to talk about. At the last meeting we had talked about a health visitor who had a patient who said before she had the baby that she wouldn't be able to breast-feed and this was linked to other feelings; but there wasn't even anything like that to bring up this time. Nobody had a case. — I wonder if anybody else has ever been in a group where nobody had a case?

Dr. I. Do health visitors ever have cases? — because they don't examine patients, do they?

Doctor B. They can examine patients, can't they? There is no reason why not.

Dr. Tunnadine 'What is a case?' is my question. I've got a fairly new advanced group and they have all got thousands of cases, all very clever and very difficult. Maybe that says something about me, or is it their expectations? I just wonder, in a situation like this, what they think *is* a case to present?

Dr. Main But why didn't they have cases? What's wrong with the seminar? They are seeing human beings, so why haven't they got cases? *They don't want to report.* I think this is the phenomenon.

Dr. C. This is what came out in *my* group. I think they don't identify what may be a case of interest.

Dr. Main If they don't want to present, they don't want to present, and they are able to find that case not suitable. If they *want* to present, they say, "It's not really relevant but I would like to talk about. . . if it's all right". It's something about the group. I don't think it's terrible. Why shouldn't the group have an off-day, or show some resistance? — Can you think of anything which happened the time before?

Doctor B. I did think about that and I couldn't. The particular nurse who produced two cases on that day had started off by saying, "I don't think it is relevant, but. . ." and they were two very good ones. This time nobody had anything from their consultations with patients which had been suitable to bring.

Dr. Main   — to that group.

Doctor B.   To that group.

Dr. Tunnadine   Our contributions in a way have represented the two sides of it. We lay on them some vision of what a case is and Dr. Main is saying they are also entitled to have their own resistance. There are two sides to this issue, aren't there?

Dr. C.   Is it a big group?

Doctor B.   No, on this particular occasion there were only four of us. Normally there are about eight.

Dr. C.   I find that although it can put the pressure on if there are very few, it can also dis-inhibit members who couldn't bring a case up in a bigger group.

Dr. Main   A case is suitable if the climate is right.

Dr. A.   How long did you wait before you took it that they really didn't have a case?

Doctor B.   Quite a while; perhaps not long enough.

Dr. Main   You would like to know that for some reason.

Dr. A.   I find that if you wait, somebody says, "I've got a case which isn't really a case" and brings something that is perfectly satisfactory, but I've had to wait five or seven minutes before they would actually say that.

Dr. Main   That's a technique.

Dr. Tunnadine   On one occasion I said, "We can go home if you like".

Doctor B.   In the end I talked about someone I had just seen before coming to the group, which I didn't really think was the right thing to do, but it was either that or we all went home.

Dr. Main   Just tell us what happened.

Doctor B.   Well, I was taking over in a teaching role.

Dr. Main   No, what happened with the group from the beginning? You were faced with a problem. There you were — four people, plus you?

Doctor B.   Yes: two health visitors, one practice nurse, one family planning nurse. I sort of said brightly, "Well, who has got a case?" They each thought a minute or two and then shook their heads and said they hadn't; and by the time it got to the fourth person they felt they had to produce a reason and said it had been the Christmas holidays — as if they had to have an excuse. Then I said, as it was the first meeting of this term and we seemed to be a small group, did anyone know if people were going to continue to come? One person said that one nurse would not be coming any more: "If you'll excuse my saying so, but she didn't think she learned anything". So then we looked at what we were trying to do and it went on a bit from there.

Dr. Main   Then what happened? There was the leader — how much up a gum tree and so on?

Doctor B.   I said something like, "I have often found in my own work, if I stop and think over people I have seen recently that there is something which is useful to talk about": some vague statement like that. Then we had a long gap. We just sat and still nobody came forward with anything. Perhaps I didn't leave the gap long enough. It seemed an awfully long time!

Dr. Tunnadine   I notice you made a group observation and I would like to propose that we never talk about the group at all. You were off the work task. We have never really looked at how far making observations about the group is a good idea. You felt the need to verbalise something about the small group and you felt the need to verbalise something about the nurses, and not much more work was done. I am not saying that was the cause, but just noticing that it happened.

Doctor B.   We talked and made observations to some extent about the nurse who thought she hadn't learnt anything; about what we were trying to do and what we were there for.

Dr. N.   But what goes on in a group is of no great importance. It's important for the leader to observe but not comment on, unless it is interfering with the work of the group.

Dr. Main   In this case the group couldn't get started on the cases. One reason might be that it is because the group is too small; another is that people didn't want to produce cases; or thirdly that the definition of a case is too high-powered for them — their concept of proper cases doesn't match that of the leader. All sorts of things are there, but to say, "It's such a small group, you see" is taking it away from the whole. Why the hell haven't they got cases? Why don't they say, "I haven't got a case but I would like to talk about something that is not quite relevant". What is it about these people that they are not free to talk in this group? That would be a more important question, I think, than the others. If there's an obvious group phenomenon then of course we will pay attention to it — say, obvious personality difficulties — but in the absence of evidence of this, it is not an explanation to fly to.

Doctor B.   I don't think there was anything odd going on in the group. It was more, as you say, that they felt that the patients they had seen were not the material to bring.

Dr. Main   Well, there's none so blind as those who don't want to see.

Doctor B.   But isn't that why they are at the group: so they can see more?

Dr. Tunnadine   The leader found herself going on to say something like, "I can sometimes think of cases" and giving an example.

Doctor B.   I was trying to get them to see that probably what they thought was not relevant would be something worth looking at. I was saying that I think back over something that would have been interesting to talk about in the doctor/patient relationship in that particular incident, and I was hoping that it might trigger them to think of something.

Dr. Tunnadine   But what I'm getting at is that you were responding to your idea that they thought their cases weren't good enough or something. It might be somewhere in that area that you were saying, "Oh come on, your cases are good enough for me!" Perhaps I'm pushing it.

Dr. K.   Perhaps this idea of the nurse/patient relationship is a bit overpowering for them at the moment. You have used it two or three times this afternoon. Maybe it's early to make them think they've got to present cases about the nurse/patient relationship.

Dr. Main   That phrase doesn't mean anything much to people: "Oh, we got on very well. . ." In this technique Dr. B. led them — you were the model.

Doctor B.   I think it was my own anxiety, enhanced by the fact that I am paid for it. This worries me a lot — scraping together a group almost, who haven't got cases. . .

Dr. Main   — And they're letting you down, the swine! It's the hatred of them not fitting in with this idea. You could say, "You bloody liars! You're seeing people — come on! Don't be so damn blind and stupid!" That's one way. You were dealing with that phenomenon when you said, "Look, stop being so blind!" The other thing to do would be to interpret it; make a remark about, "You've seen cases in the last week, and if you haven't there's something wrong with you".

Dr. C.   Sometimes I think the word 'cases' is wrong.

Dr. Main   Very good point. We're not really discussing cases, we're here to discuss the doctor/patient relation; and that is the doctor's experiences, an incident of the doctor's or nurse's experience which she wants to report, or was puzzled about, or was pleased with.

Doctor B.   I think I did start by saying, "Has anyone got *anything* they want to talk about?"

Dr. Main   Yes, that's very good.

Doctor B.   But they didn't even want to talk about *anything*!

Dr. Main   What — with you?

Dr. I.   What was their reaction to the gap while you were waiting for someone to come up with something? Were they sitting there embarrassed? There was this five-minute gap.

Dr. Main   Five seconds. . .

Doctor B.   They were still expecting me to take over, and I went and did just that!

Dr. Main   Teacher will show how easy it is.

Dr. I.   I'm sure this is what I would probably do, whereas others are much wiser, waiting five or even eight minutes.

Dr. C.   It's a terrible long time, five minutes.

Dr. Main   It's not *your* silence, it's theirs! *(Laughter)*

2. Another silent group

Leader Nurse Mrs. R.

In a nurses group, one case was presented and discussed at some length, but when this came to an end no-one else offered anything.

Mrs. R. There was a longish silence. I actually timed it because there's a clock I can see out of the corner of my eye, and it was seven minutes. But it wasn't an angry silence. I kept thinking, "What is this? I think it is a *lazy* silence". They just did not want to work. I thought, "What am I going to do with them?" So I used something which I've picked up from the group here. I said, "Well, has no-one seen any patients?"; at which three piped up very quickly, "no, we haven't". Then someone actually said, "Oh yes, can I talk about seeing a sixteen-year-old girl?", and launched into an extremely interesting girl she had seen and how she felt about this girl. But I've been wondering about this lazy silence and whether I did the right thing, and whether you just let them sit it out. Seven minutes is quite a long time, isn't it? Is it my anxiety? There was a bit of shuffling; there wasn't a lot of movement.

Dr. Main One feels uncomfortable, doesn't one!

Mrs. R. One does, yes!

Dr. Main We haven't a lot of time. Let's discuss what we've heard so far.

Dr. S. I think it's a mis-diagnosis. I don't think there are lazy silences. I think there are frightened silences and the longer it goes on, the harder it is to be the one who breaks it.

Mrs. R. It shouldn't have been me?

Dr. Q. You can make it easier, I suppose.

Dr. Main You can get it out of the way with a short lecture. Do you want a short lecture? If you let this go on for a long time, it adds certain group dynamic complications. The group becomes a thing and you get frightened and you daren't speak. You project your brain into this space in the middle of the group, and you feel stupid and humble and waiting for someone else to speak or pounce on you because you're so stupid, so you'd better keep quiet. Everybody is the same, more frightened. I won't elaborate on this. It's a secondary phenomenon which begins after some time, and before that time has elapsed, the leader should say something, even if it's only "Good afternoon!"

Dr. S.   Goodbye! *(Laughter).*

Mrs. R.   That went through my mind, because we'd only got about twenty minutes left and I very nearly thought, 'Shall we finish here?'

Dr. Main   It would have been better, because a couple of minutes is long enough. One minute is a very long time. You could have said, "Has no-one got any cases?" You could have said it earlier.

Mrs. R.   I obviously left it too long and it was my anxiety at thinking — and I was obviously getting more frightened, but I realised it.

Dr. Main   You don't know what the silence was about? Can we talk about the earlier work quickly?

In the discussion that followed it was not easy to find any obvious reason for the silence in the work that had been done before.

3. Group depression

Leader Doctor Y.

The leader described three doctors in a fairly early group who had all presented a rather disappointing encounter with a patient. The first was a woman who had had a cervical erosion treated and since then could not stand her husband near her. Although the doctor felt the woman wanted to be examined, she had not done so because she was very busy, but had made a future appointment which the patient failed to keep. The second case was of a man who brought his baby to the well baby clinic and complained that his wife was not interested, and again the doctor somehow did not want to get involved. The third case was a very disturbed young man who had just come out of the local mental hospital. He complained that he couldn't make it with the girlfriend he met there, who turned out to be one of the nurses. The doctor said he felt, 'Oh no, not now! I don't want to talk about it now'. After this the patient's behaviour had become more disturbed and he had been re-admitted to hospital.

Doctor Y.   The last doctor finished his account and there was a long silence. I said, "You seem to have reduced us all to silence" and waited for them to pick this up. There was an even longer silence. My first feeling was, 'No, I'm not going to break it — *you* can do the work'. But they didn't. So I said, "If we're all silent there must be something that we can't say" and again waited for someone to take me up on that, but nobody did.

Dr. J.   If they are coming out with cases which they are not proud of, at least it's a permissive sort of set-up.

Dr. N.   There's a bit of trust, isn't there?

Dr. I.   Yes: to say, "I've made a hash of it".

Mrs. R.   One gives courage to the other as well.

Doctor Y.   You are doing what the group did, these doctors — they all reassured each other! *(Laughter)*

Dr. S.   One of them might have said, "It's because this work is so difficult". They are suddenly realising, aren't they, that it *is* difficult and they are selecting even more difficult cases. I think they were silent because this doctor was reporting an unsuitable case for this kind of therapy. If the patient is in and out of mental hospital, I suppose they were very angry with him for not choosing someone he could work with. So they were silent and didn't like to say it even when you invited them to.

Dr. Main   Suppose someone had said with any of those cases: "You did bloody awful work, didn't you?". That would have been the truth. I don't think it would have been a *tactful* truth unless something else had been added.

Doctor Y.   Are you talking about this. . .

Dr. Main   Any of them. They were all saying, "I did bloody awful work" and they were trying to get the group to say it. They wanted a beating-up, so to speak, and the group hesitates to beat them up. I would say everyone's thoughts were unspeakable.

They ignored the anger induced by the reporting doctor, who wanted them to be angry because he wanted to air his own anger and humiliation in failure. They didn't talk about the humiliation of this. The doctor's part in the whole thing was not discussed. It was just, "I tried this", "This was the patient". The doctor thinks it is a bad bit of work and is saying, "Look, I did a bad bit of work. Please blame me".

Doctor Y.   This is what I said. I said, "It seems to me as though you are asking us to slap you". But then I suppose I ruined it by saying, "But I'm not going to". We talked a bit about whether the patient was suitable or not, and he said, "Thank you. This patient was beginning to get on top of me". I think he is someone who carries the cares of the world on his shoulders.

Dr. Main   A bit grandiose about what he can do.

Doctor Y.   I think he needs permission about what *not* to do.

Dr. Main   Wants to cure people by magic. They have learned something horrible. They are in pain. They are not as good as they want to be and are fed up with themselves.

Doctor Y.   Yes, I suppose I get tarred by the same brush. I think, "My God, what have I done to make them feel that they are not getting — "

Dr. Main   I think you failed them badly. You haven't taught them how to do magic. But they want it.

Dr. Q.   Is that really what the silence was saying?

Dr. Main   Dr. Y. feels some kind of failure, personal uneasiness — but then, their aspirations are enormous, aren't they?

Dr. Q.   Is this something we should bring out, the silence meaning their anger, either with the leader or with the patient?

Dr. Main   Silence usually means repression, which conceals a kind of anger. If I say, "Let me tell you about something awful" and tell you some awful story, or admit something which is obvious, then you are bound to attack me; and I know it. But if I start saying, "Look, I feel depressed about this case because I failed with it", then you could talk about my failure with me in an inoffensive way. If I leave you to the anger and disown it myself, then I am going to get beaten-up.

Dr. I.   Do you think they necessarily see that?

Dr. Main   In one case the doctor is grandiose and tries impossible cases and doesn't see it.

Doctor Y.   I don't think it's grandiosity, really. I don't think he imagines he's going to do magic, but I do think he picked up his own impatience on this occasion. He was aware that he had given the patient the brush-off. They talked a bit more about why he hadn't done more this time and they decided it might be something to do with the fact that the girlfriend was a nurse; and he said, "Yes, we do like to protect our nurses". — You think I should have encouraged them to bring out that anger a bit more?

Dr. I.   It's very early, it's only the second term. I feel a little bit apprehensive.

Doctor Y.   Yes, *I* did.

Dr. Main   What's the group doing to the leader?

Dr. I.   Hammering her.

Dr. Main   '— This work is no damn good — let's see how *you* get on'. It's fairly typical. It's a classic presentation of bringing impossible cases: 'See the kind of work I am doing? It's all right for you talking high and mighty stuff out there, but I'm in this field dealing with these awful cases. Let's see if *you* can do any better'. And they know damn well you can't: to cut you down to size. It's fair enough.

Dr. Q.   So as a leader we just accept being cut down and don't say anything?

Dr. I.   Try not to express that.

Dr. Main   Why not? Dr. Y. has really failed to help them — and I'm not saying she *should* have succeeded, but she has failed so far in helping them to select cases. 'Is this a suitable case?' should have been expressed very early on with this crazy fellow who's in that hospital. The leader should say, "Just a minute — does anyone think this is a suitable case?" — Not that I would do that, but Dr. N. would, wouldn't you? *(Laughter)*

Dr. N.   I would have said, "This sort of case is *not* suitable!" *(Laughter)*

Dr. Main   It would save you a lot of hard work, but I'm not sure they are any the worse for it. They are taking the long route to learning.

Doctor Y.   I get very stuck because sometimes they say, "I can't produce this case because it isn't a case" and I encourage them to bring encounters rather than long tidied-up cases. Then if they start to bring an encounter like this and I cut them short, it seems a bit contradictory.

Mrs. R.   But the other two cases weren't necessarily unsuitable at all. The doctors were frightened by them and suddenly thought, "My God, I can't cope!"

Doctor Y.   I was particularly surprised with the doctor who talked about this woman coming back after having had an erosion, because it is so unlike the previous material which she had produced.

Dr. Main   But you didn't know why it was so.

Doctor Y.   Well, another doctor was trying to get her to see that it might be something to do with the patient, and not the fact that she was having a bad morning. But she felt she had done badly, not being able to work her way round the patient.

Dr. I.   Did she have any insight as to why she should have felt badly? Was it really because she was busy?

Doctor Y.   She was feeling, 'Whether I am busy or not, it's not good enough'.

Dr. S.   So she knew it was coming from the patient, really, putting her off in some way?

Doctor Y.   You've reminded me, one of the other doctors suggested that, but I said, "What do you think you were actually avoiding?", and she implied it was involvement with the patient.

Mrs. R.   Isn't this the difficulty with the work? It is *more* difficult after you have got into the training.

Dr. S.   She is saying, "Do I want to be in this seminar? Do I want to be involved in this kind of work?" There's ambivalence there.

Dr. Main   How did the leader handle this about the erosion?

Doctor Y.   Tried to encourage the doctor who was asking about, "Do you think it was something about the patient which made you postpone the examination?", hoping that they would pick this up and enlarge on it. But they didn't.

Dr. Main   It's a bit direct, that question, because the doctor doesn't know. What sort of patient was it?

Doctor Y.   I got the impression she was a middle-aged lady, not very much more really.

Dr. Main   She's a certain kind of human being, she's not just an example of cervical erosion.

Doctor Y.   Oh no, the doctor doesn't see her like that.

Dr. Main   I know, but I'm trying to get —

Doctor Y.   I'm trying to remember. I got an image of a middle-aged distressed lady. The other thing the group talked about was what the patient's phantasies were about an erosion: how it was caused and what had been done to her. Really they just showed the doctor again that there were other areas that she had not looked at.

Dr. Main   I don't think this patient is very nice, saying that she can't stand her husband near her.

Doctor Y.   I didn't get that feeling at all. I got the feeling of a distressed lady whose husband was able to laugh about it kindly, we were told, not in a disparaging way.

Dr. Main   What a happy family they sound! — There is murder going on underneath. . . What I am missing here is the leader's aggressiveness and the awareness of aggressiveness in the group and in the patients' lives and in the doctor/patient relation.

Doctor Y.   I wasn't aware of any aggressiveness in that case.

Dr. Main   I know *(laughing)*. It looks to me as though these people were at war. Couldn't stand her husband near her and he was being nice about it. The doctor was fed up with the patient and said, "Push off!", and the group was fed up with the doctor. But you go on being sweet. I don't believe it!

Doctor Y.   That is my blank, because I didn't get any feeling of an aggressive situation at all.

Dr. A.   Did the group try to comfort the doctor, or were they critical of her?

Doctor Y.   No, they weren't critical of her.

Dr. S.   *We're* critical of her, so why — ?

Dr. Main   I'm critical of the *leader*. The leader is being sympathetic and nice and concerned with the difficulties — and she is absolutely fed up with them.

Doctor Y.   I can be angry with them when I think it is appropriate, but I wasn't conscious —

Dr. Main   They are angry with themselves; and with their patients; and with each other.

Dr. N.   You had better try my technique and tell them that they'd better report successes in future! *(Laughter)* That's a ground rule!

Dr. Main   This first doctor with the case about the erosion must have felt bloody fed-up with this patient, and the group said, "Yes, you were bloody fed-up — tell us more". They didn't discuss the *clinical* failure. I don't think the doctor was the only one in that room to be angry. The patient must have been difficult, but the doctor's angry consultation wasn't discussed as a clinical feature. It was rather a reproachful 'What did the doctor get angry about?', instead of an attempt to understand the situation.

Dr. A.   The leader was angry with the group: 'I'm not going to break this silence. They can jolly well break it themselves!' — That's being a bit cross.

Doctor Y.   If you say so. *(Laughing)* I remember feeling, 'Oh Lord, what have I done to them?', rather than, 'Blast them!'

Dr. Main   That's suicide instead of murder! *(Laughter)* 'What have I done wrong?' — 'Well, we'll tell you!'. . . It's interesting, because here we have a leader who blames herself for group phenomena rather than studying the group phenomena. It isn't a matter of doing wrong; it's a matter of taking a clinical interest in what you are doing: 'What am I doing?', not 'What am I doing *wrong*?' As far as I can make out, she was being a bit quiet and a bit unaggressive and not seeing the fury with each other and themselves and with the patients. You were simply being furious with yourself at being a failure.

Dr. I.   I feel very irritated with them, as I listen to it here.

Dr. Main   They sound to be depressed because of the control of the aggression.

Dr. I.   Yes, perhaps they feel depressed because they feel they can't air their anger because it would be frowned upon or not be acceptable.

Dr. Main   Something of this sort. The doctor couldn't say, "I felt bloody fed-up with this patient and threw her out". This sort of reporting isn't possible yet.

Doctor Y. The problem is, I find it difficult to recognise anger when it's under my nose.

Dr. Main Mmm — and pleasing people doesn't work. I don't think you should be *nasty*, but you shouldn't be nice, either.

Doctor Y. I think if I recognised it, it would be easier.

Dr. Main I think you have got to give them a lead about aggressiveness. You should thump the desk and say, "What the hell do you mean by bringing this case! You know quite well it's no good!" — Outbursts like that. Once a week.

Dr. Q. Wouldn't a way of doing that be to take it back to the doctor/patient relation: that the patient was angry, the doctor was . . .

Dr. Main The doctor was tortured.

Dr. Q. The doctor didn't know how to handle the patient and told the patient to go away.

Dr. Main And these doctors will go away unless they are allowed to legitimise their anger. They will get depressed.

Doctor Y. I will write in big letters: "AM I ANGRY?"

Dr. Main No — the rule is that you must find an excuse to thump the desk once every time.

Dr. S. If I could bring up my group for one second: last time they reported all angry patients. So I went away thinking about it and realised that I had missed the anger. *They* are feeling angry but they put it into the patients. Thinking about it afterwards I thought, 'They are all angry women fed up with their mothers for making them have abortions and things'. I am sure I was missing some anger in the group, perhaps about the leader making them have —

Dr. Main Abortions.

Dr. S. Yes — abort their practices; their long-standing fallacies. I couldn't see it, until afterwards.

4. Group aggression

Leader Doctor S.

The case presented was a follow-up of a young woman who had pain on intercourse and frequency of micturition afterwards. She had been seen by a gynaecologist and a urologist. The doctor, Dr. X., had also sent her to the STD clinic to make sure there was no infection. She had now suggested that she should have Mist. Pot. Cit., after reading about this suggestion in a journal.

Doctor S.   As Dr. X. started to report this case she reminded the group that they had criticised her a lot about it on a previous occasion. The group broke into hysterical laughter and I couldn't help joining in myself. I felt I must use this somehow, so I said, "Why are we all laughing? — it must be a cover-up for something". Someone said, "Dr. X. feels hopeless about the patient" and Dr. X. said, "Yes, I do feel that I don't know what I am doing". Then the group sort of turned and said, "Are you saying you don't think there is anything psychological about this patient?" They took her in hand in a quite kind way, which was totally different to the previous occasion when they were irritated and attacking. I just sat back and didn't have to do anything at all. They did a little bit of teaching, but they somehow tried to help her to see the other point of view. So that was the end of the afternoon and we all went out much more comfortable, and I felt that was a model of how she could have been with the patient.

Dr. C.   Do you think your comment about the laughter needing to hide something allowed them to see what was going on? It seems as though that was very constructive.

Doctor S.   Maybe; I don't know.

Dr. Main   It didn't get much of a response really, apart from that sudden change of behaviour. It didn't ring a bell about the difficulty. You said it must be about something: you drew attention to it, which is absolutely right.

Dr. C.   Nothing followed it, but they worked.

Dr. Main   The laughter woke them up. It was this doctor's communication about being attacked last week. You tried to recover by saying, "It must be about something". I wouldn't say it was too brilliant a remark; but it certainly was right, although a generalisation.

Dr. I.   It would remind them that they had been nasty to her and they were relieved that she hadn't taken it badly.

Doctor S.   Yes, because she had stayed away the previous week and I thought she might have been upset.

Dr. Tunnadine   I think that's a happy result. They said, however, "Did she really believe that there was no psychological thing?" That was the only thing I wasn't clear about.

Doctor S.   She kept sticking to her point, I'm afraid, that there is a physical cause. She hasn't changed, actually. It's just that the group has changed in their treatment of her.

Dr. C.   Maybe she will be able to learn from this.

Dr. Tunnadine   We are in danger of getting good marks and bad marks here in some funny way. Dr. S. was obviously relieved that instead of being a hateful group they were now being a protecting group to this doctor and on the whole, if you care for that sort of thing, it's nicer to be caring or teaching than hateful to a patient. But the understanding of what is going on seems no further forward.

Doctor S.   But there was some sort of a model about not getting into a fight, but trying to understand.

Dr. Main   The problem is the doctor's flight from the facts under her nose, and from the human distress under her nose, into the long-standing safety of organic medicine. That was the result of anxieties which the patient generated in the doctor on the topic of sexuality and phantasies and all sorts of things. Something frightened the doctor. I would have liked to have had the detail of the report so that could have been discussed. The moment at which the doctor took flight would have been nice to identify. That would require a very detailed account of the transactions between the doctor and the patient, so you can spot the moment the doctor finds it too much and takes flight.

Doctor S.   I think it's when the patient sits there and says, "I have a sexual problem".

Dr. Main   Fine.

Doctor S.   She does it every time.

Dr. Main Sex frightens this doctor. Once the doctor *knows* that, and the group knows that, they will stand for it. Eventually the doctor will say, "And sex was mentioned, so at once I took flight", rather than saying, "The patient must have something or other". Telling the doctor to think differently isn't so good as catching the anxiety on the wing.

Dr. Tunnadine To be fair to the doctor in this case, you have heard her report before, so you know she always takes flight when sex is mentioned. But given another doctor who has a patient who has been to a urologist, gynaecologist and so on, the pressure is on all of us to do better and be terrified and rush to the journals. I certainly have been in that situation and defy any of you to say you haven't. That is something to do with the doctor/patient interaction, isn't it?

Doctor S. The way she said it was that she knew the whole group wouldn't approve of her going off and looking in the library.

Dr. Tunnadine It's a little hard to expect Dr. X. to do any better is all I'm trying to say: if six other consultants have accepted her pain as physical.

Dr. Main We can all agree that this doctor fled from the psychosexual problem, whatever it was. She said, "I am not interested in *that*, I am interested in germs; so let's have germs and organs — I much prefer that". She couldn't attend to that and took flight and went back to books and proper procedures like 'pains are caused by germs' — well, we all know that, don't we?

Dr. Tunnadine It's silly to just argue. . .

Dr. Main I am talking about the doctor's anxieties.

Dr. Tunnadine I was really wanting to get at what the leadership business is about. Doctors and patients are not in a vacuum.

Dr. Main What goes on between these two?

Dr. Tunnadine The patient said this, and the doctor believed her.

Dr. C. That's our phantasy rather than the material you presented.

Dr. Main One way of attacking it, when you have a difficulty like this, is to ask the doctor and the group to discuss the *patient's* contribution: the way the patient is using the doctor; what sort of patient is it? why is the patient using the doctor? and how is the doctor using the patient? The two things can fit together. It's not easy to get a good discussion because the group very often has the same difficulty with that kind of description as you would have if I said, "What was the atmosphere in your group?" — It's vague. It's very important, but it's difficult to describe. People, instead of describing the atmosphere as intense or bad-tempered or low-level or hard-working — they will say, "Oh, very good". You can get through this sometimes by the detailed persecution by the leader, until you get it clear how the patient was treating the doctor, and what the patient's manner was and how the doctor was using the patient. You can get enough picture to understand the transaction between the two people.

Doctor S.   Have you any tips for when the group is absolutely roaring with laughter and you can't help joining in, because I felt very bad about that. It was really infectious.

Dr. Main   I'll tell you. When that happens, if you take notice of the group and its uniqueness and get the feel of what the whole thing is about. . . Not just the defence but the underlying anxieties.

Dr. I.   Perhaps you were relieved as well.

Dr. Main   Accepting the defence is fine, but you need to know what the *anxiety* was — if you don't know what the anxiety was, then the interpretation was not complete. For example, if I say to you, "Of course, you are defending now". But if I said, "You are defending a particular anxiety", it would have some meaning.

Dr. K.   What was the remark that came before the laughter?

Doctor S.   It was, "I reported this before and you all criticised me". And I suppose the anxiety was, "And we're going to do it again", maybe.

Dr. Main   No, I think they were very much relieved. They were feeling very guilty about it and they were roaring with laughter because it had been brought out into the open. It was true and they could enjoy it and they were relieved that this woman was still alive and none the worse for it.

Doctor S.   Yes. I suppose that was it — that she could actually say it and laughed herself as she said it. She is such a smiley person.

Dr. C.   That was good for this doctor, to be able to be as open as that.

Doctor S.   Mmm. It did seem like a great leap forward in understanding, though still. . .

Dr. Tunnadine   I'm going to be really nasty, because I am not sure that this doctor made any leap forward in understanding at all. I think the *group* made a leap forward in being able to face honestly that they had some rather nasty feelings.

5. The disruptive member

Leader Doctor L.

A leader described how one member was causing her some problems. The group was a new one, but some of them had been in a previous group. At the first meeting this doctor arrived before the others and had introduced herself to them by the time the leader arrived. She chose to sit next to the leader and on a number of occasions interrupted with remarks such as, "Susan won't like that!"

One of the cases presented was of a woman with a lot of children who had finally been sterilised. Since that time she had been very depressed and refused to have intercourse at all. When the doctor examined her and asked what she felt she was like, she replied, "Ugh, this is like raw meat. I'm yucky and horrible". She had been referred to a number of different specialists who hadn't helped; and this doctor too referred her on to somebody else.

The group discussion was almost entirely about the other children, who were all in some sort of trouble; and again the difficult doctor took over aggressively and said, "Talking about this woman's vagina is not going to help these children, who should be under child guidance. This sort of work with this patient is no good".

Dr. A. Was there something about the case, or about the doctor reporting the case, that produced all this aggression? Why did it suddenly erupt from this poor woman with her raw vagina?

Dr. I. I had the feeling of wanting to say, "Do you want to lead this group, or shall I?"

Doctor L. Mary is certainly wanting to be the major person. She is a very dynamic G.P. and the others in the group seem to look up to her; and she makes them laugh.

Dr. Tunnadine It seems to me you're trying to stay calm very well and not doing badly. She's actually one of the beginners, in a funny way, and yet she's sneaking in as the host, isn't she?

Mrs. R. But the so-called 'advanced' ones are the ones who admire her.

Doctor L. It was one reason why I kept them, so I could feel my guns loaded against her a bit.

Dr. Tunnadine But they won't tick her off for you, will they?

Mrs. R. That's because they don't undertand what's going on anyhow. This is the difficulty.

Short silence.

Dr. I. Can you throw her out?

Doctor L. Well, I think if we have a confrontation, she will opt out. I must confess that I do know some personal things about her. We sometimes meet socially and I know she is having trouble conceiving herself. I feel she may have some personal psychosexual difficulties.

Dr. Tunnadine When she presented a case before, you did say something about nervousness about her own sexuality. The question is, has she come for personal treatment? If so, how does one deal with that?

Dr. I. Do you feel she should be a member of the group?

Doctor L. No, truly deep down, I don't.

Dr. Tunnadine And yet, if one wanted a devil's advocate, from some of the things you've told us about her, maybe every group should have one. She really does have a go, doesn't she, and expresses things that need expressing?

Mrs. R.   She sounds very destructive. She's totally undermining anything you're trying to do.

Dr. I.   And inhibiting others from producing work.

Dr. Tunnadine   Does she have to go, or is there any way we can think of handling it?

Doctor L.   I don't see how she's inhibiting the work.

Dr. I.   Well, I had the feeling from you that, because of her explosive remarks when others come out with something, they find this inhibiting. The fact that they all laugh. . .

Doctor L.   You mean, it's an embarrassed laugh rather than —

Dr. I.   A funny laugh? . . . I don't know.

Dr. Main   I'm not a bit surprised, because I am a bit fed-up about the whole business. — What are we doing?

Dr. I.   Wondering whether a disruptive member of the group —

Dr. Tunnadine   — should be killed off.

Dr. Main   And what light does this throw on the case?

Dr. I.   Well, if she's a disruptive member, is it going to be more damaging to the other members of the group. . .

Dr. Main   But what light does it throw on this doctor/patient relationship which is under study? Or are we a thousand miles away from it?

Dr. A.   I wondered if you could have possibly used this outburst in relation to what this doctor was telling about this patient. I was trying to understand why she burst out at that particular moment.

Dr. Main   What was she exploding about?

Dr. A.   About the children.

Dr. Main   Go on, then: what does it mean?

Dr. A.   She would rather explode about children than about psychosexual problems.

Dr. Main   *This* psychosexual problem. — Why?

Dr. Tunnadine   Because it's too close to home, or something.

Mrs. R.   No children.

Dr. Tunnadine   Very close to home, isn't it? — It is not our business.

Dr. I.   But at that point you didn't know it was very close to home.

Dr. Main   It doesn't matter if it's too close to home or not.

Dr. Tunnadine   So you're saying how to use the case *forgetting* that you know about her personal problems.

Dr. Main   Yes. It looks to me as though you're getting awfully groupy and bothered about the individual doctors in the group, and not getting on with the work. Your idea, Dr. A., is that the anxieties about the patient were taking her away into these other defensive manoeuvres. How do you get them back on the road?

Dr. A.   If nobody else in the group was going to do it, the leader would have to make some remark.

Dr. Main   Here, I have just said, "What light does this throw on the doctor/patient relation?" because I want to get *this* group back and stop worrying about these damn doctors and private lives and whatnot, and get back on to what is going on. in the group as far as the work is concerned — You would do something like that, I take it?

Dr. A.   Yes.

Dr. Main   You would make some remark like, "How does this help us understand the psychosexual problems of the mother?"

Dr. A.   Yes.

Dr. Main   Or you could say, "It seems to be a pretty frightening business, this psychosexual business, that we have to make such dodgy manoeuvres and spend time complaining about other things". . . — something like that?

Dr. A.   Yes, I wouldn't have said it quite like that because I'm not as clever.

Dr. Main   Well, it's easy to say here on a nice Wednesday afternoon. I put it that way because I would be concerned not just with pointing out their defences and running away, but what anxiety they were running away from. It's no good saying, "Aha, you're dodging!"

Dr. A.   Is that being a bit personal?

Dr. Tunnadine   Not if you addressed it to the group.

Dr. Main   Because the whole group *was* involved in it.

Dr. Tunnadine   Yes, they were going along with her.

Dr. Main   Why does she need to be aggressive? This is a frightened doctor. The best way to help her would be to get the group to discuss the psychosexual problem of the *patient*. I would have thought her problem might go away once you get hold of the fact that she is frightened of the work.

Dr. I.   There's also the feeling that she is trying to aggravate you into saying, "You shouldn't be in this group". She wouldn't wish to say, "I don't want to come any more" herself, because that would be a let-down.

Mrs. R.   But Dr. Main isn't saying that. He's saying you must let her continue.

Dr. I.   I have a feeling she doesn't want to.

Dr. Main   I think she does want to, but she daren't come out into the open and say, "Look, I don't know anything about this". She's got to show what a cleverdick she is. She would be all right if she could get on with the work. The other thing is, the leader had been knocked off her perch by this doctor, who is pushing her in the direction of considering the doctors, treating the doctors. I am all for the group being thought about, not just the patients; but if you think about nothing *but* the group then the doctor/patient relation is never discussed. This can go on and on about the various doctor interactions and all this stuff which is irrelevant to the main task.

Dr. Tunnadine   The one chance on that level was the fact that everyone had pushed this patient on to someone else. No-one could stand her.

Dr. Main   Absolutely right. In the last century this woman would have been advised to take a trip to Australia. You can't get any farther away than that. "I know the very person for you" — all this sort of thing. There are signs of uneasiness with this woman.

Dr. Tunnadine   It could have been looked at in terms of that doctor dealing with that case.

Dr. Main   One more thing. If you talk about this woman's problems — she's got four children; she's had this, that and the other; when she was 16, a year later she was 17 — you get this sort of very interesting stuff — and then she became 21 and had another baby. . . — it doesn't matter! What is important is: what the hell were that doctor and that patient doing together? — We haven't heard a word about it, we really haven't. We've heard some frightening jigsaw puzzle. Did the doctor see the patient? *We don't know*. The main target area of our work was never brought into their discussion. They were waylaid, and that's presumably because the doctor was too frightened to talk about what had happened. The answer to this question of 'Why did these other people send her away?' would be the kernel of the problem. How to get them back to it? . . . I am liable, after the doctor has had a real go at it, to say, "Now tell us what's happened". After a long half-an-hour history, I say, "So far you haven't begun to speak. Now let's have something of the encounter". It would have been quite appropriate after that case had been discussed: "Tell us what happened". Or I might say, "Start again in this way: there you were, sitting in your office one fine afternoon at about 3 p.m. when the door opened and in walked. . . — Tell us what you saw, you heard and what went on".

Dr. Tunnadine   When faced by a doctor who could never do anything but talk about his case, I would quote Dr. Main and say, "That's one kind of story — now tell us the facts!" In other words, that's just stuff really. It's just what other people call facts.

Dr. Main   Or if I'm being quite savage — "Tell me, was there a doctor there?" The point is: get the work focussed on this task.

Dr. Tunnadine   There's another way the Master does it and that's by going to sleep and waking up and growling, "And what's that got to do with it!"

Dr. Main   Occasionally I pretend to go to sleep — *(yawning)* — when things are right off target; but this is with a group I know.

Dr. Tunnadine   I think really you're absolutely right and Dr. L. has been blinded by anxiety about this doctor, which made the case less interesting than it might have been.

Dr. Main   There's another thing which no-one has mentioned yet, a funny thing about this group. — Come on! . . .

Dr. Tunnadine   I don't know.

Doctor L. Don't tell me if it's more bad news.

Dr. Main. Susan will tell us about it. Good old Susan!

Dr. Tunnadine. First-name business.

Doctor L. Why — do you disapprove of that?

Dr. Main Not disapprove. — What's the effect of it?

Dr. Tunnadine That's right. I felt it very strongly as Dr. L. was talking.

Dr. Main Dr. L., are you conducting a group, or is Susan conducting the group?

Doctor L. I have been remiss in this.

Dr. Main No — I'm trying to *illustrate* something.

Doctor L. I always address the doctors in my group by their christian names.

Dr. Main Well, what's the effect on the group and its relation to you?

Dr. Tunnadine You're apt to get somebody telling you about their personal fertility problems.

Dr. Main That's a personal relationship. You have to jack it back and talk about the relevance to the work. You can be great friends with someone, personal friends, and have no respect for each other's professional work; or you may respect each other's professional work and not like each other. We are concerned about professional relations and how to keep it professional and not personal. — Is this making sense to you?

Doctor L. Yes, actually I'd never thought about it. Of course it makes sense. It has never been threatening before. No-one has ever attacked me before.

Dr. Main In the Medical Society people who know each other quite well will get up and say they would like to thank Dr. So-and-so for his very interesting whatnot. Or, "I am pleased to announce that Dr. So-and-so" — addressing them professionally.

Dr. Tunnadine Or The Honourable Member for Such-and-such.

Dr. Main I am addressing you in rôle, not as a person, and telling you how well you perform your rôle. There are all sorts of rôles — father, husband, gynaecologist, church warden or whatever; but you're not talking about *those* rôles. You're talking about the doctor rôle.

J

D. GROUP DYNAMICS AND THE TRAINING TASK

One of the most important tasks for the leader of a group is to observe the group behaviour and think about what this means in terms of the doctor/patient relationship, the doctor/group relationship and the group/leader relationship. The theory of group dynamics is not taught in a formal way by the Institute, but is studied in detail as the particular groups are discussed.

The danger of allowing the work to become group therapy for the individual members, rather than focussing on the training of their professional skills, has been mentioned already in several digests. However, occasional interpretation of feelings occurring between the group and the doctor, or between the leader and doctor/group, may be necessary. The most common reason is so that the group may be freed to work better. This may lead to clearer understanding of the patient's problem, or it may help individual doctors in their work (see III C 4).

Ways in which the leader can do this, and the importance of making the remarks about the group rather than about the individual, are explored.

1. INTERPRETING GROUP BEHAVIOUR TO FREE THE GROUP TO WORK.
Extract from Dr. Main's Weekend talk.

2. THE GROUP HAS DIFFICULTY STARTING WORK.
The problems of getting the group to start working, and the underlying reasons why this is difficult, are discussed.

3. INTERPRETING THE FEELING BETWEEN DOCTOR AND GROUP.
The leader is faced with a doctor who contributed well on other people's cases but presents her own badly. Ways for the leader to get the group to tackle this are suggested.

4. ANGRY LEADER IN TROUBLE WITH HER GROUP.
The leader finds herself expressing the anger of the group instead of helping the members to express their own anger.

1. Interpreting group behaviour to free the group to work

Extract from Weekend talk.

Dr. Main   The group will not be challenged to think if the leader thinks for them and pre-empts discussion. Better he leave the group to conduct the discussion, reserving his own remarks until every doctor in the group has had the opportunity to offer his contribution. When the group has exhausted its own ideas, the leader may seek to help the group to think further, about the reporting doctor's understanding and handling of the case. His remarks should aim to illumine learning not only for the presenting doctor but for the other group members also, as to the nature of the clinical events.

One way to achieve this is to draw attention to the facts of the doctor/patient relation. Another is to comment upon what is occurring in the group.

Example: Some time after a desultory discussion, a group fell silent, as if they had finished, but it was fairly clear that this was not a contented silence. I thought about this and realised that the discussion had been falsely congratulatory to the reporting doctor. Apparently supportive and encouraging, there was something dishonest about it: comment on the doctor's uselessness had been omitted. I came to the conclusion that the group was critical of this useless doctor but dare not say so, because they were trying to be only civilised and nice; not owning their own negative feelings. But I did not understand what this was about.

I made a not well focussed remark about seeming quiet and depressed; perhaps this was about something. This was enough for two members to talk about what they were fed up with: they were angry with the reporting doctor's long-suffering acceptance of his patient and his refusal to see that this was because he feared and denied his own anger, though this was obvious to them. The patient, impotent with his wife and harmless with his doctor, was a furious man who was punishing them both by being sweet and useless. The group then did some work on something which was obvious to me: the doctor was doing the same to the group as his patient to him, so that all became involved in a display of "nice" negative impotence under which, clearly, lay irritation and anger. The whole subject of transmission of uselessness via identification was opened up for study by my open observation of the group's silence; a very vague one.

So there are two levels at which the leader can work. To understand the doctor/patient relation is the group's task as well as his. Studying the group's behaviour is the leader's task. I recommend sparing use of remarks about the group such as the example above, for they contain many dangers. The group may be diverted from studying the doctor/patient relationship away to a different task; of the examination of group dynamics or of an individual's behaviour in a group setting. It may be a short step from here to group psychotherapy. These interests are seductive — who does not find them fascinating? — but to confuse them with the training of doctors is to avoid, to defend against the primary work task, the development of professional skills.

2. The group has difficulty starting work

Leader Doctor P.

A leader doctor made some general remarks about the development of her group over its first two terms. There had appeared to be a lot of group work that had to be done to clear the air: first, about the difficulty of doing the work as a married woman, having children and careers and being too busy; and then about how men, and the men in the group, see these problems differently. At the beginning of the third term, they seemed to find it difficult to start work, and spent a lot of time discussing the keeping of notes and other peripheral subjects.

Dr. Main   You have presented something which is worth taking notice of. You have discussed the group dynamics and how it was difficult even starting work. I bet you didn't handle that perfectly! *(Laughter)* How can you? We should pay some attention to this. We have been going for a quarter of an hour and *we* haven't started work until just now; and this is something about groups that we should take notice of. Groups don't start bang, like that, very easily. The work task seems to be deferred in almost every group. People usually talk about things outside: 'who's not here?' There is a reluctance to get going and to form a working relationship. It sounds as though it's happened for some weeks in your group. They wanted to talk about anything except work, and wanted to learn about what I call the pleasure principle.

Doctor P.   They tied it to the case, this business about being a woman, but somehow they seemed to manipulate the case, or tried to, to talk about how difficult it was to be a woman doctor with a young family and doing a job and coming to seminars.

Dr. Main   Let's have a think. . . — Any ideas about that problem?

Dr. I.   It's almost patronising, isn't it, saying: "Aren't you honoured to have us here?"

Dr. Tunnadine   That's one possibility. Another one that occurred to me is: "Don't expect too much of us. Life is difficult".

Dr. Main   They are stating the problem that work is difficult: 'For any of us, to get going on the work task is difficult. It's very difficult for us — let's see why — I know, it's because we are married. The fact is, it is difficult anyway; and it's very difficult because we've got a man here'. To talk personally — 'How are your children getting on?' — is another dodge. Another one is to turn to your leader and say, "What do you want us to do?", or "What ideas do you have? — Do you think we should do something other than work, like write notes and have a lovely doctor/paper relationship". These dodges are legion, but the problem is, they are doubling the work task. They lead to people talking to each other on a two-person basis, people taking flight to other topics. If I talk to you about my work, I am going to expose all my weaknesses. This delays the beginning of every group, because of the problems of working, especially as you are not sure what the orientation of the other person is. How many people in this room? — six for me, seven with the secretary. I have to relate to six people at once. A single person is much easier. I can find out what you are like this afternoon, and what your mood is, and how far I can go, or how far I shouldn't go. When one person faces you, that can be established very quickly; on a two-person basis, more difficult; on a 20-person basis, you cease to be yourself and you speak with rather more elaborate and involved sentences than is customary; you improve your accent a bit, dress properly — that is, you are setting up a projected monster that you have to behave properly towards.

Dr. Z. Do you think the original discussion is to establish a relationship?

Dr. Main Yes, absolutely. — 'Are you really the same person I met last time. Yes, you are. .'. 'Are you two quarrelling or not? — You're not: that's all right'. All sorts of things are going on in the first few minutes. We have to tolerate it and see it and watch it, but wonder what it is about, and how much anxiety is about work, and who is putting off work longest, and for what reason. That is what is going on in your group, isn't it? They are uneasy about work. Does that make sense? Do people recognise it?

Dr. Z. Do you ever get someone who says, "Let's get on with it".

Dr. Main The leader can do that.

Dr. Z. Sometimes you get it from the group.

Dr. Main You are not there to analyse the group's difficulties, but you are there to recognise them and try and make interventions; because once you start talking about the group's difficulties, you are into group therapy. I quite often say, "What about some work?" or make a teasing remark like, "All this gossip is great. It's better than work, isn't it?", or something like that: simply to draw the attention of the group to the fact that it is not working.

Dr. Tunnadine We haven't heard what Dr. P. has done about hers. There's a bit of contradiction amongst the group because they are all meeting eagerly and want to meet more often and are presenting cases, she says; although we haven't heard.

Doctor P. Would you like me to tell you about some cases? They do present cases all the time. — We had better start some work here!

3. Interpreting the feeling between doctor and patient — an infrequent technique

Leader Doctor N.

Doctor N.   I am concerned about one member in my hard-working group. She has a supply of good cases, is enthusiastic and picks up interesting images when other people present, but she is a poor raconteur and puts her own cases over badly.

The leader then described a presentation by this doctor of a patient who came and said she had felt no interest in sex since the birth of her baby. She never denies her husband, but he feels she is missing out and ought to get something done about it.

Doctor N.   The group took it up and they talked about whether this woman really just wanted to have sex to have babies; whether she was being sent to the doctor by the husband; and then, of course, inevitably some discussion about the husband. I tried to bring it back. The group is a bit nonplussed by this, but that is really because the doctor was a bit nonplussed by it. She had said to the woman at the end, "Come back and see me another time and we'll discuss it more". The doctor/patient relationship was one of putting-off the problem, just as the patient had been putting it off. I feel there is some deficiency in me as a leader that I haven't got a better technique for getting into these cases and to point out to this doctor that she is not letting us in on the whole picture. I will say to her, "You were there. What was it like when she came in?" and she'll give us a description of her clothing; but then you still haven't got any closer than that.

Dr. P.   Does she always present women with frigidity?

Doctor N.   She always presents women. I think there is a higher degree of frigidity in the cases that she produces.

Dr. I.   So, when asked how she feels about it, does she just stall you off again?

Doctor N.   Yes, we get on to the case history again. We get a repetition of how she was dressed, or a bit of history like "her mother said. . ." She is an excellent doctor for producing case fodder, but the sort of ammunition she gives you is damp!

Dr. P.   I would have thought it was frozen!

Doctor N.   She isn't a frozen woman; she is a very warm-hearted woman. I think she must be frightened at looking at the feelings. She can look at *other people's* patients' feelings.

Dr. S.   She's paralysed in *her* feeling.

Dr. Tunnadine   It would be different if she only did it once. If a doctor does something persistently, I suppose one can find a way of drawing attention to it — "Here goes Dr. X. again!" — I don't know what phrase you could find.

Dr. Main   Let's put the same fact another way. The fact that the doctor is persistent in this allows one to fairly safely come to the conclusion that this is not a product of a particular patient.

Dr. Tunnadine   Yes, so you can't say, "How did this particular patient get you to do it?", can you?

Dr. Main   You can't just say that the patient had some part in this, or it was something in the interaction between her and the patient. This is a personal characteristic which is revealing itself in her behaviour with her patient, and with her behaviour with the group. You can make remarks like, "You seem to have no feelings about this"; you can draw attention to that. Dr. Tunnadine's idea is to bring it out in the open: "We here in the group know you have a problem about this: here is Dr. So-and-so at it again". But have you actually had any remarks from the group which would allow you to say this without it becoming personal?

Doctor N.   The group subside into silence with her. That is something I *have* brought out — "The group has got stuck, like the doctor has got stuck", and things like this.

Dr. Main   In a situation like this, what choices have you got? There is a phenomenon which has been very clearly described. What is the woman doing to the group? What is this group doing to the woman? That is, instead of looking at the doctor/patient relation, look at either the woman's relationship with you, the leader, if that's the disturbance; or at the relation between her and the group. It sounds as if it's the group, rather than you. In public, she can't have any feelings because her insights and sensitivities are observable. Is it the group doing it to her, or is she doing it to the group? Is the group making her so shy that she hides from it? — "I wonder what we are doing to Dr. So-and-so?" Or is it, "I wonder what Dr. So-and-so is doing to us?" This last one is the least desirable thing to say, because it's a highly personal remark. If one can possibly say it as a group phenomenon, then one should.

Dr. Tunnadine For instance, would it be possible to say something like, "Isn't it interesting that we all find it difficult to find anything to say about Dr. So-and-so's case, which was a very similar one to the last".

Dr. Main You've just given an example of how to do it without a personal attack.

Dr. Tunnadine That's one way.

Dr. Main ". . . We seem to be paralysed with this discussion with Dr. So-and-so. There must be reasons for this. . ." No-one wants to say, "Pull your bloody socks up!" You are left with this danger that you might have to say it. It's the group's responsibility, not just yours.

Dr. A. Do they never ask her what she is actually feeling in the interview? Haven't they said to her, "What did you feel when this patient said that?", and did she just say nothing?

Doctor N. I can't actually remember the group putting it as bluntly as that to her. Whenever I have tried, she reverts back to this defence mechanism — covers up again.

Dr. Main It's a group problem.

Dr. Tunnadine I think it's interesting, too, that Dr. N. has brought it here and I just have a feeling somehow that, because she paralyses not only him but the group, that he is a bit bothered by taking responsibility for being the nasty.

Dr. Main Well, he can share it — "What are we going to do with Dr. So-and-so?" It pinpoints and shares the problem.

Dr. Tunnadine On your theory, that if the leader is feeling something, then everybody else is too, you can't be the only one.

Dr. I. But even if you put the responsibility on the group, it still is somehow denigrating to the doctor, or criticising the doctor. I don't see how you can do it.

Dr. Tunnadine I think you are right. But the woman does come every week, presumably wanting to be criticised — not in the sense of attack.

Dr. Main   You must criticise the doctor.

Dr. I.   How do you do it without making them feel. . ?

Dr. Main   ". . . This group does not seem to be able to discuss the fact that this doctor doesn't report very much about the patient. . ."

Dr. B.   ". . . She shows sensitive feelings when discussing other people's cases. . ." — I wonder if you could do it the positive way.

Doctor N.   It is as though the patients themselves paralyse this doctor, rather than the group or myself. It really seems that when she is put in an interview situation with a patient, she is frightened out of her wits and clams up; as though maybe she is frightened of giving too much of herself away to the patient.

Dr. Main   The rest of the group must know this, too. Why don't you discuss it in the open?

Dr. I.   Could it be, "Isn't it odd how this doctor seems to attract these awful patients?"

Dr. Main   No, that's quite dishonest. You can't save the doctor from awareness of her limitations. There is no way of saving her from that. She should be hit and hit hard, and if she gets hurt and depressed about it, that's excellent. She has got to change and there is no way of changing unless she gets really depressed about her present behaviour.

Dr. I.   She is warm with the other doctors.

Dr. Main   That's true, but her behaviour with patients is not good enough. It's an awkward fact, but it has to be faced. It is painful for her.

Dr. Tunnadine   The leader seems to be in some doubt about whether she is actually like that with her patients, or whether it is just the reporting.

Doctor N.   One thing that gives me a clue here is that she very seldom gets follow-ups.

Dr. Tunnadine   Ah — so there is some work to be done.

Dr. Main   Depression is a very helpful thing. It means that you review what goes on inside yourself and change — it's a painful matter, but it's the only way anyone can ever get any advance. You look at what you're doing and think, "Oh my God — I'm going to change!" It's painful to face facts that demand change, and it's depressing, but it's also hopeful.

Dr. Tunnadine I was just wondering if the fact that she was so good in other people's cases couldn't be used — draw attention to what a waste it seems, that someone who is so warm and contributing with other people's cases doesn't seem to be able to share her own.

Dr. Main She seems to be quite good at long distance, but not good in close contact. These are the kind of remarks that your group can make. It has to get to the stage that, when she does it again, the group will say, "You are doing it again!"

Doctor N. The other thing is that the group talk among themselves, and we have discussed some cases this last week; and I was able to sit back and not earn my money and just listen; and they were chatting away. . .

Dr. Main It's when you talk that you're not earning your money!

Doctor N. I have a picture of her talking to one of the newer members who was asking questions; answering her and looking at me, as though I was going to give her marks.

Dr. Tunnadine I don't understand that. Was she looking at you to defend her, or looking at you, "What is Sir going to say?"

Doctor N. No, I think she looked to me as though to say, "Asking a silly question like that! — You and I know that the answer is so and so". I couldn't say anything at the time. She has done more training than the others.

Dr. Tunnadine You didn't enjoy it very much, did you? It made you uncomfortable?

Doctor N. Yes, well I like it when the group talk amongst themselves: that is what you want them to do.

Dr. Tunnadine I'm not letting you get off the hook like that! — You don't like it that she was doing this teacher's pet thing with you. . .

Dr. Main It's often an example of someone who is remorselessly honest, but not concerned with damage. It requires that you and the group face this doctor with the fact that she does this, and get the group to share it. But what's it about? What can they do to help? Leave her *out of the discussion*. She can listen in to the group discussion about herself. The group will tackle her every time she does it. If it has been done without bad temper, it can only have a good effect, because they won't let her off the hook. How to get the group easy about facing this awkward truth, and what are their comments. . .

Dr. B.   I was wondering if she had never had a follow-up, and it would have been obvious that there would have been a follow-up — whether *that* couldn't be commented on in the group, or by you initially — "Why do you think that patient didn't come back?"

Dr. Main   Or: "I notice nobody in this group is pointing this out; they're all denying the problem". I am very reluctant to do these kind of things. Personal discussion on individuals is very painful. If you do it through the group, it's not so bad. — "We are not noticing that this doctor hasn't reported a follow-up. Isn't it a funny thing that we are not discussing this?" It gives the doctor a breathing space and the doctor hears it and the doctor knows that you are talking about her, but you are also taking responsibility for *doing* something about that doctor. It can only be done through the group, not just the doctor and the leader. It would be terrifying for the group if you did.

Dr. B.   I think you are a little frightened that it may dry up your source of cases.

Doctor N.   I don't think so. She's not a disruptive influence. The cases are paralysing, but when the discussion on other cases comes along, she joins in well.

Dr. Tunnadine   It sounds basically as if the leader feels there is gold in there being wasted.

Dr. Main   Why not say just that, and say she is bloody infuriating because she is hiding the gold?

Dr. I.   So perhaps you are angry with her?

Dr. Main   No question about that, but then the rest of the group is too. Anger is not enough. There is a reason to be angry because the phenomenon is there; but anger will not do as a response.

Dr. I.   One feels irritated with oneself that one can't bring out this gold.

Dr. P.   There is also this paralysing thing about needing to be clever, and it sounds as though when she is discussing other people's cases, she is able to produce fairly clever remarks: things that teacher will like. But when asked to expose the awfulness of sitting with a frigid woman, it is too awful because you can't be clever. There is no cleverness to do, in a sense.

Dr. Tunnadine   I am getting more and more interested in this 'teacher's pet' business. It makes it even more difficult for Dr. N. to be nasty in the group. What I mean is, she is having your balls as far as teaching her anything by these sort of games, isn't she? — 'You and I know the answer, so you are not going to be nasty to me, are you?. . .' She's defeating her own wish to learn if she's doing this, isn't she. . ? It must make it very difficult for you.

Dr. Main   There is a certain contempt, as well, for the other doctors.

Dr. Tunnadine   That's right. I rather liked the way you dealt with it: just ignored it, apparently.

Doctor N.   That's not dealing with it!

Dr. Main   Having a quiet life! *(Laughter)*. It's an interesting problem.

4. The angry leader in trouble with her group.

Leader Doctor M.

Doctor M.   It's not so much my group. I'm just being dreadful. I seem to have lost my wits.

The case was of a girl who could not consummate her marriage, and it had already been discussed several times in the group. Both the patient and the doctor tended to discuss the husband. When the patient did manage to voice her anxieties about something being wrong inside, the doctor reassured her and was not able to explore her anxieties.

Doctor M.   I was awful. I waited and tried not to say anything, but to think of all the material so that I could remember it when my moment came. The two good members of the group both chipped in with dreadful pussyfooting — "I wonder why you didn't ask her what she thought might be wrong with her inside" — in a very controlled voice like that.

Dr. Main   She was so bloody angry!

Doctor M.   That's right. Then the other one said something equally to the point, but equally pussyfooting.

Dr. Main   It's called 'sensitive!'

Doctor M.   Then there was silence. A couple more people came in and I had several goes with it — "Can we understand what is going on between the doctor and the patient?" We still weren't able to get any useful discussions going. What I am trying to say is that I was having to do all the work and it was driving me up the wall. Finally, like a fool, I lost my temper and began laying down the law and teaching. It seemed that the doctor had bashed the patient with her reassurance and sweetness, and it was clear that she had been pretty nasty to this patient; and so I said, "Look, now I am doing it to you and it's paralysed the rest of the group, hasn't it?" — so they all burst out, "Yes!" So I abandoned that case and tried to shrink back into my shell. They are not a bad group but they are doing something to me. Help me!

Dr. Main   What was going on?

Dr. I.   It's a battle, isn't it?

Dr. S.   Yes, but with someone who won't see the light, or won't understand what you are trying to say to her. She brings her own defences again and again, doesn't she?

Dr. Main   You will go on about the bloody individual, won't you! *(Laughter)*. Gently, I mean. *(Laughter)*. What is going on? Groupily, what was going on?

Dr. I.   They all seem to be ganging up.

Dr. A.   Yes. They are protecting this doctor instead of doing some work with her.

Dr. Main   And guess who fell for it!

Doctor M.   Of course! — This is what bothers me.

Dr. Main   It's very clear. It's a beautiful account of a group phenomenon and the leader has described how she felt. The more angry she got, the more they sat back and watched with great satisfaction and let her get on with it.

Doctor M.   I said two or three times, "Can anybody help me?"

Dr. Main   It was too late. That was after you had botched it up. It's a simple matter: you are *so impatient*. If the doctor feels something, then the ordinary rule is, 'Don't act on it. Write it down and think about it'. In ordinary clinical work it's not a bad rule. And let it tell you something about the patient. Well, what did this leader feel?

Dr. A.   Exasperated.

Dr. Main   Yes. All right. Now, instead of being exasperated actively, suppose she had looked at it and thought, 'I am exasperated — how interesting! What in the hell is going on here?' She would have had her wits about her, and could have seen what was going on. What *was* going on?

Dr. I.   One almost gets the impression they are there to bate you.

Dr. Main   No no, these other people were *furious* with this doctor.

Dr. A.   They are afraid to show it.

Dr. Main   These doctors also show the same fury. But this idiot leader *acted* on her fury, thinking, 'I am the leader: I must do something about it!'

Doctor M.   These other two did much better, but they did it politely! *(Laughter)*.

Dr. Main   This idiot of a leader, instead of realising, 'Oh yes, I'm getting angry; I bet the others are getting angry too. It's funny, they are being quiet; I'd better do something about their silence: "I see everyone is so angry that they are keeping quiet".. .' — *Instead of that*, shut up! Let them alone, see what they do with the intervention. Do something to *free them* to be angry, instead of taking on the responsibility for the group and leading it. She led like a good brave cavalry leader. Miles out in front of the cavalry. . . — gets killed, and is therefore no use.

Doctor M.   How to do it, you see? — I was even in the beginning thinking things like this. And yet I didn't manage to do what you say, somehow.

Dr. Main   Can you imagine yourself just shutting up and saying, "I notice people aren't discussing this very much?"

Dr. I.   But would they?

Dr. Main   No, they would have got worse and worse. . .

Dr. I.   They would have said, "No, we're not angry".

Dr. Main   Suppose you had left them alone until it was quite clear they were in difficulties, and *then* make your contribution.

Dr. S.   The patient is always blaming the husband and not owning her own difficulty, isn't she?

Doctor M.   Yes, it was like that; and the patient and the doctor were very like the doctor and the group; and I had drawn attention to that in various other reports of the same case.

Dr. I.   They wouldn't buy it, would they?

Dr. B.   The other members of the group did, I think. It's the reporting doctor. . .

Doctor M.   Yes, the doctor reported her continuing deafness, and I dealt with it badly. These two who could see it did try to verbalise it, but in a terrible pussyfooting way.

Dr. Main   Let's say it was a non-consummation. They had a go but were quickly discouraged; like the husband is discouraged in a non-consummation case every time. And you were more and more fed up with them all not consummating, and then you fucked the lot of them!

Doctor M.   Yes *(laughing)* — but it was very bad technique.

Dr. Main   No, look — not very bad technique.

Dr. I.   If you had turned round and said, "You are all angry with this doctor, aren't you? . . ."

Dr. Main   That would have been absurd.

Dr. I.   Well, not quite like that.

Dr. Main   You have to wait until it's clear that they are.

Doctor M.   And then say what?

Dr. Main   Say, you realise that you are angry, but there are other people as well angry. — You don't have to worry about that. Leave it until it's clear.

Dr. B.   Surely the group saw why you were so exasperated, did they not?

Dr. Main   They deserted their own anger once she took the burden.

Doctor M. They did laugh with relief when I finally got around to it at the end. But it was too late. It was bad work. I shut them up.

Dr. Main She was the peer point of the group.

Doctor M. They were relieved when I said that I had been angry, but it was a waste of a case report, because it was an interesting case, actually. I find myself doing it more and more with these people. That is why I am worried.

Dr. Main May I help you a bit? I have personal knowledge of one of your doctors, who is a keen thinking and highly intelligent doctor of great modesty, and she tends to keep quiet, particularly about being aggressive. She tends to kill you with sweetness, rather than just get up and hit you. But she does have feelings and does get angry. But you can't count on her to tell you how bloody fed up she is.

Doctor M. At least she said something.

Dr. Main But it's typical of her that she would be like that. — That's one I know about. . .

Doctor M. The trouble is that none of the group attack anybody fiercely.

Dr. Main That's what your trouble is as a leader; and you've helped them along by taking the responsibility for being the nasty one.

Doctor M. That's what I am fed up about. I would hope that I am helping them by being a model, but it isn't working out like that.

Dr. Main No, they are leaving you to it.

Doctor M. That's right.

Dr. Main It's the old business of the Roman circus. All the peaceable citizens watch while the others fight each other and kill each other; and they are very happy to sit and eat their bananas.

Dr. A. Did you *tell* them that they leave it to you?

Doctor M. I have said it on various other occasions in various other groups.

Dr. Main It's not fair to say that. She *took it* from them.

Doctor M. Yes, that's the trouble.

Dr. A.   Well, they did leave it first of all. They didn't get on with it.

Dr. Main   Two of them did a bit; and the interpretation would have been to have pointed out the aggro about it.

Dr. I.   The problem is, shutting up while waiting for them to come out with it themselves.

Dr. Main   Mmm. It's the old business: if *you* feel something, then you can bet that the rest of the group is feeling it.

Doctor M.   I think perhaps I need to take a rest from this group. I've lost the trick.

Dr. Main   It's all right saying you've lost the trick — I don't like this breast-beating stuff! *(Laughter)*.

Doctor M.   I'm just demoralised. . .

Dr. Main   I think what you have to recognise is — and don't tell anybody this — *not all groups are the same (Laughter)*. Don't spread the news. — Can't you see that it is a particular group?

Doctor M.   It's a challenge to me, but I'm just not doing very well with it.

Dr. Main   The group isn't doing very well with you, all right.

Dr. B.   One wonders what makes a group unable to express any anger with each other.

Dr. Main   Well, I've had experience of this in other groups. Some of the proudest moments I've had in any training were to get the group to see the rage of aggression. I can't remember the year — I wish I could, then I could boast about it — because it was the day one of our members saw that she slid the knife in every now and then with the patients, and the group were jeering at her for being so aggressive — she of all people! But it's very hard work and they are all sweet, nice people and so full of compassion and other bloody malicious blindness. I think they are so aggressive that they can't be honestly aggressive with each other.

Doctor M.   That's an interesting idea. That's given me food for thought.

Dr. Main   The defensive processes of being gentle and so on are in full operation. They are not friendly enough to be aggressive.

Dr. B.   Not enough trust amongst them. . .

Dr. Main And what is happening now is that they have an aggressive leader, and they are such nice people — "Oh, there's that aggressive leader again!"

Doctor M. They do, you see. Oh dear. . .

Dr. Main Next time you feel aggressive, think, 'Ah, the bastards!' — and leave it to them, I would think.

Doctor M. I think I'll have to.

Dr. Main Does that make sense to anyone? *(General agreement)*

Doctor M. I've tried interpreting it more than once, you see, and they just laugh at that and enjoy that; but that lets them off the hook again.

Dr. Main You don't let them get in a big enough fix about it. Let the discussion go on for an hour and a half. Let them get in trouble, and then you might have some chance.

Doctor M. I am afraid that I am a bit like Dr. S. — I like them to get on and I am impatient.

Dr. Main You know the story about Freud when he was asked why he didn't hurry? He was asked why he couldn't get on quicker and he replied with this story: there was a man who was going out for the evening with his wife. They got into the car and his wife said, "Look, we're in a hurry; we have got no time for short cuts". — It's no good hurrying.

Doctor M. I think you are right. I will just have to try and sweat it out, because there will be other occasions. I have been busier and busier for about the last four meetings. You know how it gets.

Dr. B. It's like with the patient, isn't it? It's no good *saying* it.

Dr. Main The other thing is: the leader is angry with herself.

Doctor M. I am, because it's awful.

Dr. Main I think you've got the wrong target.

Doctor M. Well, I'm not too pleased with them either, you won't be surprised to hear.

Dr. A. It seems that the presenting doctor in that case creates such an atmosphere that it is very difficult to criticise her.

Dr. I. Can you turn round and say, "What is this doctor doing?" I am wondering how you can actually make the rest of the group say, "God, that's awful work!"

Doctor M.   That's what I am wondering.

Dr. Main   Have people got any ideas about bringing the husband in and then sending him out?

Dr. I.   I feel they are sitting there paralysed.

Dr. Main   I know, but it's no good taking on the task for them.

Doctor M.   I have to keep saying, "What was going on between the doctor and the patient?": not only with this doctor, but with the group in general. I have to — directively, if you like — keep on bringing them back to that; and then, sometimes they do some work and sometimes they don't. I think you are right about this gentleness business.

Dr. Main   This particular problem requires one of those rare things: a remark about the group behaviour. It is highly personal, such as what that doctor is doing to the group, or what that group is doing to that doctor. I think it is very much easier and less personal if you talk about *what the group is doing to the doctor.* "The group is failing to discuss the material: it hasn't taken up the discussion on the husband coming in; the group hasn't discussed so and so — what is this group doing to this doctor? Why is it protecting her from these troubles? . ." — That is one way. The other thing is to talk about how this doctor, by her gentleness and sweetness, tolerates and speaks to christian charity and high-sounding principles and paralyses the group from using its critical powers.

Doctor M.   Yes, this is something I hardly ever do. I think, "Shall I comment on the group behaviour? No" — and then go back to what is going on between the doctor and the patient. You think one can occasionally do that?

Dr. Main   It is all right to do it. If you can get the group to wake up to the fact of what it is *not* doing, funny things can happen.

Doctor M.   It's worth a go. I'll have a try.

Dr. Main   I remember one occasion when I drew attention to the fact that the group was half asleep. I knew it was half asleep because I was feeling half asleep myself and this doctor was droning on. It was quite plain that something queer was going on and I had to think: 'Do I say, "What has she done to the group?" or do I say, "What has the group done to the doctor?". . .' The thing was saved for me by the case coming to an end and the doctor said, "And the patient died this morning"; and they were terribly pleased. *(Laughter)*. It was clear that she was subjecting the group to the utter weariness of having a patient who is complaining all the time but wouldn't die. She went on and on, living with this case for months — every day — it was awful; and it was wearisome for her, and she made it wearisome for us. If I had pointed out what she was doing we would have got on to this earlier. It will come round to the case eventually. The lack of discussion of open aggression in *this* case between the doctor and the patient is clear.

Doctor M.   It was clear to them by the end of the afternoon. It wasn't that bad from the actual case study point of view. It was just that I had to do it all, from beginning to end, including the bad temper — and it was awful!

The importance of interpreting the group behaviour when there is excitement, especially when this excitement has been provoked by the sexual nature of the material, is discussed in Sexualising the Interview II B. *Readers interested in this technical leadership problem are referred back to those discussions.*

E. MIXED GROUPS — Rivalries?

Two pioneer nurse leaders use the seminar method of training nurses. One of them takes part in these workshops. In addition, some doctors lead groups of nurses, or mixed groups for nurses and doctors. It is likely that many of the training ideas explored in these digests would be applicable to the training of other professionals. Some experience has already been gained in the training of nurses and of physiotherapists working in Obstetrics and Gynaecology.

1. DOCTORS AND NURSES.
Some of the difficulties than can arise in a group containing different professional workers are explored here.

2. THE LOCUM LEADER.
Rivalries can be within groups, but also between leaders. The work and possible feelings about a locum leader are studied in this digest.

3. NURSES TRYING TO FIND A COMMON LANGUAGE.

4. THE SETTING AFFECTS THE WORK.
Even within one profession the different languages spoken by those working in different settings can make it difficult for a group to work effectively.

5. INHIBITION OF PHANTASIES.
An unusual situation is discussed in this digest. The patient had been seen by a doctor and a nurse, both of whom attend the same group.

1. Doctors and nurses

Leader Doctor K.

A mixed group of family planning doctors and nurses had been running for just over a year when there was a meeting to which none of the doctors came. A case about a woman who had lost interest in sex after a baby was discussed. This patient had been discussed before, and one of the doctors in the group had been asked to see her; but the patient had not kept the appointment. The presenting nurse said she was glad that none of the doctors was there, because it was easier to discuss the problem of how much of the work the nurse was allowed by the doctor to do in the clinic.

Doctor K.   So then we had a discussion in the group about the problem of having a mixed seminar; the problems about nurses taking on this kind of work with a doctor in the clinic who probably is not trained in such work, who is an expert contraceptor but not trained in this; and the relationship between doctors and nurses working in the same field but in a different way. I think I said something like, "We have to take a look at this, because we are now working in a field in which we are not experts. We are working *with* patients and trying to learn a skill that isn't based on knowledge. Perhaps it is possible for the nurse to feel that we are all learning together, and she is therefore just as well able to take on these problems as the doctors". That was the theme: it was about hierarchy and traditional rôles of doctors and nurses.

Dr. Tunnadine   So the nurses were able to raise this when the doctors were out of the way?

Doctor K.   Yes, in this particular seminar.

Dr. I.   Presumably the doctors haven't raised this issue?

Doctor K.   No.

Dr. A.   Are the nurses allowed to treat patients by the doctors?

Dr. Tunnadine   You are beginning to believe that, too. — Let's stick with Dr. K.'s report.

Dr. Main   I agree. Let's look at the seminar. We can reform the National Health Service later. *(Laughter).*

Dr. Tunnadine   And yet this is a content of what's happening, isn't it? — there's something about these people who don't allow people to do things.

Dr. I.   Do some of the nurses in the group see the same patients as the doctors in the group?

Doctor K.   Yes.

Dr. Main   You can't discuss it with the other ones away. The nurse shouldn't discuss the case with the doctor away.

Doctor K.   No.

Dr. Tunnadine   So while the cat's away, these nurses have something to say to the leader about this thing, don't they?

Dr. Main   I'm a very sensitive person and I think maybe they are talking about difficulties between doctors and nurses. — Could it be about the doctors and nurses in the group?

Dr. Tunnadine   It is the only thing we have any control over anyway, as far as I can see. Can we postulate that at least? It's difficult for you, who are wondering what you have got into, whether they are all going to come on alternate weeks, separately! *(Laughter)*.

Doctor K.   I don't think they will, but there is this problem about territory.

Dr. S.   As I heard it, the nurse picked up a patient and made an appointment for her to see one of the doctors, and the patient chose not to turn up to see the doctor. I think the nurse was saying: "That patient wanted to see *me*. I was the right person to look after that patient".

Dr. Main   Mmm. — 'I'm *better* than doctors. . .' — And the doctor belongs to this group?

Doctor K.   Yes, she does. She spoke about it the time before.

Dr. Main   Let's divide — those for the nurses and those for the doctors! *(Laughter)*. Let's look at the fight.

Dr. C.   I wonder if the doctors were at all crippled in the group by the nurses.

Dr. Main   There are no signs of that.

Dr. C.   They haven't turned up very much.

Dr. Main   Look — there's trouble here, isn't there?

Dr. N.   You say there was an edict by someone that nurses weren't to see patients. Was that the doctor in your group, or was this just an administrative doctor? Are we dealing with that particular doctor in your group?

Doctor K. No, we're not; because I think the nurses and doctors, by consenting to come to the same group, showed there was an understanding that nurses would be able to see people. But certainly in some clinics, some doctors don't like the nurses doing this.

Dr. Tunnadine They are all beginners in this unlearning way of working and both lots feel uneasy about it in their different ways. It would be a mistake to let them accept their formulation, the traditional one, at face value; because there are different doctors and different nurses. In the tug-of-war they don't weigh the same as the other lot; like rugby players against athletes — they take the rugby player off. It would be a pity to get into that balance of power; and yet the nurses are inclined to think the doctors aren't better than they are; and the doctors are clearly frightened that the nurses are going to be better than they are. It's great that the leader has opened it up, but you only had half of them and maybe it needs to be opened up when they are all there.

Dr. Main The leader said, "You are wrong to feel inferior; you're just as good in my opinion". That was her method: it's called 'reassurance'.

Dr. Tunnadine That's right.

Dr. Main The other way is to bring the anxiety out ; face it — that they feel they are not as good as doctors in that group.

Dr. Tunnadine And of course the doctors, too, presumably need to be able to say something about, "It would be awful to think that we are not better than nurses".

Dr. Main The trouble about this mixed group is that you are clearly not going to be able to go ahead with the discussion of cases. There is a danger of getting into group therapy because of the tension between the nurses and the doctors; not only over cases, but in the group itself. . . The nurse took one look at the patient and said, "Oh, how interesting for the doctor! I'm not permitted to do this, thank God!" It's a very great thing to say, "Of course, I would love to treat it, but the doctor won't let me". It's guilt.

Dr. B.　Interestingly enough, in another group that is *all* nurses, one of the nurses actually said, "Well, I know that whatever I do will be much better than whatever my doctors do". She's a general practice nurse. She actually said that, didn't she? She had been describing a case that she had been treating.

Dr. Main　She wanted to treat cases, but this one didn't. She said, "Ah, that's for the doctor".

Dr. Tunnadine　This was a sort of non-case, because it was the doctor's case, and the nurse couldn't talk about it because it was behind the doctor's back.

Dr. Main　The leader might have helped the nurse to have faced the fact that she got frightened and ran away with a good excuse. Why didn't she run away earlier, for instance? You can face the nurse's difficulty with the patient and what was going on, and the nurse thinking, "My God, it's bigger than I thought!" That's one way: to stick on the nurse/patient relation. But the group thought, 'the poor nurse can't treat the case, so we can't talk about it'. The case wasn't discussed. The nurse's rationalisation about not being allowed to treat was followed. — It sounds as though this business of the doctors and nurses needs to be got out of the way fast or it will become a chronic issue.

Doctor K.　I said I thought we could discuss it with the doctors.

Dr. Main　In this case the nurse panicked at the amount of material she was getting and said, "This is doctor's stuff". If a nurse is prohibited from working she shouldn't really be in your group. — If you take the individual and look at it from that point of view, you can start to make sense of it, rather than get occupied with issues: 'The real trouble in the world after all is between men and women;. women have a raw deal in the world' — you can have this sort of stuff if you want to, instead of getting on to the doctoring.

Doctor K.　Nurses in the group do have high anxiety about taking on the cases, and in the first nurses group where we have been meeting longer, I think we are just getting through that a little bit; but it is still there.

Dr. Main　Their anxiety — yes.

Dr. Tunnadine　And the four doctors of course, being doctors, have no such anxiety!

Dr. Main 'It's a proper case for a psychiatrist really' is the doctor's cop-out. It sounds to me like an ordinary basic anxiety of anybody. I think we can get really occupied with this nurse/doctor business and do no work.

Dr. Tunnadine This might actually put pressure on the anxious doctor members of the group, too, that they will be set-up like this. They have to be the clever ones and the whole thing could go round and round for ever.

Doctor K. They are exposing themselves as being cleverer than anyone else.

Dr. Tunnadine But how to cope with it?

Dr. Main If I were in that group, I would be interested *not* in the similarities in the nurses' and the doctors' work, but the dissension between the two settings. The nurse very often has someone she has to refer her work to; the doctor very often doesn't; and this makes for different types of anxiety. The blaming of the boss for deficiency in one's own work — the 'I could be so good if it weren't for my boss' defence — and the fact that the nurses do feel restricted in their work, could be brought out as typical of their anxiety. There's an awful lot of room here for studying the different settings in which they work. The nurse hasn't got the same training as the doctor, and the patient doesn't have the same expectation. They are much more on the ground level, sisterly stuff. I think the nurses probably have singular opportunities which are not given to doctors. People tell their troubles to the cleaners and stuff like this goes on. Often it's thought it's too trivial to trouble the doctor with; all sorts of things go on and it would be very interesting to get the distinction clear. All parties would be interested in it.

Dr. I. I suppose they have different opportunities, too, because you implied that it was a midwife, who wouldn't necessarily have much opportunity to see the patient many more times, so perhaps she would feel under pressure to do something quickly.

Dr. Tunnadine That would emerge, wouldn't it if as Dr. Main suggests, we are positively interested in the *difference* and not needing to say, "Look, we're all the same" and reassuring. With G.P.s and family planners we draw attention to the fact that the set-up is different; and people who have referrals in an advanced group are again in a different situation. You are saying, "Make a virtue of this".

Dr. Main   Yes. I sometimes tease my Welsh friends by telling them that they shouldn't worry about being Welsh, they are just as good as anybody else; and that is what the leader did with those nurses!

Doctor K.   I am wondering whether I should do what I said I was going to do and talk about it in the next group; or whether it's better, as you say, to let it come up on an individual basis, which I know it will.

Dr. Main   I think you should feel free to do anything you like, so long as it is concentrating on the doctor/patient or the nurse/patient relation.

Dr. N.   Having said that you were going to bring it up at the next group, you can't just forget that. You have to say that you have thought about it and decided not to; or "We are going to see what happens and bring it in as the cases bring it in"; or go ahead and do it. I don't think you can just leave it.

Dr. Tunnadine   Well, you and I couldn't, anyway! *(Laughter)*.

Dr. Main   It's very easy to have a group defence against case study. And anyhow, that situation — you know, in the Middle East — very important. . . — Anything will do.

Dr. I.   I wonder whether your real anxiety is that having got the nurses to come in order to make a big enough group, you are now losing the doctors.

Dr. Main   Dr. K. hasn't got any anxieties like that! *(Ironically)*

Dr. I.   You did say one of the doctors was a good attender before the nurses came.

Dr. B.   He's been the only man in a doctor's group and I wonder if it's much more difficult to cope with, being the only man in a doctors and nurses group.

Doctor K.   Time will show.

Dr. Tunnadine   It depends what his work is like, really. We haven't heard about that yet.

Dr. Main   Well, I think women doctors aren't nearly as good as men doctors, myself! — The common thing we have is *doctoring*. If you go all over the world you will find you have professional brothers and sisters. The same is true of other jobs. A Chinese carpenter has far more in common with a British carpenter or a North American carpenter than he has with any engineer that lives next door. This is an international business and it doesn't matter about sex or race. We have this job, a professional area of competence, and we share it. *That* is what they meet for, not because they are men, or women, or whatever.

Dr. N. Is one of the anxieties in this feud with doctors pulling rank and nurses grumbling and so on — is it a competition for cases? Is there a limited amount which the doctors feel they must get their hands on? Or are they overwhelmed with cases?

Dr. Main This is a general thing, flight from cases in the discussion, isn't it? Or is there a real economic problem?

Dr. N. I don't know, you see. I think if there were a lot of cases, then there wouldn't be this hierarchical structure: it wouldn't matter. Someone can get on with the job. But if there is a limited number of cases and you are keen to improve your technique, and you're going to a seminar and must have something to present — you try and squeeze the other chap out a bit.

Dr. C. There doesn't seem to be a dearth of cases in your area?

Doctor K. Well, there isn't — but there is when you *begin*, isn't there? Yes, this has occurred in some of the other groups. — Anyway, thank you. I feel — what shall I say? — less anxious and able to have a go at it.

———————

Three months later this leader reported to the group again.

Doctor K. At the next seminar I brought up this question of the doctors and nurses and their different rôles. From then on we have managed to work much better as a group on a fairly straightforward basis.

The leader then went on briefly to describe three follow-up cases that had been discussed. One was a woman who had been worried because her husband masturbated in the bathroom with girlie magazines; he had only done this since the arrival of her baby. The second was from a member who also worked in marriage guidance, who presented a complicated story of marital strife, and sexual

*difficulties when the woman was with her husband but not with her
lovers; and the third was a case of non-consummation. The group
discussion was lively and everyone joined in.*

Dr. S.   Do they have equal opportunities to carry out the work,
or are they going to be the chalk and the cheese a bit?

Doctor K.   They work in clinics together and now the doctors
have seen that the nurses want to do the work, I think they will
allow them to have the time to do it.

Dr. Tunnadine   It's very interesting: would any of you be able to
say which was the nurse and which a doctor?. One did one case
and one did another. . .

Mrs. R.   One was a marriage guidance counsellor.

Dr. S.   She was a nurse.

Dr. Tunnadine   It's interesting you say she was a nurse; because
my feeling about her was that, whether she was a doctor or a
nurse, she was a marriage guidance counsellor and not in touch
with the nurse/patient relation yet; and that was what I missed.
What impresses me is the difference between this report and the
previous one which was all about the doctors and nurses. That
seems to have disappeared.

Doctor K.   It is much better.

Dr. Tunnadine   And you did this apparently by tackling it head
on. It's interesting that this technique seems to have worked.
They seem to be just individuals now, good, bad and indifferent;
but they *are* working.

Mrs. R.   Has your one man come back?

Doctor K.   Not yet.

Dr. Tunnadine   It's a pity our one man today has had to leave *this*
group as I would have liked his views. To be the one man among
equals is bad enough; but to be the only man in a group where you
feel you have to be better than people would have been even more
difficult, don't you think? If he shows himself less competent even
than nurses, if you see what I mean. . .

Dr. K.   He may have left because we were all women; or because
we were mixed doctors and nurses; or because we were all family
planners.

Dr. Tunnadine   Yes, many reasons. So you shouldn't mourn for him too much; perhaps find another group where he could come back and not be the only man.

Dr. B.   It's a bit difficult, I think, with the nurse who is a marriage guidance counsellor, because she's not sure if she's there as a nurse or a marriage guidance counsellor.

Doctor K.   It's a bit difficult to blend her in.

Dr. A.   Can she examine patients vaginally?

Doctor K.   Yes.

Dr. Tunnadine   The interesting thing about her case was that she was on fairly good ground dealing with couples. It's what she knows about, and their relationship and all that. One of the other patients sounds as if she was in difficulty with her own sexuality. This poor chap with the magazines: she's suddenly become a mother, and he prefers young dollies; it didn't sound frightfully pornographic to me, did it to you?

Doctor K.   He was drawing tiny women's genitals; or women's tiny genitals.

Dr. Tunnadine   Isn't it sad? Obviously he preferred her before, but *her* feelings about it weren't really explored. — But it sounds a great group to me and I think you're going to forget which they *are* before long, don't you? I've certainly forgotten which they are already. It wouldn't be surprising if some of the nurses had more feel for it than some of the doctors, and vice versa.

Postscript: *Eventually all the doctors left this group, but more nurses joined and worked enthusiastically and well.*

2. The locum leader

Locum leader Doctor S. (Regular group leader Dr. K.)

A doctor went as a locum to lead a mixed group of doctors and nurses. The first person who wanted to present a case was a doctor, and one of the nurses said, "We can always depend on him to have a case". The case was presented and discussed, and the leader continued as follows:

Doctor S. The next case, which I won't describe, had one of the nurses saying, "I wish I had been the doctor, then the patient wouldn't have spoken to me like that". Somebody said to her, "But it was only *that* patient who made you feel you should have been a doctor not a nurse. Other patients don't make you feel like that'. As this went on I was thinking, 'and I am not the legitimate leader, either'. Something made me feel that I wasn't quite as good as Dr. K. in their eyes.

Dr. Q. You had to be very careful how you handled it. In your own group you would —

Doctor S. — be a bit more forthright, probably.

Dr. Tunnadine I think we are all sharing this feeling that Dr. S. is treading on eggshells, and it sounds as though they were, too; as though they were all on their best behaviour.

Doctor S. I was rather fed up with the nurses' reporting, but was afraid to say so, and got into this difficulty between the doctors and the nurses. I suppose I could have attacked the doctor, but I couldn't have attacked the nurse. I came away feeling how difficult it was to lead a group with people who have very strong feelings about each other.

Dr. E. It came out even earlier, didn't it? The doctor said, "I've got a case" and the nurse quipped, "Oh, you can always depend on him to have a case".

Dr. Main Thank God there are no rivalries in *this* group!

Doctor S. One nurse said, "I've got this nice new job and I'm afraid I am taking on more than I can cope with". She showed her great hesitancy in this field, although she gives the impression of being very good: sensitive and non-directive.

Dr. Tunnadine But kind of apologetic for it, at this stage?

Doctor S. Yes. Made me want to encourage her.

Pause

Dr. Main Nobody is helping Dr. S. They are patting her on the back and saying, "Well done. It's difficult, isn't it?"

Dr. Q. Do you think that is because it's this mixed doctor/nurse group? You feel you can only bash the doctors and you have got to protect the nurses.

Doctor S. I did feel like that, yes.

Dr. I. That came through to you, so presumably they must have felt it too.

Pause

Dr. Y. Are you going back to this group?

Doctor S. No. I said before you came in that I was just asked to lead it as a locum.

Dr. Y. Is that why we are all a bit silent?

Doctor S. Yes, it's a bit of a non-starter in a way. I'm afraid I wanted to report so that I don't get too out of practice, but I notice that I was out of practice. I couldn't remember.

Dr. Tunnadine The leader has reported how she tried to remain silent, but how she found herself being clever and solving the case at the end. This seems a nice illustration of the difficulties with nurses. One the one hand you pussyfoot, but on the other hand you cannot resist delivering the goods and telling them. I am bothered by this 'doctors and nurses' thing. At one level Dr. Main will say that to compare the work of people from different settings is not comparing like with like. That's true technically, but there is a kind of arrogance about treating nurses gently when they might be a damn sight better at the work than the doctors. I have heard the same sort of thing about 'these poor men G.P.s who come into our marvellous family planning'. Just another example of rivalry difficulty for the leader. It's very nice to have the mugs, you see. They would have to be invented, these vulnerable nurses, if they didn't exist — and suppose they are better than the doctors? We have all suffered this in different groups.

Dr. B. My group is mixed nurses and doctors and the two nurses are better than the doctors. They have done a previous seminar and they make more useful contributions in the group.

Dr. Main You mean, they are better *nurses* than the doctors, or better *doctors* than the doctors are?

Dr. B. I mean they are better at this work.

Doctor S.   And often they know they are better. I think the reporting nurses on this occasion didn't feel as good and kept apologising.

Dr. Tunnadine   Whether you are better nurses or better doctors or better whatever shouldn't be our concern as leaders. If it is, there is a danger that the group believes they have got to know a lot about everything. The object of our training is to help people to realise that is *not* the object; it is not about knowing a lot, or about doctors having some sort of hierarchy of sexual expertise. Yet it seems as though these people played this game with you, the poor innocent nurses.

Dr. Main   I once met a doctor who was a good deal better than another doctor.

Dr. Tunnadine   Exactly.

Dr. Main   I dare say a nurse and a doctor could do equally good work, couldn't they, and there would be no rivalry between them. — They are all paid the same, aren't they! No need for any rivalry.

Doctor S.   It seemed very obvious to me and I wasn't even looking for it.

Dr. Tunnadine   There are rivalries in other groups between doctors and doctors, but it's what one does about it that I am puzzling after. Dr. S. didn't make any interpretations about it, as far as we've heard.

Doctor S.   Oh, no.

Dr. Main   If it's stopping the work, it should be interpreted; but it doesn't seem to be troubling the work as far as it was reported. The other thing about which a remark might have been made was that they were treating Dr. S. as if she were a kind of substitute for a better doctor. If that is holding up the work then that, too, should be brought out into the open. If it is not holding up the work, then it needn't be.

Doctor S.   I didn't think it was holding up the work.

Dr. Main   No. I thought the group was pretty good before a strange leader who had come in out of the blue. In fact, I thought they were showing off a bit to keep you out. But you did draw attention to one thing: they addressed the reporting doctor, they didn't discuss it with each other. It wasn't really a discussion, but

questions and answers. What to do about that? It's a
phenomenon that Dr. S. noticed, but did nothing about. Should
attention have been drawn to it?

Dr. Q. I have a feeling that you would have intervened, but you
were hindered by thinking that you were only there as a locum
and you'd got to watch and just see that everything went all right.

Dr. Main Yes. Do you mean the ugly question of rivalry
between leaders? — There was nothing like that, was there!

Dr. Q. No, I didn't mean —

Dr. Main No, of course not!

Doctor S. There was a moment when the reporting doctor
quoted the regular leader at me and I thought, "Oh, she says
that, does she!"

Dr. J. But by the same token, the group might have protected
Dr. K. and not wanted the incomer leader to go away with a bad
impression of the way the group was working.

Dr. Tunnadine They are not very successful if that is the case.

Dr. J. You mentioned the idea that they might be showing-off,
but I thought there was a feeling of, 'This is our work and you are
only here for one occasion and we have got to show you. We are
not going to let our leader down'.

Dr. Main Yes. "F.H.B."*

Dr. Y. It might have been a freeing experience, too, mightn't it,
to have somebody who is totally strange to them? — a fresh
start?

Doctor S. Yes.

Dr. Tunnadine I think the direction this discussion is taking is
because Dr. S. has these thoughts in her head about who is the
best leader and so on. Whether there is any evidence in the group
work is thin, to say the least. Perhaps showing off a bit; perhaps
playing games a bit; but I suspect it was more your feeling about
being the outsider, by the sound of it. The other assumption we
should question is their total devotion to their regular leader, as
most groups hate their leaders at the same time as being devoted
to them. Maybe it was not a good thing to assume you were
worse than Dr. K. *in their eyes.*

*F.H.B. = "Family hold back", i.e. be on best behaviour with a visitor present.

Dr. Main '. . . Wish we could have Dr. S. every week. . .' is the other possibility.

Dr. Tunnadine There is some evidence for that, you see. The one quote from Dr. K. was made in such a way that it was not a compliment to her. It isn't all idealisation, is it?

Doctor S. No. The feeling I came away with was, 'I like to go and see what goes on, but I wouldn't like to lead that group for ever, because of the rivalry between the nurses and doctors which is so evident'. I shook the dust off my feet with some relief.

Dr. Main It's a limited topic because the short-term visiting leader can't cope with that, can't take the lid off it.

Dr. Tunnadine It sounds as though it needs taking off, though.

Dr. Main What do people think about the work of this locum?

Dr. I. Easy to criticise but a difficult situation, nevertheless.

Dr. Main You mustn't be too good and you mustn't be too bad. How long is Dr. K. away for?

Dr. K. I'm back with them next week.

3. Nurses trying to find a common language

Leader nurse Mrs. R.

A leader reported a group of nurses who were working in District Nursing; as Health Visitors; family planning nurses; and in a hospital for young chronic sick patients. In a fairly early group four cases had been presented by different nurses and it seemed that the leader was having some difficulty focussing the discussion.

Dr. Main I am confused about the numbers of cases and I don't understand the discussion. I am wondering what this is about, because we don't usually get this from this leader. I think this group is in difficulties about having nurses from so many mixed, different backgrounds. There are about four languages being spoken and they are different languages and I think you are in a difficulty about this. Whether it will ever become a working group I doubt. A certain amount of disparity in the settings in which they work is all right; but beyond it. . . — I can't understand what this nurse is doing from the hospital unit. It must be very different material from that which the Health Visitor would produce.

Dr. Tunnadine The disparity between the two cases we have heard, the awful business about who is the patient when there is somebody crippled with MS and somebody who can't put a cap in — there is an enormous disparity.

Mrs. R. Do you not get this in doctoring? Clinical techniques as opposed to psychosexual techniques, isn't it?

Dr. Tunnadine I don't think so: you see, I think they are of a different order of emotional disturbance.

Dr. Main I wonder if you are in difficulty about this.

Mrs. R. Perhaps I am.

Dr. Main Unless you feel it, it is not true.

Dr. Tunnadine It's fairly clear that if the report meant anything, the leader felt swamped by all this stuff.

Dr. Main None of the cases was adequately discussed. Could they be adequately discussed by the people in that group?

Mrs. R. Yes, I think they can be.

Dr. Main Time will show, won't it?

Dr. P. I feel that the nurse who was doing the vaginal examination must have had terrific feelings about the difficulty of getting her finger in, and fury with the doctor who referred such a difficult case to her.

Mrs. R. Oh, that came over, yes. She was furious with the doctor for giving her this case.

Dr. P. Are there similar situations for nurses working in other settings about fury with other professionals — was it similar enough for that to have meaning?

Mrs. R. Oh, I think so, yes.

Dr. Main And did the group discuss it?

Dr. P. We haven't been told.

Dr. Main We know that they didn't. The leader is interested in the case, but getting the group to discuss it is another matter.

Mrs. R.   I shall have to look at this question of the different work areas.

Dr. Main   They are not talking with each other about the case, they are talking with you and the presenter.

Mrs. R.   No. There is quite a lot of cross talk, which I haven't presented, presumably.

Dr. Tunnadine   It sounds to me as though there was too much; as though they were interested in learning each other's languages instead of jointly learning this new language. It was difficult for you to get the emphasis on to the nurse/patient relation in any of the cases we have heard.

Dr. Main   That's what I mean: there was no group discussion; or if you like, you can say there was too much.

Dr. Tunnadine   They have only met four times and they are a disparate group, aren't they? It's how the leader can get them on to it, is what we should be concerned about here.

Mrs. R.   They certainly said, when someone went on to generalisations, "That's not what we are here for; we are only here to look at that patient and that nurse and the relationship between the two". That didn't come from me at all, but from one of the nurses.

Dr. Tunnadine   I don't know, I think they are probably still discussing patients, aren't they? That's what happens to begin with. And the different settings in which they are working seems to be making it even more difficult for the leader to direct their attention to the nurse/patient relation.

Mrs. R.   Several of the group were not family planning trained, so the problem of vaginal examination before fitting a cap was quite new to them. Some did not know what was involved in fitting a cap, and whether one always wears a glove or not.

4. The setting affects the work

Leader Doctor Y.

A leader described the composition of her group, which included a G.P. trainee, who left after three sessions.

Dr. Main Could we pause for a moment? Has anyone ever had any luck with general practice trainees?

Doctor Y. I've had two others, actually. But one was more mature.

Dr. Main The disadvantage about the trainees is that they are not fully invested in. . . I just wondered if the others had any general experience of this.

Dr. L. Yes, and they dropped out. They are on this rotation thing.

Dr. Main I know. That's the trouble.

Dr. Tunnadine I haven't had them, actually.

Dr. Q. I have got one.

Dr. Main Is he all right still, and still with you?

Dr. Q. Yes.

Dr. D. We turned ours down.

Dr. Main Yes.

Dr. A. We have three who have completed their two years and I thought two of them were very good; and I am disappointed that they haven't gone on, but I think it's mainly because of husbands moving. But they were in the sort of work where they could pick up cases — either G.P. work or obstetrics.

Dr. Main What age — can you remember?

Dr. A. About 28 to 30.

Dr. Main Doctor S?

Dr. S. No, I've never had trainees.

Dr. N. I had someone who was interested, but she could never arrange a suitable time. She's joined us now that she has become a partner.

Dr. Main Anyhow, going back to you. . .

Doctor Y. One of my health visitors has also left. I wondered if it was someone who was very over-burdened by the workload she was getting and seeking help in all directions. She tended to rather paralyse us when she produced her cases. They were always very complicated — patients with gross social problems — and it was quite hard to pin her down to the psychosexual element in them.

Dr. Main   She was a health visitor?

Doctor Y.   Yes.

Dr. Main   But patients don't come to health visitors. Health visitors go to the patient.

Doctor Y.   Yes, but several of her patients have approached her with their sexual problems; but it's usually part and parcel of —

Dr. Main   As a result of her coming to *them*. It's a different situation, isn't it?

Doctor Y.   It was. It became very apparent that the sort of families she was seeing were very different. Most of the group felt in awe of the load this woman was carrying and how well she was coping.

Dr. Main   It's important to understand that it's a different field of study.

Doctor Y.   Very. We did try to get a nurses group going first, because I put this to her before we even began, that I would much rather it was a nurses group.

Dr. Main   But health visitors aren't just nurses. They are health visitors. It's a very important, separate and unique job.

Dr. Tunnadine   Yes it is. But some things are more unique than others. The distinction, I suppose, between a health visitor and a family planning nurse would be comparable to a G.P. and a family planning doctor: they are different, but not as different as all that. They still see the patients.

Dr. Main   But they see the patients in utterly different settings. Different opportunities. . .

Dr. Tunnadine   Not different to a G.P. who goes to people's homes.

Dr. Main   G.P.s get called in.

Dr. E.   Health visitors get called in quite often.

Dr. Main   And quite often they aren't.

Mrs. R. Could I just make a point here? I have had health visitors in my group, over the last three years, and I have had to discuss with them that "we are not here to discuss the social problems of that patient, we are only here to discuss the psychosexual problems". They don't do vaginal examinations, either. You have actually got to dismiss the social problems, because they are enormous and you cannot deal with them in the group.

Dr. Main What they may or may not do is absolutely essential. You have given one example with vaginal examination.

Dr. Tunnadine From a leader's point of view, surely there is not a fundamental difference in saying "We have got to get away from the social problems" as in saying "We have got to get away from traditional medical history-taking".

Dr. Main My point is that you get them mixed up if you think they have the same opportunities. The setting is an indissoluble part of the technique a person uses and needs study in its own right.

Dr. Tunnadine Of course. But for every doctor, even in a mixed doctors group, the settings in which they work are different, aren't they? I would quarrel with them, not because they say, "We can't get away from social problems on to the psychosexual problems". I would have thought our task was to get away from the social problems on to the nurse/patient relation.

Dr. Main My inclination is not to mix up different kinds of doctors, or different kinds of people, but to study singular opportunities and go in depth into them.

Dr. Tunnadine But we can't help it, because everybody works in different settings nowadays.

Dr. Main A Health Visitors group would be a great one to run separately. I am wondering about the difference in professional settings. The language the other people speak will be foreign to her, and hers to them.

Doctor Y. Yes, that came over quite clearly.

Dr. Main So it was a mistake to have her in — that's the point.

Doctor Y. Yes, I think it was, and perhaps I wasn't tough enough to say, "I'm sorry"; but it's very difficult when somebody is asking to join a group and they can't join a group of their own.

Dr. Main   Mmm. It's very difficult when it's useless, too.

5. Inhibition of phantasies

Leader Doctor B.

In a mixed group of doctors and nurses a woman who had seen one of the nurses in the group was presented by the doctor who had seen her afterwards. This happened in a family planning clinic, and the patient was asking to change from the cap to the pill, because her boyfriend didn't want to make love to her very much. The nurse felt it was because the relationship was breaking up, but the patient told the doctor that it was because the boyfriend could feel the cap. She wasn't too happy about the pill because it had given her headaches before.

Doctor B.   The group wondered why she was prepared to martyr herself for her boyfriend. if she was going to get headaches again. They also felt that they didn't know much about the relationship and that the doctor had responded to the request without looking behind the facts.

Dr. E.   The nurse's instant diagnosis didn't seem to be challenged at any point. She told the doctor what it was; the doctor did as she was told; the group was presented with it; and finally wound up by saying, "Yes, that must be so", without any indication of what sort of girl this was. The only thing was that she was very panicky or something.

Doctor B.   That's true. It was just presented as this incident: "He has gone off sex. I want to keep him". Why she felt she must do anything to keep him at all costs wasn't looked at.

Dr. F.   I might have misunderstood you: did you say that the nurse who had seen the patient is also in your group?

Doctor B.   Yes.

Dr. F. So this is a very unusual situation, with two people involved in that particular presentation.

Doctor B. Yes, I think it is.

Dr. F. I think there are all sorts of difficulties there. Maybe the doctor did want to challenge the nurse's instant diagnosis, and needed to do it through the group. It doesn't sound as though that happened, though.

Dr. Tunnadine I love the word 'diagnosis'. It seems to be the one fact about this case: that nobody knew what this girl thought about it. The girl was presenting, "My chap doesn't like me any more. Please help me. What's the matter with me down here?" It was a question mark and the question mark went right down the line. They didn't discuss the nurse/patient relation, or even the fact that she was shot through the door from one to the other.

Dr. Main What's going on between that pair?

Dr. Tunnadine I don't think the pair is anything to do with it.

Dr. Main It is — the central point of the whole thing.

Dr. P. I think the material feels dead because the person presenting it was the second person to see the patient. If the nurse who saw the patient first had presented the patient's story we might have got some feel of what was going on.

Dr. Main No, look — I don't mean the man and woman pair. Discussion of that is a waste of time. What has gone on between *that* pair? There was no discussion of it here.

Dr. Tunnadine I was trying to. Because the patient thinks there is something awful about herself that is driving people away; and in fact managed to achieve that right down to the group.

Dr. Main What's she doing to the doctor? First of all, I think it's fairly clear what sort of young man she has got. We all hate him, don't we? — and we have never met him! So it's quite clear she was doing that to the doctor. She was doing something to the doctor and the doctor is not studying it.

Dr. F. The group talked about her 'martyring' herself.

Dr. Main Yes, and this was from the doctor's account. There is room here for discussion of the doctor/patient relation. Should the girl go on with this relationship, or is it better to part? — all this stuff is irrelevant. What the hell is this doctor doing with this patient? What kind of hot potato is she? What is she doing with the doctor? . . . They didn't get anywhere near it, did they?

Doctor B.   Nowhere near it, and I felt that the doctor was being rather dependent on the nurse. And yet it was very difficult to say, in that setting.

Dr. Main   They were discussing the case.

Dr. Tunnadine   The interesting thing about the case is that the nurse couldn't wait to get rid of her, as far as I can see. That was actually what happened.

Doctor B.   I don't think that was so. Because it was the pill, she therefore needed a prescription, and had to go on through the doctor.

Dr. Tunnadine   The patient's certainty that she was doing the wrong thing was pretty well confirmed, I think. It went back down the line again, didn't it?

Dr. Main   I think there may be something wrong with that patient, you know.

Doctor B.   You can't make a group take it up. I tried hard, but no-one would follow up.

Dr. Main   The study of the interaction between the doctor and the patient wasn't looked at.

Dr. P.   I think that had been mucked up in the first instance by the nurse.

Dr. F.   It is a very unusual thing that these two people are, in a sense, rivals for the patient, even though it may not have been acknowledged like that. It strikes me that when people begin to produce cases in groups, one of the things they do is let out their phantasies about what might have been going on — 'This patient made me feel very x, y and z'. You can't really do that when someone else, who *saw* the patient, is also in the group. It might inhibit you from saying, "I think this is an irritating, angry, demanding woman"; that sort of thing.

Dr. Main   Yes.

Dr. F.   For both the doctor and nurse who presented that woman.

Dr. Main   It might have been as well to have said this.

Dr. Tunnadine   It is quite an important point.

Doctor B.   I don't think I would ever have chosen to have them in the same group.

Dr. A. If they had both presented it, it would have been very interesting.

Dr. Main They both work in the same clinic? Then they will never tell the truth!

F. UNCONSCIOUS MATERIAL "GOING DOWN THE LINE"

In this last chapter I have collected a number of digests which illustrate the complicated way in which unconscious material can be carried in both directions between the patient and the doctor (1 & 2) and between the doctor and the group (3, 4, 5, 6). Just as an understanding of what the doctor is feeling may throw light on the patient's problem, so too the group behaviour can illuminate both the doctor's and the patient's behaviour. Finally, the material the group members choose to present may unconsciously express their feelings about their work and the group at that time (7 & 8).

1. SHYNESS AND THE DOCTOR'S ANXIETY.
Some of the doctor's anxiety is expressed through the patient and this prevents the group from studying the patient's hidden fury.

2. GUILTY PATIENT AND GUILTY DOCTOR.
The doctor presents her own guilt, and the failure to see that this has been aroused by the patient prevents the doctor or the group from tackling the patient's own guilty feelings.

3. PREMATURE EJACULATION.
A passive woman produces an anxious husband and a directive doctor. The report creates great activity in the group, but the leader fails to see that this behaviour has been provoked by the patient through the presenting doctor.

4. PASSIVITY IN THE PATIENT AND GROUP.
The passivity of the patient, waiting for the doctor to do the work, is seen in the passivity of the group, which eventually provokes the leader into case-solving activity.

5. 'MANIPULATING' PATIENT'S DISTRESS GETS LOST.
A report of an angry patient leads the group to attack the presenting doctor, and the non-aggressive leader finds herself defending the doctor as she in her turn has defended the patient. It seems that both the attack and the defence 'go down the line'. The distress of the patient is not understood.

6. PATIENT AND DOCTOR ARE ATTACKED.
A patient feels she is too small and it is suggested that the doctor feels professionally 'small' in relation to her own mother and the other doctors. Both get attacked, but the leader cannot get the group to recognise or study the violence.

7. CASE MATERIAL AND UNCONSCIOUS FEELINGS IN THE GROUP.
The members of a group, which has suddenly got very small, present material which is suggestive of their own anxieties about their work and their fear of closeness.

8. ENDINGS: HOW TO STOP BREAST-FEEDING.
This final digest has been chosen from several dealing with the endings of groups. 'How much is enough?' has been touched on in a previous digest (III B 5). Perhaps the reader also feels this book has not provided the answers, but perhaps it has whetted the appetite?

1. Shyness and the doctor's anxiety

Leader Doctor A.

A new doctor had recently joined the seminar and talked about a patient complaining of impotence. He was a large, well-built man with a moustache, who worked as a travelling salesman covering a large area. The doctor was surprised that such a manly-looking man should be complaining of impotence, but he also described the way the patient looked at the floor throughout the interview. The doctor asked a lot of questions and the patient admitted that things were all right when he had one-night stands away from home, but no good with his wife. In the past it was very frequent with her, and sometimes in the mornings as well. The doctor asked if his wife enjoyed it and the reply was, "She never refuses me, but she is prudish". The doctor suggested that the problem might be due to anxiety and the patient eventually asked for a repeat prescription for anti-depressant tablets, which the doctor gave him.

The group started by thinking it must be the wife's problem, but then they noticed that she had been acquiescing apparently happily for sixteen years. Then they noticed that the man kept on trying, even although he was not getting any erections. They asked the doctor how he had felt discussing this with a patient who could not look him in the face, but he denied any discomfort and said he was surprised that the man had given him so much information about it.

Doctor A.   I can't remember all the rest of the discussion. There was quite a lot of discussion but they didn't find out the sort of things I thought they would want to find out from the doctor. They never went into what actually happened in intercourse, or when he became impotent, and could he get erections by masturbation, or did he have nocturnal ejaculations, or what actually went on in the loveplay. None of these things were discussed at all and the group didn't ask. I don't know whether it was my job to say, "I notice you are not really taking a great deal of interest in what actually went on between the husband and the wife", but I didn't say that.

Dr. S.   Perhaps they didn't need to as he had reported that he was O.K. with the one-night stands. If they believed that, they wouldn't want to know too much about the physical side.

Doctor A.   Yes, perhaps that is so. But you'd think that they would want to know what actually happened in intercourse: whether they were doing any petting or whether it was just in and out. Finally, we'd had quite a bit of discussion and there was a bit of a lull and I was in confusion. I said, "You haven't tried to find out from the doctor something that you usually try to find out from doctors, especially when their reports are about women". Then somebody piped up, "Did you examine him?" He said, "Examine him? — I never thought of examining him. I didn't see any need to examine him". Then I'm afraid a bit of teaching went on. The group started telling him the sort of things that you find when you do vaginal examinations: apart from finding what the uterus is like, and the vagina, you find out about the women's feelings and how they feel about their genitals and so on. He was really terribly interested in this — it hadn't occurred to him at all. They did a bit of discussion about what was happening in the interview, but I'm not sure that it was very constructive. However there is something they did pick up: they said, "This man is not giving much to the doctor, is he? So he probably didn't give much to his wife". That was talked about, and the fact that he probably didn't do much petting or anything, but of course the doctor couldn't answer because he had never asked. He didn't know what actually went on in intercourse when it had been all right. Nobody knew what sort of intercourse it was. I felt a bit dissatisfied at the end of that and I don't feel that I used my leadership skills properly.

Dr. P.   It seems that as a leader you had a problem with a new member in a group that had been going for a while: that is, how much to let the others teach him, or ask him questions. Were they protective about him — I mean the fact that he didn't know about examining people?

Doctor A. No. They weren't attacking, but they weren't protective.

Dr. Tunnadine It's interesting that this is a beginner doctor. It isn't only about finding out about patients; it's thinking on behalf of the patient, 'What is going on?'; and the doctor is not at that stage yet. He's just a traditional ask-a-question doctor and with a depressed impotent man you don't get any answers. The group has to think on the doctor's behalf about what he and the patient are doing together. It sounds as though something about his presentation didn't help the group to do this. They weren't even picking up the obvious things like why he had a job that took him so far from home. His enthusiasm for this wife of his is very clear, isn't it? And yet he wants to please her. The ordinary level of discussion that your group are usually good at didn't seem to operate in this particular presentation, as if they were stunned by the doctor's impotence with the patient.

Dr. Main They seemed to be discussing the *treatment* of this man; like, "Did you examine him or not?" The doctor had been asking the patient a lot of questions and the patient had been doing the usual thing which follows questions: giving answers. Then they discussed, "What else should you do?" — discussing *treatment* rather than discussing what on earth was going on between these two characters. It might have been useful if the leader had cut short this business about, 'Was the treatment right and what more could have been done?', and said, "What do you think is going on between these two people?" and ask them to work on that; work on the doctor/patient relation. I notice that you didn't do this, but kept on with this business about, 'Should you examine them?', or 'Do you know about his sexual life?' These things are not bad technique: they are the product of the doctor/patient relation. But the fact is that certain things were not happening. You might have got how the doctor felt about this chap, rather than asking these nice safe questions. The doctor is very frightened to ask this man about the sexual details; so he swallowed hook, line and sinker the fact that this man had intercourse every night.

Doctor A. The group did question that.

Dr. Main Mmm. It's a funny thing that he's a travelling salesman!

Dr. Tunnadine   I don't know how he managed it, do you?

Dr. Main   It's impossible. And why do people take up this sort of job? It gets them away from danger spots like home. — They didn't discuss this.

Doctor A.   They discussed the fact that they didn't believe that he had it night and morning, and was this a sort of statement of, 'How powerful I really am?'

Dr. Main   Yes, but the man's been impotent for quite a long time. What form does the impotence take? It wasn't known.

Doctor A.   I was dying to know.

Dr. Main   Why was it not discussed, do you think, between the doctor and the patient? What is your own personal idea?

Doctor A.   I think the doctor is just not used to discussing sexual matters with his patients.

Dr. Main   Mmm.

Doctor A.   I think maybe he did pretty well for a first shot.

Dr. P.   There's something too coming from this patient, because he tells his doctor he's been impotent for six months and we know from the notes that he had been impotent for at least two years. There's something about the difficulty with this big, masculine man who cannot fully admit his difficulty.

Dr. E.   I think that was very much so: the picture of a man who couldn't face it, who couldn't look. Then there was a point at which the doctor was asked, "Did you feel awkward?" and he said, "No, of course I didn't feel awkward!" *(Laughter)* The group was feeling awkward — the shame of this chap the doctor couldn't face somehow.

Doctor A.   Although I saw that, I didn't really use it. I wouldn't have wanted to jump down the doctor's throat when he was presenting his first case.

Dr. Tunnadine   That's the trouble.

Dr. Main   It isn't a matter of jumping down the doctor's throat. It isn't a matter of saying, "You are good" or "You are bad" and making the doctor feel good because he has done some work, or bad because he hasn't. It's a matter of getting at the truth about the doctor/patient relation and a beginning glance at that wouldn't have done him any harm.

Doctor A.   '. . . I notice that the patient made you feel a bit awkward about asking about these things. . .'

Dr. Main   '. . . Because the patient. . .'

Doctor A.   '. . . Because the patient is so shy and nervous'.

Dr. Main   Yes. — They could have got to that, couldn't they?

Doctor A.   Yes.

Dr. Main   Had the leader said something like, "What do you think is going on between these two characters?", or "What about the doctor/patient relation? How is the patient treating the doctor? How is the doctor using the patient?" I would have thought that to draw attention to that might have been useful.

Doctor A.   They did discuss one little bit of that in that they said, "He is not giving much to the doctor, so it looks as if he doesn't give much to his wife — compliments or petting or whatever".

Dr. J.   It was difficult for the doctor because he had denied the discomfort at an earlier stage and it would have seemed a bit of an attack upon him if they then said, "It's not really so comfortable as you think. It's really much more uncomfortable".

Dr. Tunnadine   That's right. And the sad thing is that the leader tried to draw attention to the fact that he had not examined him, because the feelings that would have emerged would have been terrible, a revealing of this sad, shameful business. But all that happened was that the doctor got attacked in the process of showing how much cleverer the others were.

Dr. Main   To focus attention on the doctor/patient relation would have been a very different thing to discussing the defects of the doctor's technique. Any defects of technique are due to failure of one unconscious to understand the other unconscious. The success or failure rests on the understanding of the doctor/patient relation.

Doctor A.   Previously in the group they have been able to say, "I see that you didn't examine this patient. What was it about *this* patient that put you off examining him?" They have said this to each other, but they couldn't say it to him, because he was new in the group. I don't think it would have occurred to him that it could have been a useful thing to do.

Dr. Main   He was put off by the man's shyness, wasn't he? So he said, "Let's tackle this by not going through these difficult areas, because the man might feel bad about it". But that's exactly what the man was doing to *him* — putting him off. I think drawing attention to that might have encouraged the doctor to think, "I see — Mmm. . ." Next time he would recognise the shyness instead of running away from it, or colluding with it. The thing is, the group didn't go for this.

Doctor A. No.

Dr. Tunnadine It is the patient, too, who invited it in a way: different from many impotent men, who say, "Aren't you going to examine me, doc?" You can blame the doctor, if you like, in his ignorance. But the patient didn't invite it either: he wanted to shut up, please.

Doctor A. — 'Give us a prescription, and I'll be gone'. Yes, I could have done something about that.

Dr. Main There's a hint too. . . the man did say something about his wife not being very keen, or his wife wasn't very interested — something like that.

Dr. Tunnadine 'Prudish. . .'

Dr. Main Wasn't he talking about the doctor? That was a hint that the doctor wasn't very keen either; a bit prudish.

Dr. S. The doctors had never refused a prescription, had they — "She never refuses me!" *(Laughter)*

Dr. B. The prescription was a sort of reward. It was the first time he had talked about feelings with this man, so he felt he ought to give the prescription.

Dr. Main It is a sign of the doctor's dissatisfaction with his own contribution that he has to give a prescription *as well*, because he hasn't done anything.

Dr. Tunnadine I think Dr. E.'s earlier remarks about it being too good a group make some sense. Maybe they are not only too good a group but too good in relation to this newcomer. The intruder into an established group can cause protectiveness.

Dr. Main The job of the group isn't to be nice to its members but to do some work.

Dr. Tunnadine It is nevertheless a general technical difficulty when beginners come into a going concern. I agree with you that handling it by protection isn't any answer.

Doctor A.   Yes, if he hadn't been a beginner I would have wanted one of the group to say, "I wonder what it is about this patient that stops you from doing a physical examination". But as he was a newcomer. . .

Dr. Main   What difference does it make?

Dr. Tunnadine   I think your intervention about the examination backfired, because you invited criticism by saying, 'We do this all the time with women', and it allowed the group to show him what an ignorant idiot he was, or that was the effect of it. I am just noticing that it didn't work in the way that you were hoping it would.

Doctor A.   No, that's right.

Dr. P.   The other difficulty with the group is that they have learnt some clever answers and they cling to them desperately and show them off. He had brought other things which they could have used without talking about the technique: he brought his shame, this discrepancy between what was actually in the notes and what the patient said to the doctor, and all sorts of things they could have worked on if they had wanted to; and yet they had to cling to their own clever things about examinations.

Doctor A.   That was my fault, because they hadn't said it. It was me that said, "You haven't made a comment".

Dr. Main   That's the first half of a good comment: "I notice that you didn't do some examination". The other half is: "The group must have some ideas about why this didn't occur" — not as a flaw in technique, but as an event.

Dr. B.   You say you feel he didn't do it because it would never have occurred to him, because he was new; but it was something that was coming from the *patient* that prevented any talk of what was happening in sex. That could have been raised in the group — "You weren't able to talk about what actually happened to him", or something.

Dr. Main   Yes — "Has the group got any idea why that didn't occur?. . ." It would have opened the discussion about what was going on between the two of them, instead of saying, "Now the correct thing to do would have been to examine him".

Dr. Tunnadine   I wonder how much this came back from the patient because, after all, the doctor went for *anxiety*. The fury of this man with his wife was far from discussed at all and I wonder if some of that came down the line — the *doctor's* anxiety rather than this furious salesman who just hates the prudishness of his wife. That is far from the discussion and anti-depressants are not the treatment for that.

Dr. Main   It's a bit of magic, isn't it, to say, "Of course, this thing must be due to anxiety". Anxiety is good stuff. It's like stress: it saves thought, it dismisses the whole situation; and I am tired of saying that you can't be anxious. It's an incomplete concept. You have to be anxious *about* something. — You suggest the possibility of rage, or self-castration, or whatever?

Doctor A.   He tried to find out what the anxiety was about.

Dr. Main   But why was the doctor sure it was anxiety?

Dr. Tunnadine   He diagnosed anxiety before there was evidence for it.

Dr. Main   Yes, but *why* did he do it?

Dr. Tunnadine   He was a bit anxious.

Dr. Main   Yes — he didn't know what else to do.

Doctor A.   He was anxious because the patient asked for a prescription and had been getting prescriptions all this time; he was anxious, so he thought, "What'll I do? — I'll have to say this is anxiety".

Dr. Tunnadine   — but didn't, I might point out, switch it to a tranquillizer. *(Laughter)* This is the kind of aura of the whole thing.

Mrs. R.   He was probably also anxious about this new type of work.

Dr. Main   The doctor didn't know what to do. He somehow felt useless and came up with, "It must be due to anxiety".

Dr. B.   Interestingly, the word 'anger' was never mentioned in the group or by anybody at all.

Dr. Tunnadine   Or 'humiliation'. They just hit him, that's all.

Dr. Main   It's no good giving them ideas like, 'It must be anger', or 'It must be due to anxiety'. The only thing is to have a look at what is going on. The doctor didn't do very much except ask questions and I suppose he asked questions in an attempt to show his potency. He must have felt pretty useless with this man, puzzled and uneasy, and if he'd said, "God, I didn't know what to do when this man came in; I have never handled a case like this one before", that would have been an honest discussion of what was going on. In fact he just described what he *did*, not really what was going on.

Doctor A. He wouldn't let us probe that, because the group said to him, "How did you feel? Did you feel a bit nervous about talking about sex with this big potent-looking man?"

Dr. Main Ask silly questions and you'll get silly answers! *(Laughter)* They knew damn well he was anxious. Why didn't they tell him?

Doctor A. Somebody should have said, "It seems to me that you felt jolly anxious, because we were feeling the anxiety".

Dr. Main Yes. On the other hand, it is no good the group behaving as though they are a lot of sophisticates about this; that *they* are never anxious when a chap like this comes in.

Dr. Tunnadine In a way, the doctor must have set it up to some extent. He got what he asked for in a sense: a bit of a ticking off. He got some teaching.

Doctor A. He showed us that he was a bit nervous about presenting cases because he had said, only the week before, "I don't know if I'll get any suitable cases to present".

Dr. Main You never found out how impotent the man was?

Doctor A. No, that was what I was dying to ask. The group didn't ask; they were inhibited from asking.

Dr. Main Why did they not know then, do you reckon?

Doctor A. The doctor was inhibited by the patient from asking such things.

Dr. Main It was in the room, wasn't it? — You might have shown it. The doctor didn't discuss it; the patient didn't discuss it.

Doctor A. That's right.

Dr. Tunnadine There was just a hint that he wanted to go on pleasing his wife, but didn't get erections.

Dr. Main It was very difficult for the man to discuss it and therefore very difficult for the doctor. The man said, "I'm impotent. Please can I have a prescription?" It was like looking the problem boldly in the face and then going "Aarghh!" and running away *(Laughter)*.

Dr. B.   It's always easy to think of the right leadership things you should have done in the car on the way home, isn't it, rather than in the there and now.

Doctor A.   I was aware of all this unknown material but didn't somehow know how to make use of it — couldn't think quickly enough to point out to the group that this was the patient doing this to the doctor and therefore doing it to them.

Dr. P.   I wonder if one couldn't have somehow shared with the doctor the awfulness of having to open your eyes to this, when you've sat there writing your prescription for anti-depressants for years and years; and suddenly you feel guilty and feel you're inadequate. It is really a very major step for a doctor who has felt competent to cope to have to suddenly start again, admitting he doesn't know.

Dr. Tunnadine   That's right and the fact is, as I'm sure we all agree, that passive impotent people, just like passive frigid people, are the most bloody awful of all. There isn't any quick answer except sweating out the awfulness of it. Don't you agree? — It's a rough one for him to have to start with. For the leader too.

Dr. Q.   It affected me. I felt the impotence coming over and I was wondering how it was going to go. It didn't surprise me that Dr. A. felt this difficulty. But it's recognising at the time that it must be there, sitting in the room, between the doctor and the patient — and you couldn't use it. You thought, "Good, he's doing *something*. I mustn't stop him. I mustn't knock him on the head".

Doctor A.   Especially when he said he didn't feel awkward at all. I found that very difficult to deal with.

Dr. Tunnadine   And to give the doctor his due, he didn't say, "Oh, I shouldn't worry about it, old boy!", which is really in a sense what this kind of patient invites.

Dr. Q.   He has made the first step.

Doctor A.   Yes, I was pleased he had presented a case.

2. Guilty patient and guilty doctor

Leader Doctor F.

The patient came to a Youth Advisory Clinic and asked for the pill. In reply to questions from the doctor, she said she was sixteen years old, had no regular boyfriend, but wanted the pill "just in case". She confessed to having had intercourse "a long time ago" (when she was fifteen years old!), but said she certainly wouldn't be seeing him again.

The doctor described a difficult interview, with no eye contact and monosyllabic replies to questions. She felt unhappy about prescribing the pill, but eventually gave her one month's supply and arranged to see her again soon. She felt the girl had problems that she had not been able to discuss, and also that it was wrong to encourage intercourse in young people.

Doctor F.   The group took hold of this. They were fairly gentle, because it seemed that they understood there were two things going on here. There was the interview situation: how she had handled it, whether or not there was a problem which needed to be discussed, and what the evidence was for there being a problem. But they seemed to sense that the doctor had a personal dilemma in this area with regard to work with young people. They didn't launch into asking direct questions, although she was begging them to ask her what her feelings and views were. They stuck quite well to, "What was it like with the patient? Why did you sense she had a problem? What was the evidence? After all, it's not that unusual to sit at sixteen with your eyes down. It is very difficult. Who are we to ask young people, 'Have you got a boyfriend and are you having intercourse?' It's very intrusive stuff we ask them. The patient could have played the game and said, 'Yes, I have a lovely boyfriend who my mother would love to meet at tea on Sunday' — but she didn't. She was honest. . ." The doctor was very torn as to whether or not this was an acceptable and 'normal' sort of request, or whether she was making a request for some other sort of help. As they gently explored this, she agreed that it was possible that she sounded as though she disapproved of that sort of sexual behaviour, but she did actually disapprove of it. One person said, "It sounds as though we are putting this doctor in the hot seat and asking her to defend her attitudes, which is what she did to the patient. It's a very uncomfortable situation". Someone then said, "You wouldn't always feel like this with a sixteen-year-old. You would feel perfectly happy for some sixteen-year-olds to take the pill. What was it about this particular woman?" Despite this, they didn't begin to link up the fact that maybe this sixteen-year-old actually felt like a slut, so finally I said something to that effect.

Dr. Main   Right. . . Thank you very much.

Dr. S.   She didn't describe the girl so that we have got a picture of her.

Doctor F.   She didn't describe her very well at all. The doctor said, "Frankly, if people knew that in a Young People's Advisory session doctors behaved as I did on that occasion, they would be quite right to criticise us, because I think it is a bad thing I have done". The group did a lot of, "Well, what did you do? She had a blood pressure check; she was weighed; she had a proper history taken; she had a chance to speak; you tried to establish a relationship. You decided to give her the pill because you didn't want to see her pregnant and you therefore have a way into bringing her back for a check-up very soon. So why do you feel badly about that?" "You are unhappy about something", one of them said, "and I don't think it's to do with the way you actually treated this girl. I think it's to do with something else".

Dr. A.   You think it wasn't coming from the patient? It sounds to me as if it was an uncomfortable sort of patient.

Dr. I.   Although the group criticised and then reassured, it doesn't sound as though she was able to say why she felt she had done badly.

Dr. A.   They didn't really explore why she had to do a lot of questioning. Did they really discuss what about the patient had made her do all that questioning?

Dr. Main   They didn't discuss that at all. There was no discussion. They were talking to *her* all the time; they weren't discussing amongst themselves. They were either telling her she was a lousy doctor, or telling her she was a very good doctor and there was no need for her to worry so much. But they weren't discussing amongst themselves.

Doctor F.   But you see, she was very much drawing attention to herself in this.

Dr. Main   What was the problem?

Dr. I.   What the patient was trying to say and couldn't get through.

Dr. Main   Why did the doctor bring the case at all?

Mrs. R.   I wondered if it was a psychosexual case, anyhow.

Dr. Main   It doesn't matter — the doctor wants to discuss it with her colleagues. Why does she want to discuss this?

Dr. S.   She wants to be bashed.

Dr. Main   She said, "I did very badly with this"; and they said, "Yes, you did do very badly!" She asked for a beating-up, and by God the group, instead of spotting this, gave it to her; and then thought, "What have we done?" and said, "You're all right!" and tried to patch her up again. But they didn't discuss the doctor's distress.

Doctor F.   They did a little bit. One said, "It is terrible in that sort of situation".

Dr. Main   I know, but that's soft soap.

Doctor F.   Yes, general soft-soaping sort of stuff.

Dr. Main   Yes, she said, "I'm narrow-minded and did very badly with this patient. Please tell me I am narrow-minded and did badly with this patient". And they obliged, and then said, "No, you did very well. Life is very difficult, isn't it?" — It wasn't a *group discussion* at all. It was a lot of doctors discussing with the presenter rather than discussing amongst themselves. It is very easy to do that when the doctor asks for it and, my God, the group does it! The job of the group leader is to do something about it.

Dr. B.   I thought you were right to bring it back to that particular case.

Dr. Main   Yes. That was a very good intervention by the leader. — As you know, girls of sixteen are mad keen on sex, and have no moralities about it, and no hesitations or doubts — have they? Of course, we doctors *have* to stop them because they have no doubts themselves. It's a crazy view of things, isn't it? Discussion of the patient's own conflicts and problems is what you tried to start, but the group didn't worry about the patient. I think this patient *had* a psychosexual problem, myself.

Dr. S.   Yes. The anxiety of the doctor made all the rest of the group too anxious and too afraid to criticise her; or felt they were going to be too damning and moralising.

Dr. Main   But they did to start with. They went for it.

Dr. S.   Yes.

Dr. Main   They moralised about her morals.

Doctor F.   They did, in the nicest possible way, saying, "We know you have the best interests at heart".

Dr. Main   Mmm. — "You're sweet really, but we don't like you. . ." — So what is the problem for the leader in the group?

Dr. I.   To get it back to the pain of the patient and the doctor. ·

Dr. Main   And trying to get the group to have a look at it. *(General agreement).* Or at least to illumine for them what they were doing when they were ticking her off and then patting her.

Doctor F.   I did very directly allude to that in various ways, like, "We are all having a bash at Dr. X. on the grounds of her morals in this area and we are all sitting here as though we live in a vacuum. Come on, let's get back to this and what is going on. How on earth was it that she had ended up so perturbed with the interview?"

Dr. Main   Not even the leader discussed the possibility of technique. I thought the best intervention was made by Dr. F. on the point of, 'The patient has guilts of her own and is stirring them up in the doctor'.

Doctor F.   I didn't really feel I should have to make that, though.

Dr. Main   They hadn't seen it.

Doctor F.   I know they hadn't. That's why I did it.

Dr. Main   It is bad in the sense that you shouldn't be there for problem-solving. All the same, it seemed to be the only remark that got anywhere near that.

Doctor F.   I feel a terrible sense of failure when I have to do that.

Dr. Main   Yes, yes.

Dr. S.   That is your job as a leader. If they skate round the doctor/patient relationship, then surely the leader has to point it out.

Dr. Main   But you could ask why they don't see it. For example, insead of saying that is what the girl is doing, you say, "It's an odd thing that the group isn't doing this; it's not looking at the possibility that this girl has doubts of her own. When you say it like that, it's so obvious, isn't it?

Doctor F.   That's right; and one feels a twerp actually saying it, ultimately.

Dr. Main   But you can point out that the group doesn't see it.

Dr. J.   Isn't it also true that the group is having these doubts as well? The whole thing is a chain reaction.

Dr. Main   Yes.

Dr. J.   The group also is worried about sex at a young age and what should we be doing.

Dr. Main   Yes, and is blaming the doctor for containing all these doubts. But none of the group was able to discuss why it was that none of them had seen this girl's double-edged attitudes towards sex.

Dr. J.   Because of their own doubts, I would have said.

Dr. Main   Yes, but the point is they should have been *working at* why they hadn't seen it.

Doctor F.   I think it is to do with this doctor.

Dr. Main   No, they should have been discussing what might have been done — if you had drawn their attention to the fact, "Funny thing, none of us has discussed this, that the patient must have a few difficulties about sex and is putting them into the doctor".

Doctor F.   Yes, and she had given clues about that: in fact, she'd said, "Not that first boyfriend, not *that* one".

Dr. Main   Let's turn to the matter of technique, because after all they are not there to study patients, they are there to study doctors. On the matter of technique, none of them suggested how to deal with this girl hanging her head and not speaking and saying 'Yes' and 'No'. What should the doctor do? The doctor's actual technique was to say, "I didn't want to give her the pill" — but why not? You know that if you hold up whether or not you give her the pill, the patient will fight you. Why not say, "Sure you can have the pill. Now, what is this about. . ?"

Doctor F.   One of them did actually say that. She said, "What about looking at it as though it was a request for a termination, and you say, 'Sure you can have the pill. Now let's talk about it'.

Dr. Main   One of them did?

Doctor F.   Yes. The others said, "Yes, that might have been more productive".

Dr. Main   The rest of them took that up. That's discussing technique.

Doctor F.   Yes, they did actually — I'm sorry, I'd forgotten that.

Dr. Main   But they missed out altogether that the doctor might have discussed this girl's unhappiness and silence and fears of talking to the doctor about how uneasy she was about the whole thing. There are all sorts of possibilities; different doctors says different things: "I see you seem to keep very quiet about this. It must be a deadly secret that mustn't be spoken about. It's not easy for you"; or, "I notice that you are unable to tell anyone about it, you are uneasy about this"; and so on. The doctor didn't discuss this girl's unhappiness; she was simply concerned about the girl's sex. The girl has immense sexual problems: she is against it. She was hanging her head and saying, "Aren't I terrible?" The group didn't want to discuss the technique apparently, these guilt feelings and unhappiness about sex. They wanted to talk about the sexual highjinks of these dreadful youngsters. The doctors can't see the youngsters are in terrible trouble: they are most unhappy, guilty, anxious, frightened, boastful. But they didn't discuss this; so I would criticise the leader for not pointing out that they are meant to discuss various techniques instead of ticking the doctor off.

Dr. B.   The doctor had got clouded in looking at what she was doing, by her own guilt and unhappiness. She was unable to deal with the normal doctor/patient relationship. She got in the way of herself, almost.

Dr. Main   Mmm. She gave the pill and was most unhappy about it; and my guess is that the patient got the pill and is most unhappy about it.

Dr. B.   You suggested saying, "Fine, you can have the pill; and now let's discuss it", but the doctor didn't feel like saying, "Fine, you can have the pill".

Dr. Main   The leader drew attention to the fact, 'This girl is unhappy about things', but I would have liked her to have gone on and said to the group in discussion, "And what is the doctor to do about that?"

Dr. I.   But the way the doctor first presented the patient, she didn't say, "I have a patient with a problem". She presented as, "I'm worried about the way I handled this patient" — almost as though the patient had nothing to do with it, in a sense.

Doctor F.   The patient was almost a vehicle for her anxieties.

Dr. Main   I think the doctor must have had second thoughts about the case, and had all sorts of worries and thoughts about what she might have done.

Dr. S.   How to help that doctor with her inhibitions. . ?

Dr. Main   The group can discuss that, but they don't have to tell her off about it. The important thing is, Dr. F. can see this girl wasn't just a bundle of wild sexual impulses, but worried in case she was a slut. If they took *that* back from that case, it really is something, isn't it?

3. Premature ejaculation

Leader Doctor P.

A couple came to the doctor to show her the sub-fertility charts they had been keeping. The woman had been on the pill, but after stopping had developed amenorrhoea. They had been told to come for help if they had not conceived in six months, so they had dashed along for help. There was also a complaint of premature ejaculation which had come on twice: once about a year ago when his wife had irritable bowel syndrome, and once fairly recently since they had been trying for a baby.

The doctor told how the man had come into this particular interview with his wife and had produced a very tidy, neat, perfect record of her periods, little crosses when they had made love and everything graphed and beautiful. It seemed that the doctor felt there was anxiety and suggested it might be easier if he tried to do it again a second time, but that was really the only positive suggestion she had made. She had made another appointment for them to come back.

Doctor P. The group got terribly active and full of bright suggestions. There seems to be something about premature ejaculation. They all leapt in and talked to each other and I said nothing — "He's all right when he uses a sheath and he's not all right when he stops using a sheath". . . "Why don't you tell him to use a sheath with a hole in it?" . . . "Why don't you tell him to do it in the morning?" Someone said, "What about the squeeze technique?" One of the doctors said she used this technique and the others asked her to describe what it was. Then I said, "Are you having great success with this method with your patients?" and she said, "Oh, I haven't done it for a long time". I said, "I think the theory behind these techniques is that this is a re-training, behavioural method which is to do with people whose early experience of intercourse has been in unsatisfactory situations. I wonder how appropriate this might be for this couple? In this case it seems that there are certain situations where this man has difficulty and other situations where he doesn't have difficulty, so it doesn't sound like early learning difficulties". They sort of accepted that. They thought it was all due to his anxieties and they didn't seem to be able to get further than that. So then I took it back and got the doctor to describe again the consultation, which she did better. Apparently the woman had come in first and had sat down and started telling the story. The man had mentioned, "I'm afraid I can't satisfy my wife". So I went back to that and said, "Tell us what happened when he said that. What did the wife do?"; and she said, "Oh, the wife sat there nodding". Then she let out that this woman actually makes her feel quite irritated, that she's rather a sort of plump lump who just sits there, and when she walks in through the door the doctor thinks, 'Oh no, not you again!'. She complains in a lumpish sort of way without saying much. As her husband was sitting there saying, "I feel so awful because I can't satisfy my wife", she was sitting there nodding her head. Then I began to get a bit of dynamism out of the group, but eventually I had to say, "Perhaps he was a bit angry about it?" One of the group said, "No no — not angry: anxious and upset".

Dr. S.   She did say, "This woman irritates me". So that presenting doctor is able to talk about her feelings already.

Doctor P.   Yes.

Dr. S.   And you picked it up and gave her confirmation that that was what is wanted.

Doctor P.   Yes: and also to try and see that if the patient was irritating *her*, maybe this was what she was doing to her husband, too.

Dr. S.   Did she see that? — because that's the next step, isn't it?

Doctor P.   Yes. But I had to say it. The group didn't say it.

Dr. Main   We should watch it a bit about the doctor's feelings, because what the hell do the doctor's feelings matter?

Dr. I.   It depends on the doctor's feelings how she reacts and what she says and what goes on between the patient and the doctor, surely?

Dr. Main   If she has got this feeling, what does it matter?

Dr. I.   Being aware of being irritated by the woman, you've got to curb it before you come out with a remark.

Dr. Main   Do you think *you* can curb it?

Dr. I.   Oh yes — you don't just come out blatantly with anger, do you?

Dr. Tunnadine   It's this word 'feelings' that Dr. Main is in a bad temper about this afternoon. If the doctor is aware of her own feelings and can conceptualise it as an interesting fact. . .

Dr. Main   That's another matter.

Dr. Tunnadine   That's what you're talking about.

Dr. S.   Yes.

Dr. Main   The point is, we're talking about the doctor/patient relation, not about the doctor's feelings.

Dr. Tunnadine   I see what you mean.

Dr. Main   The doctor's feelings don't matter. It's the *patient*

L

relationship we ought to be studying — what does it say about the patient, what is the patient doing? We may learn why the patient is irritating, you see. We've said the doctor is irritated — and so am I — but it won't do. In what way is this woman irritating? — It wasn't in the discussion.

Dr. S.   Except that it was the way she sat there like a lump, complaining about the husband.

Dr. Main   Yes I know, but there was something which *angered* the doctor, too. I don't know what it was.

Dr. Tunnadine   On the evidence of that one interview, she was waiting passively to be put right. My guess is that it was the patient and her passivity that provoked the directive doctor. What she *didn't* do was relate this to the way the doctor herself had been provoked into being busy. You did report that they always do this with premature ejaculation. So they do.

Dr. Main   I have only one complaint about the leader: that she didn't underline what she was doing. It's like one of these things — 'She was cured, you know'. There was a time when Jung was visiting in the RSM and somebody went up and said, "Have you got any good tips for obsessionals?" . . . Or like saying, 'I once operated'. 'Oh yes, what did you operate for?' '250 guineas'. 'No, I mean what had he got?' '150 guineas!' *(Laughter)*. The concern was with the treatment, not with the *trouble*.

Doctor P.   Actually, it's quite extraordinary because I was determined that I would be very honest and confess, and I still forgot it — what I did do, I regret to say, was tell them about a case of mine about anger.

Dr. Main   You were on to this idea about anger with the group, then?

Doctor P.   Just that they all looked at me when I said it was conceivable that the man might be feeling a bit cross. I justified it by giving them a little lecture about my own case.

Dr. Main   That's terrible — but what I did admire was the way the leader saw these people scooting around for treatment without having made a diagnosis; then she turned the whole thing to a discussion of the facts which need to be thought about. My complaint is that you didn't put into words the difference between rushing into treatment and making a diagnosis. — What about this other feature of the leader, when she let them rabbit on for quite a long time before she intervened, let them get on with the magic stuff? What do you think about the way she handled the squeeze technique?

Dr. Q.   I think that was good, because it's going to come out at some point. I would have thought that letting it be aired, and showing what relevance it has here, getting it back to what is under your noses — I was impressed with that.

Dr. Main   The atmosphere in which it was done I thought was impressive.

Dr. Q.   Yes, I wouldn't have thought that the doctor felt criticised by that, or put down, but thought — 'Oh yes, perhaps it *was* inappropriate then'.

Dr. Tunnadine   It seemed to me a triumph of self-discipline for a leader who we know had all sorts of angry thoughts buzzing around in her head. She didn't say, 'That treatment is a bloody waste of time', but 'Tell me!' in a sweet tone of voice.

Dr. F.   There was quite a kick in the way you said it: the business of, 'It's a sort of technique for early learning problems'. That understanding doesn't come from that seminar. It comes from your superior experience. So in a sense it was a bit punitive to hit them with that, which was outside their own experience. It could have been conceived as a bit of a lecturette. Maybe they could have come to it in, 'What reference does it have in this particular situation?'

Doctor P.   I just feel that I have to lay down some of my boundaries and I'm not terribly prepared to sit down and talk too much about behavioural techniques. My last group was almost ruined by somebody who wanted to teach us the whole time about behavioural techniques; and if they are not prepared to look at the behavioural techniques in an honest way, then they might just as well go elsewhere.

Dr. Main   There's a difference between someone who wants to talk about it and someone who wants to teach; because the problem with the teacher wasn't the behavioural techniques at all. The problem was the *teaching* and that's the thing to go for, rather than behavioural techniques. I felt that the lecturette wasn't given for any other reason than to require them to think a bit. It's getting them to think rather than passing moral judgments about it. It was very much in the working area of the ego, I think, not the super-ego end of it. I thought that showed in the way the group discussed it.

Dr. Tunnadine The thing that interested me technically was that the group did reflect the way the doctor had got busy and made suggestions to the patient. As you quite rightly say, he's a premature ejaculator and you want to feed them some good advice — 'Slow down!' We were very interested in saying what the patient did to the doctor, and what the doctor did to the group; but how far is it useful to take it *back down the other way* — 'Isn't it interesting that we are doing here just what the doctor found herself doing to the patient?'

Dr. Y. I can hear a voice saying, 'That's a bit groupy!' — Sometimes it's very tempting to comment on what the group are doing.

Dr. Main We should be aware of it, this pitching in: it *was* a group phenomenon, wasn't it? — I thought it was dealt with pretty well. . . What else? — It was an interesting case of premature ejaculation, wasn't it? *(Ironically).*

Dr. Tunnadine No, it was an interesting case of a man under pressure.

Dr. Main Interesting case of a wife. . . — She got away, didn't she? — They all pounced on this premature ejaculation. This chap only had premature ejaculation some of the time. Sounds very reactive. Easier to treat *him* than the wife. The group didn't discuss that at all, did they? — Neither did this group.

Dr. Tunnadine It wasn't very clear to me. I don't remember who was the presenting patient.

Dr. Main She was there and she dragged her husband with her. He was being a co-patient.

Doctor P. I'm not quite sure. She was coming and I'm not sure if he was dragged or whether he pushed.

Dr. Main No, she came first for . . .

Doctor P. She was coming routinely for the pill and then she developed amenorrhoea and all the fertility anxiety started. But he, I think, wanted to bring his beautiful little chart with all its crosses about when they had done it.

Dr. Main But why did they turn up together? — I have a vision of a small man with a big woman.

Dr. Tunnadine   Nevertheless, I thought a *small* man, who burst in, you see — perhaps I am reading it wrong — saying, 'I am not untidy!' — squirting about all over the place.

Doctor P.   We did talk a little bit about his need to be in control: how neat he must be, and how difficult it must be for him not being able to be in control.

Dr. F.   It's interesting that the group produced the idea of a sheath with a tiny hole in it! *(Laughter).* I think that's the best solution I've heard!

4. Passivity in patient, doctor and group

Leader Doctor S.

A 29-year-old patient was seen at the end of a family planning clinic, but not examined because the trolley had been cleared away. Her complaint was that she had never had an orgasm, or any sexual pleasure. The doctor said, "Tell me about yourself", and the patient said she felt very resentful towards her mother because her father had gone off when she was six years old and the mother says nasty things about the father, of whom she is very fond. The mother said things like, "Sex is a dirty thing. Don't let that nasty thing inside"; so she had very negative feelings about her mother. After the father had gone off, the elder brothers and sisters babied this woman and looked after her.

The reporting doctor said, "She irritated me because every time I made an interpretation she said, 'Yes, I see that, but how does that help me? Tell me what I should do'. She kept putting it back to me and I felt irritated, as though I wasn't getting through to her".

Doctor S.   The group said the patient seemed a very controlling woman. I noticed that there were a lot of questions to the doctor. Someone asked, why did she come *now?* and the patient had said,

"I'm 29, I'm nearly 30, and I read somewhere that you are in the prime of life when you are 30 and if I can't get this right and feel something, then it will be too late!" At the end I summed it up by suggesting the doctor might be able to say something like, 'You always have to be told how to run your life. You keep asking me to tell you the answers. Maybe your elder sisters controlled you after your father left and needed to look after you'. And I just added, "Maybe you will be able to notice if she has some negative feelings coming out in the interview with you".

Dr. Main   The effect of the questioning technique was evident, wasn't it? The patient told her what the trouble was and the doctor said, "Now tell me about yourself", pushing it aside; and after that they went to fathers and mothers. We don't know what this woman's sexual problems are. She says she hasn't got any interest in sex. What goes on in her sexual life? Did it begin at some time? — My guess is, it did; and I wonder how. We don't know anything about what is going on. Does she have a lot of intercourse and hate it? Does she have none at all? What difficulties are there if she does have it? We know nothing about the woman's problem because the doctor wouldn't listen to them.

Doctor S.   She did, actually. She reported —

Dr. Main   Oh!

Doctor S.   It's the bit I forgot! *(Laughter).*

Dr. Main   Well, it's missing, anyway. To hell with her brothers and sisters and how they feel at home! — *What is the woman's sexual problem?*

Doctor S.   She had spelt it out.

Dr. Main   How did it come out?

Doctor S.   It came out that she doesn't feel anything. She does respond to her husband three times a week because she loves him and she wants to do what he wants. She is just worried because she has never enjoyed any good feelings and she has never had an orgasm; so she puts up with it. I think that was how it was reported. There isn't any pain. She just doesn't have any feeling.

Dr. Tunnadine   I think that's clear. But the doctor's response was, "Tell me about yourself". You would think that was open-ended enough and showed that the doctor had noticed that she didn't talk about herself; she talked about her mother. But as Dr. Main suggests, it was away from this business of orgasms and so on, which she had plucked up the courage to bring. For this patient, talking about the *past* somehow let her off the hook.

Dr. Main The patient waited for an hour and made no complaints; and during that hour the trolley was taken away and the doctor did nothing about that, either.

Dr. Tunnadine The patient then at some time in the conversation made the remark, "It's going to be too late by the time I'm 30". I'm not terribly surprised! *(Laughter).*

Dr. J. You seem, from your report, to have been a fairly silent leader and allowing the group to have its own pattern and you were watching it.

Doctor S. I think I decided to just let it happen and observe really.

Dr. Tunnadine I think you were not all that passive when you actually solved the case with about three sentences at the end!

Dr. I. You didn't say how they reacted. Did they just sit there and say, "Thank you very much"?

Doctor S. They looked as if they wanted to be told!

Dr. Tunnadine I love your style: 'You were blind — one, two, three!' No, you didn't say that; you said, "It would be very interesting next time to see whether you could not be so bloody blind". — I think you were a bit fed up with this doctor's passivity.

Dr. Main So there were lots of things going on that the leader might have made a comment on, but instead you solved the case. Is that a good idea? Dr. Tunnadine, you made a savage attack on Dr. S. just now.

Dr. Tunnadine Yes, that's right: rather politely, as she did on her doctor.

Dr. Main You accused her of solving the case. That is, it wasn't a group discussion; it was a consultation with an expert.

Dr. Tunnadine The leader did try not to, I must say, for quite a long time. But by the end it was irresistible. You thought you'd had enough of it, you said.

Doctor S. I suppose I just feel that I can't go there all the way from London and not give them *something*! *(Laughter)*.

Dr. Tunnadine   Like a slap in the eye!

Dr. Main   I have come all the way from Barnes and I am not going to let you get away with it! *(Laughter)*.You have come to help?

Doctor S.   If we model our leadership on leaders we have known, I would say that *you* always tie things up at the end of a case. I just can't forget that. You have been thinking all the time about what was going on, but I realise that my thoughts were not so much what was going on in the *group*, as what was going on between the patient and the doctor.

Dr. Main   I am trying to point out to *this* group that there is something to be thought about.

Doctor S.   The discussion did cover what kind of a woman this was, and why she was irritating the doctor, because she was waiting to be told answers.

Dr. Main   That's another point we haven't discussed.

Doctor S.   They discussed that a bit.

Dr. Main   Yes, it was mentioned — but what to do about it? What is the doctor doing about it? What is going on? It was worth discussing in the group further, I would have thought. It's a funny business: *she wants to be told.*

Doctor S.   Her ideas were that she always *was* told.

Dr. Main   I know.

Doctor S.   Always told by other people in her family and doesn't have a right to think for herself. Somebody actually said, "She seems to be wanting you to give her permission to get some feelings".

Dr. Main   So the woman said, "What's the use of that?" It didn't strike me as asking for permission. What do people think?

Dr. Tunnadine   I think she is someone who needs to be told; that is to say, she thinks the answer *needs* to come from outside herself; and she gets the doctor and the doctor got the group to tell her. Somehow the passivity of the patient who needed to be told was carried into the group; and whether you had come a long way from London or not, you still fell into the trap. If you had been able to relate the passivity of the patient to the group, you might not have been tempted to do the same sort of problem-solving at the end.

Dr. I.   I was wondering about the response of your group to your comment, because the patient responded, "What is the point in telling me that?" I am wondering if the group felt, "Where is the point in telling us?"

Doctor S.   No, they looked sort of open-eyed and — 'Oh! — *that's* it, is it?'

Dr. Main   Let's look at what Dr. S. did tell the group for the solution of this case.

Dr. E.   "Look out for negative feelings"; or, "perhaps you will notice if there are any negative feelings". There certainly were quite a lot in the presentation.

Dr. Tunnadine   That was what was completely missing in the discussion. The girl reminded of the hatred of the mother was the real living thing in the doctor/patient relationship, wasn't it?

Dr. Main   If you don't think for yourself, you do what you are told.

Dr. Tunnadine   And what you are actually told is, "Don't enjoy this horrible thing". All that was out of the discussion.

Dr. Main   — Or, by the doctor, "*Do* enjoy this horrible thing!" It's an interesting moment. I am impressed by the fact that this woman came, you brought this matter out — 'Why did the patient come now?': that was a very fruitful response — that this woman had said, "It's my last chance". It's now or never and she's thirty and the smell of wanting to break away from this mother is in the air, isn't it? But they didn't take it up much. That's odd to me — that they didn't discuss this mother more.

M

5. "Manipulating" patient's distress got lost

Leader Doctor S.

*A doctor who works in hospital and does day-care abortions under
local anaesthetic talked about a patient who she felt had
manipulated her. The patient was upper class, well turned out, and
said she had to have an abortion because she already had three
children. She had not been able to use a satisfactory method of
contraception. They had intercourse very infrequently and had
attended a behavioural sex therapist who had given her husband
some testosterone. The woman sounded dismissive of her husband
and felt the sex therapy had not helped.*

*The doctor felt she had to do what the patient wanted, but hoped
to explore the sexual problem more at the time the patient had the
abortion.*

*The group were rather attacking of this doctor: wondered why
she had let herself be manipulated and why she had not done more
about the sexual problem at that interview.*

Doctor S.   I said something like, "It seems that the woman
attacks the husband in a way. Perhaps he is frightened of her.
You're a bit frightened of her, and perhaps now a bit frightened
of this group attacking you" — something like that. I didn't
quite get it out.

Dr. Main   Here's Dr. S. very discontented with herself. — You
can have your conscience back — I don't want it. The other thing
is that Dr. S. didn't *report* her work in this group. It was an
anecdote of what was said. The thoughts of the leader and the
dilemmas of the time were not reported.

Doctor S.   This is what I find hard to do, because I am always
trying. I thought I did give you a certain amount of what I
thought as it went along.

Dr. Tunnadine   Yes, I think you did actually, to be fair; but
perhaps it is mainly about whether you got the case sorted out,
trying hard to do that.

Dr. Main   I didn't hear you thinking about the group: the group
response to the patient, the group response to the doctor. I didn't
hear you discussing with the group the various views that they

had about this, that and the other. It was about the cases, really, rather than the doctor/patient relation. There wasn't much about the group. What was going on?

Doctor S.   Well, the group was ganging up against the reporting doctor, and she felt that.

Dr. Main   Ganging up for some reason or other — which was. . ?

Doctor S.   I don't know. I didn't see it clearly enough to comment at the time. All I was aware of was that they were ganging up and I commented on that fact.

Dr. Main   You didn't know why they were?

Doctor S.   No, I didn't sort of think. . .

Dr. Main   Let us gang up on Dr. S. One thing I noticed at the beginning of this case is you didn't describe how the doctor got the case. Let's take it apart. Let's get it really clear here, because I think this didn't come out in the group.

Doctor S.   I think it did come out.

Dr. Main   It was discussed and criticised, but was it studied? — Just tell us what happened.

Doctor S.   The doctor was sitting in her clinic and had a woman come requesting a termination, and it's her job to make sure that it's best for that woman. . .

Dr. Main   She'd never met the woman before?

Doctor S.   No.

Dr. Main   The woman came off the street, or was sent?

Doctor S.   Came with a letter from her G.P. with one part of the Abortion Certificate signed. Actually the patient said to this doctor, "I have had to ring round all of London to find you", and that sort of made the doctor feel good, because she had been found and had a service to offer.

Dr. Tunnadine   That's what I thought was interesting when I heard you reporting the first time. You said that the doctor had noticed that the woman might be bitchy about her husband, and *not* that she might be bitchy about all these therapists who hadn't done her any good, or the fact that she had had to ring round all London to find her. I heard it quite differently, and yet the doctor felt that this was a sort of compliment or something, and missed the fact that she had got a pretty angry patient; which I presume is why she got tempted to sign the form, because the patient was going to make her anyway. It sounds as though it went right down the line: to you, to me. That's what I missed about it, that somehow this woman had come absolutely seething: "Sign this form — or else! I am not having any more of this mucking about!"

Dr. Main   And the doctor's response to that was?

Mrs. R.   "Have you got a sex problem?"

Dr. Tunnadine   Ultimately, it was just to agree. She was pretty ashamed of being manipulated.

Dr. N.   I thought the group was really fed up with this. You summed it up just now when you said, "The woman came in and sat down and the doctor's job was to sort out if there were any problems why she should or shouldn't have this abortion". And the doctor ended up by saying, "And I am going to discuss it when she comes back to have her abortion"; which really seemed to negate everything she was doing.

Dr. Tunnadine   But they did get on to the fact that the doctor hated being manipulated. That was kind of all right.

Dr. Main   The woman desperately wanted an abortion, but we don't know why. It seemed to be a very important matter to have this abortion, and she was most anxious to be sure to have it. Why was it so important? What does it mean?

Dr. Q.   Or her anger at everything failing up to now.

Dr. Main   Do *you* know why the woman wants an abortion?

Dr. I.   She's already got three children.

Dr. Q.   From a chap who has sex with her once since November and made her pregnant. There's a lot of unresolved anger about this treatment that didn't work.

Dr. N.   But now we're getting into the problem of solving this woman's case, aren't we?

Dr. Main   I am trying to point out that the doctor didn't know. She didn't inquire into the urgency.

Dr. Q.   Didn't get through to the patient.

Dr. Main   Didn't see the plight of this woman. Saw the *vehemence*, but it's like 'panicky people are always dangerous, they do damn silly things, don't they, doctor?' *(Laughter)*. This didn't come out in the group.

Doctor S.   No it didn't, and now you say that, I think the group felt that and that is why they were cross with the doctor.

Dr. Tunnadine   And she was pretty cross with herself, too.

Doctor S.   Yes, she was.

Dr. Q.   She rationalised by saying she would do it when she saw her next — didn't face her with the here and now in the examination?

Doctor S.   No. Somebody said, "How was she when you examined her?" and she said, "Ordinary".

Dr. Tunnadine   I think the leader's report suggests to me that she didn't feel in control of this group.

Doctor S.   I think I felt there was something going on that I didn't see quite quickly enough.

Dr. Main   The group started bashing her with hammers, and the leader said, "I think the group is angry with you and you feel attacked"; stating the obvious. The fact that the group attacked the doctor is clear enough. *Why* they attacked wasn't discussed, was it?

Doctor S.   No. So if I could get it back, I realise I could have gone on a bit there.

Dr. Main   . Yes. "If" doesn't exist.

Doctor S.   I think I didn't know how to handle it, so I moved on.

Dr. Main   This group was attacking the doctor. Is attacking one of your strong points? Is it one of your strong interests?

Doctor S.   No, I defend a lot. Yes, I felt for her, I think; and I moved on.

Dr. Tunnadine   I think, in one way, that you are right to think of her in this sense. There was a lot of interest in what a rotten doctor she was, to allow herself to be manipulated; but you don't get manipulated if you are in good shape. One sign of manipulation is helplessness and that wasn't there, was it? And so it wouldn't be surprising that you would feel this a bit.

Dr. Main   She's had an awful patient; but we don't know why.

Dr. Tunnadine   That's right — why the patient, too, was helpless to let her feelings come out.

Doctor S. Another thing: after I'd said, "This group is attacking this patient", the doctor said, "It makes me feel protective towards her when they do that". So there was a sort of protecting and defending going on in her interaction as well.

Dr. Tunnadine I think Dr. Main is right. We have actually heard of people who have requested abortion before, and the "baby" inside either this woman or this doctor is quite missing from the discussion, as far as I can see.

Dr. Main No feeling of suffering. . . The woman was not understood; and the doctor's behaviour wasn't looked at very much, just criticised. The doctor was very dissatisfied with herself. Here was an aggressive woman and she wasn't being examined, just fought and wrestled with, and then said, "Hard luck, doctor, I would have done just the same". It was very unsatisfactory for the whole of the group, and for the doctor and patient. Nobody was treated or looked at.

Dr. Q. She really manipulated you all.

Dr. Main I propose that for Christmas we have a wooden sign for Dr. S. which says *not* "God Bless Our Home", but "Take an Interest in Destructiveness".

Dr. I. But how do you criticise adversely without flattening everything?

Dr. Main I am not suggesting criticism. The doctor *was* criticised.

Dr. I. Yes, but then you felt you needed to defend her up to a point. You can't just go along with the criticism. . .

Dr. Main Why not just face that here is a bloody awkward patient — we don't know why. The doctor has responded to the awkwardness; that is all that has happened. You could have said, "This patient is very awkward. I wonder why? Anyone got any ideas?" It's a very interesting case, because quite a large number of people are in a panic and want it done and don't give a damn what the doctor wants: "What's the trouble, my dear?" they say, "Are you insane, or not?" It's a routine thing and to get over that and do some work isn't so easy.

Dr. I. No, but this is a doctor who is doing this work week after week. Perhaps some of the antagonism is because she's handling it badly.

Dr. Main Yes. And the group criticised her doing it badly, but didn't help her in any way; didn't look at the patient's aggressiveness and wonder why this was. This is a story of human endeavour and trouble. I don't like this word "manipulate". I think it's horrible. Who *doesn't* manipulate? — everybody does. I manipulate everybody I meet. I'll tell you another thing — so do you. — It doesn't mean anything! It condemns rather than understands. Another word I hate is 'attention-seeking'. An attention-seeking manipulator — that's me!

Dr. Q. So somehow the leader here, in this situation, was affected by the doctor/patient relationship to the extent that she was unable to show the doctor what was happening: that she was unable to get at the distress of the patient.

Doctor S. The doctor was just, somehow, in touch with the distress of the patient; and this was why she said she wanted to defend her when the group were all attacking her. She herself admitted that she hadn't got very far.

6. Patient and doctor got attacked

Leader Doctor I.

A leader was worried about a doctor in her group who did not seem to be making as much progress as the others. She tended to produce cases at the end of the seminar when there was not time for them to be discussed properly. She is very keen, partly, it seems, because her mother is a counsellor doing social work.

The most recent case was a follow-up of a woman who could not consummate her marriage. The doctor had tried to examine her, but had only managed to get the tip of her finger in, so she had referred her to a gynaecologist.

Doctor I. The group members were very critical and said, "You're not getting at the patient's feelings; you are confirming her idea that she is too small". The feeling in the group was that she had done it wrong, and everyone was hyper-critical. I am anxious about her, and my ability to encourage her to. . .

Dr. S.   Is that *your* job, or the group's job?

Doctor I.   I felt quite pleased with their response, because I felt they are grasping what we are trying to do. On the other hand. . .

Dr. Main   They hate her as well, you mean?

Doctor I.   They felt, 'What a stupid thing to do!' because she wasn't helping this particular patient and if anything it almost looked as if the group, myself included, were saying, "How awful can you get!" — which isn't actually very encouraging to any doctor, is it?

Dr. Main   We could discuss endlessly why this doctor is so awful — and there must be reasons for it — but why this thing is being presented to us is because the *group leader* has got a problem.

Doctor I.   Well, she always presents so precipitately at the end of the time; and doesn't say beforehand that she has a case, so that I could allow her more time.

Dr. Main   But you *know* why she didn't say at the beginning.

Doctor I.   She's done this before. Yes, I should have said. . .

Dr. Main   She's been bashed before, I suppose.

Doctor I.   Yes, I think she's been bashed before. I think she's beginning to think, "I'm not doing this very well".

Dr. S.   That's a good thing, isn't it, if she *isn't* doing it very well?

Dr. Main   All she learns from this is: bash the patient at every opportunity. . . *(Pause)*.. The doctor thought the patient *was* too small?

Doctor I.   Yes. She said, "I really thought that this patient was small". So one of the other doctors said, "What do you mean, she's small? She can't just be small. Do you mean she has a tight hymen?" "Yes, I think she has a tight hymen". "Not a small vagina, then?" "Well, I think she was all small". "Do you mean she has a tight hymen, a small vagina, or what?" — So we had a bit of interplay as to whether it was a tight hymen or not. Eventually she thought it was just a tight hymen. This *was* a physical problem and she would send her along to the gynaecologist. The patient had been to the gynaecologist and was told, "There is nothing wrong with you and you can stretch yourself". The doctor thinks that if she is still tight in two or three weeks time, they will do a hymenectomy. Again there was criticism from the rest of the group.

Dr. Tunnadine   I have some sympathy for this doctor, because yesterday I nearly hit a non-consummation. You think you learn, but some of them are like that. 'You *can* stretch yourself' should be interpreted as, 'You *can't* stretch yourself'. I am just wondering how far the patient and the doctor go down the line. It sounds as though the doctor has some problem, not to do with her hymen but to do with her sense of a rigid hymen as regards the work; a newcomer getting herself treated just like she treated the patient.

Dr. Main   Let me put it another way. The doctor was concerned with the patient and not with the doctor/patient relation. The group was concerned with the doctor and her deficiencies and delinquencies, but not with her work with the patient. The group leader was concerned with the aggressiveness of these doctors, which she thoroughly enjoyed because she felt the same way; so there was no examination of the relationship.

Doctor I.   No. It got sidetracked.

Dr. Main   So, let us attack the leader, shall we? *(Laughter).* — Or shall we do the other thing, which is wondering what it is about this group that somehow has got this leader into the situation where she was pushed off the track. This so-called 'stupid' doctor knows damn well that's not the ordinary way of treating a non-consummation. After some time in the seminar, she would have got the idea that this isn't quite the ticket. So what is she doing reporting it to the group?

Doctor I.   I have the feeling she was saying, "There are physical reasons too", you see.

Dr. S.   I don't think so. I think she was saying, "Bash me! — I've done bad work".

Dr. Main   She has other allegiances. Her mother is a counsellor.

Doctor I.   A social worker.

Dr. Tunnadine   It is clear that she is *wanting* a bashing. But it is interesting that the patient who got the bashing is one this doctor is convinced is very small. I am just feeling that must be important in relation to your visions about the doctor's mother, isn't it?

Dr. Main   Come on, take some more bread out of my mouth — there's some more there! *(Laughter)*

Dr. Tunnadine   Isn't that enough?

Dr. Main   Go on. This doctor presents a case of non-consummation. What does that mean in group terms? — that she hasn't consummated this relationship. I don't think that is anything to interpret at all, but something to have in mind and notice. She thinks the only way she can be consummated is violently.

Dr. Tunnadine   And is anxious about her smallness in relation to you.

Dr. Main   Yes — not big enough yet; and the interesting thing is, that is just what she reported. These other doctors — very experienced, very good. *This* one is an amateur and rigid.

Doctor I.   On the other hand, how do I help her grow up?

Dr. Main   Well, not by doing a violent hymenectomy!

Dr. S.   Giving a model of gentleness: waiting, listening. . .

Dr. Main   Not gentleness — *common sense.* Hard common sense, which isn't cruel — neutral.

Doctor I.   The last time she did just the same thing: said she had no case, then in the last five minutes brought one up.

Dr. C.   Was it a premature ejaculation?

Dr. Tunnadine   Should have been.

Dr. Main   The doctor reported precipitately.

Doctor I.   Yes, she does. It all comes out in a rush — in fact, I said, "Hold on a minute! — can you just go back?"

Dr. Main   If it was a child, what would you think was going on? Incontinence, isn't it? — anxiety.

Dr. S.   I was just trying to think how the better doctors might be with that unconsummated patient. They would just sit there and think, "I wonder what's going on? It's funny that we're not getting very far. Let's try and understand it further". They would sort of wait, wouldn't they? and not back out, but stay with the difficulty. So it seems to me that your group has to stay with this difficult doctor and be patient and be encouraging, rather than bashing. — Well no, I suppose you have to interpret that she *wants* to be bashed.

Dr. Main No, that's a group interpretation. Can you refer it back to the clinical work? What about Dr. Tunnadine's idea? This patient has been treated pretty violently and this doctor has been treated violently — what is going on? The leader sits on her like this. If she hadn't been so involved with her she might have said, "It's very interesting, this sudden violence. Is it because this patient has ideas about violence and being hurt?" Or, "What is it about the patient that affects the doctor like this?" This is your point, isn't it?

Dr. Tunnadine Mmm.

Dr. Main "What sort of patient is it?" Ask then about the people in the room, not the condition or its treatment. This doctor has feelings. You know — have you heard of those? — feelings? She's got some and they weren't taken seriously. They weren't discussed, nor the feelings in the room generated by the patient, or what the patient was feeling; just about the hymen.

Doctor I. She puts you off, because she tends to give the impression that she knows she's doing the right thing, even although she is aware. . .

Dr. Main I know, poor soul, of course she does. Your job, as a model to the group, is to get into the feeling situation between the patient and the doctor.

Dr. Tunnadine This patient had really convinced this doctor she was small and therefore violent rape was required, preferably under anaesthetic. The doctor was seduced by this, not because she was a stupid doctor, which was what she was told by the group, but because somehow the patient had really converted her to deny all the gynaecology she'd ever learnt over many years.

Dr. Main That's right. That's what these other doctors attacked her for. What should the leader do and say?

Dr. S. 'What's happening in this group? This doctor is getting attacked. . .'

Dr. Main Go on.

Dr. S. — 'It must be something about the patient that makes the doctor want to attack her by sending her off to the gynaecologist, and we are waiting to attack the doctor. . .'

Dr. Main   '. . . Dr. So-and-so is feeling awful about the way she treated this patient. She is asking for a bashing: should we let her have it, or not?'

Dr. S.   Yes, that's a better way of putting it. I'm not sure that they can understand that. It took me a long time to understand it.

Dr. Tunnadine   The other option is: 'Isn't it interesting that this doctor is getting attacked by the group; it sounds very like that was going on between the doctor and the patient'.

Doctor I.   You see, she doesn't give the story as evidence that this is what is going on between her and the patient.

Dr. S.   She hasn't thought of that yet, has she?

Doctor I.   No. She hasn't seen it from an aggressive point of view yet.

Dr. Main   Well, if you're going to get bashed in a group, you wait until the last bit; and she knew that. 'You expected to be bashed like this, didn't you, and so you other clever doctors fell into the trap.' There are all sorts of ways of coping with that. — Although it's a bit groupy, that remark.

Dr. C.   Can you do that so early in their training?

Dr. Main   I don't know. I'm just saying I'm a bit doubtful about making remarks like that which are a bit groupy; but certainly that was the group event. Whether you interpret it or not, at least you should have seen it, instead of joining one side and saying, "Cor, this is good — bash her again!"

Dr. Tunnadine   I think the group is picking up the two sides both of the doctor and the patient. The patient with all the ill-recognised wish for violence in fact presents as frail and too small, so it's not surprising to me that you would pick up the protective side.

Dr. Main   You have to leave the doctor to go at her pace. If the doctor kept away for several weeks, you could say, "I'm not surprised this doctor isn't talking about these cases, because these other clever doctors are so insensitive, talking about how she was violent with her patient when *they* are being violent with their colleague".

Doctor I.   I don't know if they're really ready to be told that they are insensitive yet.

Dr. Main   I'm sure that they aren't insensitive, but they got hooked on that occasion. Even Dr. Tunnadine has been known to make mistakes!

Dr. Tunnadine   Oh, surely not! *(Laughter)*. I would like to put forward the theory that daughters, husbands, etc. of experts in our field, or allied fields of work, need *more* training than others.

Dr. Main   I would go further than that and say: all kinds of doctors, from Medical Officers of Health to paediatricians, neurologists — the most difficult of all are orthopaedic doctors and the second most difficult are psychiatrists — they really are *wooden*: they have been trained in the opposite direction and there is an awful lot of backtracking and built-in resistances. They have been offered all sorts of reasons for the organic stance.

Dr. Tunnadine   It isn't fair to them if we have expectations that they know what they are doing.

Dr. Main   No, it's quite unfair to them.

Dr. Tunnadine   I think it's more difficult for them to acknowledge that they have to learn.

Dr. Main   They do acknowledge it and they come for help; but they put up their defences and have to go back to their long-established premises.

Doctor I.   I wonder if there is any point in letting her continue to be bashed.

Dr. Main   Of course there is not. You've got to do something about it.

Doctor I.   Precisely. So either she stays and I try to do something to help her. . .

Dr. Main   Help the *others*, who are awkward people. — I'm being mischievous about this, but the others aren't without their problems if they can bash somebody like that.

Dr. Tunnadine   That's right. They wouldn't have done very well with this patient, for example.

Dr. Main   So I'm not so sure they are so splendid as all that.

Doctor I.   No, I don't know that they are that splendid yet; but I think they have potential, the way they present their cases.

Originally, of course, all they did was to bring cases and facts, but now they are talking about feelings, whereas this particular one is still talking about the grandmother when they've finished giving the case.

Dr. Main I know what's wrong with the leader — I just realised: she wants to hurry them on! — You are liable to be a *teacher!*

Doctor I. Yes. I get hooked into it, too.

Dr. Main Well, let's attack the leader!

Dr. Tunnadine I seem to remember Dr. Main saying on more than one occasion something about 'paying tribute to the defences'. It seems to me that's the area we should be in with these beginner groups.

7. Case material and unconscious feelings in the group

Leader Doctor I.

A leader reported that at her last seminar only three out of the eight members had turned up and only one doctor had sent apologies.

Dr. Main Can you just hold on? Your observation is about the five not turning up. Can that be linked to the previous seminars?

Doctor I. I don't know. One dropped out after the very first session; I think because she felt threatened by the discussion of what was going on between patient and doctor. She didn't come any more — well, that was fair enough: she phoned me about it. But these others — no.

Dr. Main Any upsetting case or incident?

Doctor I. No.

Dr. A. It wasn't half-term, was it?

Doctor I. Unless they thought it wasn't worth coming to, which was my immediate reaction: had it been so awful? But the three that did come are keen, and in fact the others had appeared to be reasonably keen. I don't know. . . I must say, I felt a bit peeved that they hadn't bothered to give their apologies for not coming.

Dr. Main What is it about? I am sure you can blame yourself, but it may be. . .

Doctor I. I am wondering whether to contact them and say, "The next one is in a fortnight. If you can't come, please let me know".

Dr. Main They have every right to stay away if they want to.

Dr. Tunnadine It's very difficult to know, but I am sure that Dr. Main is right: you are hurt and angry, of course, but there may be some clue in the content of the previous meeting, if you could remember.

Doctor I. I don't know that they had been going well enough, because it's very difficult to get them away from facts. Practically all the cases so far have been factual and when you try to say, "What's going on?", you come back with the feeling that they don't really know how to report yet. So I'm wondering whether perhaps I haven't got this across.

Dr. Main You're rushing them.

Dr. Tunnadine There's something about the *style* of getting it across. As you report it to us, it sounded as if you implied, "What's the matter with you? I'm not interested in what you've got to say". I know you well, so I'm sure that *wasn't* how it was.

Doctor I. No, in fact I had been thinking I wasn't getting down to anything very much, and had thought to myself already, 'I had better start getting them working'.

Dr. Main There's plenty of time.

Doctor I. But I hadn't done so yet. In fact, we did more work last night with only the three of them, because I felt they were more relaxed.

Dr. Main Anyhow, you can't link up the absences with the session before. Let's go on and see what happened.

The leader then went on to describe the first case, which was of a woman of 23 years. It was a sub-fertility case. The woman had been married for a year, but had been trying to get pregnant for the last five years, although her divorcee husband had a three-year-old child; so it was all rather odd. There was not much group discussion, which tended to lead on to reminiscences about other cases.

The second case was of a girl who couldn't let her boyfriend near her, although she had started taking the pill in the hopes that she could make love. The doctor had been unable to examine her, so she had given her some K-Y jelly and suggested that the boyfriend should use it to dilate her. This produced quite a lot of group discussion about the difficulty of exploring this woman's feelings.

Dr. Tunnadine It's very interesting. I always like to fly kites about whether the case material itself in early groups has anything to do with the doctors themselves. I mean the first case, I know, sounded a nonsense, but the first word that came into my mind was that it was a *competitive* case. It was about somebody else having a baby while she was still screwing — something like that. I don't know whether that's anything to do with their feelings about the group. Then of course, this lovely next one, about. . .

Dr. Main I don't think you've been understood. Can you spell it out?

Dr. Tunnadine The case as I recall was crazy, because this girl had been trying for a baby for five years, and this bloody man had got *somebody else* pregnant in that time, which is kind of competitive, really.

Dr. Main The theme, then, is competition. That theme is in the patients.

Dr. Tunnadine And I am making a suggestion that it is something to do with the feeling of a kind of competitive *group*, or something like that. . .

Dr. Main The kind of *case* is referring to something going on in the *group*.

Dr. Tunnadine Then the second case is a totally different train of thought; but an anxious doctor who presents a case about the difficulties of getting too close, even when you're keen; being hurried along with K-Y jelly, or something like that. — It's stretching it a bit, but I think it's interesting to wonder about these things. Does this make any sense?

Doctor I. The types of case that are presented?

Dr. Tunnadine Yes. It may be saying a little bit about what they're feeling about the group.

Dr. Main Early case material is *usually* about non-consummation.

Doctor I. The first one I had, of course, was the dying woman; and the death was overtaking everything else.

Dr. Tunnadine That's right. — I was just really thinking whether the case material this time threw any clues on why the other five weren't there; because the ones who *did* turn up produced this sort of stuff: anxieties about getting too close too fast, and whether they were going to be as good as other people; this missing wife/mistress in the other case. — I don't know. I'm phantasising a bit.

Dr. Main After all, the whole purpose of the group is to make them all pregnant with knowledge.

Doctor I. One doctor hasn't presented any case yet, although he is very keen and offers very relevant remarks about other people's cases.

Dr. Main It's nice and safe to comment on other people's work. — What about this problem of reminiscences? The first case. . .

Doctor I. Yes, it reminded others of cases. Each time I said, "Yes, but what about this one?". Then somebody else would come up, "It's very similar to another one I had".

Dr. Main Yes, that's the problem. It takes away from the presenting case.

Doctor I. Perhaps I'm pushing them too quickly.

Dr. Tunnadine Good heavens, it's only the fourth meeting, and people do this. — *I'm* going to reminisce if I'm not careful! Look, how to deal with it is the question, isn't it?

Dr. Main One of my most sensitive ways is to say, "No reminiscences!" The other thing I will say is, "Has this got any relevance to this case? Would you like to tell us about this case later, when we've finished?" Either they report properly or they don't, because reminiscences are a pack of lies; they are just abstractions, summaries, omissions and selections.

Dr. Tunnadine I've heard you do both those. I've also heard another Dr. Main do something which isn't as direct, which is something like, "Isn't it interesting that we are running away from this into reminiscences?" — which is yet another trick of yours.

Dr. Main   That is the one I prefer. Reminiscences occur when the case has been exciting — "Oh, that reminds me of so-and-so!" Something ripples, runs through their minds. It's an exciting case. It's sometimes so exciting that it breaks the group up. But the thing is to *return* to the case and discuss the excitement.

Mrs. R.   But this case wasn't particularly exciting, was it? So therefore, one could possibly use another way of doing it.

Dr. Main   There was something about it that made them think of their own cases.

Mrs. R.   It didn't seem very exciting.

Dr. Main   Was it the difficulty?

Doctor I.   I wondered whether it was, because we got gaps and therefore they felt they needed to come in with something, because the doctor reporting the case had very little to offer other than the bare facts.

Mrs. R.   It was embarrassing.

Doctor I.   They felt they ought to contribute something, because we were such a small group. I don't know.

Dr. Tunnadine   Or if my phantasies were right and it was all about identifying with this feeling of. . . people who had been trying since they were sixteen years old to become proper women doctors — that it might have made those sort of ripples.

8. Endings: how to stop breast-feeding

Leader Doctors J. & E.

The leader started by saying that the group was coming to the end of the second year. The first case was of a woman with an eighteen-months-old baby who asked for the pill in order that her milk would dry up and she could stop breast-feeding. The doctor agreed to this, and the patient then went on to tell her how she couldn't bear sex since the birth of the baby. In reply to questions, she told the doctor about a termination when she was fifteen years old, and also a memory of having an injection in her bottom when she was eleven years old. She appeared very young, and complained about all the examinations when she was pregnant, which made the doctor feel she could not examine her at this time, even although she had in fact asked to have an I.U.D. removed before starting the pill.

The group asked a lot of questions, and also realised that the pill wasn't likely to dry up the milk at this stage. They felt there were discrepancies in the story. The leader continued:

Doctor J. Someone said something about denial. At that moment I said, "Denial? — What do you mean by denial? Can you develop that a little bit?" Almost immediately another doctor came in and did a waffle which was well away from the idea of denial. So we went back and said, 'No, could we talk about the denial?' She said she thought there was quite a lot of denial in the story. For instance, she wasn't talking about how awful it must have been to have the termination; at which point, I think Dr. E. said, "I can't help saying she didn't actually talk about getting pregnant at fifteen". We were both trying to encourage them to see what this girl was enjoying. That didn't seem to us to be getting anywhere. Eventually, we used the word 'excitement', because we didn't seem to be able to get to it any other way. It was quite interesting. There was almost a gasp, and a sort of recognition. One doctor said, "No way. You couldn't possibly say to the girl that she was excited by that occasion when she was eleven. What was exciting about that? It was all traumatic. How are you going to go about saying this to the girl?" I thought, 'Here is a question, and it is important really for everybody to answer it'. But everybody at that stage was slightly muddled, I think — at any rate, breathless; not able to respond to her. I can't remember what I said, but something like, "It is important to recognise what goes on in order to be able to talk to your patients with knowledge, not with confusion. You are not necesarily going to spell it out to her, but it is useful to know what it is all about". Then we went off on to something else, and Dr. E. said, "I want to go back to that question, about how you can spell it out to the woman concerned". I think you said something like, "You don't have to ask her to change. That is not the point. The point is, you are going to try ultimately to share this with her. We are not in this business for changing, but for *interpreting*. — is there something to add?

Doctor E.   I feel the things which you have been describing slightly differently, and therefore. . .

Dr. Tunnadine   I think one would sincerely hope that all eight members present would be hearing things differently; otherwise there would be something very strange. This is a dilemma, isn't it? We don't want to be muddled up.

Dr. Main   *(to Dr. J.)* Let's hear about *your* group.

Doctor J.   I don't think very much happened. We talked about the excitement inherent in the story, and how the doctor had been led away from it. They said, "Isn't it interesting that the doctor said, 'Oh, that's quite easy. We can easily arrange that. It's quite usual'; whereas in fact it is quite *unusual* to take out a coil and put the patient on the pill to dry the milk up. They agreed they had never done it in their lives, and why had the doctor fallen for this? They got on to the idea that maybe she was trying to cover up her sexual excitement, and I think at that moment we made another mistake. Dr. E. said, "An interesting thing is, why does she want to be respectable now?". Whereupon I said, "She's getting married in April and she's got a baby"; and we then had a conversation together, which is another bad thing we do — it must be very annoying. I hadn't actually seen the bit about, she was getting married, and she's got the child, and she loves having the child, and she is changing from being one person to another person. At the end, the presenting doctor said she felt she did understand a bit more.

Dr. Main   Thank you very much.

Dr. I.   I didn't quite get that last remark. You said it helped you to understand. . .

Dr. S.   Not the leader: the presenting doctor. It was her way of winding it up.

Doctor J.   Yes.

Dr. Tunnadine   To understand what?

Dr. I.   I don't quite see why she said that. That seemed to have come like a bolt from the blue. It didn't seem to follow on.

Doctor J.   It didn't make sense at all.

Dr. Tunnadine   It seems that the emphasis is on case understanding rather than the doctor/patient relation. I wonder if that is just the group emphasis, or whether it is to do with your first remarks about coming to the end of the time. — Is there pressure on these leaders to deliver the goodies before it is too late? I thought they were a bit busy.

Dr. I.   I got that feeling, but I didn't get that related to the presenting doctor.

Dr. Tunnadine   Nor did I, except that I heard a phrase about 'understanding'. What she was going to understand was what was going on in the patient: about whether she was excited when she was young, and not excited by the time she was having a baby and breastfeeding it, still unmarried. I thought the track was right, but it was to do with case understanding. I didn't have any evidence that the doctor/patient relation was discussed, in terms of the denial of excitement.

Doctor J.   Yes it was, because the doctor said that she didn't think she could possibly examine this girl. She knew that there was a reason why she couldn't examine her. They did talk about the distance that the patient kept from the doctor.

Doctor E.   She felt she would be an intruder, and the patient said, "These examinations were so awful in pregnancy: don't examine me". There was a tremendous feeling of, "Keep your distance"; so much so that it was only later that she remembered that the patient had asked to have the coil out.

Doctor J.   The group were well aware of the distance, weren't they? They got on to it quickly, that the patient hadn't allowed the doctor to be a doctor.

Dr. Main   There seems to have been an attempt to get the group to think on the topics that interested the leaders. The group in fact had some interests of their own, which might have been picked up. For instance, there was an opportunity, when one of the doctors rather drily remarked, "Eighteen months is a long time to feed — I've never heard of it"; and it gave the leader an opportunity to say, "What do other people think?" This doctor, while making a dry comment, was nevertheless making an observation: "There is something funny about this". My guess is they would have got on to the fact that, if she wanted to stop breast-feeding, she didn't need the pill. What is going on? It would have been quite plain that this woman didn't want to stop her kid from breast-feeding; didn't want to be nasty to her kid, just wanted the milk to dry up; didn't want to say, "No, you can't", but "No, I haven't got any". A non-aggressive kind of woman who daren't say 'Boo'. The group could have gone on to talk about this, if the remark had been picked up. It means that you've got to get the group to start doing some thinking. I think they are a bit stifled by the leaders doing the work.

Dr. I.   I thought it was fascinating. How can you both decide to try and get them going along the same lines? You were both trying to get them to do one thing, which they weren't able to do. Is that telepathy? *(Laughter)*.

Doctor E.   No — agony! *(Laughter)*.

Dr. Main   When a single leader is with the group, it isn't the leader versus the group. You are in the group, you learn from the group, and you are in there with them. But these two leaders don't have to do that: they have each other. There is a group of two watching this other lot out there — "How is that group getting on? What do you think? What shall we do with them? . . ." Whereas, if you are *in* the group you are no more important than anyone else in the group in so far as the *case* is concerned, but only in so far as you are observing the group, looking after the group; which is a somewhat different function from the other members of the group. I was very interested in the relationship between these two leaders. They are protecting each other from the group. . . — "What is the right thing to do?", instead of being in there, feeling things about the group and having to cope with them. Does anyone agree with this?

Dr. I.   I was just struck that you were both agreed on the same thing to do, or what would be a useful thing to do.

Dr. Main   They are thinking about each other such a lot.

Dr. Tunnadine   There was an instance when one made an opening remark, and the other answered it, and then you were in trouble, as I am often here with Dr. Main. It is a very difficult thing.

Dr. Main   Another thing which we haven't discussed here are the initial remarks of the group. They were talking about breaking up and how much they had learnt, and the topic was,

"How long do you go on breast-feeding a child?" This thing was in the air, in the discussion, it seemed to me. How many more meetings have they got?

Doctor J.   One.

Dr. S.   That was the penultimate one.

Dr. Main   So, how do you stop people breast-feeding? You don't just say, "Stop it!" but "Go on the pill and make it easy". I thought this concern was in the group and I wondered how you deal with this? — Just go on ignoring this anxiety, or bring it out in the open? They must have ideas about what they have got and what they haven't got from the group themselves. They must have many discontents because they haven't gone far enough; and yet there was the remark which one of them made: "Oh yes, we have got past that", or "learned this": kind of reassuring themselves that they are not so bad. It seems to me that now is the time for them to be able to grumble about what they *haven't got*.

Dr. I.   There was the remark about, "I've sat here for two years and not quite grasped something. . ."

Dr. S.   No no — she was saying, "I *have* grasped it. Don't think I haven't".

Dr. Main   That's right.

Doctor J.   It was about another case, actually. She said, "I haven't sat here for two years and not got *that* understood".

Dr. Main   If that was on another case, that again reinforces the idea that they are preoccupied with this.

Dr. S.   In this case she said, "I couldn't examine her anyway. I was running out of time"; as though, 'I can't go into this any more. . .'

Dr. Main   Yes — 'Let's not examine things too much'. What about doing a kind of assessment, saying, "What have we got out of this? What have we learned? What is missing here? What is disconcerting or disappointing?" — so they have some shared ability to say, "Thanks for doing what you did. Sorry you didn't do more. Goodbye!" Really bringing out the negative feelings about it; because unless the negative feelings *are* brought out, the positive ones will be embarrassed. If the negative feelings are brought out, then they can appreciate what they've got. I think it is an important matter, this: the ending of a group.

Dr. Tunnadine   As I hinted earlier, in this account I suspect that the leaders are somewhat pressured to say, "My goodness, please understand this. . ."

Dr. Main   The leaders must realise that, relatively speaking, they have failed this group's highest hopes, and face the music. We all fail our groups' highest hopes.

Dr. S.   It seems to me it would be valuable to do that in the context of that first case, and at the end of that you could say, "Well, as a result of two years' work, what do you think you know about a case like that?"; because when you were giving your preamble about 'they have learned this and that', I was thinking, "When are you going to get to the case?" I think all this generalisation is just waffle. I think in that case you could have discussed, "Now, how might you have approached that two years ago, and how have you learned to do it now?", because she did say she saw it more clearly. I felt dubious about whether she did see it more clearly.

Dr. Main   She wanted to keep it on the surface. She wanted to take it at face value. The handling of that could have been to have offered it to the group — "That's what the doctor did. What do the group think about it?" On the first level, I imagine they would say, "I think it's the wrong treatment", but when they began to think a bit, they would begin to wonder why. What is it about this woman that the doctor can't say No. The situation of those people at the end of two years must be attended to. You are suggesting that the leaders' response to this situation is that they have spotted this and are trying to give as much as they can.

Dr. Tunnadine   Yes — 'None of these pills! . .'

Dr. Main   Let's pursue this awkward thing. What do the leaders think they have achieved in two years?

Dr. S.   I think they have some satisfaction that they have managed to find some niches for these people to continue. They've looked after their future growth a bit. They are not high and dry.

Dr. Main   Well, that's a pity. Some of them should be.

Doctor E.   Some are. One has said, "This is it for me".

Dr. Main   Some of them are left high and dry, and some will come to my group. Will I be left high and dry with people who have come under false pretences? The defence against saying 'Goodbye' is, "Ah, well — it needn't be goodbye. It's all right — we'll look after you. . ." But the other thing is to say, "Goodbye — you've had it!" It isn't necessarily a good thing to say goodbye, but it is difficult, and the postponement or the watering down of it, or dodging of it, is a danger. There is another element in this. How do you feel about saying goodbye to *this* group? Good, or bad, or easy, or 'Thank God!' Are you glad to see the last of them, or what?

Doctor J.   About six different feelings, I think! *(Laughter).*

Dr. Main   How far should the leader say their piece — what they have enjoyed and what they haven't? Is that wise? — Not that they are there to have a nice time. I am just wondering about the usefulness of it.

Doctor J.   I think a discussion on how we have got on for two years might be rather a thin discussion, because there aren't very many people there.

Dr. Tunnadine   I thought you said there were seven or eight. Does that include you two?

Doctor J.   No. Last time six people came. There could be seven next time.

Dr. Main   I don't wish to set any ideal about what is going to happen. If you present them with the opportunity of discussing it, then they will either take advantage of it, or not, with your help. They will have their own limits about it. I think it might be nice for them to be able to say, "I've enjoyed working with you. I get a bit fed up sometimes about so and so, and I think you might have done more about this, but I think we did pretty well about so and so". This is a possible way of discussing it in the group. They'll say, "I'm sorry we won't be meeting again. Goodbye". — Why shouldn't they? When a group breaks up there is hell to pay, usually. They miss it. Some groups that break up have a party afterwards, bring drinks for the last occasion. Groups don't like dying, or being slaughtered.

Dr. Tunnadine   If the leaders offer this at the next meeting, what often happens is that the group bring five more cases.

Dr. Main   That might be the denial of the break-up.

Dr. Tunnadine   I notice that we are not discussing whether we think the leaders have done satisfactory work on the basis of this report, and I think Dr. J. is saying, on the basis of this one report, that she isn't very satisfied with this doctor anyway — although the group discussion she *was* pleased with — a little uneasy that she was caught up with this patient's confusion between excitement and denial to the extent she was. — Is that fair?

Doctor J.   The doctor was very unclear about it in her own mind.

Dr. Tunnadine   She was, wasn't she? And I think it was to do with the fact that the patient was presenting all this excitement that the group picked up.

Dr. I.   But where was all the excitement coming from? You say the group were all excited, and yet the way the doctor presented, it was all cut and dried — "Yes, dear, we will take your coil out". I didn't hear excitement going on in the doctor's presentation and yet it seems to have developed in the group.

Doctor J.   I thought there was quite a lot of denial of this thing which the group actually were aware of but couldn't put into words.

Dr. Main   On the report of this case, the group seems to be not bad about discussing; not marvellous, but not bad at having a go. The doctor herself has left the questioning technique aside, but she is not doing much with her listening, and therefore not interpreting or conducting anything except at a superficial level.

Dr. Tunnadine   Interested in what was going on between her and the patient, but a bit of a straw in the wind. . .

Doctor E.   She seems to think that if you bring something like this to the group, it's an appropriate case. She's got that more or less worked out. She presents a certain amount of her feelings when she talks about what it was like. She gives quite a flavour; gives you what the patient said, and the colour of it — and that's it. And she thinks that is enough.

Dr. I.   And yet she stirs up all that excitement.

Dr. Tunnadine   It was a vivid and marvellous account and the group clearly felt from the reporting doctor the other side of the patient.

Dr. Main   The doctor was saying more or less, unconsciously saying to people, "Look, I've got a funny case — God, she's odd! She's been breast-feeding for eighteen months and she wants to stop it with the pill: God knows why! She is getting married in a few months. She seems very young indeed. She was pregnant when she was fifteen. Very odd girl! She's gone off her boyfriend ever since she's had this baby. I think she likes the baby more than him. . ." She was really saying this to the group. Screaming at them, but not saying a word.

Doctor J. I didn't understand why the doctor's difficulty seemed to affect the group. The group then did something rather similar to what she had done.

Dr. Main The person who came in and said, "I have never heard of a patient breast-feeding as long as that" was really saying, "That's a bloody queer thing! I wonder what that is about: any ideas?" — It wasn't out in the open. You were on the edge of excited inquiry of the problem under their noses, but they didn't go over the edge.

Doctor E. I think that also had something to do with the fact that there was a flavour of something pretty nasty, some shameful thing that this patient had produced; because she was so repulsed and her feelings were so very strong. At the same time, there was an awareness by the group that you don't get so strongly repulsed for nothing.

Dr. Tunnadine The link between 'the more excited you are, the better behaved you have got to be, and therefore the more repulsed by your own sexuality after you become a mother' was not made clear. — It's not an easy case, not an easy history; but it is easy as far as the doctor/patient relation is concerned. One could criticise the leaders for not pointing out the contrast of the excitement in the group and where it had come from, and the patient's denial, because she was a saintly little mother now. She was more promising when she started: a little raver getting things stuck into her when she was eleven, apparently. They started to talk about trauma instead. But I was reminded recently by a leader that it is perhaps unrealistic to expect interpretations in a basic group.

Dr. Main Two years is about time that they were beginning to do more than just question and listen. It's about time they were making a shot at understanding.

Dr. Tunnadine Some of them are, by what we have heard of their interventions.

APPENDIX: PSYCHOSEXUAL PROBLEMS AND PRESENTING SYMPTOMS

There are many ways of classifying psychosexual difficulties, all of which are open to criticism. The following list is not intended to be a formal classification, but is offered in the hope that it may be helpful to readers who wish to locate areas of particular clinical interest in the text.

Presenting in connection with the following symptoms:

Pain on intercourse, p. 93, 129
— with fiancée but not lover, p. 98
— associated with female circumcision, p. 154
— with history of incest, p. 158
— and frequency of micturition, p. 279
Vaginal discharge, p. 121
Pain during vaginal examination, p. 253
Penile rash, p. 230
Heavy periods, p. 47
Abdominal pain and spastic colon, p. 86
Breathlessness, p. 51
Red eye, p. 73
Depression, p. 134

Presenting as a prescription request:

— to calm husband down, p. 60
— for tranquillisers, p. 232
— to dry up breast milk, p. 378

Presenting in relation to fertility control:

Request for contraceptive pill, p. 345
Problem revealed when collecting sheaths, p. 237
Change of contraceptive method, p. 330
Abortion request, p. 98, 362
Problem revealed during vasectomy counselling, p. 138
Depression following sterilisation, p. 283

More overt psychosexual complaint:

Impotence, p. 109, 151, 271, 335
Premature ejaculation, p. 34
— associated with sub-fertility, p. 351
Non-consummation, p. 110, 115, 246, 301, 367, 376

Sexual dissatisfaction in women, including loss of interest and lack of orgasm, p. 224, 230, 237, 357
— following treatment of cervical erosion, p. 271
— since marriage, p. 233
— following birth of a baby, p. 295, 311
— since death of a baby, p. 76

Others:

Psychosexual problem associated with terminal cancer, p. 80
Mother bringing daughter for check-up following rape, p. 28
Wife worried about husband masturbating, p. 317
Husband complained wife wasn't interested, p. 271
Patient asked doctor to show her where her clitoris was, p. 57
Patient refused vaginal examination, p. 125
Woman worried because her boyfriend wanted to live as a homosexual, p. 68
Patient complained her husband made unreasonable sexual demands, p. 173
Man of sixty complained he was under-sexed, p. 144

Thirty-three patients presented in general practice, 14 in family planning clinics, and one in each of the following settings: youth advisory clinic, vasectomy counselling clinic, hospital abortion counselling clinic, well baby clinic.